COMPUTER SECURITY:
The Practical Issues in a Troubled World

Third IFIP International Conference on
Computer Security
Dublin, Ireland, 12-15 August, 1985

NORTH-HOLLAND
AMSTERDAM • NEW YORK • OXFORD

COMPUTER SECURITY: The Practical Issues in a Troubled World

Proceedings of the Third IFIP International Conference on Computer Security, IFIP/Sec '85
Dublin, Ireland, 12-15 August, 1985

edited by

Jane B. GRIMSON

and

Hans-Jürgen KUGLER

Trinity College
Dublin
Ireland

1985

NORTH-HOLLAND
AMSTERDAM • NEW YORK • OXFORD

ISBN: 0 444 87801 7

Published by:

ELSEVIER SCIENCE PUBLISHERS B.V.
P.O. Box 1991
1000 BZ Amsterdam
The Netherlands

Sole distributors for the U.S.A. and Canada:

ELSEVIER SCIENCE PUBLISHING COMPANY, INC.
52 Vanderbilt Avenue
New York, N.Y. 10017
U.S.A.

PRINTED IN THE NETHERLANDS

PREFACE

This volume contains 38 papers, which were presented at the IFIP/Sec '85 Conference in Trinity College, Dublin from August 12-15, 1985. IFIP/Sec '85 was the third international computer security conference sponsored by the International Federation for Information Processing (IFIP), under the auspices of IFIP's Technical Committee on Security and Protection in Information Processing Systems (TC 11).

The theme of IFIP/Sec '85, *practical issues in a troubled world,* was addressed by papers which covered all major aspects of Computer Security. The Conference Programme was divided into 16 Sessions: *Database Security, Vulnerability 1 & 2, Security Management 1 & 2, Communications/Encryption, Software Security 1 & 2, Computer Audit/Crime, Office Security/Education,* together with 6 Plenary Sessions. The Plenary Sessions were addressed by invited speakers – international experts in the field of Computer Security.

We would like to thank all those who helped to make IFIP/Sec '85 a success and look forward to meeting in Monte Carlo next year.

Jane B. Grimson & Hans-Jürgen Kugler
Editors

Trinity College Dublin
Ireland

ACKNOWLEDGEMENTS

IFIP/Sec '85 was held under the auspices of the International Federation for Information Processing's Technical Committee on Security and Protection in Information Processing Systems, through its Irish member, the Irish Computer Society. The preparatory work was shared among the following volunteers:

Steering Committee:
Dudley Dolan, Chairman

Organising Committee:
Mide Fagan, Chairman
Ala Al-Zobaidie
Jimmy Finlay
David Jameson
Roger Latham
Paul Moran
Dave Murray
Jacqui Stokes
Patrick Sweeney

Programme Committee:
Hubert Kearns (Ireland), Chairman
Bill Bound (U.K.)
James Finch (Canada)
Jane Grimson (Ireland)
Harold Hyland (U.S.A.)
Hans-Jürgen Kugler (Ireland)
Herbert van Tongeren (France)

EDITORS' NOTES

The papers contained in this volume represent the Proceedings of IFIP/Sec '85. Three papers have been included which, although accepted, were not actually presented. Four papers are not included because no complete written version was submitted for publication in this volume, although they were presented at the Conference. Finally, one paper has been revised since the Pre-Prints were issued.

Papers not presented:

Integrating Security Activities into the Software Development Life Cycle and the Software Quality Assurance Process, by F.G. Tompkins & R. Rice
A Fault and Intrusion-Tolerant File System, by J. Fraga and D. Powell
The Development of a Specification Language for a Computer Security System, by J.H.P. Eloff

Papers not included:

Computers as Targets of Transnational Terrorism, by W.S. Bruschweiler, Sr.
The Data Security Problem, by A. Grissonannche
Security Considerations in a VM Environment, by C. Molloy
Can We, or Should We, Trust Data That We Acquire From Others?, by P. Capek and W.H. Murray

Paper revised:

Design of a Secure Relational Data Base, by J.M. Carroll & H. Jürgensen

CONTENTS

Preface v
Acknowledgements vii
Editors' Notes ix

I. **PLENARY SESSION 1**
Chairman: Jim Finch

Emerging Privacy Issues
W. Ware 379

II. **DATABASE SECURITY**
Chairman: Jane Grimson

Design of a Secure Relational Data Base
J.M. Carroll and H. Jürgensen 1

Design of a Relational Schema for Database Dynamic Authorization Management
M. Fugini 17

III. **VULNERABILITY**
Chairman: Hans-Jürgen Kugler

Computer Assisted Reduction of Vulnerability of Data Centres
B.T. Cronhjort and A. Mustonen 397

The High Mortality of Data
I.S. Herschberg and R. Paans 27

IV. **PLENARY SESSION 2**
Chairman: Per Hoving

Software versus Hardware Encryption –
Is there any Difference Today?
V. Fåk 35

V. **SECURITY MANAGEMENT 1**
Chairman: Sean Connolly

Security Management in Large Organisations –
Two Case Studies
K.D. McLean 39

The Bofors-Model for Working ADP-Security
J. Essén and B. Lindberg 47

Problem Quantification – Its Importance to Cost-Effective
Computer Security
R.H. Courtney, Jr. and M.A. Todd 55

Integrating Security Activities into the Software Development
Life Cycle and the Software Quality Assurance Process
F.G. Tompkins and R. Rice* 65

VI. **COMMUNICATIONS/ENCRYPTION**
Chairman: John Beatson

Communications and Network Protection Practical Experiences
O.S. Rasmussen 107

Authentication in a Heterogeneous Environment
J.M. Power and S.R. Wilbur 117

IBM Dynamic Signature Verification
T. Worthington, T.J. Chainer, J.D. Williford and S.C. Gundersen 129

EFT/POS Network Architecture – A Canadian Perspective
W.J. Byrne 155

VII. **PLENARY SESSION 3**
Chairman: Harold Highland

Computers as Targets of Transnational Terrorism**
W.S. Bruschweiler, Sr.

VIII. **SOFTWARE SECURITY 1**
Chairman: Herbert van Tongeren

How to Control MVS User Supervisor Calls
R. Paans and I.S. Herschberg 179

Concepts of Protection in the IFIP WG 2.7 Reference Model
for Command and Response Languages
H.-J. Kugler 191

How to Use the DES Safely
D.W. Davies 371

A Fault and Intrusion-Tolerant File System*
J. Fraga and D. Powell 203

IX. **VULNERABILITY 2**
Chairman: Harold Highland

Systems Design and Data Security Strategy
T. Osvald 219

The Relative Impact Measure of Vulnerability –
A System in Practice
R. Mäkilä 225

Security of Electronic Transactions
I. Ekebrink 233

Security Vulnerabilities in the Automated Office
M. Schaefer 427

X. **PLENARY SESSION 4**
Chairman: Donald Davies

Computer and Network Security Policy: A Challenge to Organizations
L.G. Becker 241

XI. **AUDIT/CRIME**
Chairman: P. Garvey

Development and Organization of the Audit and Security Functions
J.G. Beatson 251

DP-Security: Attacks against Data Processing and Preventive Measures
H. Pohl 261

Decision Support Systems – A Necessity for Effective Auditing of Controls
W.T. Tener 269

The Audit, Control and Security of the Project Life Cycle – Pre-Implementation Stage
R.T. Doswell 277

XII. **OFFICE SECURITY/EDUCATION**
Chairman: Kevin McLean

Multifunction Workstations and Multidimension Environments
E. Orlandi 283

Security for Small Business Computers
P.P.C.H. Kingston and M. Goulbourn 297

Security in the Automated Office
R.R. Moeller 305

Educating Computer Crime Investigators
P.M. Stanley 313

XIII. **PLENARY SESSION 5**
Chairman: Jim Finch

Information Security in the Framework of the International Information Flow Debate – A Business View
H. van Tongeren 323

XIV. **SOFTWARE SECURITY 2**
Chairman: Hubert Kearns

Producing Reliable, Secure Software
G.E. Murine 329

The Development of a Specification Language for a Computer Security System*
J.H.P. Eloff 337

Security Considerations in a VM Environment**
C. Molloy

Can We, or Should We, Trust Data That We Acquire From Others?**
P. Capek and W.H. Murray

XV. **SECURITY MANAGEMENT 2**
Chairman: Jane Grimson

Establishing Technical Systems Security Standards at a Large Multinational Bank
C. Cresson Wood 347

The Formidable – If not Insurmountable – Organisational Problems of Disaster Recovery Planning
V. Lane and J. Step 361

Disaster Recovery for Online Systems
M. Nolan 163

The Data Security Problem**
A. Grissonannche

XVI. **PLENARY SESSION 6**
Chairman: Willis Ware

Security for Security against Computer Interaction
D.B. Parker 175

Author Index 439

* denotes paper accepted, but not presented.

** denotes papers presented, but no written version submitted.

COMPUTER SECURITY
J.B. Grimson and H.-J. Kugler (Editors)
Elsevier Science Publishers B.V. (North-Holland)

Design of a Secure Relational Data Base[1]

John M. Carroll and Helmut Jürgensen

Department of Computer Science
The University of Western Ontario
London, Ontario, N6A 5B7
Canada

A relational data base structure in which access is controlled by cryptography can provide a model for information systems that are attractive since control can be enforced by hardware as it is in traditional military communications systems thereby avoiding the uncertainties that surround the security of computer operating systems. Simulation of the system suggests that deficiencies exist not in the enforcement but rather in the formal security models that these mechanisms are trying to enforce.

1. Introduction

We shall first discuss the structure of the proposed cryptographic access-control mechanism for a relational data base, then show how the conventional formal models of security policy can be enforced by this mechanism, carry out a simulation to observe the (undesirable) consequences of using the resulting system, and finally develop a generalized formal model within which viable systems might be designed.

2. Data Base Structure

The relational data base structure appealed to us because it would afford maximal precision in access control and avoid the complexities inherent in using the container concept as may be required when coarser data granulation is the rule [12]. (One of these complexities is the need to specify when container clearance is required [CCR] and when not.)

In a relational data base, data atoms, that is the most elementary items of data, can be visualized as residing in one or more matrices at the intersections of rows and columns. The matrices are called tables (or relations); the rows are called records (tuples); and the columns are called fields (attributes). See Figure 1.

In our example, there could be K tables $T(1),\ldots,T(K)$. We consider one of these that has N records $R(I)$ and M fields $F(J)$. Usually N is much larger than M. The cells of the tables contain encrypted data messages $E(M(I,J))$. Each data message consists of a pointer $P(D(I,J))$; it points to an encrypted data element $E(D(I,J))$ that resides elsewhere in storage. The data message also contains a cryptographic key $K(M(I,J))$ that can be used to decrypt the data element.

3. Access Control Mechanism

There are L sets of cryptographic keys $KR_1,\ldots,KR_L$ and L sets of keys $KF_1,\ldots,KF_L$. These sets of keys are associated with records and fields, respectively. A pair of key sets exists

[1] This work was partially supported by the Natural Sciences and Engineering Research Council of Canada, Grants A0243 and A7132.

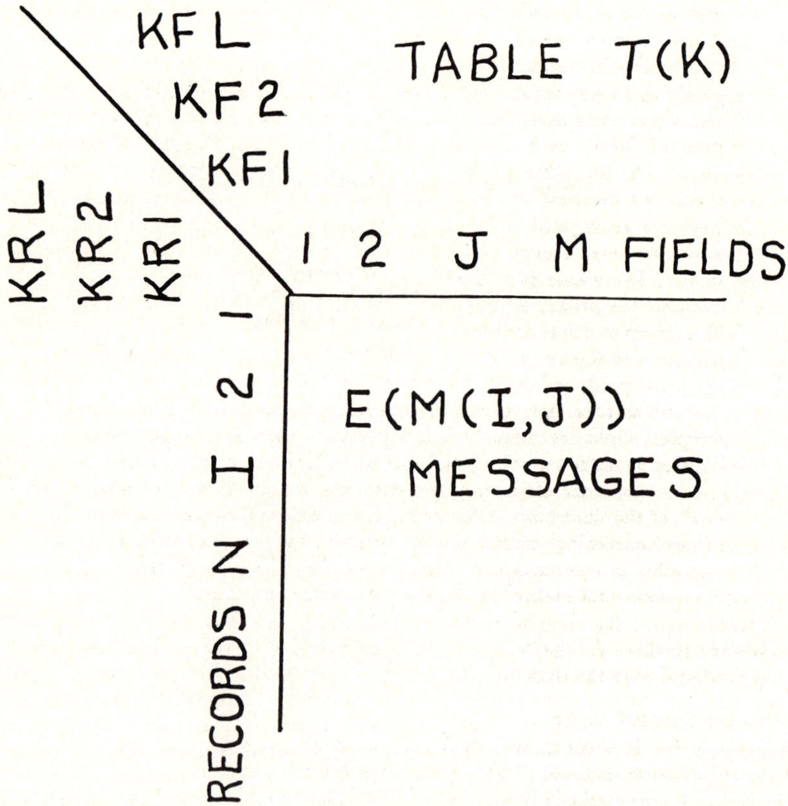

Figure 1
Structure of the data base

for every security domain: classifications (such as *secret*, *confidential*, etc.), compartments (such as *nuclear*, *crypto*, etc.), caveats (such as *Canadian-eyes-only*, *Canadian/UK-eyes-only*, etc.), discretionary access classes (also known as "need-to-know", that is individuals or groups who are granted or denied certain kinds of access), and sensitivity levels (such as *operator*, *user*, etc.).

"Classification" is an atribute of data elements corresponding to "clearance", which is an attribute of users. Similarly, "sensitivity" is an attribute of data elements corresponding to "integrity" on the users' side. Classification connotes vulnerability to intelligence; sensitivity connotes vulnerability to sabotage [4].

We elect to use a comprehensive system of security keys to avoid situations in which incompatibility between access permissions to records and fields may have to be resolved arbitrarily – possibly in conflict with the desired security policy [9].

Every field and every record has L unique keys associated with it. Every data item is encrypted $2L$ times using these keys applied in an implementation-determined order. If the data elements are short – such as "employee salary" – $2L$ cryptokeys constitute a relatively high overhead. On the other hand, if the data elements are reasonably long, 300-word summaries, say, the overhead would be small compared to the data protected.

The keys are aggregated into 2^N or 2^M, or fewer, proper subsets corresponding to user access permissions. The system grants or denies key sets to users depending on their security profiles. Every user can have a unique security profile. Figure 2 shows that, when a user is granted the proper aggregation of keys to access a requested data element, the system will perform multiple decryptions of the indicated message retrieving the pointer to the data element and the key needed to decrypt it. The data element will then be obtained from storage, decrypted, and delivered to the user. The hardware to accomplish these tasks would be located so that exposure of sensitive data is minimized. The user profiles could also be encrypted – in a key that could be a one-way encryption of the user's credentials. If the user is going to make repeated queries to the data base it may turn out to be efficient to decrypt at sign-on time all data elements to which the user has access and thus deliver a total "view" of the data base to the user's work space. The efficiency considerations are similar to those concerning storage management in a computer operating system. Use of a data-base machine in conjunction with pipe-lined decryption employing a large number of (micro-)processors could make this process fast enough.

Depending on the security environment it might not even be necessary to resort to encryption. In this case the "crypto" keys would simply be tokens symbolizing the user's access privileges over the data elements.

4. Access-Control Logic

Control of access involves three parameters: subsets of cryptographic keys, the user's profile, and the access method. These parameters are related by logical rules. Our parameterization of access methods could explicitly address the problem of differentiating between "viewing" and "copying" a data item [14], for instance. When microcomputer workstations are equipped with removable disk drives and/or printers the privilege to "read" implies the privilege to "view" and "copy". The only answer we have seen to this problem is to keep all printers and removable disk drives in registry areas and exert close physical control over the terminal area. There is a similar problem concerning the clearance of technical staff. Conventional security models seem to require that they (at least some of them) be cleared to the level of the most highly classified information stored. However, we must trust them not to leak highly classified information to data spaces having lower classification or withold the writing privilege from them. Neither of these may be acceptable.

5. Key Subsets

In each security domain, a proper subset of keys exists for every level, that is, classification, compartment, etc. There are two kinds of key subsets: *unique* and *non-unique*.

A particular key can reside in one and only one *unique subset*. Subsets appropriate to different levels of classification or sensitivity are unique. The corresponding base subset is

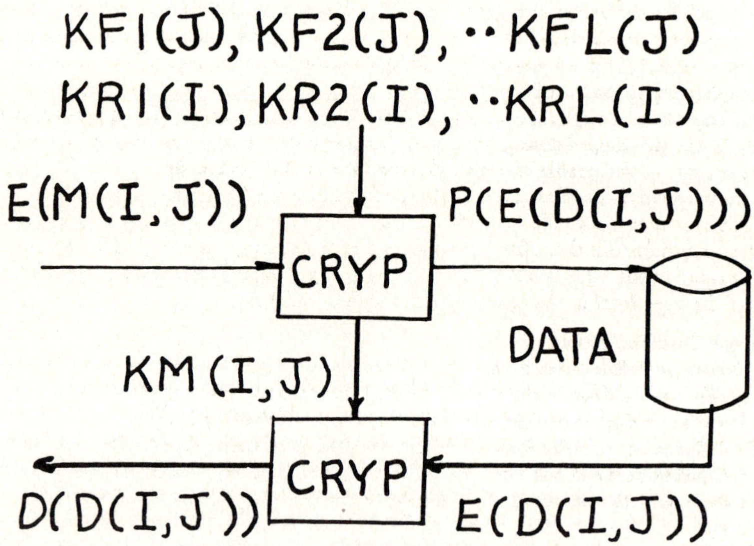

Figure 2
Data access via multiple decryption

composed of all keys not found in other subsets of the respective domain. The base subset for classification would be *unclassified*; for sensitivity it would be *user*.

A particular key can reside in any or all *non-unique subsets*. Subsets appropriate to compartments, caveats, and discretionary access classes are *non-unique*. In this case the base subset is the universal set of keys in the domain in question. In our implementation, we shall, for simplicity, regard caveats and discretionary access classes as compartments.

6. User Profiles

A user's security profile consists of a binary vector for each security domain. There is one component for each level; it corresponds to a proper subset of keys. If the value is 1, all keys in that subset are available to the user. User profiles are either hierarchical or non-hierarchical. Hierarchical profiles are appropriate for unique key subsets. In a hierarchical profile components form an ordered set with "→" denoting the order relation. A clearance profile is hierarchical as is an integrity profile. In the case of a clearance profile,

$$confidential \rightarrow unclassified$$

means that permission to access confidential data elements implies permission to acccess unclassified ones as well. The relation "→" is transitive. Owners of unmodified hierarchical profiles always possess access to the base level.

Over hierarchical profiles, the operation of complementation is defined as follows: to form the complement of a profile, all zeros are changed into ones, and all ones are changed into zeros safe for the vector component which defines the user's privilege, that is, the highest order component in which a 1 appears. For example, the clearance profile of a user cleared for *secret* is $(0,1,1,1)$ if we assume four levels: *top-secret*, *secret*, *confidential*, *unclassified*. The complement of that profile is $(1,1,0,0)$.

The operation of upper limit is defined over hierarchical profiles. It consists of retaining a 1 only in the privilege-defining component of the unmodified profile vector. For example, the upper limit of the profile of a user cleared for *secret* is $(0,1,0,0)$.

Non-hierarchical profiles are appropriate for non-unique subsets. The relation "→" is undefined over non-hierarchical profiles. Also, complementation and upper limit are undefined for non-hierarchical profiles. The owner of a non-hierarchical profile is assumed to possess access to the base level. (This does not mean that the user can see everything, the fact that the base level is the universal set notwithstanding.)

7. Access Control Rules

In this work, we define three access control methods: *read*, which we regard as subtending *execute*, *write*, when done without the possibility of reading, and *read/write* where the user or a process executing under the user's control can both read and write.

We define a set of rules for each access method over each security domain. The rules concern matches between non-zero entries in the user's security profiles and some modifications of these, and the presence of the key of the desired data element in the corresponding key subset.

There are two kinds of rules: *Existential rules* require only that a match exist; they are appropriate to all subsets and profiles. *Universal rules* may require matches on all profile components, all key subsets, or both. They are appropriate to non-unique subsets and non-hierarchical profiles.

The rules for *read* are:

> *clearance/classification* – read if there exists a match between the user's profile and a classification subset (existential, existential).
>
> *compartments* – read if there exists a match between the user's profile for all of the compartment subsets (existential, universal).
>
> *integrity/sensitivity* – read if there exists a match between the complement of the user's profile and a sensitivity subset (existential, existential).

The rules for *write* are:

> *clearance/classification* – write if there exists a match between the complement of the user's profile and a classification subset (existential, existential).
>
> *compartments* – write if for every component of the user's profile there exists a match with a compartment subset (universal, existential).
>
> *integrity/sensitivity* – write if there exists a match between the user's profile and a sensitivity subset (existential, existential).

The rules for *read/write* are:

clearance/classification – read/write if there exists a match between the upper limit of the user's profile and the classification subset (existential, existential).

compartments – read/write if for every component of the user's profile there exists a match with every compartment subset (universal, universal).

integrity/sensitivity – read/write if there exists a match between the upper limit of the user's profile and a classification subset (existential, existential).

These rules enforce four security models: (1) the simple security model (*read* with respect to *clearance/classification* and *compartments*), (2) the ⋆-property (*write* with respect to *clearance/classification* and *compartments*) [3], (3) the integrity model (*read* and *write* with respect to *integrity/sensitivity*) [4], and (4) the lattice model (*read/write* with respect to *clearance/classification* and *compartments*) [7].

8. Simulation

We ran a simulation experiment with a rapid prototype of this system to determine the consequences of its use. The data base had one table with 50 records and 20 fields. We specified three security domains: *classification* with 4 levels, *compartments* with 4 levels, and *sensitivity* with 3 levels. As shown in the structure chart representation in Figure 3, the main elements of the simulation are initialization, retrieval, evaluation, and output.

8.1. Intialization

The initialization section is expanded in Figure 4. The major parts of initialization concern simulating a data base and a set of users.

Simulation of a data base consists of selecting the subset sizes for each security domain for records and fields. The sizes were randomized but selected such that they formed a rough geometric progression from highest to next-to-lowest level with respect to classification and sensitivity. The subsets were then populated with record and field designations.

We cycled the creation of users through all four clearance levels having 1, 2, 3, or 4 compartment permissions (that is, 16 users). Permissions of cardinality less than 4 were randomly chosen.

At the maximal level of *read* privilege (*top-secret* clearance and all compartments), and at the maximal level of *write* privilege (*unclassified* and no sensitive compartments) we cycled the creation of users through all three levels of integrity (that is, 6 users).

8.2. Retrieval

Retrieval consisted of fetching all 1,000 data messages and unlocking them in accordance with the user's three security profiles, the subsets of 4, 4, and 3 key tokens for both records and fields, and the corresponding access rules. These procedures are illustrated in Figure 5.

8.3. Evaluation and Output

For every one of 20 users and 1,000 records we determined whether or not access should be granted for *read*, *write* and *read/write*. Our results, in terms of average numbers of records successfully retrieved are tabulated below.

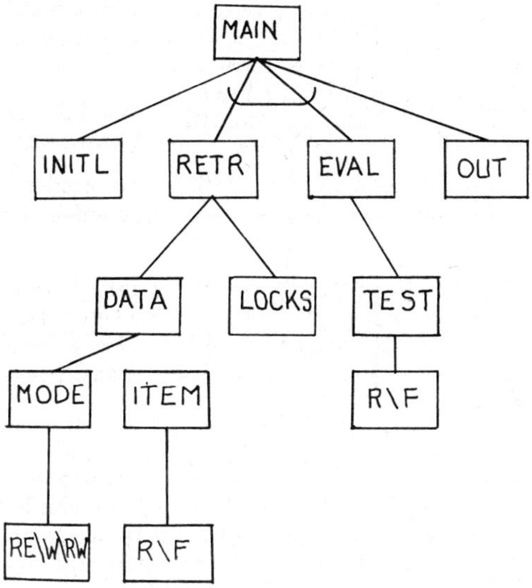

Figure 3
Simulation structure chart

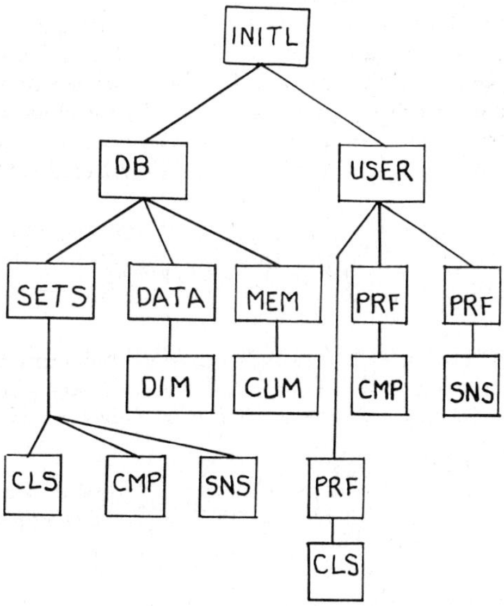

Figure 4
Initialization of simulation

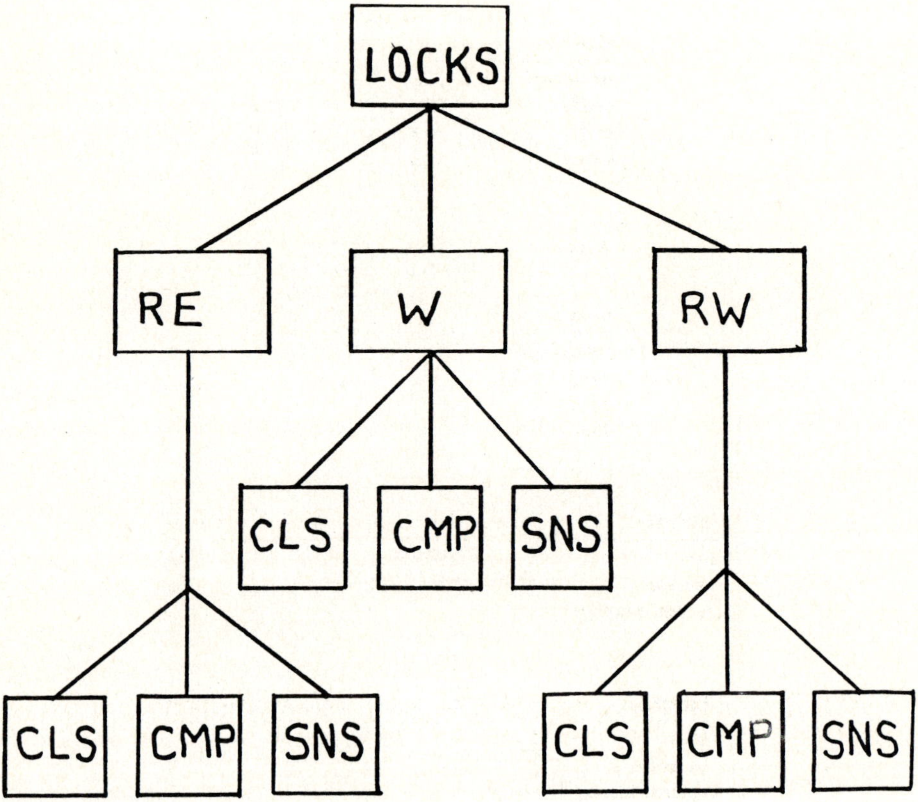

Figure 5
Retrieval of data items

9. Results of Simulation

Access = *read*

classification:	compartments: 1	2	3	4
unclassified	78	84	114	189
confidential	176	207	290	456
secret	234	297	462	736
top-secret	290	360	540	1000

Access = *write*

classification:	compartments: 1	2	3	4
unclassified	494	8	0	0
confidential	138	2	0	0
secret	60	1	0	0
top-secret	0	0	0	0

Access = *read/write*

classification:	compartments: 1	2	3	4
unclassified	55	0	0	0
confidential	5	0	0	0
secret	4	0	0	0
top-secret	0	0	0	0

integrity:	*read* (max *write*)	*write* (max *write*)
user	55	495
operator	2	828
system manager	1	1000

integrity:	*read* (max *read*)	*write* (max *read*)
user	1000	0
operator	84	0
system manager	8	0

10. Discussion of Simulation Results

The results of the simulations are plotted in Figures 6 and 7. They suggest that enforcement of the $\star$-property can be highly restrictive even if the system designer can guarantee that the access method *read* shall not imply *write*.

Perhaps the worst aspect is that highly privileged systems personnel have vast privileges to read within the data base but would be able to write little or nothing, and, therefore, be unable to maintain the system in any practical sense.

In actual systems, compartments are usually employed with information already classified as *top-secret*; it is called *SCI*, sensitive compartmented information. There are three prescribed ways to handle it:

(1) *Dedicated mode:* The entire system handles only information having the same set of compartments.

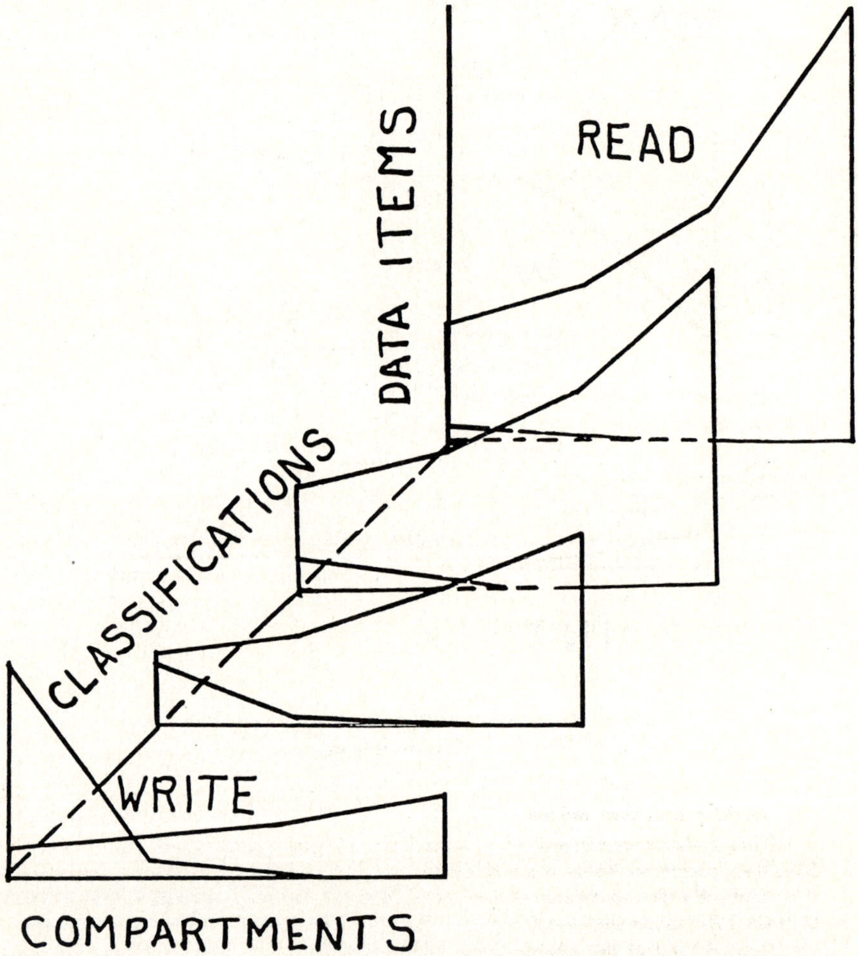

Figure 6
Results: classification and compartments

(2) *System-high mode:* All people working on the system are cleared for all compartments being handled.

(3) *Controlled mode:* Some people working on the system all not cleared for all compartments being handled and physical restraints are employed to prevent them from seeing

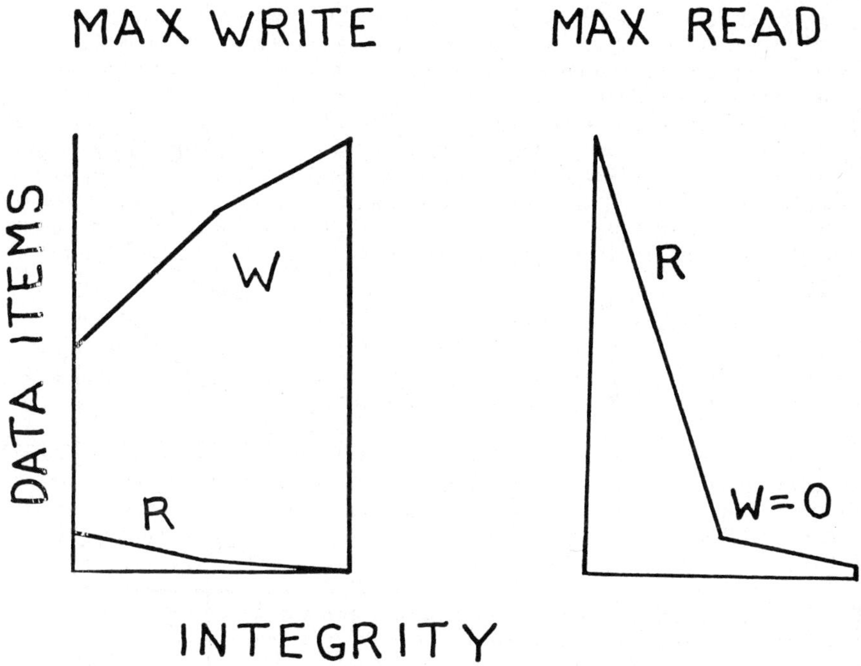

Figure 7
Results: integrity

anything that they are not entitled to see.

These policies are expensive and sometimes awkward to implement. Accordingly, means have been sought to realize a *multilevel secure mode* (MLS mode) in which computer hardware and software can assume the responsibility for preserving security within a system. It is in the MLS mode that the ⋆-property dilemma becomes a serious design constraint.

One way out of this dilemma has been to allow users to assume different personae so that a trusted user can assume any security profiles needed to accomplish a job at hand [17]. This practice can lead to all kinds of abuses and totally destroys any institutionalized accountability.

In some realizations, a certain amount of "writing down" is permitted, the ⋆-property notwithstanding [1].

Another way out has been to declare that "trusted" software can be permitted to accomplish various necessary tasks that entail violating one or more access rules [15]. However, the lack of progress in verifying and validating software especially in the form of object code together with substantial progress in attacking the trustworthiness of software by Trojan horses [10, 2], rogue programs [8], selectively gated compilers [16], and, especially, viruses [6], suggest that trusting software may be a snare and a delusion. An interesting side-effect of these irregular implementations of security policy is that in a contested case of espionage it might be impossible to prove guilt beyond a reasonable doubt.

It has been suggested that applation-specific models should be generated [12]. The earliest prototypes, however, have tended to ignore the roles of "technician", "system manager", "systems programmer", and "operator" while attending to the roles of "down-grader", "releaser", etc. There can be a large number of specific applications and this suggests that there should be a coherent and automated procedure for generating specifications for secure environments, say, by use of expert systems [5]. However, a unifying formal model will be required.

11. Formal Model of Systems Security

In this section we develop a formal model of security systems based on the discussions of the previous sections. The theoretical analysis confirms the simulation results obtained before. In particular, our model will specialize to the Bell-LaPadula model and Denning's lattice model.

The basic difference between our model and the ones proposed in the literature [11] is that we do not assume any prior structure on the set of security classes; instead whatever structure these sets have is induced by the enforcement policy for various data access methods. This allows us to avoid the controversial – and inherently so – discussion about the relation between access methods by introducing the enforcement policy as an additional parameter.

Admittedly, this will allow for models which do not make any sense whatsoever, practically. On the other hand, this approach enables us to derive general expressions for the quantitative behaviour of arbitrary strategies. The logic of such systems and practical enforcement using cryptography will be addressed in a future paper.

As in the example discussed in the previous paragraphs, we distinguish between security classes that are uniquely assignable only and classes which can be assigned in combinations. Some arguments in favour of this distinction will be given below.

A priori, the sets of security classes will not have any structure assigned to them – the lattice model [7] will turn out to be a special case –; instead, whatever structure these sets have will be induced by document access rules which really form the major component of the security scheme.

We make no distinction between security classes assigned to documents or data and security classes assigned to users of these data. If such a distinction turns out to be required for special applications, it would not be difficult to incorporate it in the model.

11.1. Access Methods

At the basis of our model are data access methods and their mutual relations. Actually, the set of access methods is a finite and partially ordered set $(A, \rightarrow)$.

For $\varrho_1, \varrho_2 \in A$, the statement $\varrho_1 \rightarrow \varrho_2$ is interpreted as saying that the ability to access data via ϱ_1 implies the ability to access at least some of these same data via ϱ_2.

As an example, consider the set

$$A = \{r(ead), p(rint), e(xecute), w(rite), d(elete), m(odify), a(ppend)\}$$

On A at least the following implications seem pausible:

$$p \rightarrow r, e \rightarrow r, a \rightarrow m, d \rightarrow m$$

Depending on the particular interpretation of the system and the implementation of these functions other relations may be holding true as well, of course.

That A is partially ordered by $\rightarrow$ rather than just pre-ordered is motivated by this interpretation of the relation $\rightarrow$.

11.2. Uniquely Assignable Security Classes

Let S be a set, the elements of S being considered as security classes such that each data object and each user will be assigned exactly one element in S. Such a set of security classes will be referred to as a *unique classification* in the sequel.

An *access strategy* for S is a mapping

$$\alpha : S \times A \times S \rightarrow \mathbf{B}$$

where $\mathbf{B} = \{0,1\}$ is the Boolean semiring or the set of integers $\{0,1\}$, depending on the context of how α is used. The interpretation of α is as follows: A user assigned class s is allowed access to a data object assigned class s' via access method ϱ if and only if $\alpha(s, \varrho, s') = 1$.

Given the partial order on the set A of access methods, an access strategy has to satisfy the following condition:

$$(1) \quad \forall s, s' \in S \; \forall \varrho, \varrho' \in A : (\varrho \rightarrow \varrho') \Rightarrow \alpha(s, \varrho, s') \leq \alpha(s, \varrho, s')$$

This axiom says that if access via ϱ can simulate access via ϱ' in some cases – at least – then the authorization for ϱ must always imply the authorization for ϱ'.

Instead of α consider the mapping

$$\bar{\alpha} : A \rightarrow \mathbf{B}^{S \times S} : \varrho \mapsto \bar{\alpha}(\varrho) = \lambda s, s'.\alpha(s, \varrho, s')$$

where, as usual, $\lambda s, s'.\alpha(s, \varrho, s')$ denotes the mapping of $S \times S$ into $\mathbf{B}$ which maps (s, s') onto $\alpha(s, \varrho, s')$. One sees that $\bar{\alpha}$ is in fact monotonic.

At this point it seems useful to note that the assumption of A being partially ordered rather than just pre-ordered can also be argued from axiom (1). For

$$\varrho \rightarrow \varrho' \rightarrow \varrho$$

implies

$$\bar{\alpha}(\varrho) \leq \bar{\alpha}(\varrho') \leq \bar{\alpha}(\varrho)$$

componentwise. Hence

$$\bar{\alpha}(\varrho) = \bar{\alpha}(\varrho')$$

Thus, there is no need to distinguish between ϱ and ϱ' in such a case.

11.3. Non-Uniquely Assignable Security Classes

The standard example of non-uniquely assignable security classes is the set of compartments. Let T be a set – of security classes – to be referred to as a *non-unique classification* in the sequel. Typically a data object or a user would be assigned a subset of T, that is, an element of 2^T.

However, one cannot simply replace T by 2^T in order to remove the distinction between unique and non-unique classifications. First, an encryption based enforcement method will use keys for each element in T and then combine them according to the particular subset of T at hand – if it was for no other reason then at least in order to reduce the number of keys required –. Second, access to data items with non-unique classifications is quite different from the case of unique classifications.

For instance, consider the operations of *r(eading)* and *w(riting)* in the Bell-LaPadula model [3], assuming that r and w are really incomparable in A. If a data item has the non-unique classification $T_d \subseteq T$, then every user assigned a set $T_u \supseteq T_d$ may read the document. On the other hand, he may write the document only if $T_u \subseteq T_d$.

This comparatively simple situation changes when one has to assume the existence of some implicational structure on T – several subareas together defining a compartment – which would have to be captured by a fairly complex consistency axiom or – as we prefer – again by the access strategy.

Observe that the potential for this kind of difficulty exists with the unique classification as well; however, it seems to be more easily removed there.

An *access strategy* for a non-unique classification is a mapping

$$\beta : 2^T \times A \times 2^T \to \mathbf{B}$$

The interpretation of β is as follows: A user with privileges $T_u \subseteq T$ is allowed access to data in compartments $T_d \subseteq T$ via access method $\varrho \in A$ if and only if $\beta(T_u, \varrho, T_d) = 1$.

Again, if $\varrho \to \varrho'$ then

$$(2) \quad \forall T_u, T_d \subseteq T : \beta(T_u, \varrho, T_d) \leq \beta(T_u), \varrho', T_d)$$

Very little else can be said about β in general. Only the following axiom seems to be natural:

(3) β is isotonic or antitonic in the first and third components

This axiom is motivated by the following observation: Suppose that

$$\beta(T_u, \varrho, T_d) \leq \beta(T_u, \varrho, T_{d'})$$

where $T_d \subseteq T_{d'}$. Then if $T_{d''} \supseteq T_{d'}$ one would assume

$$\beta(T_u, \varrho, T_d) \leq \beta(T_u, \varrho, T_{d''})$$

to hold.

To be quite plain – there is no absolutely compelling reason for accepting axiom (3). However, most of the situations seem to satisfy it.

12. Security Schemes – An Example

A *security scheme* is a quintuple

$$(\{S_i \mid i \in I\}, \{T_j \mid j \in J\}, A, \{\alpha_i \mid i \in I\}, \{\beta_j \mid j \in J\})$$

where I and J are finite index sets, each S_i is a unique classification, each T_j is a non-unique classification, A is a set of access methods, and α_i, β_j are access strategies for S_i and T_j, respectively.

In contrast to the lattice model and other related models, the structural details of a security scheme according to this definition allow for a greater flexibility in defining access strategies and access restriction enforcement mechanisms. The precise relation between our model and the lattice model will be treated in a forthcoming paper.

As an example of a security scheme consider the scheme discussed in the previous sections. There we have, for instance,

$$S_1 = \{\textit{top-secret}, \textit{secret}, \textit{confidential}, \textit{unclassified}\}$$

$$S_2 = \text{the sensitivity levels}$$

$$T_1 = \text{the compartments}$$

$$A = \{r, w, r/w\} \quad \text{with} \quad w \rightarrow r, r/w \rightarrow r, r/w \rightarrow w$$

The functions α_1, α_2, β_1 are given by tables as described by the binary vectors discussed before.

The important observation to make at this point is that the security classes do not have a structure on their own; whatever structure they may have is really induced by the partial order on A via the mappings α_i, β_j. This is not just the "hen-and-egg problem". It seems that only in this way can one adapt to various situations arising in computerized document processing.

13. The Statistics of a Security Scheme

In the simulation it was shown that the Bell-LaPadula model is unusable in a computerized document processing environment. In the formal model we provide the theoretical justification of these simulation results, which would allow one to perform analogous evaluations for this and other models without carrying out a simulation.

We assume that the probability distributions of assignments of security classes and compartments to documents (data elements), and users are the same. For $i \in I$ let $P_i(X_i = s)$ denote the probability that a document or user is assigned the class $s \in S_i$. Similarly, let $Q_j(Y_j = T')$ denote the probability that a document or user is assigned the compartments in $T' \subseteq T_j$.

Then, assuming independence, the probability that a user with security classes

$$\{x_i \mid i \in I\} \quad \text{and} \quad \{y_j \mid j \in J\}$$

can access data items via access method $\varrho \in A$ is

$$\text{Prob}(\forall i \in I \ \alpha(x_i, \varrho, X_i) = 1 \wedge \forall j \in J \ \beta(y_j, \varrho, Y_j) = 1))$$

$$= \prod_{i \in I} \mathrm{Prob}(\alpha(x_i, \varrho, X_i) = 1) \cdot \prod_{j \in J} \mathrm{Prob}(\beta(y_j, \varrho, Y_j) = 1)$$

$$= \prod_{i \in I} \sum_{\alpha(x_i, \varrho, s)=1} P_i(X_i = s) \cdot \prod_{j \in J} \sum_{\beta(y_j, \varrho, T')=1} Q_j(Y_j = T')$$

One easily verifies that with the data used in the simulation this formula confirms the simulation results. Of course, it can be used to evaluate other security policies. In fact, its main advantage is that it allows one to assess the usability of such a policy without having to carry out empirical or simulation tests.

References

[1] Ames, S.R., Jr., *User Interface Multilevel Security Issues in a Transaction-Oriented Data Base Management Model*, The Mitre Corp., MTP-178, Bedford, MA (December 1976).

[2] Anderson, J.P., *Computer Security Technology Planning Study*, USAF Electronic Systems Division, ESD-TR-73-51, Bedford, MA (October 1972).

[3] Bell, D.E., and LaPadula, L.J., *Secure Computer Systems: A Mathematical Model*, USAF Electronic Systems Division, ESD-TR-278, Bedford, MA (November 1973).

[4] Biba, K.J., *Integrity Considerations for Secure Computer Systems*, USAF Electronic Systems Division, ESD-TR-372, Bedford, MA (April 1977).

[5] Carroll, J.M., and MacIver, W., *COSSAC: Computer Systems Security Analyzer and Configurator*, Proc. IFIPS/SEC-1984, Toronto (September 1984).

[6] Cohen, F., *Computer Viruses: Theory and Experiments*, Proc. IFIPS/SEC-1984, Toront (September 1984).

[7] Denning, D.E.R., *A Lattice Model of Secure Information Flow*, Comm. ACM **19** (1976).

[8] Dewdney, A.K., *Computer Recreations*, Scientific American **250**, 5 (1984), 14-22.

[9] Graubart, R.D., and Woodward, J.P.L., *A Preliminary Naval Surveillance DBMS Security Model*, Proc. IEEE Symp. Security and Privacy, Oakland, CA (April 1982).

[10] Karger, P.A., and Schell, R.R., *MULTICS Security Evaluation: Vulnerability Analysis*, USAF Electronic Systems Division, Bedford, MA (June 1974).

[11] Landwehr, C.E., *Formal Models for Computer Security*, ACM Comp. Surveys **13** (1981).

[12] Landwehr, C.E., Heitmeyer, C.L., and McLean, J., *A Security Model for Military Message Systems*, Naval Res. Lab., MR-4925, Washington, DC (September 1982).

[13] McGettrick, A.D., *Program Verification Using Ada* (Cambridge Univ. Press, Cambridge, 1982).

[14] McLean, J., Landwehr, C.E., and Heitmeyer, C.L., *A Formal Statement of the MMS Security Model*, Proc. IEEE Symp. Security and Privacy, Oakland, CA (April 1984).

[15] Nibaldi, G.H., *Specifications for a Trusted Computing Base (TCB)*, The Mitre Corp., Bedford, MA (November 1979).

[16] Thompson, K., *Reflections on Trusting Trust*, Comm. ACM **27** (1984), 761-763.

[17] Weissman, C., *Security Controls for the ADEPT-50 Time Sharing System*, AFIPS Conf. Proc. **35** (1969), 119-133.

COMPUTER SECURITY
J.B. Grimson and H.-J. Kugler (Editors)
Elsevier Science Publishers B.V. (North-Holland)

DESIGN OF A RELATIONAL SCHEMA FOR DATABASE DYNAMIC AUTHORIZATION MANAGEMENT

Mariagrazia Fugini
Dipartimento di Elettronica
POLITECNICO DI MILANO
Piazza L.da Vinci, 32
20133 MILANO ITALY

Database authorization management often encompasses treatment of grant and revocation of access rights. This paper discusses discretional authorization to access to database resources, and presents a relational schema of data which are needed by the DBMS to handle dynamic authorization introduced by rights propagation. The schema is derived from a conceptual description of the policies of access authority distribution inside the organization.

1. INTRODUCTION

Large database installations are more and more demanding that database management functions be distributed among several individuals. One aspect relates to authority of regulating access to the database. The decentralization of this authority reflects a distribution of administrative and operational functions among different persons, each concerned with some portions of the database. In fact, the responsible for a group of data and applications is likely in charge of distributing access rights among users of that portion of the system. Also, his authorization to grant these privileges is typically delivered by a central database administrator, or by authorities which are higher in the organization hierarchy.

Automatic handling of authority distribution requires a database authorization mechanism able to manage dynamic authorization.

The problem of authority distribution and grant and revocation strategies connected to it is discussed in [1]. Grant and revocation of rights is managed by some existing database systems: in System R [2, 3], dynamic authorization is handled through system catalogs describing grantability of access rights; the creator of a relation has all privileges on it and can propagate a subset of these; an access right may be granted with "grant" option.
Ingres [4] manages dynamic authorization allowing to grant access rights through the "define permit" QUEL command: rights can be granted on relations only by their owners under conditions, such as content-dependent or time-dependent conditions, name of the terminal on which the grantee should be logged in, etc.

In this paper, dynamic authorization is tackled from a design point of view; the aim is to devise the module of the Data Base

Management System (DBMS) which is in charge of managing the privilege to deliver and revoke access rights. Two levels of authority are considered; the authority to grant access rights and the authority to deliver the right to grant access rights. This reflects a hierarchical distribution of administrative roles in several enterprises.
We present the basic features of a logical schema for management of this two-levels dynamic authorization: in particular, a relational schema is shown for those data which are needed by the DBMS in order to check authorization of users to deliver access or grant rights.
This schema is obtained from the authorization policies of the organization [5]; these policies state authorization of users, protection of resources such as data and programs, and establish which users have the discretion to deliver privileges.
We suppose that authorization policies have been collected and analyzed in a former phase of the authorization system design, namely a conceptual design: in this phase, authorization policies are collected and represented in an implementation-independent way through a conceptual model: conflicts and ambiguities in authorization policies are solved. This multilevel approach to database authorization, also discussed in [6], derives from the idea of treating security information in the same way as information describing the database: thus, a multiphase methodology similar to database design methodologies can be employed for database authorization design.

In section 2 some policies of authorization are discussed. In section 3 a description of rights propagation policies at conceptual level is given. In section 4 the relational schema of data needed to handle two-levels dynamic authorization is shown.

2. POLICIES OF AUTHORIZATION

Policies of authorization can be classified as:
access policies, which state how database resources, such as data and programs, can be accessed, i.e. read, updated, created, by the users;
rights propagation policies, which define authority of individuals to distribute access rights and grant rights in the system.

We are concerned with this second type of policies: an example of rights propagation policies is given in the following.

- Each resource in the system must have at least one owner.
- The owner of a resource has all types of access rights on it; also, he can distribute authority on the owned resource. We say that he is endowed with rights propagation privileges.
  Thus, a user who owns a set of resources is allowed to manipulate directly some of them, and to distribute authority on some others.
- The owner of a resource can distribute authority on it in two ways. He can deliver access rights on the resource to other users, and we say that he holds grant rights. He can also deliver the privilege to grant access rights on the resource to

users; in this second case, we say that the owner holds delegate rights on the resource.

An example of these policies is shown in fig.1, where the system is assumed to be composed of 10 resources (a-j) and 9 users (A-K); in the figure, only grant and delegate rights are shown.

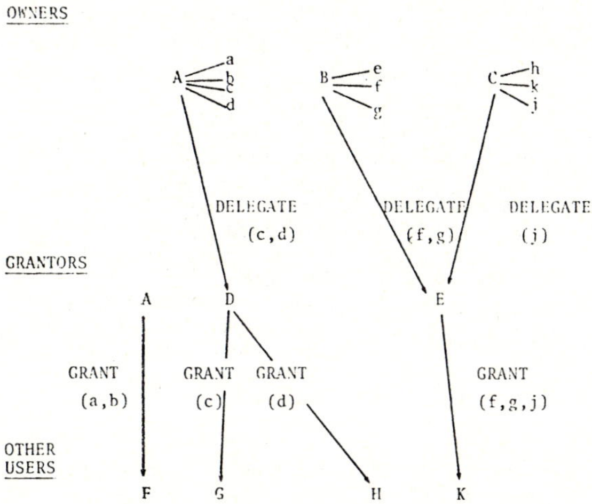

Fig. 1. Example of rights propagation

In this figure, all the resources are distributed among three owners: A,B and C. Users D and E can be delegated by A, B and C to grant access rights on some of these resources; for this reason D and E are named grantors. Namely, D is delegated by A to grant rights on c and d to users G and H; E is delegated by B and C to grant privileges on f, g and j to user K. Note that owner A can grant access rights to user F on a and b, without delegating any right to any grantor user.

3. CONCEPTUAL DESCRIPTION OF RIGHTS PROPAGATION POLICIES

As explained in the previous sections, rights propagation privileges allow a user to deliver and revoke access and grant rights; therefore, authorization checking requires that access and grant rights be run-time updated, according to the dynamic delivering and revoking of rights. This problem is known as dynamic authorization management [7, 2]. The design of an authorization system able to manage dynamic authorization requires that rights propagation policies be fully described to the system.
A conceptual, implementation-independent description of such policies is an effective design tool, because it both allows to understand which information is needed to the system to handle dynamic authorization, and to solve conflicts and ambiguities.

We refer to a conceptual model for authorization developed by the authors [8], where access rights and propagation rights are represented on two distinct graph frameworks. We consider the framework related to rights propagation privileges.
Let us introduce the conceptual description of rights propagation policies.

<u>Delegate rights</u> are specified as follows:

1.DELEGATOR 2.DELEGATED_USER 3.ACCESS_RIGHT 4.DELEGATED_RESOURCE 5.GRANTEE_USERS

This means that a user (delegator) who owns a resource (delegated resource) can deliver another user (delegated_user) the privilege to grant an access right to a set of users (grantee users). The specification of the set of grantee users is needed by the system in order to control the parameters of the subsequent "grant" operation performed by the delegated_user.

A delegate right delivered by a delegator U1, to a delegated user U2 on a resource R with grantee users U3 and U4 is shown in fig.2.

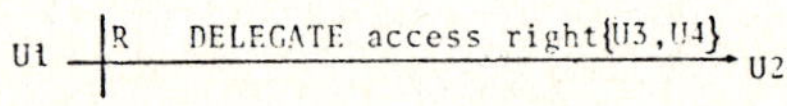

Fig. 2. Delegate right

<u>Grant rights</u> are specified as follows:

1.GRANTOR 2.GRANTEE_USER 3.ACCESS_RIGHT 4.GRANTED_RESOURCE

The grantor may or may not be required to hold the access right he can grant, depending on the authorization policies.

Graphically, a grant right delivered by a grantor U2 to a grantee user U3 on a resource R is represented as shown in fig.3.

Fig. 3. Grant right

Fig.4 a) is a graphical representation of the conceptual model relating to the following rights propagation policies.
User U1 owns R and S; R is also owned by U7; U1 can delegate user U2 the READ access right and the UPDATE access right on the resource R. The READ right is grantable by U2 to users U3 and U4; the UPDATE right is grantable by U2 to users U5 and U6. Also, U1 can grant to user U6 the right to READ S. User U7 can delegate to U2 the UPDATE right on R; this right is grantable by U2 to U5.

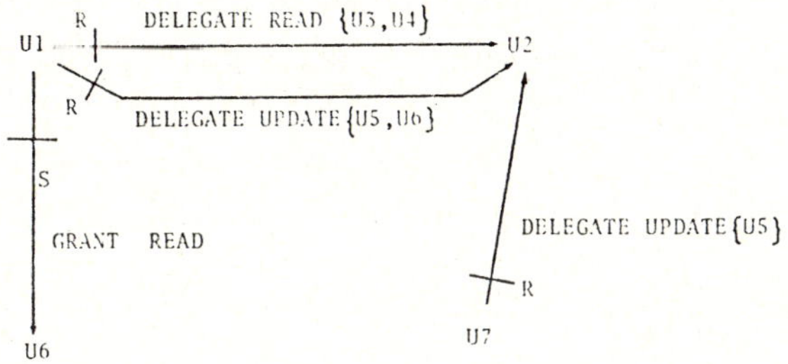

a)

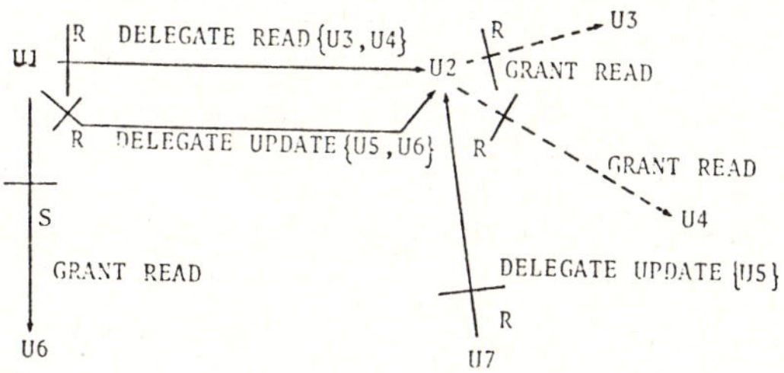

b)

Fig. 4. Conceptual model of rights propagation policies

In fig. 4 b) it is supposed that U1 has actually delegated READ to U2 and the corresponding grant rights acquired by U2 (dotted-line arrows) are shown.

The conceptual model is intended to be a semantic framework which shows information needed to automatically handle users requests of delivering and revoking rights, and how this information must be managed by the system. As such, it is useful to check the consistency and completeness of authorization policies. This view of conceptual modelling is now widely accepted in the database research area [9].

In the remainder of the paper, it is assumed that the distribution of propagation rights and the consequent modification of users authorization and of resources protection has been tested to be the desired ones on the conceptual model, and that all conflicts of policies have been solved at the level of the conceptual design.

4. THE LOGICAL SCHEMA OF RIGHTS PROPAGATION PRIVILEGES

This section illustrates a relational schema of data which are needed to represent grant and delegate rights and to handle dynamic authorization. This schema is derived from the conceptual representation of rights propagation privileges illustrated in sect.3. However, this paper is not concerned with a procedural description of conceptual-logical mapping; we only show how conceptual information about dynamic authorization can be organized into a relational framework. Also, the relational schema can be improved on a performance basis; anyway, optimization is not considered in this discussion.

The relational schema is accessed by the authorization module of the DBMS in charge of checking access and rights propagation privileges. Upon each request performed by a user to delegate or grant rights, the authorization system checks the user authorization profile against the system relations describing user's discretion to delegate and grant privileges. On a positive result, information about the delivered rights is recorded by the authorization system in the schema.
We suppose that authorization to access to database resources is checked by the authorization module against a set of system relations, which describe access rights. This set of relations is updated by the authorization module, according to grant and revocation of access rights performed by grantors.

This presentation is framed in the structure of rights propagation policies described in sect.2. These policies can be more constraining (e.g. a resource can have only one owner) or less constraining (e.g. also ownership can be delegated), depending on the type of organization under exam.

In sect.4.1 the system relations needed by the authorization system to handle dynamic authorization are presented.
In sect.4.2 the basic functions performed by the authorization system for dynamic authorization checking are shown.

4.1. RELATIONS FOR DYNAMIC AUTHORIZATION MANAGEMENT

Entities represented in the relational schema are users, programs and data. Users and programs are known to the DBMS through a unique identifier (user_id or program_id). Data are user relations, set of relations, portion of relations, such as sets of tuples or attributes whose values satisfy a fixed condition.

The authorization schema is constituted by two relations:

DELEGATE (OWNER, OWNED_RES, DELEGATED, AC_RIGHT, GRANTABLE_TO)

This relation describes delegate rights: a user (owner) who owns a resource (owned_res) can delegate another user (delegated) an access right grantable to a specified user (grantable_to).

GRANT (DELEGATED_BY, GRANTED_RES, GRANTOR, AC_RIGHT, GRANTEE)

This relation contains information about grant rights: a user (grantor) can grant to a user (grantee) an access right on a resource (granted_res).

According to our policies, the grantor may be the owner of the resource or must have been delegated by the owner. Consequently, the GRANT.DELEGATED_BY attribute may be empty or contain the delegator's user_id. All the tuples with a user_id in this attribute can be inserted into and removed run-time from the schema by the authorization system.

4.2. THE DYNAMIC AUTHORIZATION MANAGEMENT PROCEDURE

In this section, the dynamic authorization checking procedure is illustrated (see fig.5).

The authorization system filters the requests performed by users to delegate or grant access rights.
On a request performed by a user U1 to delegate an access right AR to a user U2 on a resource R, the authorization system tries to retrieve from the DELEGATE relation one (or more) tuple with attribute values equal to the parameters (users_id, name of the resource, type of access right , etc...) of the user request (see fig.5 a). Referring to the example in fig4 , and supposing that U1 requests to delegate the READ right to U2 on R, the tuples:

```
-------------------------
U1 | R | U2 | READ | U3 |
-------------------------
U1 | R | U2 | READ | U4 |
-------------------------
```

are retrieved from DELEGATE.
As a consequence, U1 can delegate, and two tuples corresponding to the dotted-line arrows of fig. 4 b) are inserted into the GRANT relation.
This relation is directly accessed by the authorization system when a user U2 requests to grant an access right (see figure 5 b). If the corresponding tuple is retrieved, the authorization procedure inserts information about the new access right in an ACCESS relation, which can be of the form:

ACCESS (USER, TYPE_OF_ACCESS, RES, GRANTED_BY)

Let us show the procedure of revoking access and grant rights.
If a delegate right is revoked to U2 by U1, all the tuples with GRANT.DELEGATED_BY=U1 are removed from the GRANT relation, and all the tuples with ACCESS.GRANTED_BY=U2 are removed from the ACCESS relation; if two identical tuples are found in ACCESS, only one is removed. In fact, U2 may have granted AR to U3 on R twice, since two different owners of R may have delegated the same right AR to U2. This case is shown in fig.6, where U1 and U10 can delegate the same AR on R to U2. As a consequence, U2 can grant AR twice to U3, as

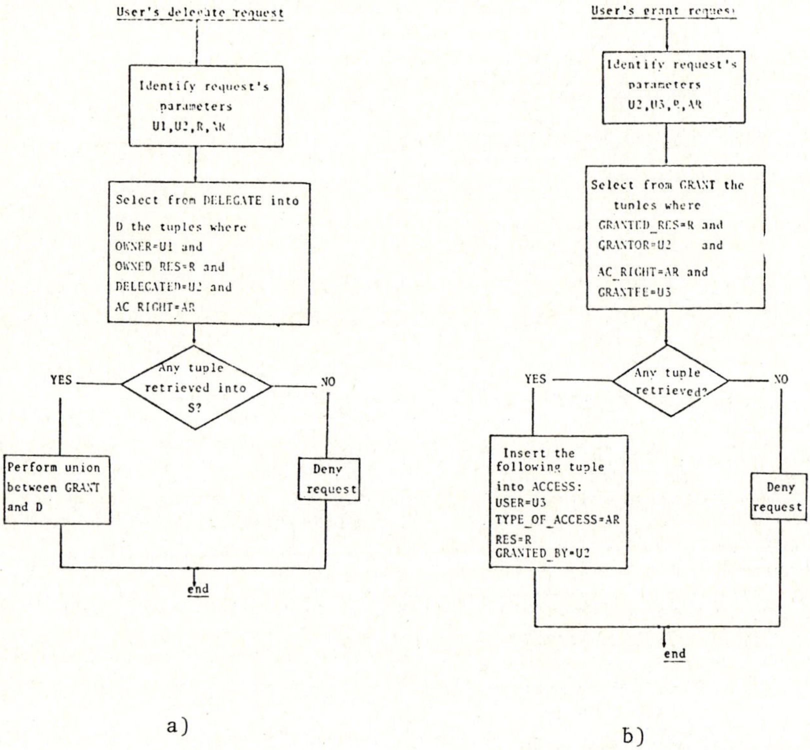

Fig. 5. The dynamic authorization procedure

shown by two dotted-line arrows between U2 and U3.

If a grant right is revoked by a grantor U2, all the tuples with ACCESS.GRANTED_BY=U2 are removed from the ACCESS relation.

5. CONCLUDING REMARKS

Some users of a database system may be allowed to grant and revoke access rights to other users. Also, some organizations may require that some users discretionally deliver authority on the portion of database for which they are responsible, still maintaining the privilege to revoke such authority.
These issues introduce the need to design an authorization system able to dynamically manage access rights.
The basic features of an authorization system able to manage two hierarchical levels of responsibilities have been presented.

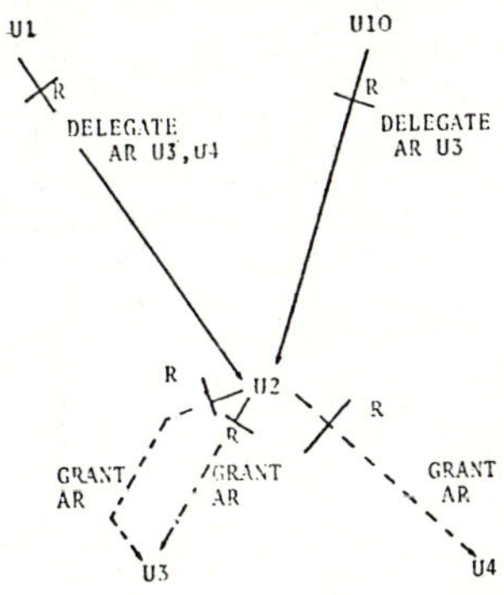

Fig. **6.** Multiple delegation of rights on a user U2

Information needed by the system has been focused, on the basis of a conceptual description of authorization policies which guide the database administration.

REFERENCES

[1] J.A.Larson, "Granting and revoking discretionary authority", Information Systems, vol. 8, n. 4 (1983)

[2] P.P.Griffiths, B.W.Wade, "An authorization mechanism for a relational database system", ACM Trans. on Database Systems, vol. 1, n. 3 (Sept.1976)

[3] P.F.Wilms, B.G.Lindsay, "A database authorization mechanism supporting individual and group authorization", in Distributed Data Sharing Systems, ed. Van de Riet, Litwin, North-Holland, Amsterdam (1982)

[4] M.Stonebraker, E.Wong, P.Kreps, G.Held, "The design and implementation of Ingres", ACM Trans. on Database Systems, vol. 1, n. 3 (Sept.1976)

[5] C.Wood, E.B.Fernandez, R.C.Summers, "Data base security: requirements, policies and models", IBM Systems Journal, vol. 19, n. 2 (1980)

[6] E.B.Fernandez, R.C.Summers, C.Wood, "Authorization in multilevel database models", Information Systems, vol. 4 (1979)

[7] E.B.Fernandez, R.C.Summers, C.Wood, Data Base Security and Integrity, Addison-Wesley, Reading (1981)

[8] U.Bussolati, M.G.Fugini, G.Martella, "A conceptual framework for security systems:the action-entity model", Proc. IFIP 9th World Computer Congress, Paris (Sept.1983)

[9] M.L.Brodie, J.Mylopoulos, J.W.Schmidt eds., On conceptual modelling: perspectives from artificial intelligence, databases, and programming languages, Springer-Verlag (1983)

COMPUTER SECURITY
J.B. Grimson and H.-J. Kugler (Editors)
Elsevier Science Publishers B.V. (North-Holland)

THE HIGH MORTALITY OF DATA

Prof. dr. I.S. Herschberg[1] and Ir. R. Paans[2]

The high reliability of present-day computer equipment, constructed for technical near-immortality, is contrasted with the much lesser reliability of its software, subject to disease and decay. Data is even more ephemeral and prey to mortal corruption.
A first, coarsely quantitative, analysis of the causes of the pollution so engendered in data will be given. It will be concluded that what is (re)produced by any computing system should be handled with extreme care and scepticism.

The ultra-reliability of hardware

It is hard to exaggerate the reliability of present-day hardware. Let us take some current large systems as examples. It is well known that in a large system there are between a few and a few tens of millions of operations going on each second, or, in popular parlance, we deal with machines ranging from, say, three to some twenty *M*illion *I*nstructions *P*er *S*econd (MIPS) or over. What is more, this rate can be maintained for twenty-four hours a day, week in week out, throughout the year and, even more surprisingly, it can be maintained over the years. If it had not been for economic obsolescence, many of the mainframes of the seventies would still be with us because, in a technical sense, they would not have deteriorated significantly. In this respect they are reminiscent of airplanes which, also technically speaking, seem to have life eternal: the propeller planes which have become economically obsolete in the West still run happily in less well-favoured countries showing that, technically, they are as good as ever.

Mainframes, too, leave nothing to be desired given technical maintenance. To quote an example (hard to substantiate but correct in order of magnitude) just a handful of hardware errors occur during normal operation in the course of a year. For convenience's sake, let us approximate this handful by the constant π. Working out the sum, we find that in a year, that is some π * 10**7 seconds, there are some π * 10**14 operations per system. Now if we allow π errors in a year, this boils down to the order of magnitude of one error in 10**14 operations, an achievement which has never been equalled before and which corresponds to a resolution hard to equal anywhere else, except in mainframes, in today's world.

If one is allowed a slightly poetical interpretation of the signal-to-noise ratio, one error in 10**14 operations equals a signal-to-noise ratio of 140 decibels (dB) which amounts to such absence of noise as is not found anywhere else, we believe, in technology. Moreover, this signal-to-noise ratio is not even the ultimate limit. It is due to John von Neumann [6] that such a ratio can always be

[1] Delft University of Technology, Department of Mathematics and Informatics, P.O. Box 356, 2600 AJ Delft, The Netherlands.
[2] during this research, Mr. Paans was with Delft University of Technology, Department of Electrical Engineering.

doubled, barring five dB, by simply triplicating the hardware which in turn means that, with present-day equipment, something like a 275 dB purity of signal can be achieved. We posit that, going back to chemistry which is part of our background, this purity is incredible: it would mean, roughly speaking again, that a ton of iron could be made so pure that it would not hold more than one single atom other than iron and, even in these days of sophisticated solid-state technology, such a purity is not even dreamt of in chemistry.

Let us express the incredible reliability of our present-day hardware in different terms, say in terms of thermodynamics. It is easily shown that such purity corresponds to a minimal, in fact subminimal, increase of entropy due to the hardware's operation. Now a very low increase of entropy, or rather the absence of any measurable entropy at all, corresponds to being very close to absolute zero (0 K), in fact much closer to this ultimate limit than can be reached by any other known process. The comparison to such an ultimate of low temperature is also significant because, as is well-known, cooling to such temperature requires a lot of energy and it is not therefore surprising to learn that this hardware, performing superbly and ultra-reliably as it does, requires some 150 kilowatt (kW) for its operation. This corresponds very closely to what a similarly sized attempt to achieve these ultra-low temperatures would in effect require; that the dissipation therefore - one must heat in order to cool - should be so high is not surprising.

Of course, this ultra-reliability is not achieved without trouble. Even within the circuitry, many additional measures must be taken to preserve it. Error detection is quite efficient and is, moreover, supported by error-correction circuits so that the π errors per annum we referred to are, in fact, achieved owing to retries and other corrective actions. It is, so to speak, then by sleight of hand that is unbeknown to the user. But why worry about that? So long as the reliable effect is achieved it is not for the user to enquire how it is achieved. The occasional retry when accessing memory and the occasional error correction occurring automatically and behind the user's back should not detract from the picture we have sketched: the hardware is ultra-reliable. This applies, to a lesser but still quite significant degree, even if the hardware observed is extended with storage devices still having some mechanical components that is, for instance, some rotating or linearly moving devices. Even there the reliability, while not quite reaching one error in 10**14 is still within, say, two orders of magnitude of this figure, yielding a still quite astonishing error rate of one in 10**12. We can therefore safely rule out hardware errors, in whatever guise, as a factor significantly contributing to lack of data integrity.

Control software: always in control?

Still and all, crashes occur more often than to the tune of π per annum. At the outset, let us state that most crashes, unfortunately, cannot be traced to their origin. In those cases which *are* traceable to their origin and are in effect so traced, we arrive, estimating roughly, at crash frequencies amounting to some one occurrence per month. This, rather optimistic, estimate applies only to those systems enjoying a stable environment, that is, essentially dealing with the same application spheres, and hence they do not apply to installations where the type of application may be dependent on the time of day or to those hyper-complex installations which attempt to be all things to all men. If 'general purpose' is driven to its extreme, it is not unusual for these crashes to rise in frequency to a few a day.

The reason for these crashes is not far to seek: present-day control software is of almost unbounded complexity [5,7], where neither the term 'unbounded' nor 'complexity' should be taken in its strict mathematical sense. Let us take them, rather, in a workaday sense when dealing with control software, that is with the operating system and its various appendages driving peripherals and telecommunications consisting, in quite normal cases, of some ten millions statements and suffering, at any given moment, from the occurrence of 100 to 200 known errors at any time. This is a lamentable state of affairs. However vigorously the correction of these errors is being pursued, it seems an impossible race because at best one has to run very fast to keep up - at some distance - with the rate of errors being signalled. Even so, the crash rate attributable to control software (of which may be stated that, at least in the purist sense, it has gone out of control) still makes no very significant contribution to data error, at least not in relation to further types of error with which we shall be dealing in the sequel.

The application software is accident-prone

Even so, control software, with its many known errors, is a model of probity when compared with application software. It is generally known that about 70% of an application programmer's activities is devoted to what is euphemistically called 'maintenance'. Now the notion of 'maintenance' covers a multitude of sins, and we shall not state categorically that maintenance, so understood, only amounts to the deletion of errors found to exist in applications. Rather, maintenance often covers minor modifications not arising from errors shown but simply from meeting new requirements, notably new user requirements. Still and all, a great deal of 'maintenance' is designed to correct errors, shortcomings, lapses, call them how you will, in applications. It is almost impossible to quantify the percentage contribution of application-program errors to data pollution, to data mishandling or by whatever other term one wishes to refer to data corruption. It is, however, a certainty in the experts' view and it is common ground among all programmers that application errors *do* contribute significantly to data pollution. To quote just one amusing example: it was an application programming error which caused, in an experimental system in The Netherlands, a seventh child of a parent to be correctly recorded as a seventh child, but also caused the parents' names to be entered among their own children, thereby leading, through a program error, to the biological impossibility of parents being their own child. (The programmer had not included families with more than six children in his test cases.)

Other examples with less amusing and much more serious consequences abound and will spring to mind to anyone in our audience. Unfortunately, we are not in a position to quantify the contribution of application errors to the corruption of data. EDP-auditors generally are justifiably weary of program errors in applications, precisely because, until the error has been brought to light and has been corrected, its effects can be devastating even while they are unquantifiable.

The corrupt birth of data

It is not always realized to what extent data, when first recorded on some medium to be eventually transferred to a computer memory, internal or external, are tainted at their origin. The authors have some crass examples of this. To mention an innocent instance once more, it was found during an investigation in The Netherlands that three in any thousand personal records in an experimental population registry system contained either a biological impossibility or, failing that, were in conflict with the explicitly stated rules of that same registry. Now three in every thousand may seem an excessively low score. It is *not*: when evaluating this experimental figure, it should be kept in mind that data were prepared and entered by those in charge of the population registry, a profession which does not make for a lax or lackadaisical approach to lapses in general and to data in particular. One should shudder to think about their actual occurrence in less exacting, less consciously precise environments. Again, quantifiable data are lacking, but at least in our experience roughly one in a hundred statements emanating from a bank is completely corrupt in the sense that the addressee has no apparent relation to the account number actually affected, which is to say that some booking in a statement simply has been ascribed to the wrong account. By the nature of things, most of these errors are eventually corrected. Even so, this is far from always being the case, because, as we shall show later on, it is *not* in the nature of man to act to his own best advantage. Even so, the figure of one item going astray in a hundred of bank statements or similar could give rise to a great deal of fraud.

Even where punch-cards are still in use, and where, by tradition, they are verified independently, the authors find that, while a great many errors are caught, a great many also still slip by. Incidentally, one may arrive at a very good estimate of the percentage of the original errors caught by looking at the back of the Dutch Postgiro transfer cards: in about one in twenty of them, you may find at the back a bit of silvered sticking paper indicating that, even this day and age, a hole has been pasted over and repunched by hand.

To summarize the argument: data, even when cross-checked by verification or other means, is corrupt. It has a very high percentage of errors when entered by hand, as most data still must be: automatic data capture, though on the increase, is still a rarity. We arrive, very crudely, at a probable estimate of data corruption rate arising from their very birth, that is from the moment of entry, of one percent. This applies to the best-controlled environments. There is definitely more than this single percentage point in a more humdrum, workaday environment.

True, countermeasures can be taken and are being taken against the data being corrupted at entry-time. Check digits or their equivalents are being applied and, in our view, should be applied far more widely than they are. We are also familiar with painstaking, lengthy and often less than transparent verification programs based on checking the data entered for its inherent plausibility. Too often these techniques are applied in a less than strict manner. It is often objected that these verifications are so lengthy, so involved and give rise to so much overhead that one feels justified to omit them on exceptional occasions, such as bulk input. Even when applied, plausibility checks, e.g. checks of reasonable ranges of data entered, often fail to capture errors of this type because the error, though outrageous by human standards, still falls in the range allowed by the plausibility check. If the normal transaction in a financial environment is not subject to special checking unless it exceeds, say, ten thousand dollars, then the introduction, fraudulently or not, of an extra zero in many cases will not be sieved out by the checking program. In effect, a case can be made that complete checking of input data is impossible in the present state of the art because it would in effect expect the computer to have not just artificial intelligence but *human* intelligence, an achievement far beyond the possibilities of our present-day machines.

Corruption by birth, death and removal

If one deals with data that are related to individuals, biology in its strictest sense steps in to create sources of data corruption. To start with the simplest causes: people are happily subject to birth and unfortunately subject to death. In a roughly stable population in Western countries, these two processes tend to be in approximate equilibrium; even so, they each account for about 2‰ of modifications per annum on any given data base in so far as it deals with persons. Certainly the 2‰ effects of the inescapable death cannot be discounted even if one's data set deals with adults only and does not take the newborn into account.

However, understanding biology in its wider sense to include the migratory habits of homo sapiens, his tendency to move house and to call that removal-van every seven years or so during his life, makes for corruption. Any Dutch data base containing people's addresses must count with a rough migration rate of some

15% per annum, which implies that man is not too firmly resident and changes his premises with some predictable frequency of once every seven years. A connection with the well-known seven-year itch is suggested, though not too seriously. Also, when the data base refers to an individual's relations to an organization it is a sad fact - to some - that people *do* change their affiliation and notably that they *do* resign from organizations they belong to.

These three causes, when added together, imply a mutation rate either with respect to persons and their addresses which is conservatively estimated at 20% per annum. This is a well-known fact to all those operating and maintaining these data bases. The consequences are not always considered very carefully during the initial design phase.

Running fast to stay behind the facts

The above, gloomy but realistic, picture of a data base's corruption is completely analogous to the law of radioactive decay: at any given instant in time, the number of decays (that is changes of address etcetera) that is the rate of corruption, is proportional to the number of atoms present, that is proportional to the number of records present, that is proportional to the number of persons in the data base. When the rate of decay through the causes outlined above approximates 20% per annum (conservatively), the law of radioactive decay states that there is a well-defined half-life to the validity of the data in the data base. If one is doing no active updating of changes in affiliations, residents, etcetera, the rate of changes at 20% implies that the half-life is some three years.

This means that, even if it should be possible to have a data base completely correct, error-free and in accordance with the facts at some year t, it will unless rigorously updated, decay to being 50% corrupt at year $t+3$. It is easily seen and widely appreciated that such an updating policy therefore must be pursued for all data which, being person-related and subject to precisely this type of decay, at something like the rate indicated.

The consequence which unfortunately is not universally appreciated is that the noble pursuit of the maintenance of such a data base decaying at 20% per annum implies that for each and every workday (roughly estimated at 200 per annum), one must modify at least one datum, possibly an entire record, per workday for each thousand persons in the data base. For a data base comprising a million persons - and these are far from uncommon - this amounts to the data-base owner's willingness to modify one thousand records for each workday, and so proportionally for larger data bases.

Incidentally, even in a territory as small as The Netherlands, numbering 14 millions souls, data bases exist containing ten millions of entries, all of them person-related. This implies an updating rate which, when extended to the entire Dutch population, amounts to approximately ten thousand modifications (updates) per day. In at least a few historical examples, this updating rate was not anticipated with the direst consequences for the reliability of the data base involved. Even so, one cannot hope to be up to date at any one time. It follows that for each day one lags behind the facts, a 0.1% degree of pollution is inevitably introduced. This in fact reduces the signal-to-noise ratio in the data base by fully 30 dB which is ludicrously high, seeing that the hardware achieves 140 dB fidelity without effort. To paraphrase Alice, in data country one must run very fast just to make no progress at all: one must update furiously for the privilege of being slightly behind the times.

Practice shows that man is far from having his own best interests at heart. A large Dutch insurance company, trying to maintain a data base of its policy-holders, has found that, in spite of its honest and costly efforts, some

7% of the relevant addresses were obsolete at any given point in time. Since a major portion of its policies covered theft and fire, these policy-holders would be without insurance cover (which is site-dependent) while their addresses were out of date. Even so, this must have been the case for, roughly, one policy-holder in 14. This data pollution was caused by the 20% decay per annum. Assume premiums are due once a year and that the average client holds one policy; it follows, with the given rate, that 10% of bills would be wrongly addressed when the average delay is one half of the once-a-year billing rate. The company's best effort only resulted in a reduction of the expected 10% decay rate to a steady-state error of 7%, shocking, perhaps, to the uninitiated, but not at all unusual for the population at large.

Fraud as a data corruptor

All the above causes of impurity, corruption, pollution in data are, in a manner of speaking, 'natural' causes. These have in common that they are almost inevitable and countermeasures, though possible, are just sufficient, in the best of cases, to counteract some but not all pollution. In a different view, these pollution causes have in common that they are, for the most part, unintentional, not given in by malice aforethought.

Though we have earlier references to cite [2,5,7,8], the present authors are far from being the only ones to point out how easily applications and control software may be corrupted. If they could not, it would be pointless to hold annual international conferences sponsored by IFIP [3,4] about this type of intentional corruption, known as computer-related fraud, also known as hacking or cracking the computer system. Of course, the impact of these intentional corruptive influences is impossible to gauge. However, anyone responsible for data control or data audit should be well aware of fraud, the big corruptor.

It is not relevant in this context whether the corruption, as in the classical cases, arises at data-entry level, that is by wilfully and maliciously manipulating data or whether it arises at system level, that is by wilfully tampering with the system. Both varieties occur, both varieties cast further doubt on the integrity of data stored in a system, - and what significant amounts of data are nowadays stored unless it be *within* a computer system of some description?

What price confidence?

We offer, in conclusion, that various causes combine to corrupt data in any given data set or data base to the extent of one in a hundred in a favourable case, one in ten possibly in less favourable but conceivable cases. This forces one to the conclusion that such corruptible data bases as we have even in the absence of wilful, fraudulent corruption should not be too closely relied on for individual cases.

Whatever is recorded in any individual record has a non-negligible change of being utterly wrong and without foundation. A certain lack of definition, a certain degree of being out of focus is, we hope to have shown, inherent in any large collection of data, most especially when this deals with natural persons and their actions, affiliations and finances.

This inaccuracy is not particularly troublesome in statistical applications when the data base or large portions of it are used to extract global, summary data related to the entire (sub)population involved. Such confidence, however, is completely unjustified for individual data and we submit that the noise by natural reasons and the never-to-be-excluded possibility of fraudulent manipulation combine to reduce the contents of our data bases to a moderate degree of controllability and an even more moderate degree of auditability.

In another view of the same facts, the data contained may be just good enough for a census of which it is admitted in the United States that its results cannot be given to better than within a few percent [1]. For applications to an individual, we urge extreme scepticism with regard to anything entered into and therefore with regard to anything extracted from any large data base, in spite of the pseudo-precision. This pseudo-precision, incidentally, is shared with census data: the census, probably no more precise than to within 2‰, had a very pseudo-exact result, e.g., on April 1, 1980 the United States counted exactly 226,545,805 souls.

Finally, we suggest that in the present state of the art the following metaphor is applicable. We play back through an incredibly reliable amplifier (the hardware) data which is the output of a very mediocre turntable and stylus (the software). These in turn are fed with data of such fearful noisiness that it is best compared with an early record from the 78-rpm days. This record moreover has been played so often as to wear out all grooves to their bottom. It is honestly questionable whether such a system is well-balanced.

References

1 Hacker, A, A statistical portrait of the American people, as reviewed in Scientific American Vol 249 No 1 p 24 (July 1983)

2 Herschberg, I S, and R Paans, The programmer's threat: cases and causes, in "Computers security: a global challenge" (1984), see [4] pp 77-90

3 IFIP TC-11, "Security, IFIP/Sec'83" Proceedings of IFIP/Sec'83 Conference, V A Fak (ed) (May 16-19, 1983) Stockholm, ISBN 0-444-86669-8 North-Holland Publ (1983)

4 IFIP TC-11, "Computer security: a global challenge" Proceedings of IFIP/Sec'84 Conference, J H Finch and E G Dougall (eds) (Sept 10-12, 1984) Toronto, ISBN 0-444-87618-9 North-Holland Publ (1984)

5 Miller, J H, Characteristics of the computer environment that provide opportunities for crime, in "Computer security: a global challenge" (1984), see [4] pp 103-108

6 Neumann, J von, The general and logical theory of automata (1948), in "John von Neumann collected works" Vol V, Oxford etc. (1963), p 322

7 Paans, R and A H J Bonnes, Surreptitious security violation in the MVS operating system, in "Security, IFIP/Sec'83" (1983), see [3] pp 95-106

8 Paans, R and I S Herschberg, A topology for secure MVS systems, in "Computer security: a global challenge" (1984), see [4] pp 137-147

COMPUTER SECURITY
J.B. Grimson and H.-J. Kugler (Editors)
Elsevier Science Publishers B.V. (North-Holland)
IFIP, 1985

SOFTWARE VERSUS HARDWARE ENCRYPTION - IS THERE ANY DIFFERENCE TODAY?

Viiveke Fåk

Dept. of Electrical Engineering
Linköping University
S-581 83 Linköping
SWEDEN

Data encryption has traditionally been firmly divided into hardware and software solutions. These two categories differ very much in their characteristics.

HARDWARE CHARACTERISTICS

Hardware has been fast (although not fast enough for disk channels until recently). It has been designed as simple extensions of the line from the terminal so that it should be very easy to install. This means that every terminal, every remote site etc has demanded the purchase of a pair of such boxes. The boxes may be cheap, but that low price has soon multiplied into a very high price for the whole system. With a rather small perceived need for encryption at most installations, this kind of hardware has not been so popular.

SOFTWARE CHARACTERISTICS

Software is conveniently flexible. It can be installed in existing processors. It can be adjusted to peculiarities in the customers protocol or data. It can with relative ease provide true end-to-end encryption, thus eliminating the necessity to trust any nodes and rerouting computers. Standard algorithms are not expensive. They are, however, usually slow. Software encryption has not been given much interest among experts of cryptology. The general approach has been to develop a logically sound method consistent with all rules of cryptology. This will almost inevitably result in something which is not so very easy to do in software. Software encryption has mostly consisted of smart programmers trying to make existing algorithms run as efficiently as possible on a given processor.

CURRENT COMBINATIONS

Thus the obvious solution seems to be a combination of hardware and software. In general this is already true, since "hardware" today often means a standard microprocessor, a customized chip and PROM or something like that. This kind of equipment is, however, usually designed to do a very specific task. They contain features that make very little room for the flexibility of software. It is cheaper to design new versions of such equipment than it is to make a new customized chip (at least in smaller numbers), but still they are very far from the flexibility of a general computer, although they happen to incorporate one.

One solution, that seems natural to many today, is to mix hardware and software in the same system. The terminals have no room for an algorithm. Usually they contain no programmable part. Thus you buy black boxes for them. It is fairly expensive, but there is no alternative. At the central site you have a fairly powerful front-end. There you want software instead of hundreds of black boxes. Unfortunately this means that you can encrypt at the terminals at a very high speed. There this is not needed. At the computer end you are left with the relatively slow software. There you need the high speed. Moreover key management is no problem at the box end. Once it has got its master key installed, everything is fairly easy. At the computer side this is very different. If the devices have individual master keys, these must be stored and handled. Session keys, transaction keys etc are almost always generated at the central side. No matter who generates and distributes these keys, the central site must keep and handle every single one of them. This is also a demanding task. Thus this solution gives you efficient equipment where you do not really need it and inefficient where this is a tremendous drawback. The solution can work, but it is a highly limiting factor on traffic etc. (Or it gives high costs in size of front-ends etc.)

An "in-between" solution is to have more powerful black boxes at the central site. These are small concentrators handling several encrypted lines. They reduce the cost and raise the limitations and rigidity of the system. They are for example highly dependent of the protocol, they fix physical connections to a given pattern, precluding som changes in the front-end etc. For systems where this is already unchangeable for other reasons, they can be useful.

THE IDEAL

The solutions mentioned above also leave one problem unresolved: End-to-end encryption in a fairly complex network. From a security point of view it often makes sense to encrypt data on the relatively sensitive lines near, but not at a terminal, as well as when satellites or radio links are used etc. There is, however, yet another situation when encryption is extremely important: when data passes a computer outside your direct control. It can be a routing computer in a public or a jointly owned network. It can be a computer belonging to another organization with a right to pass some information to or from your computer. It can be a lot of other situations. Cooperation or renting of resources does not mean that all my information is yours. Unfortunately there is today no off-the-shelf equipment for these situations in general. True end-to-end encryption is definitely not a standard.

Thus the market fails to meet many real needs concerning encryption. In spite of standards and modern ways to design equipment there is no ideal solution on the market. What are then the properties of the ideal product? Well it is not one product, but a family. The characteristics are the following:

- It is based on an algorithm which is both fast and small when realized as software. This rules out the DES.

- The algorithm is usually a standard one, which happens to be an ISO standard, but it can be exchanged for a private one for security reasons. This applies to both hardware and software solutions. DES is today the only algorithm even on its way to being standardized.

- The hardware comes mainly in three versions: "The secure cable", "The intelligent cable" and "The peripheral unit". "The secure cable" is cheap, limited to one protocol/version and can not manage for example flexible selective encryption. It can reside on the other end of a cable where there is another "secure cable" device or an "intelligent cable" device. The intelligent cable contains more memory and processor power. It can handle more demanding protocols (including its own for key exchange, selective encryption etc). It can cooperate with all three devices in the family as well as pure software. It is more expensive than "the secure cable". "The peripheral unit" can be connected to a computer through a standard interface. It recognizes a lot of commands including key management, encryption/decryption for a given user and treatment of traffic from or to "the intelligent cable".

- The hardware is always securely encapsulated.

- The hardware can be simulated by fast software due to the structure of the algorithm.

- The hardware contains wired-in master keys. They may be common for a whole system or device dependent, depending on the customers choice.

- The hardware incorporates options (more expensive ones naturally) where key management and user identification can be based on for example chip cards.

- From the above it is quite obvious that the whole family of products is designed as more or less independent modules which can be left out or exchanged for other ones in the different versions.

SECURITY CONCERNS

All hardware units should be properly sealed in order to prevent any tampering. The encryption unit including key storage can be encased in a cast layer of special material, which can not be stripped without breaking entirely including what is encased in it. This technique is sufficient if the units reside in an area which is regarded as physically secure. When this is not the case, the whole unit should be sealed. Maintenance then consists of supplying a new unit. Parts of the old one may still be reused, but only as spare parts in a "new" unit with a new key. This means that the unit must not contain any moving parts, keyboards, readers etc. That is also necessary for the low price. An alternative in for example a rather open office environment is to use chip cards both for user identification and key distribution. Any tampering with the then vulnerable line between card reader and encryption unit will only yield useless intermediary data. The unit should still contain a master key in very sensitive cases, since otherwise someone could install a bug on the card reader line and transmit or record transaction keys, which are used directly without further modification. But the transmitting bug will have severe difficulties getting through the radiation proof encasing that the unit should have anyway, and recording will only work if the wiretapper can regularly come to the site and read the recordings. Thus these threats are not important in most cases.

Software is very vulnerable. It can be used with care in controlled environments with trusted people. Someone with general high responsibility and good understanding of security matters can use it for his PC. Then that person must lock away the floppy containing encryption program and keys immediately after loading. The PC should be shut off whenever it is left unattended after an encryption session, which in its turn means that encryption is used for selected tasks at concentrated, rather rare sessions. At a front-end software may also be used in trusted environments, but great attention should be paid to loading procedures.

COMPUTER SECURITY
J.B. Grimson and H.-J. Kugler (Editors)
Elsevier Science Publishers B.V. (North-Holland)
IFIP, 1985

SECURITY MANAGEMENT IN LARGE ORGANISATIONS

- TWO CASE STUDIES

Kevin D. McLean
Computer Sciences Company Ltd.
20 Savile Row
London
United Kingdom

Complex management and organisational structures can lead to difficulties in applying effective security management. The identification of significant risks and the devolution of authority and responsibility for security are two principal problem areas. Examples drawn from banking and Government department experience illustrate the problems and provide guidelines for their solution.

1.1 INTRODUCTION

There are many management problems associated with the effective running of large organisations. Mostly, these are due to communications problems across departmental and hierarchical boundaries. These problems can easily lead to a failure to disseminate high level corporate policy and, in the reverse sense, a lack of appreciation of inadequacies and weaknesses at the working level. Within a large corporation functionally delineated departments will be large themselves and co-ordination of effort across departmental boundaries is often difficult to achieve. It is often the case that the line management responsibilities for, say user and technical departments, only converge at too high a level for effective and dynamic response to problems arising.

The technologies of data processing and telecommunications are providing the means to assist in the solution of some of the problems of the management of large and diverse organisations. Information centres, management workstations, cheap and effective microcomputer based proprietary applications for financial assessment, planning, trend analysis and other management tasks are all useful weapons in the management armoury. The use of these automated aids in local and wide area networks contribute to the availability of reliable management information, its accurate analysis and the speedy distribution of management instructions. They also present security problems, some of which are discussed in this paper.

Information Systems Security is one management area which is frequently given inadequate attention in all types of organisations which use, and depend on, automated data processing. In a small to medium sized organisation with, for example, a single processing centre, few applications and short lines of communication between departmental managers, there is better opportunity of an awareness of security shortcomings than in a larger corporation. This paper presents some observations on Information Systems Security Management and uses as illustration two example organisations: a large clearing bank with diverse domestic and international business and a Government department involved in processing large amounts of personal data and making payments. (The Government department does not handle information concerned with national security). The two organisations are not identified. In fact, the examples given are based on experience gained from security consultancy in several such organisations.

Both example organisations have employees numbered in thousands, a large number of High Street public offices or branches and a small number of concentrated centralised computer facilities. Each is supported by computer systems implemented on different manufacturers' hardware and to diverse design architectures. There is a commitment in both cases to future integration of current and planned systems into corporate networks to improve consistency and provide better management information.

2.1 THE PERCEPTION OF RISK - THE PROBLEMS

In each of the two example organisations, senior management were asked their views on risks which they felt were significant to the organisation. In both cases, no formal risk assessment programmes had been performed prior to the consultancy activities, and the views expressed were based on the intuition of the managers interviewed. The main concerns were found to be fraud and adverse publicity following disclosure of personal information. The expressed concerns were summarised as follows:

Bank	Government Department
1. Major fraud	Commulative petty fraud
2. Disclosure of client's information	Disclosure of personnel information
3. Disclosure of corporate information	Disclosure of departmental information
4. Disaster (contingency)	Major fraud
5. Cummulative petty fraud	Disaster (contingency)

Other risk possibilities were, in general, not considered significant.

The security consultancy activities included a risk assessment programme which highlighted many more categories of risk, some of greater potential impact than those intuitively chosen by the senior managers. These derived from threats of human error, disruptive attack by idealogical group, disruption by disgruntled employee, failure of systems to perform to specification, excessive system and component failures and the failure to provide, in automated systems, controls at least comparable to those implicit in the original manual systems. Many of these threats gave impact potential which were less sensational than major fraud or disaster, but the cummulative cost to the organisation in wasted resources could be significant. Whereas risk analysis can show speculative annual loss expectancies against major fraud, disclosure and disaster, losses incurred against error, failure and inadequate recovery planning are real losses.

In addition to highlighting risks which had been overlooked or rejected as insignificant, the risk assessment programmes showed the managers' ranking of the risks in variance with the annual loss expectancies calculated by the risk assessment. In both example cases, the actual most significant risk was computer centre disaster. It had been assumed by the organisations that existing contingency plans and provisions could cope with disaster, but on investigation, this was shown for practically all systems not to be the case. Plans were out of date with developing systems, inadequate in the first place or in some cases non-existent. In one area, a designated standby processing centre for an on-line system could arguably have coped with the additional processing for a stricken centre, but the communication network could not have been reconfigured to handle the data traffic throughput to the standby centre.

The re-ordering of significant risks lead to a further problem. The potential impact of a major fraud was estimated to be very high for each organisation - so high that a single occurrence would impact significantly on business revenue - but the effect of the relatively low probability of occurrence of such an event was to generate a low annual loss expectancy. In presenting the results of the risk assessments to management, in order to assign priorities to further security management activities, particular attention was drawn to the high impact/low frequency risks. In both example organisations, an insurance solution was recommended as a quick and cost effective countermeasure against the devastating impact of a single occurrence of such a threat in the short-to-medium term.

2.2 THE PERCEPTION OF RISK - CONCLUSIONS

Prior to risk assessments performed by experienced security consultants, the corporate view of significant risks was deficient in failing to identify all potential risks, and to rank recognised risks in true order of significance. The effect of these deficiencies would have been to perpetuate the exposure to unidentified risks and the misdirection of resources in risk avoidance or containment.

While risk management conventionally accepts annual loss expectancy as the principal factor in assessing exposure to risk, it is necessary, if a single impact of a particular threat would be crippling to the organisation, to consider such threats on their individual merits in terms of expenditure and priority on countermeasures.

3.1 GENERIC THREATS - THE PROBLEMS

In large organisations, handling vast volumes of business on automated systems, the major threat effect is the loss of that processing capability, whether due to natural disaster, human error or deliberate destructive or disruptive attack. In the banking example, the ultimate effect of such a disastrous event would be failure to compete commercialy, failure to meet legal and commercial obligations and, eventually, the collapse of the business. The Government Department does not have worries about losing business to competitors, but the effects of a disaster would be loss of confidence in the Department, wasting of public resources and, perhaps, subsequent political implications.

Reviews of general threat scenarios for the two organisations showed almost identical threat characteristics. Both organisations as processors of instruments of payment are liable to attacks motivated by gain; banking institutions are as much symbols of 'establishment' as any Government department in terms of ideological motivation; both organisations are equally subject to errors and Acts-of-God.

In terms of deliberate attack, it was a feature of both organisations only to recognise deliberate threats originating from 'traditional' adversaries. For example, the Government Department had no trouble accepting threat scenarios involving deliberate disruptive attack by anarchistic groups. Examples of these were:

(a) Hacking attack on network to compromise data privacy
(b) Physical (e.g. terrorist) attack on equipment to inhibit public service
(c) Saturation of system by organised and concerted public demand on system

The bank found this style of threat more difficult to accept. It, in turn, found it easier to identify with potential attacks by criminals such as:

(a) Active wire tapping to manipulate electronic funds transfers
(b) Physical attacks on cash handling equipment (ATMs)
(c) Corruption of staff to perform internal fraud
(d) Theft of materials and equipment for production of credit cards and other instruments of payment

In fact, both these sets of threat scenarios have applicability to both types of organisation. The assumption by the organisation that will not be an attractive target to a particular style of threat is in itself a vulnerability in that the assumption of immunity can lead to no practical controls and countermeasures being adopted in this area.

3.2 GENERIC THREATS - CONCLUSIONS

Features of the conduct of business of the bank and the Government department are:

Integrity and Availability of Public/Client Service
Financial Transactions
Processing of Private Corporate and Personnel Information
Satisfactory Performance as judged by Board/Cabinet, and Shareholders/Electorate

These factors greatly influence management's responses to the principal threats to the integrity, confidentiality and availability of the organisation's computer systems. However, managers may consider themselves immune from certain threats and not provide adequate compensating controls and countermeasures. This effectively increases the vulnerability rating of that threat category. For example, the Government Department considered itself an unlikely target of organised crime with respect to fraud, due to the low value of typical financial transactions. This was despite an extremely high number of such transactions. The Bank took few precautions against terrorist attack, despite an increasing trend in such attacks in the U.S.A. and mainland Europe.

A wide spectrum of generic threats should be considered in any high level Risk Assessment. This threats spectrum should be independent of the organisation being assessed since the threat environment is external to business and other characteristics of the organisation. It is the impact and probability of occurrence which is a function of the organisation's characteristics.

Finally, the existence of other, apparently more threat susceptible organisations does not make one's own organisation less vulnerable.

4.1 VULNERABILITY AND ORGANISATIONAL CHARACTERISTICS - THE PROBLEMS

Both organisations exist in the same threat environment, i.e. the world of human frailty, mechanical or electronic failure, organised crime, fringe politics, etc. There was a tendency by senior management, on initial assessment, to prioritise the threats to which their organisation, with its unique functional characteristics, and business profile would be most susceptible. This resulted, for instance, in the Bank chosing major fraud as a significant risk and the Government Department's choice of cummulative petty fraud. Both these choices reflected the profile of financial transactions performed by the two organisations.

There was a general tendency in both cases to overlook threats to which the organisation was vulnerable because of the composition and corporate 'style' of the organisation. This was probably due to a not unnatural inclination to overlook weaknesses in one's own organisation, or simply being too intimately involved to take an objective view. Factors contributing to possible vulnerabilities were:

- organisational structure
- management structure
- corporate/management style
- personnel profile
- industrial relations
- associated organisations and clients

Examples demonstrating threats and vulnerabilities deriving from these categories are:

(a) In the bank, there were three separate functional groups responsible for in-branch systems, communications network and central computing systems. No one group was able to take responsibility for protection of data on the corporate network.

(b) In the Government Department, the breadth of the management structure meant that common responsibility and authority for technical, user and policy departments converged at a level which was too high for effective co-ordination between these departments.

(c) Certain aspects of the banking business involve a high mobility of a staff between rival banks (especially in currency dealing departments). This can result in employment of staff whose loyality is weak and where career and personal background may be difficult to verify.

(d) Both organisations made extensive use of contractor and supplier expertise in technical departments. This presents the dual risk of undesirable actions during performance of the contracts or the subsequent use of knowledge gained whilst with the organisation.

(e) Comparing the motivation and morale of the staff within the two organisations, the bank gave the more favourable impression; some of its staff felt themselves to be in an employment 'trap' due to concessionary low interest mortgages, but in general morale was high. The Civil Servants in the Government Department were generally less motivated; at the time of the study, the national Civil Service was suffering an attrition of DP staff which was higher than the rest of the computing industry.

(f) The staff morale problem was reflected in the Industrial Relations situation in the two organisations. The Civil Service trade unions and staff associations were more militant than the Banking unions. There had been several instances of local and wider industrial actions at the time of the security consultancy activity. There was also a history of difficulty between management and unions over job saving through increased automation.

The following table outlines some of the security implications of the corporate shortcomings listed above:

ORGANISATIONAL SHORTCOMINGS	SECURITY CONSIDERATIONS AND VULNERABILITIES
1. Management Structure	No devolved authority for security. Inadequate response to security requirements. Failure to act on corporate-high security instructions. Failure to consider return-on-investment on security controls.
2. Inter-departmental Interfaces	Transaction chains difficult to audit. Incompatible security standards between departments. Inadequate contingency for corporate needs. Difficulties in systems integration.
3. Corporate/Management Style	Poor security awareness and training. Cost cutting in security controls. Excessive use of contracted 'outsiders'. Data privacy exposures. Failure to prosecute or otherwise punish security offenders.
4. Personnel Morale and Motivation	Personal action by disgruntled employee. Fraud by employee. Excessive staff turnover. Failure to apply security controls.
5. Industrial Relations	Strike action. Boycotting of new technology. Divided loyalty of staff. Industrial support of third party e.g. refusal to handle 'blacked' material. Deliberate disclosure of corporate data.

4.2 VULNERABILITY AND ORGANISATIONAL CHARACTERISTICS - CONCLUSIONS

The structure and style of an organisation can affect its vulnerability profile. An ideal environment will provide the opportunity and mechanisms for the creation of security policy and the enforcement of effective security programmes and controls. This requires awareness and willingness at all levels to implement, enforce and practice good security. A failure by management to appreciate and respond to a return on investment approach to expenditure on security will result in losses to the organisation.

One of the most significant potential risks arising from organisational weaknesses is that of disruption of computing facilities by industrial action. The problem needs to be addressed primarily by avoidance through employee morale and industrial relations programmes and secondarily by provision of contingent alternatives. In providing contingency for industrial action, the balance must be struck between that which is necessary for emergency operations and that which may be provocative to the trade unions. A secondary risk of an extended disruption involving financial transactions is the extended exposure to client fraud due to non-available automated audit controls, e.g. the inability to clear cheques or the payment of grants and allowances without verification of entitlement.

Loyalty of individual staff at any level must not be taken for granted. Surveys of security violations in the U.K. and U.S.A. have shown a significant number of fraudulent and disruptive attacks by insiders from users, technical and management sectors. Dependance on contracted-in temporary staff should be minimised and dependence on any individual key staff avoided. One of the example organisations had used a subcontracted programmer who was convicted of fraud after his service with the organisation. An expensive comprehensive audit was performed to ensure that code produced by this individual was 'clean'. On concluding the task, the investigators concluded that it was likely that the programmer had access to all software being developed in his project area, as, being a gifted technician, his assistance was regularly sought by his colleagues. Nothing untoward was discovered but the organisation expended valuable resources in the investigation without receiving 100% assurance of 'safe' code.

5.1 SOLUTION RECOMMENDED

Both organisations were about to adopt more co-ordinated approaches to corporate systems which would lead to opportunities for improved security. This would include an opportunity to provide mutual internal contingency support, introduce common standards and practices, ensure that transactions which spanned different applications systems had cohesive audit trails and many other enhancements to corporate security.

To supplement this corporate initiative, the recommendations of the security reviews included:

(a) Creation of a security management infrastructure. This was to be centred on a senior security manager with full corporate responsibility. It involved a network of project and site security officers who encompassed the total life cycle of applications systems, including requirements, design, coding, test, acceptance, deployment and maintenance.

(b) The classification of all corporate data. This involved the identification of data owners, custodians and users. Rules were produced for putting data into classes reflecting its privacy, financial or functional value.

(c) The establishment of data and systems security policy based on data classification rules and the criticality of systems and user requirements.

(d) Co-ordination of a perpetual risk management programme to review cyclically the security situation at both high and detailed levels. One of the stated objectives of this programme was to provide an assurance of data and systems security as required by UK Data Protection Legislation.

(e) Development of a co-ordinated contingency programme based on minimum levels of service required by users.

(f) Involvement of all sectors of the organisation in the security activities. This involved the establishment of committees and forums comprising representatives from systems, users, personnel, management and other relevant departments.

(g) Development of security awareness and training programmes. These were aimed at all levels of personnel, first concentrating on designated security officers and then using the security officer infrastructure to disseminate further knowledge.

5.2 CONCLUSIONS

In a large organisation, the greatest security risk is the failure of automated systems to provide support necessary for continuity of business. The greatest vulnerabilities are a lack of management awareness, misplaced security concerns and a failure to provide uniform security management across the organisation.

The solution to the security problems is to instigate a corporate Risk Analysis review to determine priorities, establish a management and working structure to conduct a Risk Management programme and to ensure that good security is practised throughout systems life cycles.

COMPUTER SECURITY
J.B. Grimson and H.-J. Kugler (Editors)
Elsevier Science Publishers B.V. (North-Holland)

THE BOFORS-MODEL FOR WORKING ADP-SECURITY

Johan Essén and Björn Lindberg

ADP Security Department
AB Bofors Dataservice
Karlskoga, Sweden.

To much ADP security will be very expensive. To little ADP security can be catastrophic to almost all companies and other organizations. Therefore it is important to find the right security levels for an organization and to clearly describe them for different ADP environments. If one also can find out an easy way for the ADP users to recognize which of the security levels they should use, than you have a very good tool for working ADP security. This is the background for the Bofors Model for Working ADP Secutity.

INTRODUCTION

Inside the Bofors company a continuous work is going on to make the ADP-security better within all fields. An important point during this work has been to get an equable security on a level adjusted to the protection objects in question.

To reach this we have developed a working method or a model which we call " THE BOFORS-MODEL FOR WORKING ADP-SECURITY ".

The purpose of this model has been to offer a tool which in a comprehensive way directs towards an even and well adjusted ADP-security level everywhere in the company.

The model is based on some key-elements:

- An ADP-SECURITY POLICY which is established by the Managing Director of the Bofors Group.

- An interpretation of this policy into GENERAL RULES about how the ADP-security is going to be attained, also confirmed by the the Managing Director.

- INTRODUCTION of the rules by educating and motivating all ADP-users in the company and by a joint construction of detailed checklists for each computer environment and security level. E.g: For systems development in the IBM 3081 environment, for obtaining, installing and running different types of minicomputers and PCs and so on.

  The checklists consider the conditions for each environment and declare how the ADP-security is to be handled in the environments respectively.

- The use of the checklists brings up different deficiencies, which means that various MEASURES have to be taken, e.g: installation of an ACS, installation of a dial-back equipment, changed back-up routines, buying in a data medium cabinet and so on.

- Finally, all the steps in this model have to be continuously REVIEWED and new conditions must be taken into consideration. They can necessitate CHANGES of everything from policy to plans for measures.

In this paper some of the most important qualities of the elements of the Bofors Model will be discussed.

POLICY

The basis of all work on ADP-security within the Bofors Group is given in the ADP-security policy which was established by the Managing Director in 1982.

The policy is brief and written in general terms but it confirms some very important rules for ADP-security in the Bofors Group:

- SCOPE

  Functionally: all authomatic data processing

  Concerning organization: the whole Bofors Group

- MEANING

  Areas of protection: asset protection
function protection
data security
data quality protection.

  Levels of protection: a basic protection level which is to be achieved for all ADP in the Group and some additional levels shall be defined.

  ADP-security plan: a plan has to be made, describing how the ADP-security is going to be achieved.

- RESPONSIBILITIES

  Everyone who is responsible for a function where ADP is used is also responsible for the ADP-security in that function.

  The ADP-security manager is responsible for developing methods and techniques for ADP-security.

- CONTROL

  The ADP-security control is to be performed by the person who is responsible for the function in question in consultation with the ADP-security department.

The most important items of this policy is that EVERYONE WHO IS RESPONSIBLE FOR A FUNCTION IN WHICH ADP IS USED IS ALSO RESPONSIBLE FOR THE ADP-SECURITY IN THAT FUNCTION.
It is also very important that THE BASIC PROTECTION LEVEL IS TO BE ACHIEVED FOR ALL ADP WITHIN THE BOFORS GROUP.

RULES

The rules for the ADP-security, which also are the definitions of the protection levels are documented in a paper called SKYDDSNIVÅER (PROTECTION LEVELS in English).

When working with the definitions of the protection levels we found that it was absolutely necessary for our method to have information classified. We needed that to find out which protection level should be used where. Three questions arose:

- Which classes should we use?
- Who decides to which class a certain piece of information belongs?
- How should each class be protected?

After discussions with a lot of people in the Group we found out that the most suitable classes to be used within the Bofors Group are:

1 OPEN

2 INTERNAL

3 RESTRICTED

4 CONFIDENTIAL

5 COMPANY SECRET

6 CLASSIFIED STRICTLY SECRET

The OWNER of the information is the one who should classify it. That means that the owner points out to which of the six classes his or her pieces of information belong.

The rules for the protection levels describe how the information classes should be protected.

The BASIC LEVEL covers information classes 1, 2 and 3.

ADDITIONAL LEVEL 1 covers class 4.

ADDITIONAL LEVEL 2 covers classes 5 and 6.

The demands of the basic protection level are divided into the four different areas of protection:

- Asset protection
- Function protection
- Data security
- Data quality protection

and, in addition, one more area

- Organization

In the additional levels the demands are gradually tightened up for Asset protection and Data security.

INSTALLATION OF THE MODEL

When the rules had been presented and submitted for consideration to those in leading quarters of the Bofors Group, both in the formal organization and in the informal one, our Managing Director confirmed that these rules for Information classes and Protection levels should from now on be in force within the Group.

The next step was to start teaching everyone in the Group, who uses ADP, how to use these rules. In the Bofors Group that means education of about 8 000 persons, and we have just started. When we write this, about 500 of the actual staff have learned how to use the information classes and the protection levels, and they really use it with success.

The rules are in force for all ADP in the Group, CAD/CAM, wordprocessing, personal computing with and without communication, authomatic process control etc. included. Because of that and because of the fast development in the ADP area, the rules are written in so general terms that we need not change them from one ADP-equipment to another or from one application to another.
To make the rules concrete enough to really work with we are working out checklists for every new ADP environment, one checklist for each protection level. We are doing that in cooperation with those who know the new technique best. In the checklists we take into consideration the special hardware and software conditions for the ADP environment in question.

In this way we have produced, among others, checklists for systems in our IBM 3081 environment which point out the demands on filing, back-ups, authorization rules to put into the ACS and so on.

The checklists are used both as lists of demands when new systems are designed and installed and as instruments for control of old systems. In the checklists space is left for notes to be done when designing and installing the system and when controlling it. The notes are left to be used at the next control of the system.

MEASURES

As different systems are controlled, deficiencies are found about which some measures have to be taken. Then the person responsible for the system, together with the ADP-security department, makes a plan for measures. That plan contains the measures and where, how and when they should be taken. That is a piece of the ADP-security plan which the policy demands.

THE TOOL

In other words, the real tool in the Bofors model consists of the INFORMATION CLASSIFICATION SYSTEM, the different PROTECTION LEVELS and the CHECKLISTS. This tool is to be used by the information owners as shown in this flowchart.

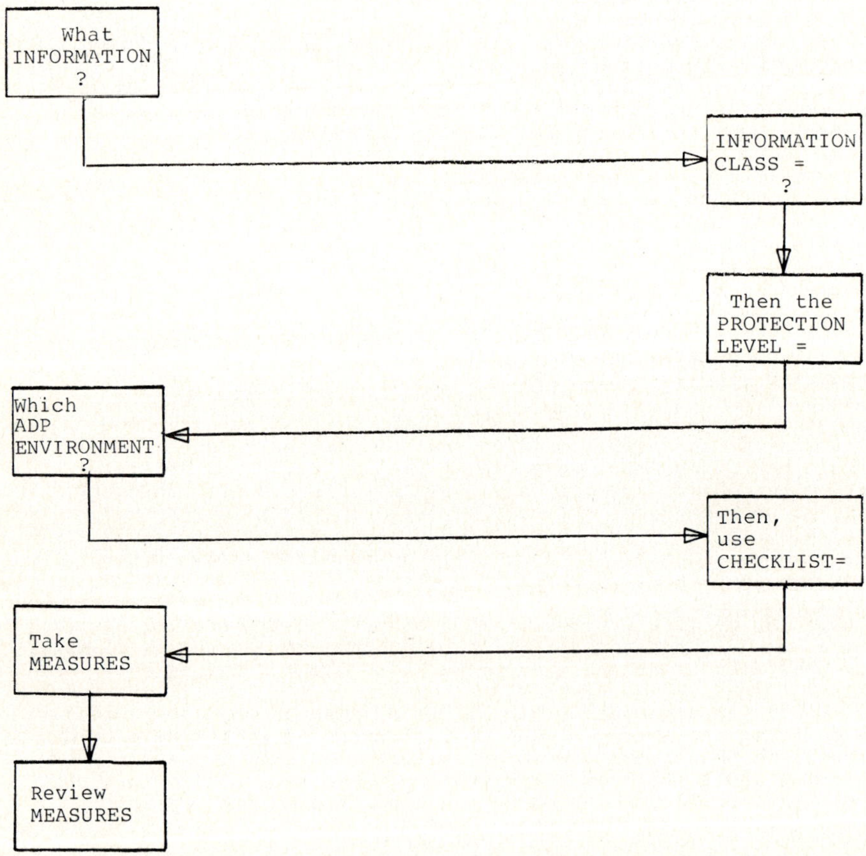

REVIEWING AND CHANGING

As this model is made to be used for directing a part of the work in a field which is known for its fast development, it is necessary that the elements of the model can be changed correspondingly.

If, for example, good authorization control functions for PC come up, the checklists for that ADP environment must be changed to make the PC users use the new functions when they are needed.

It can also be necessary sometimes to change the rules for the protection levels or even the policy. But that should not happen very often.

COMPUTER SECURITY
J.B. Grimson and H.-J. Kugler (Editors)
Elsevier Science Publishers B.V. (North-Holland)

PROBLEM QUANTIFICATION — ITS IMPORTANCE TO COST-EFFECTIVE COMPUTER SECURITY

Robert H. Courtney, Jr.
Box 836
Port Ewen, New York 12466

Mary Anne Todd
U. S. Treasury
Washington, D.C. 20226

Security measures are not inherently desirable. Most of them either cost money, impair function, reduce performance, degrade usability or maintainability, or some combination of these. They are nevertheless desirable in that, properly selected, the direct and indirect costs associated with them are less than the cost of suffering the losses which they are intended to obviate. Comparison of the costs of problems and the costs of solution is not possible without problem quantification.

THE WRONG QUESTIONS TO ASK.

When enterprise managements find themselves on unfamiliar ground or faced with problems quite beyond their areas of technical competence or experience, they are often most interested in what other organizations have done when they were faced with the same problems. This is particularly true of issues such as computer security where the executive level is often less than certain that it will get reasonably unbiased opinions from the data processing management which has induced the organization to its current high state of dependence on electronic data processing and may not now be ready to assess, with reasonable objectivity, the negative as well as the positive aspects of that dependence. For this reason, two questions about computer security frequently asked by the most senior management are (1) how much do other companies of comparable size spend on it or (2) the percentage of the data processing budget which should be spent on it.

Unfortunately, the answers to either of those questions are only rarely helpful to those trying to decide what to do about computer-related security. Organizations are too different. Even organizations about the same size in gross revenue and in number of employees, and which are in the same business in the same general geographic area will rarely need, or be able to justify, the same level of expenditure on data processing-related security measures or controls. (In this paper we use the term "control" to include all business controls of which the security measures are a subset. "Security measures" include all of the members of that whole body of things, physical, procedural, and technical, we apply to protect the safety and integrity of data and the means of acquiring, processing, storing, communicating and presenting them.)

Consider, for example, the rapidly growing organization that has achieved its current size through an aggressive acquisition program, which is heavily decentralized and possibly with several data centers run by competing management teams, with several mainframe vendors, where two or more groups of users and programmers are passionately polarized to particular architectures and where smooth working relationships between these several groups have not yet and may never be established. Such an enterprise will need a wholly different set of business controls or security measures than will a stable organization with a steady growth and low personnel turnover, which is heavily centralized, and which has been pursuing its data processing strategy with only very few and minor readjustments for ten or more years. Except in the case of rather small organizations, two companies or two public sector agencies are only very rarely, if ever, so much alike that the adequacy of the computer security program in one can be assessed through comparison with the program in another.

There is much to be learned through other enterprises' good and bad experiences. While we should reject the notion of measuring the adequacy of any total security program by comparing its cost with that of any other organization's program, we can gain valuable insight into the potential workability of particular strategies and controls by seeing how well they worked elsewhere - but only if we understand the differences in the two environments. If we cannot gauge our need for security and the adequacy of a security program through comparisons with that which is done in other, similar organizations, what then are the criteria for determining how much security is enough and, equally important, how much is too much?

It has been suggested by a highly respected authority on computer security that there are some security measures the need for which is so completely obvious that further justification is unnecessary. These wholly obvious things include, he suggests, physical security for the data center and other such fundamental things. He is quite correct as far as he goes. His contention is true for the generics such as security for the data center. But we cannot implement generics. They must be fleshed out and become real, implementable things. The problems are encountered when specific measures must be selected.

What is done about physical security for a data center must be determined by a number of quite specific factors which require study and analysis. For example, consider the variety of factors which influence the selection of suitable safeguards for a data center mid-town in a large city with heavy social unrest, terrorist activity, high potential for spills of toxic or corrosive chemicals reasonably close to the data center, unreliable or dirty power, a highly antiquated underground telephone cable network and heavy dependence of the organization on the continued support of the systems installed therein. For that company, it may well be that the most appropriate step is a move of the data center to a more suitable location. A data center supporting a similar company and which data center is already located in a more kindly place simply does not have the same security needs beyond the trivially-stated generic - that is, adequate security for the data center. But what is entailed in meeting that common goal is vastly different in one instance from that required in the other.

The list of things which should be done about data processing security without regard to the relative severity of problems in that particular operating environment and the dependencies of the organization of the data center in each specific instance - that is, without any risk analysis - is quite short. The concept of the so-called baseline measures about which there is no need to think, which you simply do, is dangerous indeed. Among the most simple and yet important measures we can conceive is the hand-held fire extinguishers in the machine room. Yet, even these cannot be selected without careful consideration of the nature of the flammables encountered there. As the sophistication of the measures which must be considered increase to include protection against communications intercept, damage by disgruntled, technically-strong employees, individual accountability, logical access control, appropriate user identification and authentication means, protection against access by hackers and against unauthorized activity by employees with take-home terminals and PC's, and many more, the improbability that appropriate measures can be selected except in the light of the cost of the problems when compared with the costs of the solutions is only greatly magnified.

We can only arrive at the satisfaction of the specific security needs of a particular organization through careful analysis of the vulnerabilities, the cost of losses which might be encountered through those vulnerabilities, and the cost-effectiveness of available means for reducing those losses. Qualitative assessments of these factors are not very helpful. Any notion of a qualitative assessment of cost-effectiveness seems a contradiction in terms.

It is our contention here that a quantification of the loss potentially avoided by a security measure and the cost of that measure are necessary to the selection of those measures which are cost-justified and the rejection of those which are not. Only if we do this can we be reasonably certain that we are spending less to solve a problem than it will cost to tolerate it and, conversely, that we have applied all or most of the security measures which do cost less than the problems to which they are applicable.

HOW MUCH SECURITY IS ENOUGH?

The figure on the following page describes, in a somewhat idealized way, the relationship between the costs of controls and the losses, both direct and indirect, potentially obviated by them.

The curves in our figure are considerably smoother than those we encounter in actual situations. There are dependencies of measures one upon the other for their effectiveness and this produces step functions in the loss curves which are not reflected in the figure as it is drawn. Similarly, the cost curves, too, are usually other than quite smooth. This idealization of those curves in no way invalidates the concept described there.

It is quite important to recognize that the losses to which we refer in the figure are not the total economic impact of something undesirable. These losses must be expressed in cost per unit time, such as dollars per year. We call them EAL or expected annual loss.

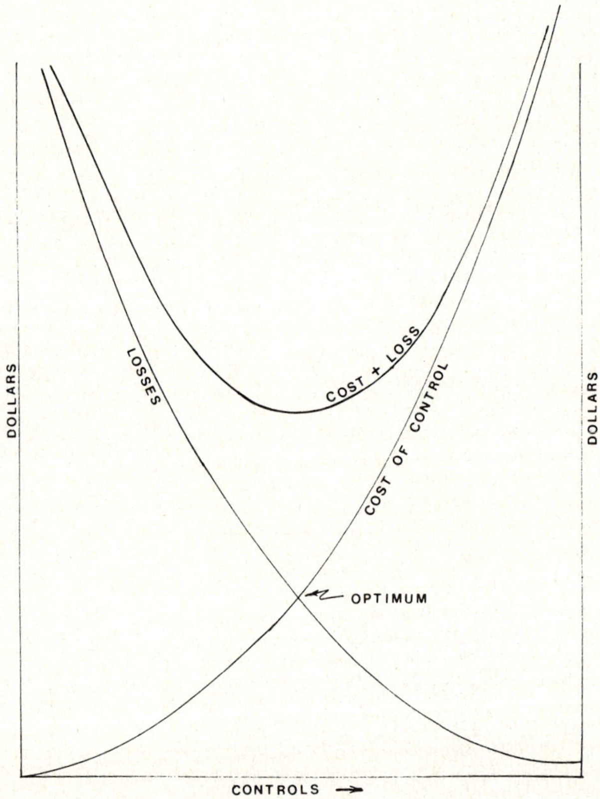

It is easier to estimate the initial and operating costs of security measures than it is to estimate the EAL attributable to some system vulnerability or the EAL displaceable as a result of adopting some security measures. Yet it is not so difficult to make adequate EAL estimates that we can afford to adopt security measures in a haphazard, intuitive manner.

The generally large difference between the cost of the corrective measure and the EAL greatly simplifies the process of selecting most measures. When it becomes quite difficult, that in itself should induce considerable caution in those responsible for selecting those measures in that the ratio between the costs and the losses is no longer large.

The risk assessment team should include a diversity of skills, talents and disciplines which will yield consideration of each vulnerability from several perspectives with the result that the estimates of the individual team members, before reconciliation - if ever, may vary by a factor of ten. Even this very limited precision is, more often than not, wholly adequate in light of the cost of the appropriate corrective measures. If the readily available precision in estimating loss is not adequate to justify controls under consideration, then it is probable that additional effort should be expended in identifying increased scope for the effectiveness of the measure under consideration, other less expensive measures, or other measures with greater scope and, therefore, greater potential for displacing loss.

Our goal in applying security measures is to approach, as closely as we can, the lowest point in the curve reflecting the sum of the control costs and the potential losses. It can be readily seen, then, that the answer to the question as to how much security is enough is that it is that amount of security which is in place when the next incremental increase will cost more than the loss displaced by it.

The statement, often heard, that "we cannot afford to do the things we should about data security" is a logical contradiction. If each security measure selected does, as it should, displace a loss greater than the cost of that measure, then the economy of that situation suggests that you cannot afford not to implement that control. If the measure does not displace a greater loss, then, without regard to ability to fund the implementation, it is not economically justified and, therefore, should not be done.

Referring again to the figure, it is fortunate that the things offering the greatest displaced loss for the least cost are almost always those things which are, in fact, prerequisites to the measures represented by the costs further to the right on the cost curves. If the implementation of a comprehensive computer security program is initiated by selecting for earliest implementation those things which are most effective in enhancing security, they will probably be things on which the effectiveness of other measures is highly dependent and the probability is also quite high that those initial steps will be the ones which cost the least while yielding the greatest security benefit. Examples may help here.

In looking at the computer security posture of well more than four hundred private sector organizations, we have seen almost none with an adequate computer security posture without also having a strong corporate-wide policy statement issued by the senior management, usually the Chief Executive Officer. Because more security variances or violations are committed by people outside of the data processing shop than by people within it, no amount of imposition on the data processing staff by its management will be very effective in providing adequate security unless those managing the supported functional areas are also directed to take the necessary steps within their individual areas of responsibility to protect data and the means of entering and accessing them. It appears that a data security policy statement is an essential prerequisite to an adequate security program and yet there are few things that can be done about security which cost less to implement than does such a policy statement.

As another example, it is usually quite difficult to put a good security program in place in most organizations without also having a strong employee security awareness program. Unless most employees, even including those only peripherally involved, are aware of the importance of observing all of the established security procedures and practices, it is quite difficult to have an adequate program. As it is in a larger community, unless a majority of the community supports a rule or law, its enforcement becomes difficult, if not impossible. This is no less true in the smaller community of the private enterprise or public agency. Again, a good employee awareness program is among the least expensive things which can be done about security while it is among the most effective.

As a final example, and in an area directly involving data processing hardware and programs, consider the relative effectiveness of user identification and logging as opposed to logical access control. It is almost universally true that measures which hold users accountable for their actions through the implementation of appropriate identification means and logging or journalling of their activities are more effective than logical means for constraining what each person is allowed to do. The reason for this is quite clear. Most dishonest conduct and most damaging errors are committed by persons authorized access to the resources which were abused. In these cases, the limitations imposed by logical access control would do little or nothing to lessen damage.

Continuing with this point, it can be readily shown that logical access control is almost always more costly by far than simply logging activity and subsequently processing those logs to find anomalies of possible interest to the security administrator. Both the administration of most access control facilities and their imposition on system performance, while usually tolerable and fully justified, are, in fact, more burdensome than is logging of activity. Further, user identification is essential to both. Thus, once again, the less costly things, properly identified and properly installed, are usually more effective than, and are often an essential precursor to, those which are to their right on the control cost curve in our figure.

ESTIMATING AVOIDABLE LOSS.

In a real, conventionally-encountered data processing environment, the expected annual loss can be decreased sharply with relatively modest increases in the cost of controls when care is taken to select those controls which are applicable to the broadest array of problems. The controls which contain the broadest array of problems usually will be those which are most cost-effective.

Because there are six undesirable things which can happen to data, accidental disclosure, modification and destruction and intentional disclosure, modification and destruction the effectiveness of each candidate control in obviating or lessening the effect of the greatest number of these is often a strong indicator of its relative economic benefit. They are quite frequently the ones which displace the greatest expected annual losses and, for that reason, are the controls which afford the greatest economic benefit.

As an example, measures which are designed solely to detect possible instances of dishonesty in the data entry/file maintenance process may not displace losses near so great as those measures which do that job but which also provide a means for holding all data entry personnel individually and specifically accountable for their actions. In this way we can not only increase our chances of finding the dishonest employees, we will also be able to identify those whose loyalty and honesty are unquestioned but whose error rate is unacceptably high and, therefore, need to be cautioned or further trained.

Mistakes by clerical employees entering data are not only expensive to suffer or to detect and correct, they also constitute a training ground for the dishonest employee. Many of the employees who have stolen through illicit manipulation of a data processing system used schemes the workability of which they learned through making mistakes and not being caught. For this reason, and in many similarly-reasoned instances, the total scope of the problems potentially containable by each measure must be considered when deciding which of several candidate measures are the most acceptable. The relative costs of those measures are of no greater importance to an economics-driven decision than are the sizes of displaceable losses attributable to each. Both are major factors in the decision. The cost of the control, however, has very little relevance except in the light of the losses to which it is potentially applicable.

Just as we should seek those controls which displace the broadest array of security problems because they are usually the most cost-effective, it is essential that we watch particularly closely when selecting those controls the need for which may seem intuitively obvious; they may well be the ones which are not cost-effective because they address only narrow and often improbable problems. They may seem indicated only because so many people are using them when, in fact, there is no real justification in terms of potentially displaceable losses when both the consequences and the reasonably anticipatable frequencies of occurrence of the appropriate problems are assessed. As an example, a guard force for a data center in continuous use may be required in some places, but it can be a needless expense in a highly benign environment.

There are many instances in which a proper contingency plan will be less expensive and more broadly applicable than is a guard force. Further, the contingency plan address a far greater problem scope and might well be otherwise indispensable. There are many times in which a pleasant receptionist will be equally if not more effective than a guard keeping out unauthorized people or in calling the law enforcement people to thwart a dissident group. The receptionist is generally more literate and amenable to and capable of and flexible in accepting a variety of tasks and, for that reason, is often far more valuable than a guard. Again, these decisions can best be made in the light of a realistic, quantitative assessment of the expected annual loss to that problem. It is not our objective here to mount a campaign against guards on data centers; they are at times needed. We want only to caution that the selection of a security measure simply because the need seems intuitively obvious or because other, respected institutions are doing it is only rarely the correct route to take.

DIFFICULTIES IN QUANTITATIVE PROBLEM ASSESSMENT.

Almost from the initial proposal several years ago of the use of quantitative risk assessment to support the selection of security measures in an electronic data processing environment, there has been confusion between the desirability or necessity for performing such risk analyses and the feasibility of doing them. We believe that we have made the case, in quite straightforward, practical terms, for performing such analyses because they are the only demonstrably rigorous means for determining the cost-effectiveness of most security measures. Most opponents of risk analyses in a computer-based information systems environment seem to base their objections more on what they regard as the infeasibility of doing such analyses than they do on the need for them. Because that seems to be the case, we will argue that it is more appropriate to attempt to overcome the obstacles to doing them, if there are, in reality, serious obstacles, than it is to reject the analyses as unnecessary.

Numerous papers, including several by one of these authors (Courtney), describing techniques for quantitative risk assessment have been published in the past ten years. A comprehensive discussion of the relative effectiveness and ease of use of the several different methods is quite beyond the scope of this paper the purpose of which is to urge the necessity for performing such assessments at all.

The arguments that we cannot do sufficiently accurate risk analyses seem to center about the problems of dealing with the statistics of small numbers. Let us, then, examine that situation. It is generally recognized that, to be sufficiently useful, a risk analysis must treat both the consequences of an undesirable event and its anticipated frequency of occurrence. Neither the consequences nor the frequency, taken individually, are of much value without the other.

For example, it can be argued that the giant catastrophes against which we too frequently postulate our contingency plans occur with frequencies so low that, even though we may be able to gauge the economic consequences of a total loss of a data center, we cannot estimate with sufficient accuracy the conditional probability or frequency of occurrence with which we might lose it. That is quite true as far as it goes. The total loss of a data center in most areas is a fairly low-probability thing. If, however, we examine concurrently all of the things which can stop the processing of the critical functions supported by a data center, we are usually no longer dealing with very small numbers. We are now treating the fairly high probability of occurrence of some one of a large number of events which individually might occur with a low probability. The more difficult task is not estimating the probability of a major stoppage; it is identifying the truly critical functions supported by the data processing facility and estimating the economic consequences of their stoppage as a function of the duration of the downtime. The probability of interruption to data processing from some cause is not at all difficult because, with many potential causes properly aggregated, the problem is now within the realm of the experience of many data processing management people.

It is often argued that we cannot possibly estimate the probability of employees in a particular area engaging in theft involving the data processing capabilities. That is often but not always true. What we can do is to use the experience that we do have to cost-justify measures which are applicable to a broad array of problems and not just to a single type of malfeasance which is hard to estimate. If there is a larger problem containable with the same measures, and there often is, then those measures need not be cost-justified by the hard-to-estimate low probability events.

In summary, what we have argued in the paragraphs immediately above is that the risk assessment must be done in the light of a broad awareness of the availability and effectiveness of the many security measures potentially applicable to the whole broad array of problems which might be encountered. It cannot be done well in isolation from consideration of the need to aggregate findings relative to the applicability of corrective measures. Our experience in taking this approach is quite positive and fully supports the contention here that problem quantification offers the best assurance of the cost-effectiveness of security measures.

COMPUTER SECURITY
J.B. Grimson and H.-J. Kugler (Editors)
Elsevier Science Publishers B.V. (North-Holland)

INTEGRATING SECURITY ACTIVITIES INTO THE SOFTWARE DEVELOPMENT LIFE CYCLE AND THE SOFTWARE QUALITY ASSURANCE PROCESS

Frederick G. Tompkins
ORI, Inc.
Rockville, Maryland, USA
and
Russel Rice
National Aeronautics and Space Administration
Washington, DC, USA

Security concerns should be an integral part of the entire planning, development, and operation of a computer application. Inadequacies in the design and operation of computer applications are a very frequent source of security vulnerabilities associated with computers. In most cases, the effort to improve security should concentrate on the application software. The system development life cycle (SDLC) technique provides the structure to assure that security safeguards are planned, designed, developed and tested in a manner that is consistent with the sensitivity of the data and/or the application. The software quality assurance process provides the reviews and audits to assure that the activities accomplished during the SDLC produce operationally effective safeguards.

INTRODUCTION

The United States Government Office of Management and Budget (OMB) Circular A-71, Transmittal Memorandum (TM) No. 1, dated 27 July 1978, "Security of Federal Automated Information Systems," requires each federal agency develop and implement a computer security program. One of the specific requirements of OMB Circular A-71, TM No. 1 is that each agency must establish a management control process to assure that appropriate administrative, physical and technical safeguards are incorporated into all new computer applications and significant modifications to existing systems. The objective of the management control process is to assure that, in addition to meeting all applicable Federal policies, regulations and standards, the security specifications (and/or security safeguards) must be adequate for the application. Therefore, security concerns should be an integral part of the planning, development, and operation of a computer application. This paper focuses on the planning and development portions of the overall life of a computer application.

TOOLS FOR THE PLANNING AND DEVELOPMENT OF APPLICATION SOFTWARE

The software development life cycle and the software quality assurance process are tools that provide structure and foundation for the planning and development of application software. The software development life cycle, commonly referred to as the SDLC, is a technique used to divide the system development process into distinct phases with formal management control points placed between and during each phase. The objective in using an SDLC technique are twofold: to provide a more structured management scheme for controlling costs and schedules; and, to ensure proper and responsive communications channels among users, auditors, hardware planning personnel, top management and the data processing personnel responsible for developing the applications system [1].

The software quality assurance (SQA) process attempts to improve the quality of computer software products produced via the software development process. SQA involves the use of various reviews and the establishment of baselines throughout the system development life cycle. The objective of employing an SQA process is to produce reliable software.

THE SOFTWARE DEVELOPMENT LIFE CYCLE

As noted previously, the software development life cycle (SDLC) is a technique used to divide the system development process into distinct phases. Figure 1 [2] shows some 15 different software life cycle models. None of these models uses exactly the same terminology for all the phases in the life cycle. However, it is important to note that the management structure represented by the models is a proven method for enabling a project manager to:

- o estimate the cost/time to complete a system or software project,
- o Make use of existing industry and government standards and guidelines,
- o assess the progress of a project at discrete points in the life cycle by conducting formal reviews and audits, and
- o control system development by requiring go/no-go decision points throughout the life cycle.

A generic life cycle, based on the model presented in the National Bureau of Standards FIPS PUBs 38 and 64 [3,4] is presented in Figure 2. This generic life cycle identifies three major phases: initiation, development and operation. The development phase is divided into four stages: definition, design, programming and test. The operation phase, for the purpose of this paper, has been divided into two stages: implementation and maintenance.

The Initiation Phase

During the Initiation Phase, the objectives and general definitions of the requirements are established. First, there is an initial user definition activity. During this activity there is a determination of what's currently being done; what needs to be done; understanding the problem; defining of the scope, objectives and operating environment; definition of functional, performance, and methodological requirements; and, acceptance criteria.

The second activity conducted during the Initiation Phase is evaluation and initiation of necessary documents to formally commence the software development project. This activity includes performing a comprehensive study of technical, operational and economic feasibility; performance of a cost/benefit analysis; analysis of general design approaches, and generation of development plan.

Documentation produced during the Initiation Phase requires user involvement to define the project and its worth. Typically, a Project Request Document is developed as a means for the user organization to request the development, procurement or modification of software or other ADP-related services. It serves as the initiating document in the software life cycle, and provides a basis for communicating with the requesting organization to further analyze requirements and assess impacts. The second document produced is usually the Feasibility Study Document. The purpose of this document is to provide: (1)

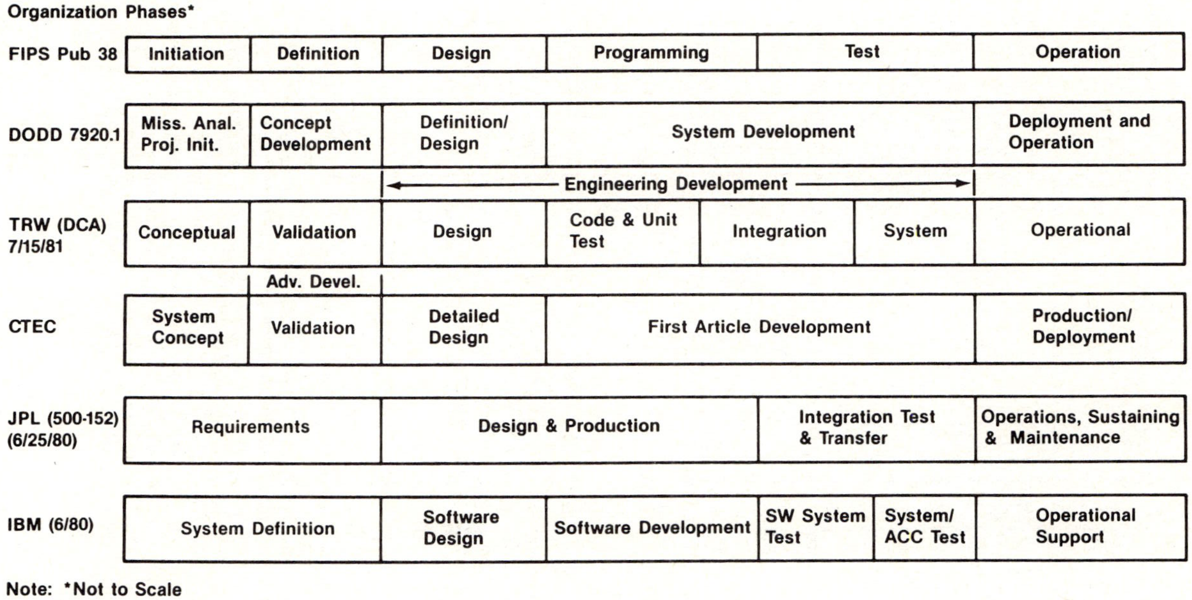

Figure 1 Survey of Software Lifecycle Models

Initiation Phase	Development Phase				Operations Phase	
	Definition Stage	Design Stage	Programming Stage	Test Stage	Implementation Stage	Maintenance Stage
• Present Request Document	• Functional Requirements Document	• System Subsystem Specification	• Users Manual			• Change Requests
• Feasibility Study		• Program Specification	• Operations Manual			
• Cost-Benefit Analysis	• Data Requirements Document	• Data Base Specification	• Program Maintenance Manual	• Test Analysis Report		
		Test Plan				

(Source: FIPS PUB 38)

Figure 2 The Software Lifecycle

an analysis of the objectives, requirements and system concepts; (2) an evaluation of alternative approaches for reasonably achieving the objectives; and (3) identification of a proposed approach. The third document, Cost/Benefit Analysis provides managers, users, designers and auditors with adequate cost and benefit information to analyze and evaluate alternative approaches.

All documentation is widely reviewed and is followed by a management decision of whether to continue on to the Definition Stage. For external procurements, a Request for Proposal (RFP) is issued, proposals are evaluated and a contract is awarded.

The Development Phase

During the Development Phase, the requirements for software are determined and the software is then defined, specified, programmed and tested. The Development Phase is broken down into four stages: Definition, Design, Programming and Test.

The Definition Stage

The activities during the Definition Stage include: translation of the user requirements into detailed functional requirements and a functional architecture defining the operating environment, functional modules, inputs, outputs, processing requirements and system performance requirements (as needed to meet user performance requirements); definition of data requirements; completion of a general top-level design; definition of functional interfaces (man/machine, system/system, function/function); identification of required equipment; and, planning for development activities. Documents typically produced during the Definition Stage include the Functional Requirements Document and the Data Requirements Document.

The Design Stage

During the Design Stage, the Systems and Program Specifications are developed. Activities at this point include: designing the system to meet functional requirements; dividing functional modules into program modules identifying the inputs, processing and outputs of each; definition of the control and data structures and protocols; and, specification of interfaces in detail. Documents typically produced during this stage include the System/Subsystem Specifications, Program Specifications, Data Base Specifications and the Test Plan.

The Programming Stage

During the Programming Stage, the software is coded and debugged. Activities may include obtaining of the required hardware; writing, testing and debugging of software programs; preparation of manuals; and, completion of test procedures. Documentation typically produced during the Programming Stage includes the Users Manual, Operations Manual, Program Maintenance Manual and the Test Plan.

The Test Stage

During the Test Stage the software is tested and the related documentation is reviewed. The software and documentation are evaluated in terms of readiness for implementation. Activities include: performance of integration and acceptance testing; training of users and operators; installation in the operational environment; data base conversion; and testing in the operational environment. Documentation produced during this stage is the Test Analysis Report.

The Operations Phase

During the Operations Phase, software is maintained and enhanced as additional requirements are identified. The Operations Phase can be viewed as two distinct stages: Implementation and Maintenance.

Implementation Stage

The Implementation Stage is that period of time immediately following the beginning of the operation of the software in a production mode. Activities during this stage include the removal of latent defects that were not discovered during development testing. Additionally, user requirements will have to be incorporated that were not generated during the programming or test stages when no additional user requirements were permitted and the baseline was frozen to permit testing. During this implementation stage, the user requirements that were generated after the baseline was frozen, are incorporated as modifications to the operational software.

The Maintenance Stage

Following the initial implementation stage on-going maintenance is required. Maintenance activities over the remaining life time of the application can be broken down into three distinct types [5]:

- o Corrective maintenance-fixing errors that had not been uncovered or fixed correctly if previously exposed in testing.
- o Adaptive maintenance--performed in anticipation of hardware or support software changes.
- o Perfective maintenance--changes to improve performance.

Software Development Life Cycle Security Activities

Much of what needs to be done to improve (or initially incorporate) security is not clearly separable from what is needed to improve the usefulness, reliability, effectiveness, and efficiency of computer applications [6]. While security concerns should be integrated in the life cycle of a computer application, the steps taken to ensure the appropriateness, adequacy and reasonableness of security safeguards should be separately identifiable activities within each stage or phase of the SDLC.

Security Activities

System planners, developers and users should accomplish a series of security-related actions throughout the SDLC. While the order in which the actions should be accomplished is presented sequentially, it should be recognized that there will be much interaction between a particular step and the preceding steps. The process for incorporating security safeguards in an application is not substantially different from the SDLC activities identified in Section 3. It should also be noted that, if during development, any change occurs in a software requirement or specification, the change must be reviewed to determine if coincidental changes are required in the security requirements or specifications.

The security activities (Figure 3) to be completed throughout the SDLC are:

- Determine Sensitivity of Data/Application
- Determine the Security Objective(s)
- Assess the Security Risks
- Conduct a Security Feasibility Study
- Define the Security Requirements
- Develop the Security Test Plan
- Design Security Specifications
- Develop the Security Test Procedures
- Write Security Relevant Code
- Document Security Safeguards
- Conduct Security Test & Evaluation
- Write Security Test Analysis Report
- Prepare Security Certification Report

Much of the information provided in the description of the security activities is presented in FIPS PUB 73 [6].

Determine the Sensitivity of Data Application

The degree of sensitivity of an application system depends upon the data it will process and/or the types of functions to be accomplished by the software. For example, data may be personal in nature, represent valuable tangible assets such as high-dollar value inventory or represent real dollars. Application processes which perform critical operations may include formulas or algorithms that must always be executed exactly the same, such as engineering calculations or on-board software for a space vehicle.

FIPS PUB 73, Section 2.3, provides categories of sensitive systems with some examples of the types of applications that would fall under each of the categories. The categories and examples are:

Activities	Accomplished by
Data/Appl Sensitivity	Users Application/DPI CSO
Security Objective(s)	Users Application/DPI CSO
Security Risks	User System Planners Application/DPI CSO
Security Feasibility Study	User System Planners Application/DPI CSO
Security Requirements	User System Planners Approved by Application CSO
Security Test Plan	QA Audit IV&V (Reviewed/Approved by Application CSO)
Security Specifications	System Developers
Security Test Procedures	QA Audit IV&V (Reviewed/Approved by Application CSO)

Figure 3 Software Development Lifecycle Security Activities

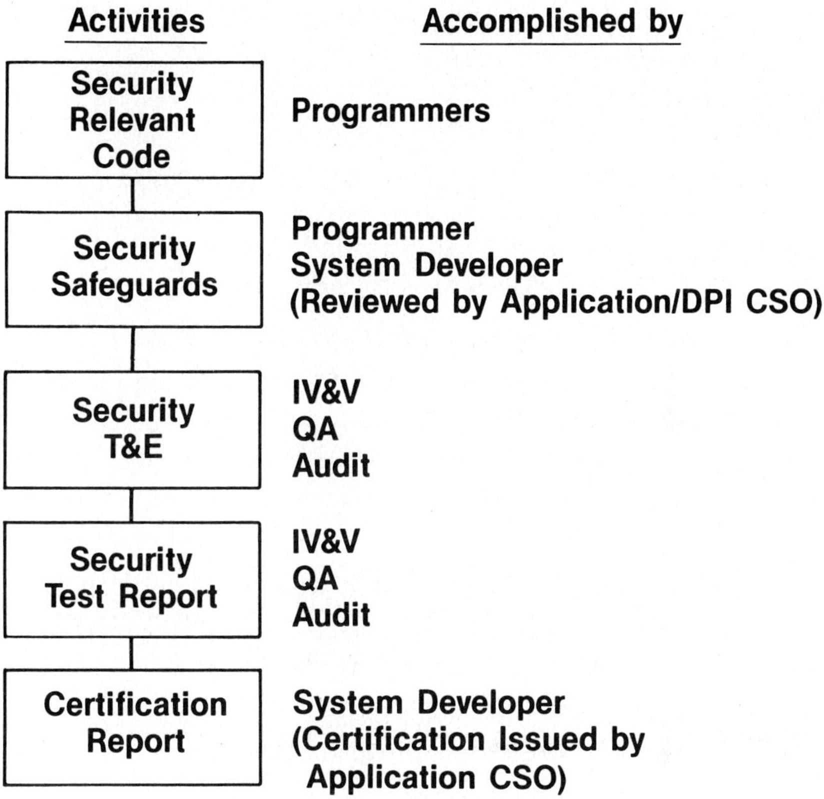

Figure 3 Software Development Lifecycle Security Activities (Continued)

- Applications Providing General Processing Support - The primary concern is for accidents, errors and ommissions. Health, safety, welfare and lives may depend on the correctness of output from these applications. Thus data integrity, including integrity of the software, is critical.

  - Engineering calculations used in aircraft design
  - Query systems that support health care decisionmaking
  - Automated wind tunnel control systems
  - Simulation of the dispersion of toxic substances

- Funds Disbursement, Accounting, Asset Management Systems - These systems frequently involve personal or other confidential data. In these applications, deliberate and accidental acts are a major concern. Data integrity is the major objective. Data confidentiality may also be required.

  - Payroll
  - Financial accounting
  - Procurement support
  - Equipment inventory control

- General-Purpose Information Systems - The simultaneous use by different user populations makes data confidentiality critical as well as data integrity. The generality of such systems and their associated security requirements also make it more difficult to design effective security controls.

  - Generalized data management systems
  - Centralized management information systems

- Automated Decisionmaking Systems - Manual review is more difficult, so that errors made by the automated systems are less likely to be detected before they lead to serious harm. The major objective is rigorous data integrity.

  - Fully automated funds disbursement and accounting systems
  - Automated inventory reordering
  - Automated scheduling for maintenance

- Real-Time Control Systems - These systems have all the security concerns of automated decisionmaking systems plus a rigorous requirement for constant availability and very rapid response times. Basic controls plus automated fault detection, backup, and recovery in conjunction with redundant hardware support may be required.

  - Air traffic control
  - Mission control
  - Rapid transit system control
  - Automated production control

- Systems Affecting National Security or Well-Being - These systems must be protected against hostile acts by unauthorized persons who have considerable resources. Data integrity, confidentiality, and ADP availability are all required plus techniques for formal development and verification of controls in operating systems as well as application systems.

  - Military command and control
  - Management of multilevel classified information
  - Integrated electronic funds transfer
  - Nuclear material control and accountability

Essentially, the objective of this step is to determine whether or not the application or the data is sensitive. If the data or application is sensitive, the rationale should be documented. When reviewing the data, one should attempt to determine the potential gain to persons from unauthorized access to or use of the data or the application process. This step should be accomplished by the owner or intended user in concert with the cognizant computer security manager.

If the application is determined to be sensitive, the next step in the process is to determine the security objective or objectives.

Determine The Security Objectives

There are two types of events that can have unwanted or undesirable effects on sensitive data or applications; advertent or inadvertent. The advertent or inadvertent events may result in the modification, destruction, or disclosure of data or applications software programs, or the unavailability of computing resources. A useful approach for assuring that appropriate and adequate safeguards are incorporated in sensitive applications is to establish security objectives that, if achieved, will reasonably mitigate advertent or inadvertent events. Generally speaking, five security objectives should satisfy all types of events and effects: data integrity, application integrity, data confidentiality, application confidentiality and ADP availability.

- Data Integrity - The state that exists when computerized data is the same as that in the source documents or has been correctly computed from source data and has not been exposed to accidental or malicious alteration or destruction [6].

- Applications Integrity - The state that exists when the source and object code are the same as originally developed and certified/accredited or, have been modified and tested in accordance with established standards and procedures and recertified/reaccredited, and have not been exposed to accidental or malicious alteration or destruction.

- Data Confidentiality - The state that exists when data is held in confidence and is protected from unauthorized disclosure [6].

- Application Confidentiality - The state that exists when application source and object code and documentation is held in confidence and is protected from unauthorized disclosure.

- ADP Availability - The state that exists when required ADP services can be obtained within an acceptable period of time [6].

Figure 4 provides a guide for determining sensitive application security objectives. First, determine the category of sensitive application. Second, refer to Figure 4 and determine the possible security objective that may have to be achieved. It should be noted that this is a preliminary determination. It may be useful to perform this determination at a lower level than the complete application (i.e., module) since different modules may exhibit different security characteristics. The assessment of risks and security feasibility study may surface concerns or limitations that would require a modification of the security objectives.

This step should be accomplished by the owner or intended user in concert with the computer security manager.

Assess the Security Risks

The types of controls that will ultimately be incorporated into an application system should be determined based upon the potential loss or harm that could be suffered if the data or the application were modified, destroyed or disclosed or is caused to become unavailable due unauthorized or undesirable events.

In the initial assessment of risk, the concern is for the impact and frequency of major failures. The impact of major failures can be described in any convenient terms--dollar value of loss, extent of inconvenience or hardship, lives lost or degree of disruption to the national security or agency mission.

The impact of at least the following failures should be assessed for each major body of information that is to be processed by the proposed system [7].

- Inaccurate Data - Data (programs) could be corrupted with errors, but the system continues to function while producing erroneous outputs. Estimate the potential impact of erroneous actions that might result assuming only that the output of the ADP system is not so obviously out of line with reality that the errors would be noticed. Consider both the impact of a few very serious errors and the cumulative effect of many small errors.

- Falsified Data - An individual could falsify data in order to gain some advantage. The falsifications may be limited only by the fact that they are subtle enough so they are not detected manually. Estimate the total impact that could occur over an extended period of time.

- Disclosed Data - Sensitive data in the system becomes available publicly or to certain individuals. The unauthorized disclosure of data is not necessarily discovered.

- Lost Data or Application Software Code or Documentation - Data, source code, object code or documentation are destroyed or corrupted. Backup versions are nonexistent or not usable, and the data must be reconstructed manually or software code or documentation must be rewritten. Estimate the impact of losing the data, source code, object code or documentation. If manual reconstruction is obviously not feasible and if backup in depth is anticipated, estimate the impact of using old version,

Effect	Type of Event	Category of Sensitive Application					
		General Processing Support	Funds Disb Accounting Asset Mgmt	Gen. Purpose Information Systems	Automated Decisionmaking Systems	Real-Time Control	National Security or Well-Being
Modification of Data/Appl	Advertent	AI	DI, AI	DI, AI	AI	AI, DI	AI, DI
	Inadvertent	DI, AI	AI, DI		DI	AI, DI	AI, DI
Destruction of Data/Appl	Advertent			DI, AI	AI	AI, DI	AI, DI
	Inadvertent			DI	DI	AI, DI	AI, DI
Disclosure of Data	Advertent		DC	DC	AC	AC	DC, AC
	Inadvertent			DC		AC	DC
Unavailability of Computing Resources	Advertent		AA	AA		AA	AA
	Inadvertent	AA			AA	AA	AA

Legend:
DI = Data Integrity
DC = Data Confidentiality
AA = ADP Availability
AI = Application Integrity
AC = Application Confidentiality

Figure 4 Sensitive Application Security Objectives

inaccuracies, and the temporary unavailability that would result while recovering from an old copy on the assumption that all current or recent backup copies have been destroyed.

- Unavailable Data Services - Estimate the impact if the computer hardware or related equipment in the computer facility is disabled and the system is not available until it can be brought up in another facility.

An estimate of the impact of a major security failure is not particularly meaningful without some estimate of how frequently it might occur. Unfortunately, during the initial planning for an application system, it is difficult, if not impossible, to estimate the frequency of a major failure by evaluating the controls in place. However, it is possible to develop rough estimates based upon experience with manual system activities and by looking at the experience of failures or disruptions with similar types of systems.

An alternate approach for estimating frequency is to use a low, medium or high frequency rather than orders of magnitude. This approach when used as part of the Threat Team Analysis should provide sufficient data to provide an assessment of the impact of major failures.

A threat team is composed of key employees within an organization who meet as a task force to search for threats and vulnerabilities in a system and who create possible scenarios for attacking the system. Use of such teams is based on the premise that people in the best position to discover how to beat the system are those who work with it every day. The objective is to capitalize on their knowledge. Threat analysis unlocks this potential through the use of a moderator familiar with computer abuse methods. The threat sessions seek a symbiosis between the moderator's general knowledge of typical schemes and the participants' specific knowledge of data processing operations and functional experience with the system under evaluation [6].

Actual threat scenario development is accomplished through a series, usually two, informal team meetings. The first meeting should be scheduled for two to two and one-half hours. The second meeting should last for one to two hours. At the beginning of the first meeting of the team, a basic set of ground rules and background information must be given. The moderator should give a brief summary of the statistics of computer abuse, an outline of major schemes that have been perpetrated against similar types of applications and how they were accomplished (modus operandi). The objective is to "prime the pump" and stimulate the participants in developing possible attacks against their system.

Flip charts should be used to record the following information:

- What is being attacked or compromised in the system?
- What vulnerabilities would permit the attack to be accomplished?
- What methods or procedures would be utilized?
- What types of safeguards or controls could be used to prevent or reduce loss?
- What is the likelihood that this scenario will work (high, medium, low)?

- What is the impact on the system or organization if the scenario were successfully executed (order of magnitude dollars, delays, etc.)? Note: Quantification of impact while desirable is not mandatory.

One alternate approach is for each threat team participant to keep notes, summarize each scenario and turn the notes over to the moderator for summarizing. The summary would be reviewed by each team member at the second meeting. Another alternative, is for the moderator, or other designated person, to act as a recorder, to keep a "transcript" of the meeting. The transcript would then be reviewed by each participant after each meeting and finalized as a consensus record.

The second meeting should be conducted within one to two weeks after the initial session. The initial session provides a "sensitizing" of the participants. Between the two sessions, participants can review the proposed system with some new perspectives and will usually provide additional scenarios. At the conclusion of the second meeting, conclusions about the scenarios should be agreed upon by all participants. A report of the sessions should be written. The report should be closely held, distribution extremely limited and copies protected.

Upon completion of the threat scenario analysis exercise, it is suggested that the security objectives be reviewed to determine if the preliminary security objectives are still valid. When reviewing the security objectives, the following items should be considered to ensure that major concerns about security have been addressed [6].

- Source data accuracy - Will the data supplied to the ADP system be accurate and complete enough to support its intended uses without harmful side effects?

- User identity verification - Can users of the systems be adequately identified and authenticated so they can be held accountable for their actions?

- Restricted interfaces - Are the user interfaces to the system sufficiently restricted so that adequate security is feasible?

- Separation of duties - Do the boundaries between ADP and related manual activities provide maximum separation of duties and independent review?

- Facility security - Is the proposed processing facility adequately secure?

The next step in the security life cycle is to determine the types of controls that should be incorporated into the application that will achieve the security objectives.

Security Feasibility Study

The purpose of the security feasibility study is to determine if controls are available to meet the security objectives, how well they will satisfy the objectives, whether the controls should be preventive, detective or recuperative in nature and what mix of administrative, physical and technical controls is most feasible. Cost, performance degradation, and impact on requirements for user friendliness should be considered. In other words, what types of controls are appropriate for the proposed application?

Brill, in "Building Controls Into Structured Systems" [8] states:

> Probably the most difficult problem facing the systems analyst or inexperienced auditor is how to identify controls efficiently in an existing system or in a system that is under development. The best way is to use an analysis tool. ...This tool is a decision tree whose branches consist of categories and questions that guide you toward the controls on the end branches.
>
> ...When used as a tool for developing controls for a n~v system, it challenges the analyst to answer a series of questions that lead to suggestions for controls.
>
> Application controls (Figure 5) can be divided into three major classes: controls over inputs, controls over processing and controls over output.
>
> The controls over input are the most important and the most numerous, as most errors are generated by input processing. There are four types of input streams: transaction inputs, file maintenance inputs, inquiry inputs and error correction inputs.

Detailed information on these controls and how to implement them can be found in "Building Controls Into Structured Systems."

The next step to consider the controls over processing those inputs. There are three major types of processing controls: run-to-run controls, file and operator controls, and reasonableness tests.

Run-to-run controls were previously discussed in the input controls discussion. Run-to-run controls in the processing area consist of data generation controls and verification controls.

Output controls include: control totals, verification controls and distribution controls.

At this point in the life cycle with the determination of sensitivity completed, the identification of security objectives, the assessment of risks and security feasibility completed, definition of security requirements is the next step.

Define Security Requirements.

Definition of security requirements takes place during the definition stage of the development phase of the system development life cycle. The term "requirements" can be used at many different levels. The requirements defined at this point should include everything that the users and other responsible parties want to require of the application software. The security requirements should be expressed in a way that permits the software designers to choose the best way of implementing them. It should be remembered that security controls can be enforced either by software or by physical or administrative procedures.

The first step in defining security requirements is to conduct an analysis of the "current system" to identify and develop an understanding of the principle functions and to identify sources of input and the flow of data through the system. When the current system is reasonably understood, the user and system requirements should be documented. The sources of input and the flow of data through the system are two of the most important sources of data for defining security requirements. Brill indicates that systems analysts can use four different sources to identify controls that belong in the new system: stated user policy, unstated user policy, the current system and external constraints.

- Stated user policy--Users should be asked how they handle errors in the present system, the kinds of errors or problems they suspect they don't know about (that is, those that are slipping through undetected). Users should also be asked about laws or regulations that affect the way system processes must be done as well as questions about the value and criticality of their data.

- Unstated user policy--Users expect comprehensive controls to be built into their system without ever mentioning controls in discussions with the analysis team. For example, the need to test check digits on account numbers may never be stated because the present manual system may not have facilities to permit it.

- The current system--New systems tend to do many of the same things as the systems they replace. While the specific controls in the new system may differ from those in the old system, there are going to be overlaps. But, you have to look for them, and have to recognize them as controls and to assess their suitability for transplantation into the new system.

- External constraints--Various laws and regulations can directly affect a system. (This area would include agency policy for security, financial accounting, etc.)

FIPS PUB 73 suggests that the following areas be addressed when developing security requirements: identification and definition of systems interfaces (to include responsibilities associated with each interface and separation of duties), identification of the sensitive objects to be processed, determination of error tolerances and definition of availability requirements.

- Identification and definition of systems interfaces--Identify each job function which is related to the application system. Consider each job function as an interface to the application. Define the nature of the interaction between each job function and the system. Also identify and define any interfaces to other automated systems. Include all job functions (or other automated systems) that are to be supported by this system--even if the people performing those jobs only receive reports from it. Also include all job functions (or other automated systems) that supply information to the application system or that support its operation. Be sure to include critical job functions such as: source data collection, input preparation, data entry, output dissemination, data base administration, system security planning and control, internal audit, application program maintenance, archival or backup data storage, computer operations, and system programming.

  Define the responsibilities of the individuals who interact with the application system through each defined interface. Identify the constraints on the use of each interface that must be enforced if security is to be preserved. Consider the likelihood of errors occurring in the use of the interface and identify the consequences. Consider the consequences of deliberate misuse of the interface. Identify the management and administrative controls that will be available to ensure that the interface is used properly.

Examine interfaces to ensure that security exposure will be minimized even if an interface is misused. Ideally, any action that could result in serious harm should be checked or approved from an independent interface.

- Identification of sensitive objects to be processed--Identify the objects to be processed--include input data, stored data and output data. Determine the sensitivity and asset value of the data objects. Identify the operations or functions that users will perform on this data.

- Determination of error tolerances--Determine the application's error tolerance by taking into consideration the expected reliability and validity of the data and the intended objectives of the application. For example, funds disbursement or electronic funds transfer systems may have a low tolerance for data error since such errors directly translate into dollars. Real-time control systems such as air traffic control have virtually no margin for error since human lives may be lost. Some management information systems, particularly those used to predict future demands and resource requirements, may not be as susceptible to errors in data. However, algorithms in the code may have less tolerance for errors. The application's tolerance for error and the requirements for maintaining error levels within acceptable tolerance must be defined.

- Definition of availability requirements--Determine the user tolerance for interruption of output data and the potential harm that could be a result due to non-availability of the application output.

The preceding discussion in this section has addressed the collection and analysis of data that precedes the actual documentation of security requirements. Requirements should define what is required by the user not how it is to be accomplished.

FIPS PUB 73 describes some basic controls that can be used to achieve security objectives. It is relevant at this point in this discussion to summarize these basic controls since the descriptions provided, with some modification, can be used as security requirements. The basic controls provided in FIPS PUB 73 are: data validation, user identity verification, authorization, journaling, variance detection, and encryption.

For data validation in a batch system a typical requirement statement might read:

> All source data will be keyed twice and automatically compared with the transcribed source data previously keyed.

For an on-line system where transactions are entered in real-time, a typical security requirement might read:

> All keyed transactions (or transactions of a certain type) will be visually verified prior to transmission to the system.

Data may also be validated during processing. Most of the techniques that are appropriate to validation during data entry may be applied during processing. An example of a requirement that related to validation during processing is:

> Transaction with errors detected during the data processing phase need to be controlled to ensure they are corrected and reentered in a timely phase.

Examples of requirements for user identification and/or verification might be as follows:

> For batch submissions, users must be visually identified by a control clerk and all jobs logged.
>
> For on-line submission of transactions, all users must have an individual identifier and password for initial logging on.

An example of an authorization security requirement might read:

Examples of a security requirement for journaling are:

> The system will log all accesses by payroll personnel to any employee's payroll record. The system will log all initial log-ons, final log-off at the end of the normal work day and all log-ons and log-offs on weekends.
>
> The system will log all opening and closings of the payroll master file and payroll transaction update files.

A security requirement for variance detection might read:

> The system must be capable of providing post-processing analysis of all or selected activity initiated from a given terminal or by a given employee.
>
> The system must provide an interaction capability to identify attempted accesses to restricted files by unauthorized users.

The preceding are examples of static monitoring. Some variances can and should be detected in real-time so that responses can be immediate. An example of a dynamic monitoring requirement might read:

> The system must be capable of real-time display at a designated console of the full interactive traffic of any terminal or user.

A security requirement for encryption might read:

> All data transmitted between the host computer and remote site will be protected from unauthorized disclosure and modification during transmission.

Following the definition of security requirements, two activities should be initiated: development of the test plan and the design of the security specifications. While they are shown in Figure 3 as sequential events, they can be accomplished in parallel since two different groups of people are involved.

Develop the Security Test Plan

Testing and evaluation attempts to demonstrate that a system is reliable, meets specifications, and meets the requirements of the user. Sorkowitz [5] provides the following comments on testing:

> The main problem in program testing becomes clear when we try to define the word "testing." To many programmers, testing is a process of proving that a program is correct (i.e., the program performs according to specification). However, experience leads us to the belief that there really is no practical way to demonstrate that a program is correct. The best we can say is that at some point in time, there are no known errors. Myers [4] gives a different definition of testing: "Testing is the process of executing a program with the intention of finding errors."

Careful and thorough testing and evaluation can improve system security by uncovering errors, omissions and other flaws in the system's design and code [6]. From a security perspective, the testing of security controls should focus on ensuring that security controls are invoked when required, that they cannot be easily bypassed, that they are auditable and that they are appropriate in view of the sensitivity of the data or the application.

The test plan for security should describe what is to be tested, the testing schedule, resource requirements, testing materials, requirements for test training, the location of the test, the functional security requirements, the tests to be performed on the software and their relationship to the functional security requirements, the testing methodology, the evaluation criteria, data reduction techniques and a description of each test to be performed. The test plan format provided in FIPS PUB 38 [3], with slight modification, can be used to develop the security test plan. A suggested test plan format is provided in Appendix A.

At this point in the system development life cycle, only portions of the test plan can be developed. If the format at Appendix A is utilized, the following sections can be generated at this time. Section 1, General Information, can be completed. In Section 2, Plan, the software description can be written; tentative milestones can be developed; and, preliminary development of the testing subsection can be started. One of the critical items in Section 2 is the area of test training. Specifically, the types of training for the test team should be identified as soon as possible. In Section 3, under Specifications and Evaluation, the functional security requirements and the security functions to be tested can be identified. Additional portions of the test plan will not be able to be developed until such time as the system/subsystem specifications, program specifications, data base specifications and security specifications have been generated.

One of the major objectives of the security test and evaluation of an application under development is to provide some of the data to support the certification of the security controls.

Design the Security Specifications

The design stage is the time to make detailed decisions about how the security requirements will be implemented. There is usually a variety of ways to achieve an adequate level of security. In designing security controls, the age-old maxim of "Keep It Simple" is most applicable. A primary source of security problems is excessively complex design that cannot be implemented easily or correctly, and cannot be maintained nor audited. Losonsky [10] and Wong [11] suggest that, for any sensitive application, a thorough risk analysis, including safeguard selection, should be performed at the beginning of the design phase to assure that appropriate cost-effective controls are integral to the system's design. The guidance in FIPS PUB 65 [12] can be tailored for a risk analysis of an application system design [6]. FIPS PUB 73 [3] provides some ideas that apply to the overall security design effort.

- o Unnecessary Programming. Terminals should be interfaced with the application system so as to minimize the danger that users can get unneeded programming capability. Users who can execute their own programs usually have the potential to bypass any security controls.

- o Restricted User Interfaces. User interfaces should be tailored as specifically as possible to fulfill the user's requirements. Unneeded flexibility makes it more difficult to train users and to get them to accept the system. Flexibility also hurts security. The greatest danger occurs when users are given unnecessary access to a general purpose programming language; ...Once the user's needs are understood, interfaces should be designed to meet these needs as simply as possible with no unnecessary capabilities that complicate things both for the users and for the security analyst.

- o Human Engineering. To preserve security and integrity, user interfaces must be designed so they are easy to understand and use. This can forestall many user errors, and it decreases the chances that users will neglect or bypass controls which they view as cumbersome and annoying.

- o Shared Computer Facilities. It is easier to protect the code and data of the application system if it does not share computer facilities with other applications. It is especially useful to exclude all program development activities from the machine that runs the application-including the development and maintenance of the application's programs themselves.

- o Isolation of Critical Code. The code and system data that is critical to security should be well identified so it can be more easily audited and protected. When possible, security controls should be isolated in modules that have few interactions with the rest of the application software. This makes it easier to audit these modules and protect them from unauthorized modifications during operations. Sometimes automated controls can be used to protect these modules:

- * Checksums of the object code can be used to try to detect unauthorized changes.

- * Hardware protection states or protection domains can protect code and data critical to security.

- * If security-critical code always resides in a fixed area of memory, then read-only memory can be used.

- * Recent experimental languages, called type safe languages, may soon be available. Compilers for these languages can protect modules and their data from unexpected interactions with other modules.

Identification and partial isolation of critical code and data are reasonably easy; however, rigorous isolation is more difficult than it sounds. Without very careful planning, all system code and data will end up being relevant to security because errors or deliberate traps elsewhere can still cause security failures. This other software includes:

* The operating system and other software that supports any of the security functions.

* All parts of the application system needed to guarantee that the security controls are invoked at the appropriate time.

* Compilers and other software used to develop and maintain any security-relevant software.

When code relevant to security is rigorously isolated from the bulk of the software, it is called a security kernel. Security kernels that protect data from unauthorized disclosure are feasible, but they require specially designed operating systems.

o Backup and Recovery. With appropriate contingency planning, the services of a computer application can usually be restored within a few hours after a failure. If availability requirements are more rigorous than that, then automatic backup and recovery mechanisms may need to be included in the application software.

o Use of Available Controls. The operating system and the facility management may already provide a variety of controls such as:

* User identity verification.

* Authorization for access to system files.

* Journaling of operating system activities.

* Backup and recovery operations.

While the application system usually needs to supplement these controls, available controls should be used to the fullest extent possible. In too many cases, controls are needlessly reimplemented because controls that are available are not understood or not utilized.

Since the security controls of an operating system are not absolutely reliable, the application system should use some data integrity checks to try to identify whether critical data has been altered; however, in general, there is no reason to believe that controls implemented in the application will be any more reliable than those already provided by an operating system.

The purpose of the design stage is to translate the security functional requirements into security specifications that can be used by programmers to develop the security-relevant code.

In developing security specifications, there should be a normal evolution from architectural specifications to design specifications. Whether there will be an explicit distinction between architectural-type specifications and detailed specifications will depend on each organization's standards for software life cycle development. It should be noted that the terms logical design and physical design, used in some methodologies, correspond to SDLC architectural design and detailed design, respectively.

In Section 2.3.1.5, examples of security requirements were provided based on the basic controls described in FIPS PUB 73. The types of basic controls included: data validation, user identity verification, authorization, journaling, variance detection, and encryption. The following discussion will provide examples of specifications for some of the security requirements previously discussed.

- Requirement - All source data will be keyed twice and automatically compared with the transcribed source data previously keyed.

- Specification - A second person will key the data into a verifier. Only those fields containing transaction code, employee name, SSN, and grade will be verified. Any record containing a discrepancy between the initial keying and the verifying keying will be recorded on a discrepancy file. The discrepancy file will be forwarded to the input control group. Each record containing an error will be visually compared to the original source document and the input control group will resolve any discrepancy. The corrected transaction record will then be submitted input to the system.

  (The operations manual would indicate the record positions of the fields to be verified and the specific instructions for incorporating the correct record/transaction into the batching process.)

- Requirement - All keyed transactions (or transaction of a certain type) will be visually verified prior to transmission to the system.

- Specification - Data entry personnel will visually verify that the transaction code is equal to a 1, 2, or 3; the name field contains no arabic numeric data (note romanic number such as I, II, III, etc., are legal); the SSN field contains no alpha or special characters, no blanks; and that the grade field contains no alpha, special characters or blanks; that grade field contains only one of the following: 01, 03, 04, 05, 07, 09, 10, 11, 13, or 14.

  If any field is not correct, the operator will check the source document for the correct data. If the source document is in error, the document will be returned to the point of origination for correction and resubmission.

- Requirement - All data transmitted between the host computer and remote site will be protected from unauthorized disclosure and modification during transmission.

- Specification - All data will be encrypted using the Data Encryption Standard as specified in FIPS PUB 46.

After the security specifications have been developed and approved, the development of test procedures can begin.

Develop Security Test Procedures

At this point in the life cycle, following the definition of the security specifications, Section 3 and 4 of the Security Test Plan can be developed. Using the test plan format at Appendix A, the next step is to complete the sections dealing with methods and constraints and evaluation.

The methodology should indicate whether static or dynamic testing or both will be used, whether live or test data and an indication of the volume of data that is required to adequately test the security controls. The method for recording test results should be identified as well as any constraints that may limit the scope of the test. Under the evaluation section, the criteria for each type of test should be identified. Data reduction methods should also be described.

FIPS PUB 73 offers some guidance on static and dynamic testing that is useful to this discussion of developing test procedures.

> Static Evaluation. These techniques, which involve examination and analysis of the systems documentation and code, represent the most effective way to detect deliberate traps or other unauthorized modifications. However, due to the complexity of most systems and the limitations of automated techniques, and tools, it is not currently practical to analyze systems completely using static evaluation methods. In addition, static evaluation does not examine the system in a "live" or operational mode so that errors in the execution environment are not detected. Specific techniques and tools include:
>
> * Code Review. Portions of the source code are evaluated to determine if they implement the design specifications and are free from errors. In most cases, it will be impossible to review all of the system's code.
>
>   Generally, samples of code will be reviewed--especially critical modules or critical portions of the code. The code review can be done by an internal test and evaluation team that is involved in the system development or by an independent (third party) team--either internal or external to the organization. Code review differs from peer review, ...in that the code review is performed by individuals who were not involved with the design and programming of the application.
>
> * Penetration Studies. A few individuals can be challenged to find unknown weaknesses in the security controls. Penetration studies to identify programming errors can be expensive and are useful only if someone believes that there are no remaining errors that can affect security.
>
> * Source Code Analyzers. These software tools aid the evaluation process by providing details about specific characteristics of the source program. Examples include:
>
>   - cross reference listings are an aid to code review and may be useful to identify "suspicious" variables and source statement references.

- the variables which can influence control flow decisions can all be identified or variables which could be read before any value has been assigned to them can be identified.

Dynamic Testing. These techniques involve executing the application system, or portions of the system, with test data and comparing the actual results with expected or known results. ...Dynamic testing is only practical for selected test cases. Fundamental questions such as, "Which test cases should be chosen?" and "How many test cases are enough?" must be answered. The answers to these questions depend upon the system being tested and upon the experience of the test team.

The following tools can be used to aid the dynamic testing process:

* Program Analyzers. A program analyzer is a computer program that collects data about another program's operation while that program is executing. Program analyzers can be particularly useful for evaluating how thoroughly the test data has exercised the program being tested. In addition, they can be used to identify extraneous code that might be an unauthorized insertion.

* Flaw Hypothesis Method. Security flaws can be hypothesized based on analogous flaws found in other systems and then tested for existence in this system. This is an effective approach for selecting test cases that are likely to find flaws.

The finalization of the test procedures will be a simultaneous activity by the test team while system developers are writing the security code and documenting the security safeguards.

Write Security Relevant Code

The precise way in which security safeguards will actually be implemented in the software code will depend to a great extent on the programming language used, installation standards, and personal programming style. Within the foregoing limitations there are some practices that should be followed to ensure that security relevant code is understandable, auditable, maintainable and testable.

The Systems Auditability and Control (SAC) Study [1] in discussing application system development controls provides some guidance that is useful to the development of security relevant code.

> The adequacy and effectiveness of controls included in computer application systems are affected by the methods and procedures used during the system development process.

One of the areas discussed in some depth is the use of structured programming. The following is a summary of the SAC discussion of structured programming.

The objective in using structured programming techniques is to develop more usable and effective programs. "Usable" implies that the program can be read and understood by technical persons who did not write it, including users and EDP auditors. "Effective" implies that the program is designed to fit into an overall application system scheme so as to reduce redundancy and ensure processing efficiency.*

Structured programming is a technique for system builders that renders systems easier to build, maintain and alter. It is a discipline that is used primarily in the detail design and programming states of the development process. As such, it uses a stepwise top-down approach, in which program modules are organized by functional specifications into a balanced hierarchical structure with minimum side effects on each module.

Structured programming involves a team approach to detailed design, with team members being used to "walk-through" the design and coding of components. The effect is that the design and code can be viewed by other than the originator to detect faulty logic, hard-to-follow code and the extent to which the design meets prespecified objectives.

Stanford Research Institute, authors of the SAC Study [1], found the following major techniques were used by many organizations:

- o Program Structure.
- o Statement Formatting.
- o Peer Reviews.
- o Team Organization.
- o Top-Down Design.
- o Segmentation.
- o Structured Coding.
- o Walk-throughs.
- o Programmer Librarian.

FIPS PUB 73 recommends the following additional practices to enhance the security of application systems:

- o Program Libraries.
- o Redundant Computation.
- o Program Development Tools.

Document Security Safeguards

Program documentation is needed during any software development; it is especially necessary for security-relevant code. FIPS PUB 73 defines security-relevant code as:

- o code that implements security controls;

---

* Security controls should meet the usable objective. To be effective, in the above context, security controls should not unnecessarily reduce processing efficiency and be implemented in a way that they are part of the overall application scheme, and do not appear or operate as an interruption to the normal flow of the program or application processes.

- o code that performs critical processing (e.g., check disbursement, real-time controls); and
- o code that has access to critical or sensitive data during its execution.

The SAC study provides the following thoughts on documentation that are applicable to the documentation of security controls.

> Documentation...is important because it helps ensure correct and efficient processing within both data processing and user areas; it increases the ease and accuracy of computer program maintenance, and it provides auditors with an independent basis for evaluating application control.
>
> In addition to verifying the existence of sufficient documentation, this technique also assesses various aspects of the documentation, including the following:
>
> - Does the documentation give evidence that processing controls will be adequate?
> - Have sufficient controls been built into the system to allow effective operation and maintenance?
> - Can the documentation be used as a basis to prove that controls over operation and maintenance are adequate?

It is recommended that the documentation of security-relevant code be contained in an independent document. The sensitivity of security-relevant code is such that it should be well-protected and access to the documentation should be restricted.

Conduct Security Test and Evaluation

Ideally, the conduct of the actual security test and evaluation will be performed by an organization independent of the system developers and users; that is, an independent validation and verification (IV&V) team, quality assurance personnel or an audit group. If such groups do not formally exist within the organization, a team of security evaluators may be formed for the purpose of conducting the security test and evaluation. Team skills that will be required include application analysts, testers, programmers, penetration specialists, VV&T specialists and security.

The actual test will consists of some combination of the following: document reviews, interviews, dynamic tests and penetration resistance tests. Each of these have been previously discussed.

Regardless of what combination of tests is used, it is important that the test team keep a list of documents reviewed, document all interviews, and document and maintain the results of any tests run against the application.

Write Security Test and Evaluation Report. The purpose of the Security Test and Evaluation Report is to document the test and evaluation results and findings; present the demonstrated capabilities and deficiencies of the security controls; and provide a basis for preparing the proposed security certification report.

The Security Test and Evaluation Report should be prepared by, or under the direction of, the security team leader. It will then be transmitted to the application computer security official (CSO). FIPS PUB 102 [13], provides a sample outline that can be used to develop the Security Test and Evaluation Report. The sample outline contains five sections. Section 1, Introduction and Summary, briefly describes the application and summarizes the evaluation findings and recommendations. Section 2, Background, provides contextual information for the Application CSO including the security standards and policies that were applied. Also, it should include a list of the general functional characteristics of the application that generally influence its certifiability (e.g., the absence or presence of user programming). The scope of the evaluation and the assumptions and constraints on the test should be identified.

Section 3, Major Findings, should summarize the controls in place and their role in protecting the data and/or the application. It should emphasize those controls that were found to be effective. Any vulnerabilities found during the test should also be documented. The report should identify those vulnerabilities which should be accepted and those which should be corrected.

Section 4, Recommended Corrective Actions, identifies what additional controls should be considered and the anticipated costs of such recommendations. Section 5, Evaluation Process, should summarize the security test and evaluation process to include the types of tests that were conducted.

Prepare the Proposed Certification Statement

The proposed Certification Statement should summarize the recommendations, the acceptability of applications' security safeguards, restrictions (e.g., applications must be run as a stand-alone system), and/or corrective actions that must be accomplished prior to allowing the application to commence running.

SOFTWARE QUALITY ASSURANCE AND SECURITY

G. H. Myers, in Software Reliability, Principles and Practices [9], begins a discussion of the definition of software reliability as follows:

> The most significant problem facing the data processing business today is the software problem that is manifested in two major complaints: software is too expensive and software is unreliable. Most computer professionals recognize the former problem as largely a symptom of the latter...
>
> It is interesting to note that the software reliability problem as it exists today was observed in the early days of computing:
>
> > Those who regularly code for fast electronic computers will have learned from bitter experience that a large fraction of the time spent in preparing calculations for the machine is taken up in removing blunders that have been made in drawing up the programs. With the aid of common sense and checking subroutines, the majority mistakes are quickly found and rectified. Some errors, however, are sufficiently obscure to escape detection for a surprisingly long time [13].

> This observation was published by three British mathematicians in 1952. Although software errors were encountered before 1952, this seems to be the first recognition of the reliability problem, that is, a considerable amount of time is required for testing, and, even after this, some software errors will remain undetected.
>
> The immediate problem encountered in dealing with software reliability is one of the definition: What is a software error? What is software reliability?

Myers provides the following definition:

> A software error is present when the software does not do what the user reasonably expects it to do. A software failure is an occurrence of a software error.
>
> Software reliability is the probability that the software will execute for a particular period of time without failure, weighted by the cost to the user of each failure encountered.

One of the areas of software where errors can be least tolerated is that of security safeguards. One of the techniques that is currently being employed to improve the reliability of software is software quality assurance. This section provides a discussion of software quality assurance, the software quality assurance life cycle, and how software quality assurance can be employed to reduce the potential for incorporating unreliable security safeguards in application systems.

The Cost of Software Errors

Sorkowitz [6] indicates that to better manage the development and maintenance of ADP systems, it is important to have an understanding of how software costs are distributed throughout the total software life cycle. Sorkowitz provides the following:

> Life cycle costs are documented as follows:
>
> a. Initiation Phase
>
> Very little research has been done in this area.
>
> b. Development Phase
>
> A number of independent studies [16] divide the development costs as follows:
>
> 1. analysis and design--40%
>
> 2. coding and unit testing--20%
>
> 3. system test and integration--20%
>
> The above figures have sometimes been described in the literature as the 40-20-20 rule.

Testing

> Studies have shown that the various testing phases can account for up to 50% of the total resources spent for the development of a software system.

In discussing the detection of errors, Sorkowitz indicates that:

> The phase in the life in which errors are detected is very important. This may sound obvious, but there are severe penalties if this simple point is not well understood. The cost of correcting an error increases with time.

Myers shows two relationships concerning error correction versus schedule times (Figure 5). The first relationship shows that the cost of correcting an error increases rapidly during the latter parts of the development cycle. However, a second and less-known relationship also follows the same general curve. The probability of fixing a known error incorrectly also increases rapidly during the latter stages.

In the first relationship, Wolverton and Putnam [14] noted that a requirement error detected in the design stage is 2-1/2 times more costly to fix than if detected in the requirement stage. This same error detected in the Unit test stage is five times more costly and if found during Integration testing is 36 times more costly. If we consider the very special case of a security safeguard that is embedded in the software and that safeguard contains an error, we can see that the ultimate potential cost can increase dramatically (Figure 6).

Not only will the organization incur the cost to fix the flawed software, but in addition, could incur a loss which may well exceed the cost to fix the flaw.

From the security perspective, the concern then is how do we ensure that the safeguards that are incorporated into application's software are free from errors and are reliable. From the system designer's and system developer's perspective, the concern is how do we define, design and develop error-free and reliable safeguards. In other words, how do we define and develop quality safeguards? One of the techniques is the use of a quality assurance process.

Software Quality Assurance

Perry, in Effective Methods of EDP Quality Assurance [15], provides some introductory comments on quality assurance that are appropriate to this discussion.

> Organizations continually quest for quality products. Organizations that achieve a high level of quality in their products first establish an acceptable level of quality and then build a mechanism that assures this level is maintained. That mechanism in manufacturing is known as quality control. ...Quality control includes more than an evaluation of the end product. It begins with the examination of the raw materials and continues throughout the manufacturing cycle.
>
> Data processing organizations must equate their function to manufacturing a product in order to see the need for a quality control function. Data processing must assume the responsibility of determining an acceptable level of quality, and then establish the mechanism (e.g., quality assurance function) to assure that level is maintained.

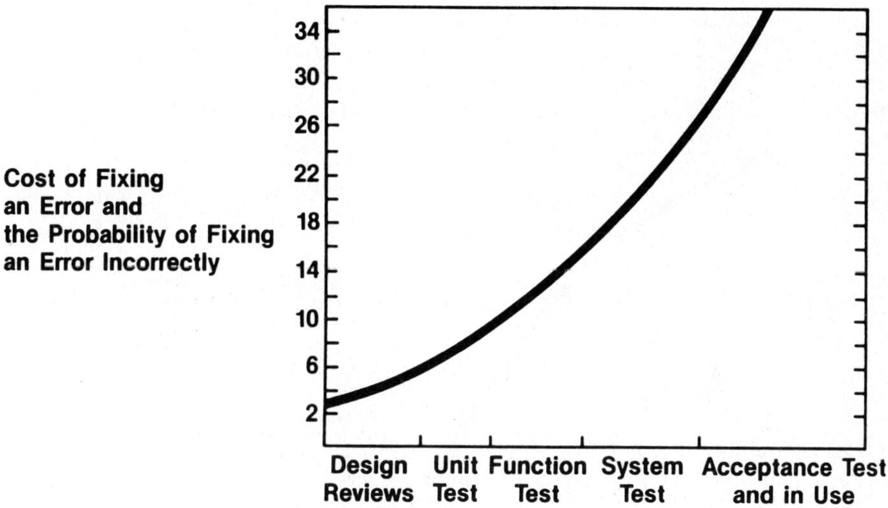

Figure 5 Relationships Between Error Corrections and Time

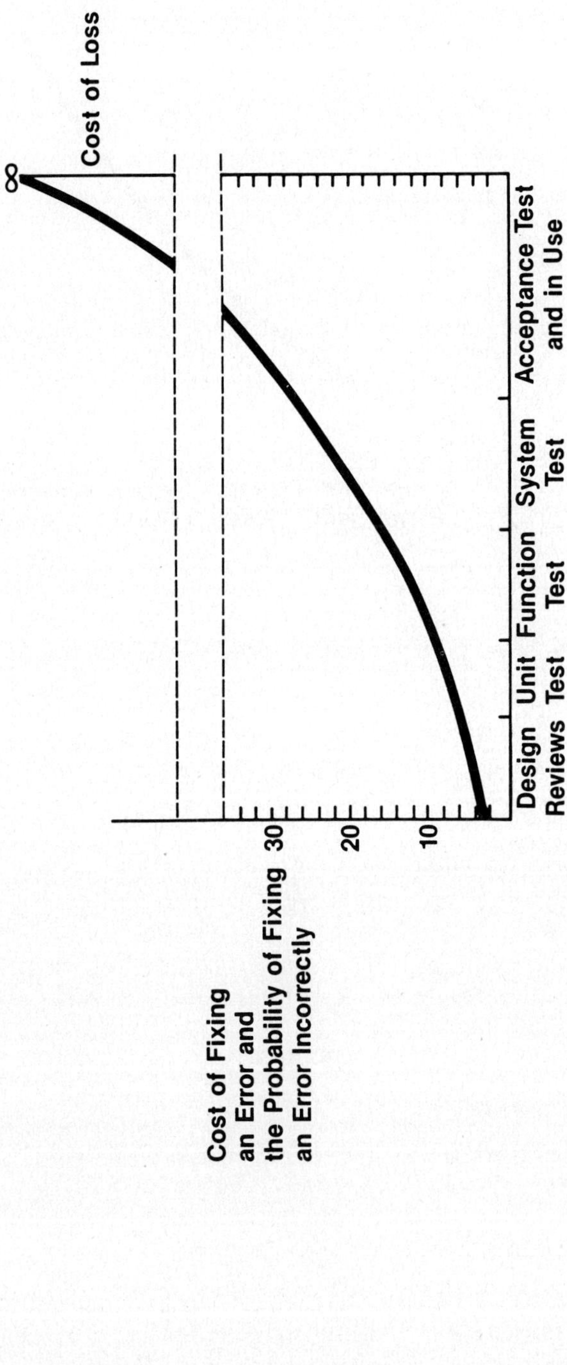

Figure 6 Relationships Between Error Corrections and Potential Loss of Exploited Software Safeguard

> ...the quality assurance function is an evolutionary step along the path of moving data processing from an art to a science.

One of the questions that comes to mind in any initial discussion of software quality assurance is: What is quality? Perry provides the following thoughts:

> Quality is defined in the dictionary as an attribute or characteristic that is associated with something. Thus quality cannot be universally defined, but rather, must be defined for the item in question. Quality becomes a stated list of attributes and characteristics.

Software Quality Factors

To improve the quality of software, it is important to have an understanding of the attributes and characteristics, sometimes referred to as factors, that contribute to software quality. Sorkowitz [18] provides the following list of software quality factors.

- Correctness - the extent to which a program satisfies its specifications and fulfills the user's mission objectives.
- Reliability - the extent to which a program can be expected to perform its intended function with required precision.
- Efficiency - the amount of computing resources and code required by a program to perform a function.
- Integrity - the extent to which access to software or data by unauthorized persons can be controlled.
- Usability - the effort required to learn, operate, prepare input, and interpret output of a program.
- Maintainability - the effort required to locate and fix an error in an operational program.
- Testability - the effort required to test a program to ensure it performs its intended function.
- Flexibility - the effort required to modify an operational program.
- Portability - the effort required to transfer a program from one hardware configuration and/or software system environment to another.
- Reusability - the extent to which a program can be used in other applications--related to the packaging and scope of functions that programs perform.
- Interoperability - the effort required to couple one system with another.

Software Quality Factors and the Life Cycle

The points in the system development life cycle where each of the factors is of concern is illustrated in Figure 7. Figure 8 [16] identifies the relationship of software quality factors to the life cycle phases in terms of

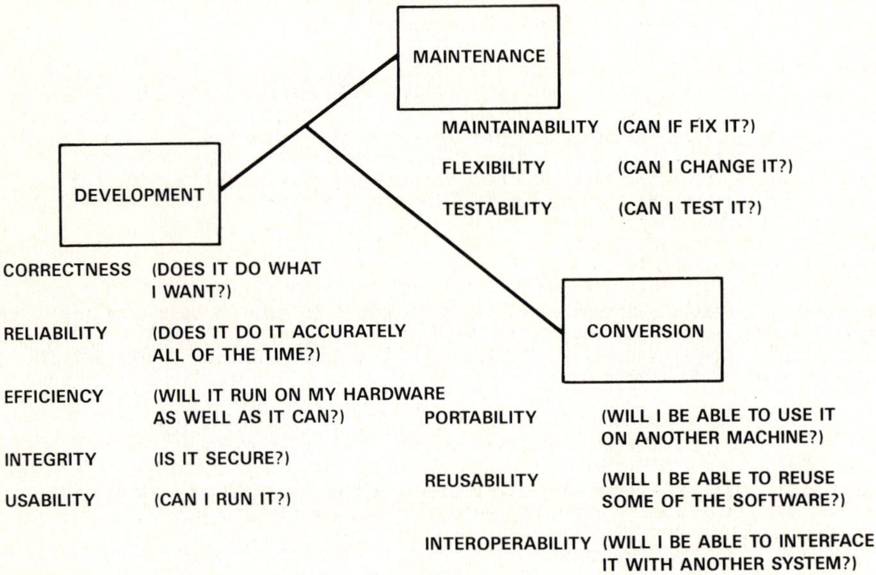

Figure 7 Relationship of Software Quality Factors to the Software Lifecycle

	DEVELOPMENT			EVALUATION	OPERATION		
Factors \ LIFE-CYCLE PHASES	REQUIREMENTS ANALYSIS	DESIGN	CODE AND DEBUG	SYSTEM TEST	OPERATION	MAINTENANCE	TRANSITION
Correctness	△	△	△	X	X	X	
Reliability	△	△	△	X	X	X	
Efficiency		△	△		X		
Integrity	△	△	△		X		
Usability	△	△		X	X	X	
Maintainability		△	△			X	X
Testability		△	△	X		X	X
Flexibility		△	△			X	X
Portability		△	△				X
Reusability		△	△				X
Interoperability		△			X		

Legend:
△ Where quality factors should be measures
X Where impact of poor quality is realized

Figure 8 Relationship of Factors to Lifecycle Phases

where quality factors should be measured and where the impact of poor quality is realized. It should be noted that software quality factors should be included in the functional requirements document and ultimately viewed as performance criteria.

The Software Quality Assurance Process

The purpose of employing a software quality assurance process is to improve computer software products that are produced via the software development process. Software quality assurance activities should be accomplished at pertinent points during the system development life cycle. Also, procedures should be established to control and track changes generated during the development cycle. Software quality assurance involves the use of various reviews and the establishment of baselines throughout the development cycle. The reviews and baselines are depicted in Figure 9.

Software Quality Assurance Baselines

The characteristics of an evolving system and its configuration items are defined and documented in increasing detail at logical transition points, or baselines, in the system development life cycle. At any time in the life cycle, all of the previously established baselines, together with approved changes to these baselines, constitutes the identification of the system and its configuration items. Five baselines are usually defined in the software assurance life cycle: functional, allocated, developmental, product and operational.

- o Functional Baseline - marks the end of the initiation phase and the start of the definition stage of the development phase.
- o Allocated Baseline - marks the end of the design stage and the start of the programming stage and is established by the detailed design specifications.
- o Developmental Baseline - marks the end of the programming stage and the start of the test phase.
- o Product Baseline - marks the end of the test stage and the start of the operations phase.
- o Operational Baseline - marks the end of the implementation stage and the start of the maintenance phase and is established by the satisfactory demonstration of the application system in the operational environment.

Reviews and Audits

The various reviews and audits that should take place throughout the system development life cycle include the system requirements review (SRR), system design review (SDR), preliminary design review (PDR), critical design review (CRD), test readiness review (TRR), functional configuration audit (FCA), physical configuration audit (PCA), and formal qualification review (FQR).

- o Systems Requirements Review (SRR) - the objective of this review is to ascertain the adequacy of the system requirements. It should be conducted when a significant portion of the system functional requirements have been established.

Initiation Phase	Development Phase				Operations Phase	
	Definition Stage	Design Stage	Programming Stage	Test Stage	Implementation Stage	Maintenance Stage
• System Requirements Review	• System Design Review	• System Specif-ication Review	• Test Read-iness Review — Unit — Module — Interface System	• Functional Configuration Audit-1 • Physical Configuration Audit-1 • Formal Qualification Review-1	• Functional Configuration Audit-2 • Physical Configuration Audit-2 • Formal Qualification Review-2	
• Functional Baseline	• Allocated Baseline	• Allocated Baseline	• Developmental Baseline	• Product Baseline	• Operational Baseline	

Figure 9 Software Quality Assurance Reviews and Baselines

- System Design Review (SDR) - this review should be conducted to evaluate the optimization, correlation, completeness and risks associated with the allocated technical requirements. Also included is a summary review of the system process which produced the allocated technical requirements of of the planning for the next phase of the effort. This review should be conducted when the system definition effort has proceeded to the point where system characteristics are defined.

- Preliminary Design Review (PDR) - this review should be conducted for each system element to (1) evaluate the progress, technical adequacy, and risk resolution (on a technical, cost and schedule basis) of the selected design approach, (2) determine its compatability with performance and requirements of the development specification, and (3) establish the existence and compatibility of the physical and functional interfaces among the other elements (personnel, equipment, facilities and computer programs).

- Critical Design Review (CDR) - this review should be conducted for each element when the detailed design is essentially complete. The purpose of this review is to (1) determine that the detailed design of the elements under review satisfies the performance requirements of the development specifications, (2) establish the detailed design compatibility among the elements, (3) assess the producibility and risk areas (on technical, cost and schedule perspective), and (4) review the preliminary product specifications.

- Test Readiness Review (TRR) - a formal review should be conducted to validate the plan and the test procedures to include the test conditions, the extent of testing and the criteria for acceptance.

- Functional Configuration Audit (FCA) - a formal audit should be conducted to validate that the development of an element has been completed satisfactorily and that the element has achieved the performance and functional characteristics specified in the functional and design specifications.

- Physical Configuration Audit (PCA) - a technical examinatiopn of a designated element should be conducted to verify that the element "as built" conforms to the technical documentation which defines the element.

- Formal Qualification Review (FQR) - this review should consist of a test, inspection or analytical process by which products at the end item or critical end item level are verified to have met specific requirements (specifications or equivalent). This review does not apply to requirements verified during the FCA.

Reviews and audits should be conducted by personnel or an organizational entity independent of the development team.

Software Quality Assurance Life Cycle Security Activities

It is not sufficient to incorporate security safeguards in application systems. Safeguards should possess many of the same characteristics previously identified in the discussion of software quality factors. Also, security concerns should be integrated into the software quality assurance process in the same manner that security concerns should be incoporated into the system development life cycle process. Like software quality, the quality of security safeguards must be build-in and cannot be tested-in.

Security Safeguard Characteristics (Factors)

Security safeguards should possess the following characteristics: correctness, reliability, efficiency, integrity, usability, maintainability, testability, flexibility and interoperability.

- o Correctness - the extent to which a security safeguard satisfies its specifications and fulfills the application security objectives.
- o Reliability - the extent to which a security safeguard can be expected to perform its intended function with required precision.
- o Efficiency - the amount of computing resources and code required by a security safeguard to perform its function.
- o Integrity - the extent to which access to the security safeguard by unauthorized persons can be controlled.
- o Usability - the effort required to learn, operate, prepare input and interpret output from a security safeguard.
- o Maintainability - the effort required to locate and fix an error in or to determine the impact of other system changes on a security safeguard.
- o Testability - the effort required to test or audit a security safeguard to ensure that it performs its intended function.
- o Flexibility - the effort required to modify an operation security safeguard.
- o Interoperability - the effort required to couple to or integrate security safeguards into the application system.

Security Assurance Activities

The security activities that should be an integral part of the software quality assurance process consist of a set of defined reviews and audits and approvals. The reviews and audits to be accomplished throughout the software quality assurance life cycle can be viewed as an integral part of the software quality assurance process but are separately identifiable actions. The security activities (Figure 10) to be completed in conjunction with software quality assurance activities are: security requirements review, security design review, security specifications review, security test readiness review, and the security test and evaluation review.

Initiation Phase	Development Phase				Operations Phase	
	Definition Stage	Design Stage	Programming Stage	Test Stage	Implementation Stage	Maintenance Stage
• System Requirements Review • Functional Baseline	• System Design Review • Allocated Baseline	• System Specification • Allocated Baseline	• Test Readiness Review — Unit — Module — Interface System • Developmental Baseline	• Functional Configuration Audit-1 • Physical Configuration Audit-1 • Formal Qualification Review-1 • Product Baseline	• Functional Configuration Audit-2 • Physical Configuration Audit-2 • Formal Qualification Review-2 • Operational Baseline	
• Security Requirements Review	• Security Design Review	• Security Specifications Review	• Security Test Readiness Review	• Security Test & Evaluation Review		
• Security Requirements Approval	• Security Design Approval	• Security Specifications Approval	• Security Test & Evaluation Plan Approval	• Security Safeguard Certification		

Figure 10 Security Assurance Reviews and Baselines

Security Requirements Review

The objective of this review is to ascertain the adequacy of the security objectives, security feasibility and the preliminary security requirements. It should be conducted when a significiant portion of the security requirements have been defined and in conjunction with the system requirements review (SRR).

The security requirements should be reviewed and approved by the application computer security official.

Security Design Review

This review should be conducted to evaluate the completeness and appropriateness of the technical security requirements. The review should also evaluate the technical risks of the safeguards that are being considered to meet the security requirements. The review should be conducted when the security definition effort has progressed to the point where the types of security controls that are proposed for the system have been identified and the initial or draft architectural security specifications have been developed. The system process which produced the architectural specifications should be reviewed. This review should be conducted in conjunction with the preliminary design review. The architectural specifications should be approved by the application computer security official.

Security Specifications Review

This review should be conducted for each security safeguard when the detailed security specifications are essentially Complete. The purpose of the review is to (1) determine that the detailed design of the safeguards under review satisfy the performance requirements of the architectural specifications, (2) establish that the detailed design of the safeguards is compatible with the application system detailed design, (3) assess the producibility and risk areas (from a technical, cost and schedule perspective), and (4) review the preliminary security product specifications.

This review should be conducted in conjunction with the critical design review. The detailed design security specifications should be approved by the application computer security official.

Security Test Readiness Review

The purpose of this review is to validate the security test plan and test procedures to include the test conditions, the extent of the security test and the criteria for acceptance. The review should also determine the readiness of the security controls for testing to ensure that the security test and evaluation schedule can be met. The review should be conducted in conjunction with the test readiness review. The test plan and test procedures should be approved by the applications computer security official.

Security Test and Evaluation Review

The purpose of the security test and evaluation review is to evaluate the auditability of the records of the procedures, the accuracy of the data resulting from the tests, and the effectiveness of the tools and techniques used during the test. A useful set of criteria evaluating the security test and evaluation report is provided by FIPS PUB 102 (Figure 11).

Resource Questions

1. How much of resources (e.g., time, money) were expanded in the evaluation?

2. Who performed the evaluation? What are their qualifications? Might there by any reasons to question their objectivity?

Process Questions

1. What technical review mechanisms were used?

2. Have the findings and recommendations been properly coordinated?

3. What major tools and techniques were used? What other experiences have there been with them? Have resources been effectively allocated to tools, analysis, and presentation of findings?

Content Questions

1. Are the findings and recommendations reasonable?

2. What are other agencies doing in similar situations? Are Federal and agency requirements applicable to this application? Are there recent or proposed policy changes that are applicable? Do agency needs override user needs? What are the penalties for not complying with policies and requirements?

3. Did the evaluation focus on the those things of primary importance? What assurances are there that major problem areas have not been overlooked? Are there safeguards not considered by the evaluation activity that might influence the findings? Are the recommendations prioritized? What was the basis for prioritization?

4. Many residual vulnerabilities will exist. Have they been identified?

5. Are recommendations and judgments supported? Is the quality of supporting data showns?

Figure 11 Criteria For Assessing Security Evaluation Report

REFERENCES

[1] Institute of Internal Auditors. System Auditability and Control Study-Control Practices. Altamonte Springs, FL, 1977.

[2] Frank Mayo, Frederick G. Tompkins, Dana L. Hall. NASA Software Development and Assurance--Survey of Problems and Practices, MTE-82W205. The MITRE Corporation, McLean, VA, 1982.

[3] National Bureau of Standards. Guidelines for Documentation of Computer Programs and Automated Data Systems. Washington, DC, GPO, 15 February 1976, FIPS PUB 38.

[4] National Bureau of Standards. Guidelines for Documentation of Computer Programs and Automated Data Systems for the Initiation Phase. Washington, DC, GPO, August 1979, FIPS PUB 64.

[5] Alfred R. Sorkowitz. Software Life Cycle Costing. Proceedings Trends and Applications 1979. IEEE Computer Society, New York, NY, 1979.

[6] National Bureau of Standards. Guidelines for Security of Computer Applications. Washington, DC, GPO, 30 June 1980, FIPS PUB 73.

[7] Brandt Allen. Threat Teams: A Technique for the Detection and Prevention of Fraud in Automated and Manual Systems. Computer Security Journal, Volume 1, Number 1, Spring 1981.

[8] Alan E. Brill. Building Controls into Structured Systems. YOURDON Press, New York, NY, 1983.

[9] Glenford J. Myers. Software Reliability, Principles and Practices. John Wiley and Sons, New York, NY, 1976.

[10] Terrence M. Losonsky. Automated Information System Security: A Comparative Analysis of Risk Management Procedures. Florida State University, December 1974.

[11] K. K. Wong. Computer Security Risk Analysis and Control, A Guide for the DP Manager. Manchester, England, The National Computer Center Limited, 1977. ISBM 0-8104-5466-1.

[12] National Bureau of Standards. Guidelines for Automatic Data Processing Risk Analysis. Washington, DC, GPO, August 1979, FIPS PUB 65.

[13] R. A. Brooker, S. Gill, and D. J. Wheeler. The Adventures of a Blunder. Mathematical Tables and Other Aids to Computation, Volume 6, Number 38, 112-113, 1952.

[14] R. W. Wolverton and L. Putnam. Quantitative Management: Software Cost Estimating. IEEE COMPSAC 77, November 1977.

[15] William E. Perry. Effective Methodology of EDP Quality Assurance. Wellesley, MA, QED Information Sciences, Inc., 1981.

[16] Alfred E. Sorkowitz. Life Cycle Quality Assurance Workshop. Potomac Forum, Alexandria, VA, 1984.

COMPUTER SECURITY
J.B. Grimson and H.-J. Kugler (Editors)
Elsevier Science Publishers B.V. (North-Holland)

COMMUNICATIONS AND NETWORK PROTECTION PRACTICAL EXPERIENCES

Ole Stampe Rasmussen
Security Manager
The Danish Banks and Savings Banks Debit and Credit Card Company
Copenhagen, Denmark

The Danish banks and savings banks have launched two nationwide EFT-systems, a POS-system and an ATM-network. Based on the experiences with developing, implementing, and operating the two systems the practical solutions for data protection and authentication are presented.

0. Table of content

1. Overview and Summary
   1.1 Introduction
   1.2 The Danish Automated Clearing House
   1.3 Debit and Credit Cards
   1.4 Cash Dispensers (ATMs)
   1.5 Concepts
   1.6 Security

2. Threats and Attack Points
   2.1 Terminals
   2.2 Data Network
   2.3 Computer Centre
   2.4 Clearing Transactions

3. Protection Means
   3.1 DES-Encryption
   3.2 Public Key Encryption
   3.3 Message Authentication

4. Implementation - Key Management
   4.1 Key Generation
   4.2 Key Distribution
   4.3 Key Protection

5. Conclusion

1. Overview and Summary

1.1 Introduction

The Danish banking system is characterized by a relatively large number of commercial banks and savings banks. Despite the large number there is a unique tradition for technical co-operation. It started at the beginning of the sixties with a wage- and salary transfer agreement followed by an agreement about cheque encashment. These agreements resulted in an explosive growth in paper based transactions. During the seventies the paper based systems were converted to electronic systems and today almost all interbank transactions are exchanged electronically. In order to facilitate the exchange and to minimize the remaining number of paper transactions three joint companies were established. The three companies are owned by a holding company, PBS - The Danish Banks and Savings Banks Payment Systems Company (figure 1).

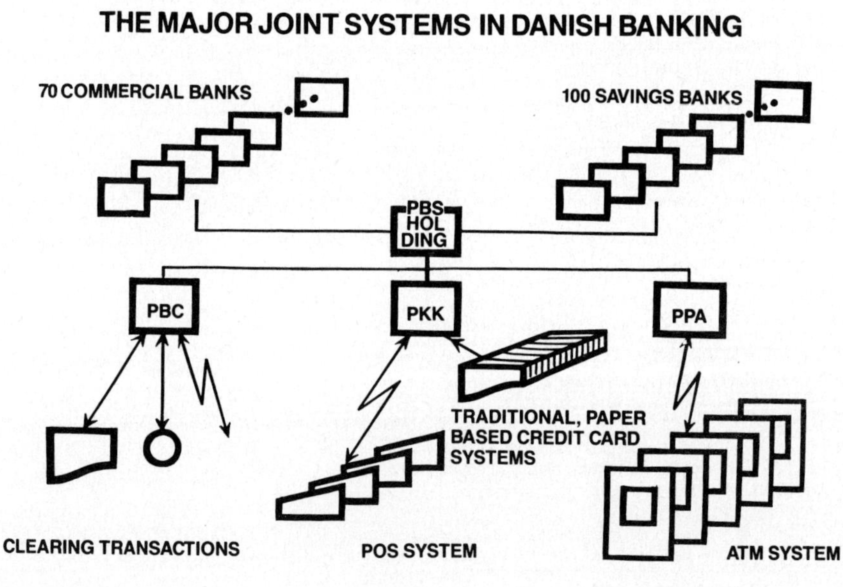

FIGURE 1

1.2 The Danish Automated Clearing House

In 1971 the Danish banks and savings banks established a joint company, PBC - The Danish Automated Clearing House, with the purpose of developing and operating a fully automated clearing system based on datatransmission.

1.3 Debit and Credit Cards

In 1979 the banks and savings banks decided to introduce a national debit and credit card, and a new joint company, PKK - The Danish Banks and Savings Banks Debit and Credit Card Company, was established.

PKK started with a traditional paper based system using a national card - The Dankort - issued by the banks and savings banks.

Besides operating the paper based system PKK has developed and implemented an on-line electronic point-of-sale system where the purchasing and payment information is captured and stored immediately and cleared between the banks within the next 24 hours.

Apart from the national Dankort system PKK is operating the international credit card systems Eurocard and VISA.

1.4 Cash Dispensers (ATMs)

In 1983 PPA - the Danish Banks and Savings Banks Cash Dispenser Company was established. The object of PPA is to develop and run a joint cash dispenser (ATM) network in Denmark with 150 ATMs installed in shopping centres, supermarkets, department stores, railway stations, airports etc. without direct connection to any bank office. The ATMs are open 24 hours a day, 7 days a week.

1.5 Concepts

The POS- and ATM-systems are designed as on-line systems where all ATMs and POS-terminals are connected to a central computer via a circuit-switching public data network. Every transaction is transmitted to the computer and verified against the card file containing all valid Dankort and their PIN-verification codes. If the transaction is accepted an acknowledgement transaction is returned to the terminal.

Once a day all transactions are delivered to the clearing system run by PBC, and the cardholder will be debited for his purchase or withdrawal within the next 24 hours.

If a card is lost, stolen or misused it can be blocked immediately via a telephone call to PKK.

1.6 Security

All transmitted data in the two systems are encrypted under the Data Encryption Standard (DES). The DES encryption keys are distributed in two different ways.

1.6.1 ATM-System

The DES-keys for the ATMs are generated and transmitted from the encryption unit in the ATM to the central computer under the protection of Public Key Cryptography (RSA-method). Since the method is rather time-consuming (about 1 minute) it can only be used for transactions with a very low frequency, e g once a week or less, thus perfectly suited for distribution of other encryption keys, i e the DES-keys.

1.6.2 POS-System

A very important design parameter for POS-terminals is minimizing the purchasing price. Therefore, the Dankort-terminal has no interface to receive calls from the central computer and no PKC-algorithm. Instead, the DES-keys are loaded directly into a Security Module in the terminals from a Key Generation Box. The keys are generated by the box and later loaded directly into the Encryption Unit in the central computer. Although the security-level for this method is by no means less than the ATM-system, the method has two disadvantages. It requires highly trusted security staff to survey the key-loading and it leaves each terminal with the same set of keys for all the terminal's life-time. A cost-benefit analysis showed clearly that the two disadvantages were less costly than providing the terminals with the PKC-algorithm and a receiving transmission port.

2. Threats and Attack Points

The major criminal threats in on-line EFT-systems are unauthorized collection of confidential data and unauthorized manipulation of data. The first one because access to confidential data, i e the data of the magnetic stripe in the plastic card and the secret PIN-code, will make it possible for criminals to produce massive volumes of fraudulent cards and thus milk any electronic system, especially ATM-systems.

The second threat is the manipulation of data where the criminals will try either to change their own identity on already authorized debit-transactions or, more serious, change the identity of the payment receiver on credit-transactions.

In EFT-systems there are four points where the data can be attacked. Fortunately the countermeasures are, to some extent, overlapping but the four points should, nevertheless, be analyzed individually.

2.1 Terminals

The first attack point is the terminals, i e POS-terminals and ATMs. They are normally placed in a hostile environment with absolutely no access control. That goes especially for POS-terminals, but also for ATMs placed outside bank branches, e g in shopping centres, railway stations, airports etc.

2.2 Data Network

The next point is the data network. It can be either a leased line network or at public network. In both cases there is absolutely no protection of the lines. It is even possible to tap the lines without physical connection just by recording the radiation from the lines.

2.3 Computer Centre

The third point is the computer centre. Here is a great variety of attacking possibilities, e g copying and manipulating data files and transactions, placing Trojan horses in computer programs etc. Although a very efficient access control can be established a great number of skilled and experienced people, e g operators, programmers, systems engineers, hardware engineers etc., necessarily must have access to the computers.

2.4 Clearing Transactions

In a joint system where a number of banks co-operate there will be a need for exchanging clearing transactions. Contrary to the terminal transactions the clearing transactions normally do not carry confidential information, i e the PIN-code. The major concern is consequently to protect the data from being manipulated. The exchange can be done either via a communication network or magnetic tapes distributed by messengers. In the first case the risks are similar to the risks in the terminal network. In the latter case a new risk element is introduced.

3. Protection Means

During the design phase of the Danish on-line EFT-systems in the early eighties it became obvious that encryption was the only way to protect the data in the systems. It was decided that the systems should be based on a proven method with a minimum of secret information, with a reasonably high performance, and commercially available either on cheap standard chips or possible to program on cheap custom-built chips. A thorough investigation showed that there were only two generally approved and accepted encryption methods, i e the DES-method and the public key method. Besides, a great number of other methods showed up, but they were all based on secret algorithms and had consequently never been examined and tested by encryption specialists.

3.1 DES-Encryption

The DES-method was chosen for all transaction encryption because the method is fast, even implemented on the cheapest chips the encryption of a transaction will only take 1/10 of a second, and because the method relies on only one pair of secret keys.

3.2 Public Key Encryption

Public Key Encryption is the most secure encryption method known today because its pair of keys do not have to be identical and only one of the keys has to be kept secret in the central computer. The other key can be publicly known without compromising the secrecy. The method could be compared with a bevelled spring lock. Anyone can lock it without a key and only the keyholder can unlock it. Whereas the DES-method could be described as a martise lock, where you need to have the same key for both locking and unlocking.

The disadvantage of the public key method is that it is rather time consuming when implemented on microprocessors. The encryption of a transaction might take about 1 minute and that is too long to wait especially for POS-systems. However the method is perfectly suited for exchanging the secret keys for the DES-method. This only has to take place, e g once a week and could be done during periods with very little traffic.

3.3 Message Authentication

One of the threats in EFT-systems is fraudulent manipulation of the data in the transactions. The protection against that could be encryption of the entire transaction. However, if the transaction has been received from the terminal, verified by the computer, and stored in a log-file, the need for total encryption is no longer ultimate since the transaction easily can be retained from the log-file if the data have been tampered with. Thus the problem is to detect any change in the data and to make sure the data are corrected before further processing. That problem is solved by adding a Message Authentication Code (MAC) to each transaction.

The message authentication code is a unique 4-8 digit number derived from the original, decrypted data in the transaction by a new DES-encryption and a special decimalization procedure.

The transaction can now be processed, e g sorted, transmitted, or used for updating account-files without time-consuming decryption at every stage. Only when another member of the network, e g a clearing centre, the card issuer etc., takes over the responsibility of the transaction, the MAC is verified by the receiver as a guarantee against any intended or unintended change.

4. Implementation - Key Management

According to section 3 the ideal solution is a system where all transactions are encrypted by the DES-method and all DES keys are distributed protected by public key encryption.

Unfortunately it is not always possible to build ideal solutions. In POS-systems the purchasing price for the terminals is a crucial factor. That means that the number of facilities must be reduced to an absolute minimum. In the Danish POS-terminals there are consequently no calling facilities from the central computer and no public key algorithm.

In ATM-systems a few extra chips in the microprocessor do not change the purchasing price significantly. In the Danish ATM-network the ideal solution has been implemented. But even with the ideal solution key management must be meticulously organized.

4.1 Key Generation

Encryption keys are just numbers. Preferably these numbers should be random and some special numbers must be avoided because they will give a weak encryption. Furthermore, the keys should not be known to any human being.

These requirements can, to some extent, be met with manual procedures. The last one by letting 2 or 3 people key-in different but complete keys and then do a binary addition of the keys inside the encryption module.

However, the best solution is to generate the keys in a tamper proof hardware Key Generation Box (KGB). Besides being tamper proof the KGB must be designed so that no unauthorized person can get access to the information in the KGB. Today boxes like that are available as standard equipment and all keys in the Danish EFT-systems are generated in one of our three KGBs.

4.2 Key Distribution

As mentioned earlier the Danish POS-terminals can not be called from the central computer, and they can therefore not get their encryption-keys via data transmission.

Instead, the keys are fed into the terminals directly from the Key Generation Box just before the terminals are ready to leave the factory. After feeding a batch of terminals the KGB is connected to the central computer and the key for each terminal is stored encrypted under a terminal master key. The physical link between the KGB and the terminals is, of course, a weak point. Consequently, the whole process must be carried out by trusted security staff.

4.3 Key Protection

All encryption keys must be ultimately protected.

In the POS-terminals the keys are fed from the KGB into a custom built Security Module. This module is like the KGB tamper proof, and it is impossible to get the keys out of the module.

In the central computer the keys are fed from the KGB into a similar Hardware Encryption Unit (HEU) protected by public key encryption. In the HEU the keys are decrypted, encrypted under a terminal master key, transferred to the mainframe, and stored in the terminal file.

Later on when terminal "i" has been installed in a shop and starts to transmit, a transaction from terminal "i" is received in the central computer. The computer will find the encrypted key for terminal "i" in the terminal file, and transfer the transaction and the key to the HEU. Here the key is decrypted and then used for decrypting the transaction, which is then returned to the computer for further processing.

The flow of the keys is shown in figure 2 where a double line indicates a secure module or a surveyed transmission link.

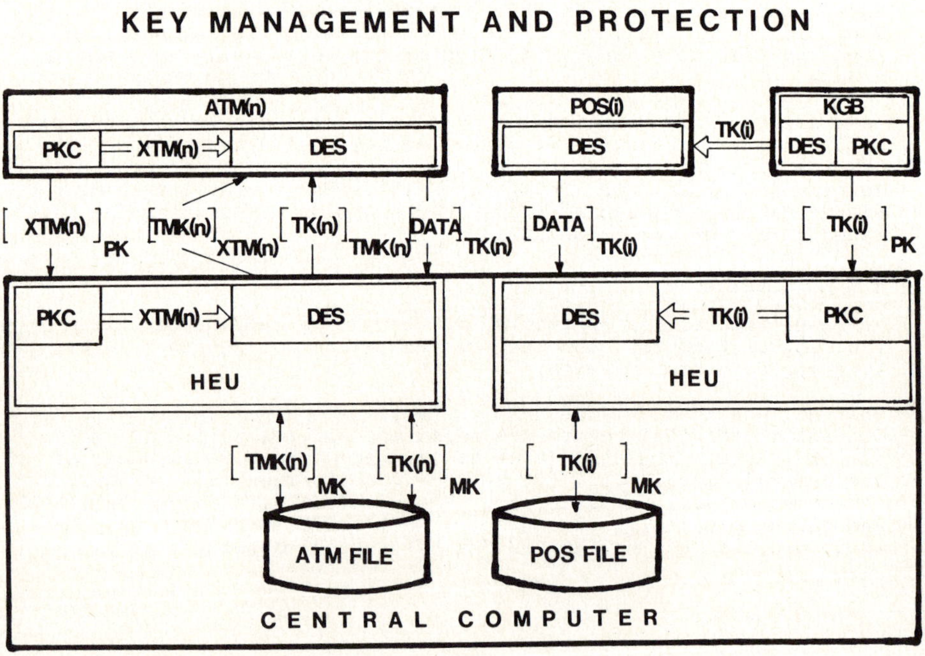

FIGURE 2

5. Conclusion

Besides the above described encryption keys the Danish EFT-systems use encryption keys for PIN-verification and MAC-control. Because of the many involved parties, i e all the banks and savings banks, the key distribution is a little more complex, but the basic concept is still the same

- no confidentiel data in the clear outside tamper proof hardware modules

- no keys known by human beings

COMPUTER SECURITY
J.B. Grimson and H.-J. Kugler (Editors)
Elsevier Science Publishers B.V. (North-Holland)

AUTHENTICATION IN A HETEROGENEOUS ENVIRONMENT

June M. Power and Steve R. Wilbur

Department of Computer Science
University College London

This paper considers how a mechanism might be set up to provide authentication of users and servers. The scheme proposed aims to deal with simple processors which are unmanaged, as well as managed timesharing systems. It would provide authentication tokens which can be included in the applications protocols. Much of the difficulty of the scheme is concerned with building a distributed secure database for private keys.

1. INTRODUCTION

In a distributed system clients on one machine may access services on another. Even if management arranges that the coded user identification (uid) is identical on both (all) machines, passing such uids in unencrypted messages may lead to penetration of important resources by unauthorised third parties. There are several forms of attack which can be made on network based systems:

- Eavesdropping: listening to conversations which are private and making use of the contents in other transactions.

- Faking: generating messages or replaying earlier legitimate messages to gain resources for which the faker is not authorised.

- Trojan Horse: pretending to offer a service, perhaps even offering it, but gathering information which allows impersonation of clients on other servers.

Our local distributed system is vulnerable to these attacks, especially faking and the use of Trojan Horses. This paper explores possible solutions.

2. THE ENVIRONMENT

The University College London, Department of Computer Science (UCL-CS) environment consists of a number of local area networks (LANs) which are interconnected and have gateways to other external networks. Various service time sharing (Unix) machines are attached to the LANs, as are a variety of communications servers, file servers and microprocessors. At present, various machines authenticate users when they begin a session. However, such authentication only serves one machine, although having been authenticated a uid is often passed between machines by specific applications. Thus, authentication currently may allow terminal access at a given time to machine A, and file transfer to machines B,C,D provided the uid is also valid there, but no terminal access to B,C,D without further authentication. The file transfer protocol itself is insecure, since users on any of the machines with direct network access could inject messages containing any uid, including the privileged user id.

Servers are found by name-to-address mapping in a name table. It is difficult but not impossible to change this table and interpose a fake server (Trojan Horse) between the client and true server. Equally, if a legitimate server moves, and another eventually takes over its old address, the client and possibly the server would like to be aware of this, rather than trying to perform an inappropriate action. Thus, besides having authentication of users, there is a need for authentication of servers too.

The environment being considered is shown in Figure 1. Mm are managed machines, in that users are authenticated when they begin a terminal session, and that access to the LAN is via a managed kernel. In principle, the kernel could prohibit access to the LAN, and certainly would provide a limited set of modes of access. The unmanaged machines, Mu, do not have any such secure network interface, thus there is no way of, say, preventing such users from listening to all transactions on the LAN or changing the node's network address if the hardware permits such functions. The server machines, Ms, may either fall into the same pattern as Mm, or may have a kernel which is available in source form to the user, i.e. the kernel may be protected/privileged at run-time to limit faults and share functions, but may be changed by the user at development time to include new functions. Finally, the gateway machines, Mg, are generally similar to Ms, except they have to impose access control between the LAN and WAN.

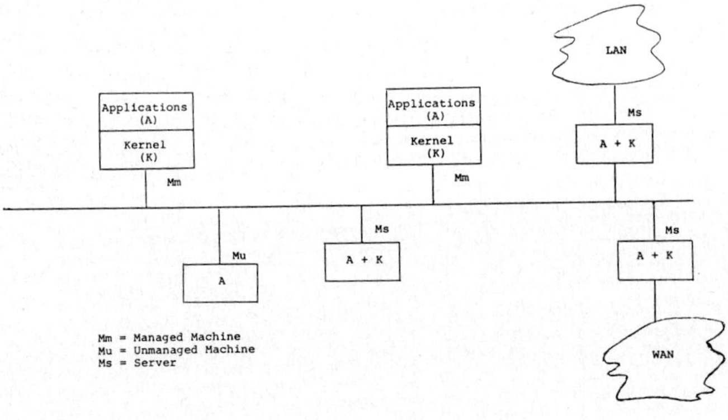

Figure 1. The Environment

3. THE MODELS

ECMA is currently working on a draft proposal for authentication [1] based largely on the earlier papers by Needham and Schroeder [2] and Israel and Linden [3]. In the ECMA document two forms of authentication are proposed, strong and simple. "Strong" is intended to resist attack, but may impose computational delays at execution time, whereas "simple" is fast but much weaker. The strong approach uses the DES algorithm for encryption. Needham and Schroeder propose an alternative based on PKC, which is interesting but even more computationally demanding than DES based approaches. PKC will not be considered further in this document, the intention being to see whether the ECMA models are adequate for a heterogeneous environment such as UCL-CS.

3.1 Simple Model

The protocol for the ECMA simple authentication model is shown below.

```
A  -> B:  A,Ksa
B  -> Au: A,Ksa
Au -> B:  b
B  -> A:  Ksa                    (1)
```

where A is the name of the initiating client, B is the name of the recipient or server, Au is the authentication service, Ksa is A's simple key and b is a boolean variable which indicates whether or not Ksa is A's simple key.

The client sends its name, A, key, Ksa, and a transaction request to the server. In turn, the server contacts an authenticator and asks for these to be validated, whereupon a suitable response is returned. Presumably to prevent fake results being returned to A, its key is returned with the results. All messages are in cleartext, i.e. no encryption is used at any point in these transactions. Ksa is private to A, and is also known to the authenticator.

Management of keys is not dealt with in the ECMA proposal, and as a minimum there needs to be a per session or per transaction exchange of the form:

```
A  -> Au: A, Pwd
Au -> A:  Ksa                    (2)
```

where Pwd is some token for authenticating A. Clearly any eavesdropper observing the plain text Ksa or Pwd at (1) or (2) can pose as A. This simple approach therefore seems to be most appropriate for distributed systems where access to protocol messages is impossible because of physical security, or where low grade resources are being protected.

Another approach would be for the authenticator to be able to generate a sequence of keys, each session or transaction having a different one. The management issues appear to be difficult, since there may be many processes owned by A and also multiple authenticators. Keeping all keys in step even in a perfectly reliable environment would be difficult, but in the face of intermittent loss of messages and re-transmission, it is felt that this scheme needs considerable further study.

3.2 Strong Model

The protocol for the ECMA strong model is shown below. It relies on encryption and assumes that all network nodes have a reasonably well synchronised clock.

```
A  -> Au: A,B,I
Au -> A:  [[Kc, Texp, A]Kb, I, B, Kc] Ka
A  -> B:  [Kc, Texp, A]Kb, [Ti XOR PIDb]Kc
B  -> A:  [Tj XOR PIDb]Kc                        (3)
```

where []Ka means the quantity between the square brackets is encrypted under A's private key and []Kb and []Kc are equivalent for B's private key and the conversation key, respectively. A and B are the names of the initiator and recipient, I is a random number called the nonce, Texp is the expiration time for a set of credentials, Ti is a time stamp obtained from the system clock at time i, Tj is a time stamp obtained from the system clock at a later time than Ti and PIDb is the processor ID of B.

The authenticator knows the private keys of both the client and server, and when the client asks to be authenticated, a conversation key Kc is returned which can be used to encrypt the data, together with sufficient information to pass the key to B and verify that the message containing the key has not been replayed.

The client contacts the authenticator (Au) giving its own name, that of B and a random number called the nonce which will not be used again for a long time, and cannot be predicted. Au then invents a new key, Kc, for the conversation, which it encrypts together with the name of A and an expiry time (several hours away, typically) with B's private key. It then takes this coded data, the name of B, the nonce, and Kc and encrypts them with A's private key. Thus, only A can decrypt it and check the nonce. The Kb encrypted data is passed to B, together with the current time of day, XORed with the processor ID of B. The purpose of this is to prevent replay of messages, in that only a small amount of time should have elapsed during the transaction between A and B.

The scheme is largely that of Needham and Schroeder, but with expiry time and transmission time included [4] [5]. The inclusion of time poses two problems, namely keeping the clocks of each machine sufficiently in synchronism for the scheme to work and making the scheme work in batch or buffered systems as opposed to directly coupled systems.

4. IMPLEMENTATION ISSUES

4.1 Protocol Hierarchy

Two broad families of protocols have to be authenticated. One is stream protocols, the other is transaction protocols. It is not considered necessary at present to cover threats at the protocol level, and indeed the scheme developed will suffer many of the deficiences outlined by Watson [6]. Thus, the authentication protocol sits above both the stream and transaction protocols.

In the case of stream protocols, the stream would be opened in the normal way. Once established, or in parallel, the client will obtain the relevant credentials from the authenticator, unwrap them and pass the conversation key to the server. The server in turn will give a handshake to this message. Both message and handshake will be carried over the newly established stream. Thereafter, all data messages are encrypted as discussed below. Protocol messages are not encrypted, so an interloper could inject fake resets or resequence packets. This kind of threat is considered to be acceptable.

For transaction protocols, there is an initial session-like binding performed by client to server in the scheme currently in use. At that stage the client asks to be bound to one of several servers for a particular service. This binding mechanism must be extended to include the exchange of credentials which then hold until the binding is terminated. It is possible for a client to be bound to several servers simultaneously. In such cases the conversation keys used should all be unique, so that discovery of one key does not compromise all servers.

4.2 Encryption Algorithm Performance

If encryption is to be used, it must not significantly degrade performance. The ECMA proposal suggests use of the Data Encryption Standard (DES) [7] for encryption, but in the U.K. the use of DES encryption chips is tightly controlled. Other encryption algorithms could be used, but they would necessarily prevent interworking with proper implementations.

Software based encryption has been considered, and according to Newman [8] software performance of around 2Kbps can be achieved on a 16-bit machine for data blocks of 16 x 8 bytes. Such performance is significantly inferior to that of our stream or transaction protocols and is unacceptable where very short messages are involved. Following Newman's work our early implementations will use additive stream cipher mode (ASC). In this a pseudo-random number generator is used to produce 64-bit values which are encrypted by DES in advance, and then XOR-ed with the text as it is being sent or received. Present 16-bit machines can perform such stream ciphering at rates of the order of 100 Kbps.

4.3 Key Storage and Distribution

Distributing keys is extremely difficult, and encipherment is useless unless the key management is secure. In terminal systems it may be tempting to have users be responsible for keys. This does not solve the problem, however, as it depends upon the individual's security system. The problem is being passed to users and they often cannot be trusted!

We are concerned about the problem of users and therefore find it useful to investigate the storage of keys in the system and their distribution. Not all the systems that we are dealing with have human users interacting with them. Servers may need to be re-booted in the middle of the night and so there is need for an automatic secure key distribution mechanism for such machines.

In general we believe this to be an intractable problem, however one solution which is being pursued is to introduce a security kernel in a front-end processor which is inaccessible to the normal user.

Another aspect of the problem is whether the key storage should be centralised or distributed. A centralised approach is attractive from the point of view of management, but it would be unacceptable for such a vital part of the system to become disabled. Thus a distributed and replicated approach is favoured. In many respects the problems of key storage are largely traditional database problems with the added complications of security.

4.4 Time

The ECMA standard includes the notion of "Universal Time" (UT), which is held accurately (unspecified but approx 1 sec) in each machine. A time server must be provided to ensure this. The time protocol should attempt to compensate for transmission delay between the time server and the requesting process.

The major problem with including time in the authentication protocol is that of synchronization. This is fundamental to the acceptable operation of the protocol so that a private key will not be compromised. A compromised key may lead to the impersonation of either a client or the authentication service itself. This in turn can lead to a security breach of the whole network.

Playback attacks can be assuaged by a sense of 'currency'. If authentication is to be current then an absolute sense of time must be introduced into the network. This requires complete synchronization of all network clocks. Synchronization may be possible within 1 second over local area networks but for long-haul networking this may not be achievable.

The prevention of playback attacks can also be obtained without the use of universal clocks and their associated penalties. This can be achieved by the use of event markers [9] which are both local and private in the sense that no external synchronization or coordination between communicants is required.

It is important when choosing event markers that the following two conditions exist:

- the sequence of event markers must be chosen so that at any point in the sequence the next marker is not predictable

- any cycles must be long so that specific event markers are used again only after long intervals of time

5. DESCRIPTION OF SYSTEM

5.1 Protection Offered

The authentication procedure relies on several assumptions which influence the protection it provides. The first of these is that the authentication service which holds all secret keys is secure. Secondly, it is assumed that the encryption algorithm itself is secure.

We are concerned with protecting our machines and services from any unauthorised access. This does not include the need for all data to be transmitted in ciphertext nor does it mean that all services will have restricted access. On the contrary, many of our services such as lineprinters and common filestores will remain unauthenticated.

5.2 Authenticated Stream Protocols

Because of the clock synchronisation problems described above, an alternative protocol using event markers has been explored. However, as described below it needs more messages to flow between the client and server to achieve the same effects as the ECMA strong protocol.

In the protocol, A requests a secure connection by sending its claimed identity and unique (and unpredictable) event marker, EMa, to B. B can then either refuse the connection or enter the protocol. If B continues then it requests a conversation key from the authentication service by sending it A's claimed identity, it's own identity, A's event marker and a unique and unpredictable event marker from itself. If both A and B are registered with the authentication service then the authentication service generates a unique conversation key Kc and sends a message to B consisting of two parts: one destined for B and another destined to be forwarded to A from B. This message could be sent to A instead or to A as well as to B.

These alternatives are equivalent in terms of the security they provide. The advantage of the authentication service sending both parts to B is that it requires fewer network messages B can decrypt the first part of this message from the authentication service to learn the conversation key, the intended communicant A, and it's original event marker because they are encrypted with B's private key, Kb. This assures that the authentication service understood B's request to communicate with A and that that part of B's request information was not modified by an intruder. If B is careful to change EMb for every connection then it can be sure that the message sent back from the authentication service was not previously recorded and played back.

Since the conversation key appears only twice (encrypted under the private keys of A and B), only parties aware of those private keys may learn the conversation key.

Continuing the protocol, B forwards to A the portion of the message returned from the authentication service that is encrypted with A's private key. A decrypts the message to learn the conversation key, Kc, it's intended communicant

B and it's original event marker EMa. This gives A the same assurance B has that the message was from the same source.

The sequence of events just described is listed below.

```
A->  B: A, EMa
B-> Au: A, EMa, B, EMb
Au-> B: [Kc, A, EMb] Kb, [Kc, B EMa] Ka
B->  A: [Kc, B, EMa] Ka                    (4)
```

A may now encrypt its request to B using Kc and the reply from B can be similarly encrypted.

5.3 Authenticated Transactions

At UCL we support distributed transactions by means of remote procedure calls. These are based upon a datagram service that operates at the Transport Service level. As mentioned in section 4, the authentication protocol sits above the transaction protocol. Remote Procedure calls have session-like bindings performed for client to server transactions. It is not possible to determine the number of calls that will be made to a particular service at bind-time. Thus, authenticating transactions is similar to authenticating connection-based services.

Besides protecting against the obvious threat of faking, the model can be augmented to provide stronger protection against replay attacks in a way that is particularly appropriate for transactions. This is achieved by the receiving side of a call returning a new conversation key (that is randomly generated) along with the data. The calling side decrypts this message with the original conversation key and uses the new key for the next transaction. The receiving side has retained the new key as the legitimate conversation key so that it will only recognise subsequent calls encrypted with this key.

5.4 Authenticating Unmanaged Services

If a communicating node on the network is not 'managed', such as a workstation that has no secure network interface, it may be restricted to a weaker form of authentication. This may also apply to managed services that have no kernel where encryption can be securely carried out. In these cases the authentication protocol described for managed services will not be applicable.

It is imperative when a request is made of a service that it can determine whether the requesting client is authenticated to a sufficient degree of confidence. When strong authentication is not available to a client, it might be acceptable for certain services to condone authenticated requests of a weaker nature.

If a machine is 'managed' and does not support a secure network interface, it is possible to employ a slightly modified version of the managed machine protocol. This would entail having a client on such a machine, A, contact a service B, which in turn refers to its authentication service to find out the strength of A's authentication. If it is strong authentication then the protocol proceeds as outlined above. Otherwise, A will be asked by either B or the authentication service to resend a password that corresponds to the one used initially for registration with that service. If it matches the registered password then the service can inform B that it believes that A is authentic. Similarly, the same procedure can be repeated with the service and B so that A can be informed that the service believes that B is who it says it is. It is up to the two parties involved, A and B, to decide if this is enough assurance to continue the communication.

For a machine where there is no trusted protection, another approach is necessary. If a client wishes to authenticate itself to a service then the strongest form of authentication it can attain is by sending a password (possibly in cleartext) together with the address of a managed network node which has a copy of its password to the authentication service. The service then forwards this encrypted information to the selected node for confirmation. If there is a match at the node then the authentication service sends a message to the requested service, B, that it believes A is who it claims to be.

This scheme could just as easily be carried out between A and a selected node before contact with the authentication service. In this case the authentication service would be informed by the managed node of the partial authentication. This could be done in tandem with the unmanaged node contacting the authentication service to inform it of its intent to request a remote service.

It is important to note that in both of these 'unmanaged' cases that the authentication is not completely secure, particularly in the latter case. This degraded form of authentication is suggested to provide some form of multiple level service.

5.5 Multiple Authentication Services

It is possible that more than one authentication service may be desired. This could be for reasons of reliability, performance or possibly for organisational demarcation and management. Bauer et al have proposed a protocol [10] that accomodates this situation which is a natural extension of the modified ECMA model we have outlined.

Given two communicants, A and B, the protocol proceeds as before but with the added addresses of A's and B's authentication services. A sends B its own identity, the address of its authentication service, ASa, and a unique event marker, EMa. B then sends its own authentication service, ASb, the identity of A, A's event marker, the address of A's authentication service, it's own identity (B), and a unique event marker, EMb. B's authentication service responds by sending to A's authentication service the identity of A, the identity of B, A's event marker and an event marker of its own, EMasb. The inclusion of this last event marker is to protect ASb from playback attacks. A's authentication service then generates a conversation key, encrypts the message eventually destined for A under A's private key and returns ASb's event marker. B's event marker is encrypted with the conversation key under a secret key, Kx, that is known to the two authentication services. If the use of exchange keys is felt to be too much of a risk for the network then further authentication can be implemented between the two services.

The extended protocol outlined is listed below:

```
A   -> B:    A, EMa, ASa
B   -> ASb:  A, EMa, ASa, B, EMb
ASb -> ASa:  A, B, EMa, EMasb
ASa -> ASb:  [Kc, B, EMa] Ka, [Kc, EMasb] Kx
ASb -> B:    [Kc, A, EMb] Kb, [Kc, B, EMa] Ka
B   -> A:    [Kc, B, EMa] Ka                     (5)
```

The transaction request and reply can not be exchanged between A and B under Kc.

6. CONCLUSIONS

The ECMA proposal considered uses two authentication schemes, one strong and one simple. Each has its own key so that penetration of one scheme does not compromise the other. The simple scheme is felt to be inappropriate in environments where network messages can be observed by intruders. Even if stronger management approaches are used, such as short duration keys, the management of these becomes difficult where multiple authenticators are involved.

The strong model is much more robust, but does rely on network-wide clock synchronisation. Dangers are seen in using the present scheme in batch systems with long queuing delays. To overcome this, schemes which use event markers are being investigated. They in turn introduce additional transactions, leading to a power performance protocol. Multiple administration authentication adds further to the message content.

References

1. Rank Xerox Contribution, "ECMA Authentication Service Standard - Draft Proposal", September 1984, .

2. Needham, R.M. and Schroeder, M.D., "Using Encryption for Authentication in Large Networks of Computers", CACM 21, 12 pp 993-999, December 1978.

3. Israel, J.E. and Linden, T.A., "Authentication in Office System Internetworks", ACM Trans. on Office Information Systems 1, 3, pp 193-210, July 1983.

4. Denning, D.E. and Sacco, G M., "Timestamps in Key Distribution Protocols", CACM 24, 8, pp 533-536, August 1981.

5. Berson, T.A. and Bauer, R.K., "Local Cryptosystem Architecture", Proceedings of Spring Compcon 1982, IEEE Computer Society Press, pp 138-143, February 1982.

6. Watson, R.W. and Nessett, D.M. and Sorkin, A.R., "Connection Management and Key Distribution Protocols", UCRL-88345 Preprint, Lawrence Livermore Laboratory, November 1982.

7. FIPS Publication 46, "Data Encryption Standard", National Bureau of Standards, Washington, D.C., January 1977.

8. Newman, B.B., "Encryption over the Universe Network", Logica U.K., April 1982.

9. Lamport, L., "Time, Clocks and the Ordering of Events in a Distributed System", CACM 21, 7, pp 558-565, July 1978.

10. Bauer, R.K. and Berson, T.A. and Feiertag, R.J., "A Key Distribution Protocol Using Event Markers", ACM Transactions on Computer Systems 1, 3 pp 249-255, August 1983.

COMPUTER SECURITY
J.B. Grimson and H.-J. Kugler (Editors)
Elsevier Science Publishers B.V. (North-Holland)

IBM Dynamic Signature Verification

TK Worthington TJ Chainer JD Williford SC Gundersen

IBM Thomas J. Watson Research Center
Yorktown Heights, New York 10598
U.S.A.

The IBM signature verification technology uses a pen with transducers to convert the motions made while signing into electronic signals. A mathematical algorithm has been developed which measures the degree of similarity between two sets of these signals. A user enrolls in the system by signing a number of times to establish a reference. At a later time, when verification of the identity of this individual is required, a signature is acquired and compared against the reference. If the required degree of similarity is achieved the individual is declared by the system to be the same person who enrolled. We have conducted a series of tests over the last two years collecting more than 28,000 signatures from more than 350 subjects. The error rates in our most recent test were: False rejects 0.19%, False accepts 0.56%.

Introduction

The need for personal identification in society has always existed and the pervasive means in western society is a person's written signature. It is used for such important and common transactions as endorsing checks, making credit card purchases and authorizing contracts, among others. However, as paper based transactions such as checks and letters are replaced by electronic funds transfers and electronic mail, the need for a person's identity to be verified by a computer rather than by another human becomes a major impediment to the establishment of the paperless society. There are a myriad of applications which require a person to be identified by a computer. They range from the simple act of "logging on" so that the correct account is billed, to complex interactive systems that require multiple levels of authorization for a variety of business transactions involving multiple computer networks.

There is a substantial body of research,[1,2,3,4,5,6,8,11] aimed at providing automated personal identification technologies. Some of these technologies have been offered as products, however, none has found a substantial market. There are a variety of possible reasons for the lack of commercial success including price, performance and human factors.

All of the possible personal identification techniques can be placed in four categories:

- Something Remembered - pass words, PIN's, names
- Something Possessed - magnetic card, key
- A physical characteristic - finger prints, hand geometry
- An action performed - signature verification, voice recognition

We believe that personal identification by means of signature verification has three distinct features that other methods cannot satisfy simultaneously. They are:

1. Signature verification will be the most easily accepted method since people are accustomed to using their written signature to confirm their identity.
2. Signatures cannot be lost, stolen or given away.

3. The technology has matured to the point where the performance is excellent, the hardware is low cost and the software can be easily integrated into any computer system from microprocessor based stand-alone units to mainframes.

The IBM signature verification technology uses a pen with transducers which measure the motions of the users hand during the signature. The system requires six signatures to establish a reference for the user (ie., to enroll the user). At a later time, when verification of the identity of this individual is required, a signature is acquired and compared against the reference. If the required degree of similarity is achieved the individual is declared by the system to be the same person who enrolled. Typically the signer is given two or three tries to achieve the required similarity since people occasionally make mistakes. In an acceptable system the rejection rate is very low and thus there is usually only one signature required per verify session. Depending upon the application, the two primary software components, signature acquisition and signature processing, may be contained in either the same physical component (e.g. an automatic teller machine), or in separate physical components (e.g. a terminal attached to a central processor).

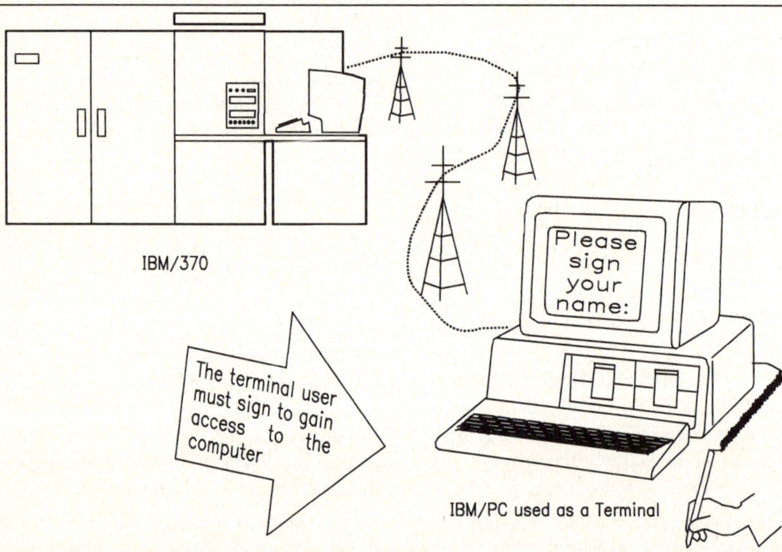

Figure 1. IBM Research demonstration system.

We have developed two prototype systems to demonstrate the technology. We have a stand alone system running entirely within an IBM-PC and a system which uses signature verification to control access to a VM network by 'dial-up' users. A schematic of our VM based demonstration system is shown in Figure 1.

Hardware Description

The design of the hardware to support signature verification is intimately related to the design of the algorithm and the realities of the environment in which the technology will be used. The prime design criteria is to measure enough information for the algorithm to distinguish between verify signatures and forgeries. The pen must be comfortable to use and reliable or the signers will find the use of the device burdensome and the consistency of their signatures could be compromised. Low component and manufacturing costs have also weighed heavily in the design of the hardware so that the system could be made available at an acceptable price.

Pen Design

The pen contains sensors that measure the two components of the acceleration perpendicular to the pen axis and the time derivative of the pressure (dp/dt) applied to the pen tip. Figure 2 shows the acceleration and time derivative pressure signals for a typical signer sampled at 80 Hz.

The design of the transducers, although required to measure signals over only a limited frequency and amplitude range, is complicated by several other constraints. First the pen must be low cost, therefore the transducers should be inexpensive and easily assembled. Second, the pen may be subject to abuse at the hands of the users requiring the transducers to withstand large inputs and still function properly at low levels. Third, the pen must be interchangeable so users can sign with any pen in a system. The interchangeability requirement establishes tolerances on the pen which can only be determined by studying the effect of changes in the pen on the performance of the algorithm. The techniques we used to establish these manufacturing tolerances are discussed in the section on pen interchangeability.

The algorithm which compares signatures is rotationally invariant about the pen axis which provides the freedom to design the pen with axial symmetry similar to a normal pen. We felt a symmetric design which would not require the signer to hold the pen in any particular orientation would make the system more comfortable and reliable. The biaxial accelerometer consists of two piezoelectric rectangular beams which are cantilevered by embedding one end in epoxy. A piezoelectric material is one which converts a mechanical stress into an electrical charge separation. This property results in a design with few components and therefore simple assembly. The charge is proportional to the acceleration, $\ddot{x}$, of the beam through a geometric factor and the piezoelectric coupling coefficient d_{31} given by

$$Q = d_{31}\frac{L^3}{2t^2}m\ddot{x} \qquad [1]$$

where L is the length of the beam, m is the linear mass density and t is the thickness. The beam acts as a capacitor so that the charge can be determined by measuring the voltage across the beam. The voltage must be measured by a high input impedance circuit due to the small beam capacitance, typically 1 nF. The pen contains operational amplifiers connected as voltage followers to eliminate problems driving the cable. The pen also contains 50 Megohm input resistors which limit the low frequency response of the accelerometers to 2.5 Hz. The fundamental vibrational resonance of the cantilevered beam occurs at approximately 1.7 kHz which is sufficiently high so that any noise due to its excitation can be easily filtered.

The force transducer consists of a piezoelectric cylinder which is epoxied onto an aluminum plug on one end and to the pen tip on the opposite face as shown in Fig. 3. The piezoelectric cylinder is poled radially and has a wraparound electrode on one end for the easy attachment of leads. A force applied to the pen tip produces a stress in the transducer. The stress which is perpendicular to the poling direction produces a charge on the cylinder walls. The same circuit used for the accelerometer is used to measure the charge on the pressure transducer, however the load resistor is much smaller. The typical capacitance of the tube is 2.7 nF and the load resistor is chosen to be 2.2 Megohm which places the corner frequency at 27 Hz. This is higher than the predominant frequency range for signatures. In the range of frequencies less than the corner frequency the output voltage is proportional to frequency. Therefore in the time domain the

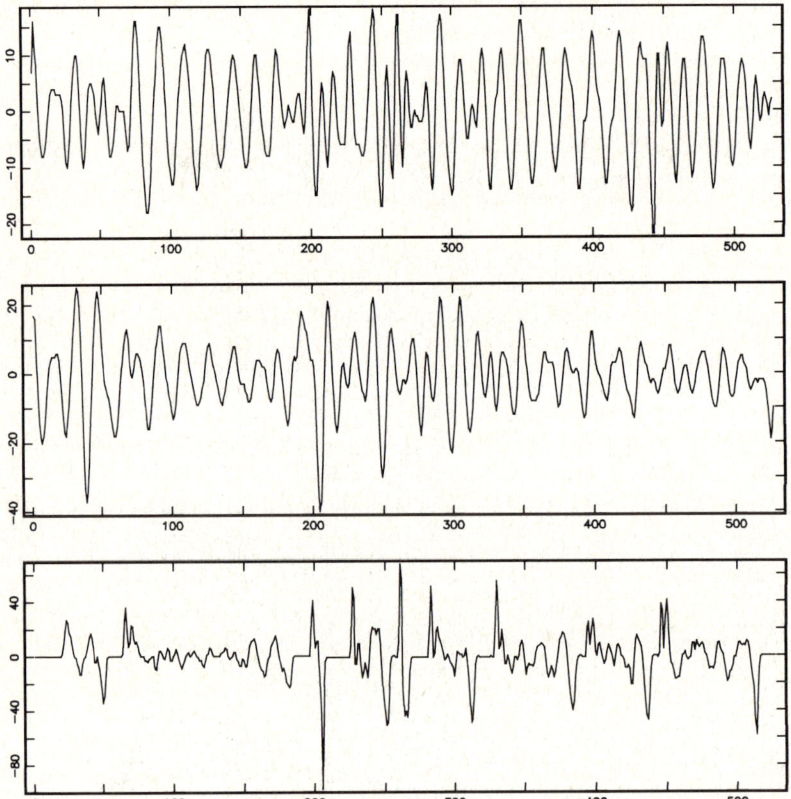

Figure 2. Typical signature waveforms. From top to bottom are displayed the x-acceleration signal, the y-acceleration signal and the rate of change of pressure.

output signal is proportional to the time derivative of the input signal for the frequency range of signatures. The advantage of measuring the rate of change of pressure in place of the absolute pressure is the reduction of the problem of base line drift.

The transducers are mounted on a rigid threaded aluminum plug. This plug also supports a plastic carriage which holds the small printed circuit card and the cable strain relief. An exterior aluminum tube is threaded onto the plug to provide a rigid structure to transfer the forces during signing to the transducers rather than deforming the pen structure. The plug is rigid enough to prevent the squeezing forces of the signer from generating signals in the transducers. The exterior aluminum tube of the pen is grounded to shield the transducers from electromagnetic noise and to protect the signer. The circuit card and accelerometers are sealed to make the pen corrosion resistant. The pen weighs approximately 30 grams and has a flexible cable so as not to interfere with the signing process.

We estimate that the cost of manufacturing the pen in quantities of 10,000 /year to be $50. Figure 3 shows the assembly drawing of the pen.

Data Acquisition

The analog signals from the pen must be amplified and then sampled to be in a form suitable for use by the algorithm. The sampling must be done often enough and accurately enough to capture the information necessary to distinguish verifies from forgeries, however, over-sampling increases the cost of the system in terms of hardware, algorithm execution time and reference storage space. Our studies of the spectrum of many signatures indicates that there is little information above 20 Hz and that most of the information is in the range 2 - 12 Hz. We chose a sampling rate of 80 Hz. The early work at IBM used a sampling rate of 100 Hz.[6] Their simulations showed that the correlation scores degraded rapidly if the signals were sampled below 60 Hz. The correlation part of the algorithm requires locating the maximum value of the cross correlation of two signature segments. An 80 Hz sampling rate introduces at most a 5% error in evaluating this maximum unless some form of data reconstruction or fractional shifting is employed. The 80 Hz rate is also conveniently far from 60 Hz, any 60 Hz noise that escapes the analog filters will alias to 20 Hz where it can be removed from the data without effecting the signal.

The data is sampled with an 8 bit analog to digital converter. The predominant noise source in the pen is from the vibrations of the pen rolling on the paper. The noise appears mostly on the accelerometers and is broad band extending to at least 1 kHz. To adequately remove this noise with a sampling rate of 80 Hz would require a very sharp analog filter. Such a filter would also contribute large phase shifts to the signals in the frequency range of interest. Any large phase shift or change in phase shift either between channels of the accelerometer or between systems will degrade the cross correlation score. In order to reduce the demands, and therefore the expense of the analog filter the data is sampled at 640 Hz and a digital decimation filter is used to reduce the sampling frequency to 80 Hz. Since the Nyquist frequency is 320 Hz, a filter with a more gradual roll off, and therefore a smaller phase shift in the signal bandwidth, can be used to prevent aliasing. The analog filter for the accelerometer is a 2 pole Butterworth filter with a -3 dB point at 30 Hz and a gain of 44 dB. One percent components are used throughout the filter and this is more than sufficient to provide interchangeability of the cards.

The voltage follower amplifiers for the accelerometers have very large input resistors (50 Megohm) and therefore significant output offset voltages due to the input offset current. An input blocking capacitor is necessary to remove this DC offset. This capacitor was selected to also remove the base line drift due to the pyroelectric effect when the signer first grabs the pen and the temperature of the accelerometers rises.

The pressure channel is subject to much larger forces and therefore produces much larger signals. Our technique for detecting penlifts requires information about the baseline which requires us to DC couple the pressure amplifier. However, the larger signal amplitude and the larger capacitance and thus smaller input resistor on the pressure channel keeps the DC offset in the pressure channel to an acceptable level.

The decimation filter averages the 16 previous samples every 1/80 th of a second to calculate a data point. It has a linear phase shift so that its only effect on the correlation is a time shift applied equally to all three signals. The A/D converter has two input ranges for each signal. The two ranges provide for increased sensitivity for light signers without clipping for heavy signers. The decision of which range to use is made by the acquisition software during the signature. We estimate that the cost of the card, including assembly and test, to be $49 in quantities of 10,000.

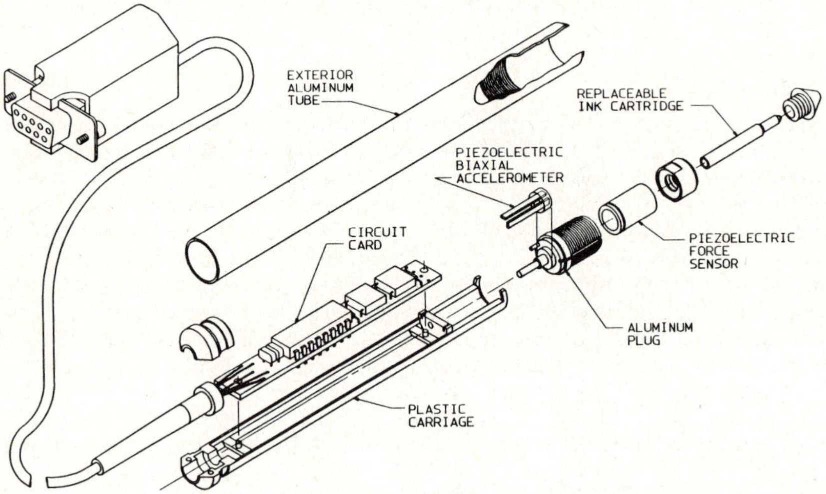

Figure 3. The Assembly drawing for the pen.

Software in the terminal, in our implementations an IBM PC, controls the signature acquisition and performs the decimation. The software uses the pressure channel data to determine the start and end of the signature. The maximum amount of data collected is 1000 points or 12.5 seconds. Approximately 1% of the users have signatures which exceed this limit. In those cases we simply stop taking data and use the first 1000 points in the algorithm. This does not seem to reduce the effectiveness of the algorithm.

After the signature has been captured, the signals are further processed to improve the operation of the algorithm. The pressure data is examined and the linear component of the baseline drift is removed. This drift is due to temperature changes that occur when the pen is first picked up. The accelerometers do not have this problem and only the average offset is removed. The high frequency components of the signals is further reduced by digital filtering after the segmentation has been determined.

Algorithm Description

This section will present the algorithms used in the signature verification system. It will be presented in the context of providing access to a large computer system through either local or remote terminal access. Software is required at the terminal to acquire and transmit signatures and at the host to perform enrollment and verification of users. There must exist a mechanism for acquiring signatures at the terminal, transmitting them to the host processor, and then performing the appropriate function at the host, either enrollment or verification. All functions must be coordinated by an associated driving application at the host processor.

Enrollment and Verification

The host portion of the signature verification system must be able to enroll and verify users. To do this it must coordinate three essential components:

- Terminal I/O - to request and receive signatures from a terminal
- Signature Verification processing - to enroll or verify a user
- Data Base Management - to maintain a reference data base

Other capabilities which complement a signature verification system include message transmissions to and from users, operators, and security administrators, system performance and transgression logging, and system installation aids. Terminal I/O and data base management are very dependant on the particular implementation and are discussed in an example of an application which controls access to a VM network by dial up users in the conclusion.

The IBM Research signature verification algorithms have been implemented in the PASCAL programming language running on both VM (remote PC as a terminal) and the IBM/PC (standalone). The signature verification portion of the system consists of 1700 PASCAL/VS statements. In the remote terminal access application, the remaining functional components, taken as a whole, exist in 500 statements.

The enrollment process consists of obtaining a set of sample signatures, creating a reference file and storing this file in a data base. We typically collect six signatures. The data returned from this process is written to a file defined as the user's reference file. The reference contains:

- a set of individualized parameters for this user
- two signatures designated as the user's primary reference signatures, and
- a dynamic set of four of the most recently accepted signatures for the user.

This latter set, referred to as the user's adaptation "bucket", is initialized to be the four signatures from the set of enrollment samples which were not selected as either of the two reference signatures. The reference is updated after each successful verify session.

When the system requires a check of the identity of an individual, it first asks the user for his ID which is used to retrieve the users reference from the data base. The verification process consists of acquiring a signature and computing the similarity between the current signature and one or more of the signatures in the reference. It was discovered early on[6] that some people had more than one signature style and that the reference must take this into account. We also found that the signature was not constant in time and that to achieve a low Type I error rate the reference must follow this drift. We have developed a dynamic reference adaptation technique which allows the system to recognize multiple signature styles and adapt to slow changes in the styles.

The similarity is computed by an algorithm described below. A sample signature is "accepted" if the similarity score exceeds a preset, empirically derived threshold. The verification mechanism allows for more than one submitted sample signature, uses two reference signatures, and maintains a recent signing characteristics "bucket" of signatures from which to automatically update a reference if required. The steps in the decision process are listed below. Throughout the session the user is accepted as soon as any one of the comparisons results in a similarity score greater than the threshold.

1. A sample is compared against the 1st primary reference signature.
2. If the sample signature is not accepted against the 1st reference signature, it is compared against the 2nd reference.
3. If the sample is not accepted against either primary reference signature, but the similarity measure is close enough to the acceptance threshold to indicate that it is not obviously a mistake or a forgery, the sample signature is compared against the signatures in the bucket.

4. If the sample is accepted against one of the bucket signatures, the user is accepted and his reference is adapted as described below.
5. If the user has not been accepted, and the number of submitted samples is less than the number of samples in a session, another sample signature is obtained and the entire process is repeated.
6. Otherwise, the session is deemed complete and the user is rejected in this session.
7. If the user is accepted, any of the sample signatures that were close are put into the bucket, replacing the oldest bucket signatures.

Adaptation is a two stage process. The bucket is continually updated with accepted signatures or signatures that were close and part of a session with an accepted signature. If a sample signature is not accepted against one of the primary references, but is accepted against one of the bucket signatures, a new reference is generated from the set of available signatures. The reference generation algorithm differs from the one described below only in that the bucket signature against which the sample was accepted, is chosen to be the first primary reference. The clustering technique is used to select the best complementary signature. The reference generation algorithm calculates new control parameters and fills the bucket with the four most recent signatures that were not chosen as primary references. The depth of the bucket used in our technology tests was 4 signatures and the session consisted of at most 2 signatures.

The adaptation technique allows a reference to continuously adapt to changing signature styles and significantly lowers the false rejection rate. It also allows us to run the system with a high threshold and therefore maintain a very low forgery rate.

The Similarity of Two Signatures

Our technique for comparing signatures is an extension of the algorithm developed by Herbst and Liu [6]. A pair of signatures, each composed of a set of three waveforms as described above are directly compared and a score measuring their degree of similarity is calculated. This approach differs fundamentally from those systems which attempt to characterize each signature with a set of measured characteristics and then compare the characteristics to measure the similarity [4]. The similarity measure is composed of five fundamental measures of the signature pairs.

- M_1 – *Segment Alignment*
- M_2 – *Pressure Correlation*
- M_3 – *Acceleration Correlation*
- M_4 – *Pressure Coherence*
- M_5 – *Acceleration Coherence*

Each of these measures has some ability to distinguish between verifies and forgeries and are combined in a way that maximizes the separation between verify and forgery similarity measure distributions. The following sections describe the computation of each of the measures and the construction of the final similarity measure. (Note: the algorithm is essentially symmetric, that is the designation of one of the signatures as the reference and the other as the sample is arbitrary. The places where this is not strictly true are noted in the text.) A major point that deserves emphasis is that techniques that increase the similarity measure of two signatures do not necessarily improve the performance of the system. The bottom line in deciding whether a given technique improves the system is whether or not the overlap of the verify and forgery distributions is reduced. Absolute values on any scale for verify or forgery distributions when examined independently mean nothing.

Segment Alignment

Signatures are typically composed of several line segments, a segment being defined as the time the pen is in contact with the paper. (Pen-down followed by pen-up.) Segments are fundamentally important to our comparison technique because the reproducibility of a signature is evident during pen-down periods, while pen-up periods show greater variability. The segments are also used in aligning the signature pieces in the other measures of similarity since they provide timing marks which can be identified in each signature. The segment alignment measure, M_1, provides a value that indicates how well the segment lengths of the sample and reference compare.

Segments are determined by analyzing the signal that is the time derivative of the pressure on the pen tip. Representative pressure signals are shown in Fig. 2. The distinctive properties of a pen-lift (pen-up followed by pen-down) are evident; the long flat sections near zero surrounded by distinctive 'peaks' from the rapid change in pressure as the pen is lifted and then later set back down on the paper.

The similarity of the segment lengths of a signature pair is evaluated by

$$M_1 = \frac{1}{NSEGS} \sum_{i=1}^{NSEGS} \frac{(seglr_i - segls_i)^2}{seglr_i \times segls_i} \qquad [2]$$

where NSEGS is the total number of segments of the signature pair and $seglr_i$ and $segls_i$ are the lengths of corresponding segments in the reference and sample signatures, respectively, in units of number of points. M_1 is zero when the segment lengths are identical. Clearly, M_1 can only be evaluated when the signatures have the same number of segments. Unfortunately a given sample will often not have the same number of segments as the reference. This is due to the natural variability of people and the nature of the segment detection algorithm. Therefore, any difference in the number of segments must be reconciled before the segmentation measure is calculated. The segmentation of the pair of signatures is modified, first by addition, and then by deletion of penlifts in a way which minimizes M_1.

The final step in the segmentation process is to subdivide large paired segments. We have observed that long segments tend to fall out of phase beyond the 0.7 second mark, even with very consistent signers. We have achieved better performance by splitting these large segments into smaller pieces, the largest allowed piece being 55 points or 0.7 seconds. This length is actually user dependent, the value being set during the enrollment and adaptation process. The splitting, being performed on paired segments, also logs the initial location within the initial segments so that the penlift timing mark information is retained. Associated with each new sub-segment is an array informing the remainder of the algorithm whether the segments should be left, middle or right aligned in carrying out the correlation and coherence portions of the algorithm.

Regional Correlation

The regional correlation function, developed by Herbst and Liu[7] is employed to obtain two input measures to the similarity measure. They are M_2, the pressure correlation similarity component, and M_3, the acceleration correlation similarity component. These functions provide information on how alike two waveforms are in the time domain. The pressure regional correlation function operates on paired segments of the pressure waveforms of a sample and reference signature. The ith segments generate

$$pscore_i = \underset{\tau}{\mathrm{MAX}} \left[\frac{\sum_t S_p^i(t)\, R_p^i(t+\tau)}{\left[\sum_t S_p^i(t)^2\right]^{\frac{1}{2}} \left[\sum_t R_p^i(t)^2\right]^{\frac{1}{2}}} \right] \quad [3]$$

where $pscore_i$ is the maximum value found over the allowed time lags τ. The time lags used are dependent upon the initial alignment position that depends on the origin of the segments. If the left or right portion of the segments correspond to a true penlift the segments are left or right aligned respectively. Segments that have been artificially created by splitting large segments might have their origin within the body of the original segment and are aligned about their relative centers. M_2 is then computed as a weighted sum by

$$M_2 = \sum_{i=1}^{NSEGS} olapp_i \times pscore_i \quad [4]$$

where the weight factor, $olapp_i$, is the amount of time the two segments overlap divided by the total pen-down time of the reference. The weighting factor effectively reduces the contribution of segments that require large shifts. The segmentation is more consistent for verifies than forgeries and therefore large shifts are less likely for verify signatures. The overlap factor can then be viewed as a means for enhancing the distinguishability of the regional correlation function. This is an example of a case where the absolute value of a measure is reduced in favor of separating the verify and forgery distributions. The normalized distributions for the pressure correlation measure is shown in Fig. 4. The curve on the left is the data from the forgery signatures and that on the right is from the verify signatures. The source of the data shown is from the Charlotte experiment and retrieved off-line from our simulator. Since there were more verify signatures than forgeries, the forgery distribution has been scaled to equalize the area under the curves.

The regional acceleration correlation function is computed in a way that is independent of rotations about the pen axis. This is accomplished by combining the x and y acceleration signals into the complex pairs

$$\begin{aligned} R_a(t) &= R_x(t) + iR_y(t) \\ S_a(t) &= S_x(t) + iS_y(t) \end{aligned} \quad [5]$$

The regional acceleration function can then be expressed as

$$ascore_i = \underset{\tau}{\mathrm{MAX}} \left[\frac{\left| \sum_t S_a^i(t)\, R_a^{i*}(t+\tau) \right|}{\left[\sum_t \left| S_a^i(t) \right|^2\right]^{\frac{1}{2}} \left[\sum_t \left| R_a^i(t) \right|^2\right]^{\frac{1}{2}}} \right] \quad [6]$$

where the '| |' symbols indicate the magnitude of the complex quantities. Rotations about the pen axis produce a phase factor that is eliminated by using the magnitude of the sum of complex correlation for each segment. The amount of shifting for the acceleration correlation function is limited to +/- 1 point from the final alignment found in evaluating the pressure correlation function since the acceleration signals are 'phase-locked' to the pressure signal. The acceleration correlation similarity component, M_3, is then found by

$$M_3 = \sum_{i=1}^{NSEGS} olapa_i \times ascore_i \quad [7]$$

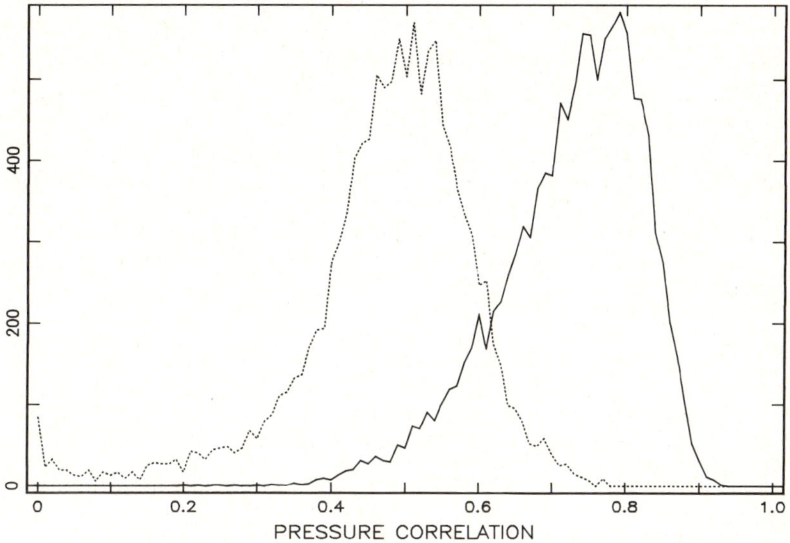

Figure 4. The normalized distributions of the pressure correlation similarity component.

Coherence Function

The magnitude squared coherence function, $\gamma^2(f)$, hereafter referred to as just the coherence function, is used by the signature verification algorithm to obtain two input measures to the similarity measure. The coherence function provides information about the similarity of the reference and sample signals in the frequency domain. The definition of the coherence function is given by

$$\gamma^2(f) = \frac{|\,G_{rs}(f)\,|^2}{|\,G_{rr}(f)\,|\;|\,G_{ss}(f)\,|} \qquad [8]$$

where f is the frequency, $G_{rs}(f)$ is the cross spectral density function between the reference and sample signals, and $G_{rr}(f)$ and $G_{ss}(f)$ are auto spectral densities of the reference and sample signals respectively. $\gamma^2(f)$ provides information on the relative power contained in the signals at frequency f. The conventional use of the coherence function is as a comparison between an input and output signal of a linear two-port system. A value of one indicates that the frequency content of the two signals at frequency f is identical. A value less than one indicates that the output signal has contributions due to random noise and/or system nonlinearities. In our system we interpret the reference as the input signal, the sample as the output signal and the system as the user variability plus any noise sources inherent in the hardware.

To obtain meaningful results from the coherence function it is necessary to construct pseudo-signatures from the input waveforms. This reconstruction serves three purposes:

- To time align each pair of segments in the reference and sample, by using the time lag that maximized the regional correlation function.

- To force each segment into an N-point segment of the pseudo-signature by truncation or padding with zeros. Choosing a power of 2 for N prepares the signals for conversion to the frequency domain by the use of an efficient fast Fourier transform algorithm.
- To taper the pseudo-signature's segments to eliminate artificial high frequency Fourier components introduced by truncation of the waveforms.

The choice of 32 point segments provides an adequate number of segments for establishing reliable spectral estimates with minimal data loss at the end of some segments. The spectral densities are computed by the Welch method [12] of time averaging the N-point segments of the pseudo-signature. A 32 point fast Fourier transform is used to provide a frequency resolution of 2.5 Hz from zero to the Nyquist cutoff of 40 Hz. The cross power spectral density is given by

$$G_{rs}(f) = \frac{1}{NSEGS} \sum_{i=1}^{NSEGS} g^{i}_{rs}(f) \qquad [9]$$

where Nsegs is the total number of segment pairs in the reference and sample pseudo-signatures and $g_{rs}(f)$ is the contribution from segment pair i and is given by

$$g^{i}_{rs}(\mathrm{f}) = S^{i*}_{f}(\mathrm{f}) \times R^{i}_{f}(\mathrm{f}) \qquad [10]$$

where $S^{i}_{f}(f)$ and $R^{i}_{f}(f)$ are the Fourier coefficients of the sample and reference pseudo-signature's i^{th} segment. The pressure coherence measure obtained from the coherence function is computed by the weighted sum

$$M_4 = \sum_{n=1}^{5} w_p(nf_o)\ \gamma^2_p(nf_o) \qquad [11]$$

where f_o is 2.5 Hz. The weighting factors have been selected to maximize the separation between verifies and forgeries.

The acceleration signals are treated in an analogous way to the pressure signals except for use of the complex acceleration signals of Eq. 5 which supplies the required rotational invariance to the coherence function. The acceleration coherence measure is then computed by the weighted sum

$$M_5 = \sum_{n=2}^{5} w_a(nf_o)\ \gamma^2_a(nf_o) \qquad [12]$$

where, in this case, the sum covers the frequency range from 5 - 12.5 Hz. The normalized distributions are shown in Fig. 5.

Construction of the Similarity Measure

The similarity measure uses a set of parameters that depend upon the distributions of the raw inputs for a general population of users. The tests we have performed have provided roughly 28,000 signatures to use as a sample population for parameter selection. In the section discussing reference generation, we will discuss the individualization of these global parameters thereby reducing the dependence on our sample. The basic characteristics of the raw inputs that we have just discussed are clearly illustrated by the normalized distributions of the similarity components. Each plot can be divided into three regions that can be characterized by the probabilities that the sample is a true verify or a forgery. These regions are:

- I - to the left of the verify distribution where the probability for a forgery is high.

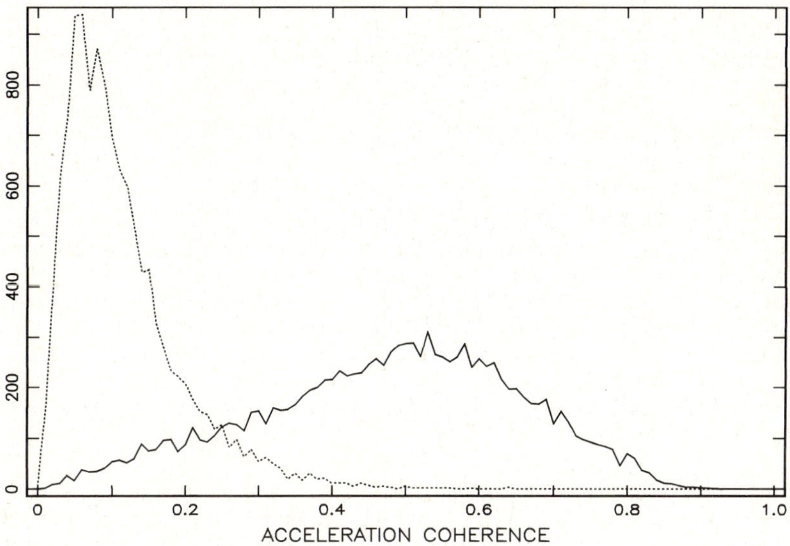

Figure 5. The normalized distributions of the acceleration coherence similarity component.

- II - between the peaks of the two distributions where the two distributions overlap and neither probability is high.
- III - to the right of the forgery distribution where the probability for a verify is high.

The similarity measure is designed to combine these probabilities in a fashion that weights more strongly the raw measures that obtain values in the more probabilistically certain regions of the distributions. This provides a mechanism that emphasizes the most reproducible measures for verifiers and requires forgers to perform reasonably well on all measures in order to be accepted. Each raw input is converted to a component, Sm_i , of the similarity measure. The preliminary total similarity measure is determined by summing the components

$$SM = \sum_i Sm_i \qquad [13]$$

The similarity component is calculated using the function expressed by

$$Sm_i = \frac{(M_i - MID_i)^3}{(HI_i - MID_i)^3} \qquad M_i >= MID_i \qquad [14a]$$

$$Sm_i = \frac{(M_i - MID_i)^3}{(MID_i - LO_i)^3} \qquad M_i < MID_i \qquad [14b]$$

The values for MID_i LO_i and HI_i are chosen to optimize the performance and the stability of the performance for changes in the threshold. The input measures are converted to a common scale by Eqs. 14 that is independent of the range of values of the input measure and allows the inputs to be combined by Eq. 13. A natural weighting of the input measures has been accomplished by this technique, since the choice of the parameters, LO_i, MID_i and HI_i, is dependent upon the separation of the distributions and therefore the range of each similarity component reflects the separation. The parameters are also fine tuned for each individual during reference generation. The final distributions are well separated, as is clear from the error rates. This technique extracts the maximum useful information from each of the measures and also has the advantage of being easily extended if additional measures are discovered.

Reference Generation

A reference file, associated with each user, is created and maintained by the signature verification system. The file contains a set of control parameters used by the similarity algorithm and a set of signatures with which the sample signature will be compared. The purpose of the reference generation algorithm is to establish the control parameters and to select which signatures will serve as reference 1 and reference 2. The algorithm is invoked during initial and adaptive enrollments. For adaptive enrollment the signature termed reference 1 has been preselected and the algorithm chooses a signature for reference 2 from the remaining signatures provided by the calling routine.

Control Parameter Individualization

The purpose of individualizing the control parameters is to recognize the difference in the degree of variability between users. More consistent signers have control parameters assigned that reduces the probability of a Type II error occurring against their reference. These parameters include:

- The required length of quiet sections for penlift identification, QUIET.
- The maximum segment length, MAXPTS.
- The shift percentage, SHIFT, for the regional pressure correlation function
- The five sets of similarity component parameters, LO_i, MID_i and HI_i .
- An overall adjustment parameter to the similarity measure, *REF*.

All of these parameters were selected by analyzing the results of simulation studies using performance measures as a guideline.

Reference Selection

The structure of the signature verification system makes use of two specially classified signatures termed reference 1 and reference 2. This section will discuss the selection of these two signatures from a set of N, where N is any number greater than 2. The method used is a slight modification of the technique developed by Herbst and Liu[6] . The scores of all pairs of signatures is calculated producing an NxN matrix. The technique is as follows:

1. For every combination of selecting a pair of signatures from the set of N, determine the maximum of the two measures versus each signature in the set. (In matrix terms, isolate the two rows that correspond to the pair of signatures selected. For each column in these two rows, select the maximum of the two measures.)
2. Save the minimum of these maximum values for each pair.
3. Select the pair that produces the maximum of the saved minimum values.

This technique allows nicely for sets of enroll signatures that contain two distinct classes of signatures since references are selected in pairs. A problem can arise if the set of N signatures contains one maverick signature, possibly an unintentional error caused by dropping the pen or some other such mishap.[10] The technique will select the maverick as one on the references. This case is tested for by demanding that each member of the pair contributes at least two of the maximum values. If a maverick is identified by this criteria, it is removed from the set and the procedure is then re-executed with the reduced set of signatures.

The implementation of this algorithm for selecting two reference signatures is slightly modified from the above picture by using two NxN matrices as inputs. The role of the NxN matrix described above is played by a combined pressure and acceleration coherence matrix

$$X^{ij} = \frac{(M_4^{ij} + 2 \times M_5^{ij})}{3} \quad [15]$$

A second combined correlation matrix, whose components are

$$Y^{ij} = \frac{(M_2^{ij} + 2 \times M_3^{ij})}{3} \quad [16]$$

is also utilized in testing for mavericks. The coherence matrix, X^{ij} is used to select the pair of signatures by the technique described above and then used to test for the occurrence of a maverick. If a maverick is discovered it is eliminated and a new pair is selected from the reduced set. The correlation matrix is then used to test for a correlation maverick and if one is detected then a new pair is once again selected from the possibly further reduced set.

System Performance

Signature Verification is a very difficult technology to test since it involves people and their reactions to the equipment and its performance. During the past two years we have conducted three major tests involving more than 350 people and collected more than 28,000 signatures, more or less evenly divided between verify and forgery attempts. There were a number of important observations that became evident in the early tests, the most notable being that user motivation is extremely important. The design of an experiment must overcome the almost uncontrollable urge of the test subjects to fool around with the system; to see what changes one can make and still be accepted. This kind of activity can easily ruin the results of a test. It is also difficult to motivate users to attempt forgeries due to the difficulty in defeating the system. We experimented with various approaches for awarding successful users, and found the best motivator, not surprisingly, to be money.

Measures of Performance

The performance of any personal identification system is simple to measure in the sense of establishing the standard error rates though it is difficult to understand what performance level will be required for any particular application. One could imagine requests for performance levels that have:

- extremely low probability of false acceptances (forgeries) at the expense of false rejections (verifies).
- extremely low probability of false rejections at the expense of false acceptances.
- a uniform distribution of false rejections while maintaining low false acceptance probability.

The final request is sensible for any application that must insist that all potential users will be able to be identified by the system and one that has been largely ignored in the literature. Our method of measuring the performance of personal identification systems by the useability rates defined below is aimed at supplying information directed at the concerns of this type of request. An additional difficulty is related to the fact that the verify and forgery error rates are inversely related to one another and can be controlled by adjusting the acceptance threshold. Any tuning of a system must rely on a good set of data that includes realistic forgery attempts. Our approach to this problem has been to design the test environment to closely simulate a realistic environment for true verifiers and to provide assistance to the forgers. In this way, we expect the error rates we obtain to represent reliable estimates.

There are two generally accepted measures of performance for personal identification systems; the Session Type I and Type II error rates. A session refers to any time a user attempts to use the system. The maximum number of signatures allowed in a session can vary, depending on the application, and we have used both two and three signature sessions in past tests. A Session Type I error occurs when a valid individual is falsely rejected. The Session Type I error rate is the percentage of sessions that result in a Session Type I error. The Session Type II error is the analogous quantity for forgers being falsely accepted. Other relevant measures of system performance are the per signature error rates which we refer to as the Signature Type I and Type II error rates and the Useability rates. The Session Useability rates are derived from the cumulative percentage of users with respect to the Session Type I error rate and are very helpful in illuminating behavior that the overall Session Type I error rate does not and evaluating whether the technology will find acceptability. If we let $CP(X)$ be the cumulative percentage of users, where X is the Session Type I error rate, then meaningful classifications, applicable to all personal identification systems are:

- $Z = CP(0)$ The percentage of users with zero Session Type I error rate.
- $U(X) = CP^{-1}(X)$ The value of the Session Type I error rate where the cumulative percentage is X%.

For example, we consider two systems used for accessing an automatic teller machine with identical Session Type I error rates of 1.0%. To simplify the comparison we will assume equal numbers of users and equal numbers of sessions for each user. System A attains its error rate by having a uniform session error rate of 1% for all it's users. System B has a 0% session error rate for 98% of it's users and 50% for the remaining 2%. The users of system A can expect to have difficulty and require the use of some backup method to obtain funds about once a year if we assume two transactions per week. While system B, having the same session error rate would have 2% of it's users having difficulty once per week on average. The difference between these systems becomes apparent if we examine the U(100) useability rate. For system A, U(100) is 1% while system B attains 50% indicating that some users will have difficulty using this system. We have chosen U(100), U(99) and U(95) as standard useful useability rates to aid in assessing the performance of both our on-line and simulated experiments.

One final important measure of performance has to do with the forgery rate obtained in a system such as ours, in which the reference adapts to changes over time. The problem with such systems is that a forger who succeeds in defeating the system once will have a greater probability of being able to repeat. With our system, the successful forger has his version of the signature stored in the bucket, so subsequent attempts only need to exceed the close threshold to eventually have the sample signature compared to the previously successful signature(s). This comparison is much more likely to exceed the similarity threshold than did previous attempts against the target's true signatures. To quantify this form of error, we define the Adaptive Forgery Error Rate as the percentage of forger-target combinations that succeeded in defeating the system.

The Charlotte Experiment

We conducted a test with a group of manufacturing employees in Charlotte NC during the fall of 1983 with 108 users. After enrollment, they were asked to sign their name twice daily for 9 weeks. The sessions generally occurred during coffee breaks or before and after lunch breaks. To mimic the point of sale environment signatures were collected with the users standing at one of two podiums and sessions consisted of up to two attempts. Motivation was provided by cash prizes, distributed as gift certificates at the end of the test, redeemable at a local catalog sales store. They were given $1.00 for each success on the first attempt, and $0.50 for a success on the second attempt. There were also bonuses for consistently good performance throughout the test. Users that succeeded on every signature received a $15 bonus, those with 95% of their signatures accepted received $10 and those with 90% Signature Type I Error rate were given $5. The bonus system succeeded in controlling user experimentation of the system's tolerances. Each podium housed an IBM PC emulating a 3277 terminal connected to an IBM 3081 host running the VM/CMS operating system. A monitor entered the users ID number at the terminal and told the users when to sign. If a user indicated that he/she made a mistake or that a particular signature was not 'good' the monitor did not transmit it to the host for processing and another attempt was allowed without penalty. A concurrent forgery experiment was carried out by allotting one day each week to forgery sessions in place of verify sessions. The users were given a copy of a target signature at the beginning of the day and encouraged to practice until they felt as comfortable as possible in attempting to forge it. The targets were chosen randomly from the other users taking part in the test. A prize of $20.00 was awarded for each accepted forgery. On days when there were no successful forgeries a $20.00 prize was given to the person who came closest to being accepted by the system. This helped maintain a high level of motivation for most participants. The forgery experiment effects on the reference files were not allowed to interact with the verify experiment. At the end of each forgery day all reference files were reinstated to their previous condition.

Figure 6 lists the measures of performance obtained from the Charlotte experiment. These are the actual on-line performance measures, not simulation results. The data from the first week has been separated because it represents a transient period during which the users were becoming familiar with the system and the system was adapting to the users.

The number of verify signatures collected was 4700 of which 4616 were accepted, 247 by the adaptive process. Only 9 Session Type I errors occurred in 4625 sessions, and no user had more than one Session Type I error. This desirable uniformity of performance across users is supported by the excellent useability rates, with the Z useability rate indicating that 91.6% of the users did not have a session failure. The Type II error rates are based on 2133 signatures collected in 1068 sessions during the experiment. The total number of forger-target combinations was 592. A total of 6 session Type II errors occurred, 3 by the adaptive process, by four forgers versus 4 different targets. The forgery rates obtained are quite low, but did illuminate the vulnerability of the adaptive nature of the system as discussed above. In three cases the forger succeeded during his/her first session of the day and two of these were able to repeat during the second session. The fourth case succeeded during the second session of the day so did not have the opportunity to repeat after the first success.

Simulations and Analysis

Simulations refer to off-line processing of signatures. This is usually accompanied by some modifications to the algorithm and is used to determine their effect on the performance of the system. This provides a powerful tool to analyze the behavior of the system due to algorithmic changes and hardware variations. The standard approach in the literature has been to present

PERFORMANCE MEASURE	OBSERVED VALUE
Session Type I Error Rate	0.19 %
Signature Type I Error Rate	1.77 %
Session Type II Error Rate	0.56 %
Signature Type II Error Rate	0.28 %
Z Useability Rate	91.6 %
U(100) Useability Rate	4.8 %
U(99) Useability Rate	2.8 %
U(95) Useability Rate	2.0 %
Adaptive Forgery Rate	0.7 %

Figure 6. Charlotte experiment performance measures.

the simulation results as the indicator of the performance of the system[4,6]. This can be a misleading technique, since it does not allow user-system interaction effects to occur. We can understand these effects qualitatively by considering a user who is being rejected repeatedly by the system. That person may get discouraged and not come back for subsequent attempts or might try to modify his/her natural signature. Such behavior is directly linked to the performance the system is attaining on-line and any off-line modifications, or worse, elimination of such data, does not represent a true estimate of the system's performance. However, useful information as to the effect of any changes made to the system is obtained and we will present the results of such studies. All simulation studies use the signatures obtained during the Charlotte experiment.

Variations of the Similarity Threshold

The first item we examine is the performance behavior as the similarity threshold is varied. The data is fed to the simulator in exactly the same order as it was obtained on-line. The fact that the number of signatures required during any particular session might vary from the on-line sessions means that signatures obtained from different on-line sessions may become mixed within one session during a simulation. Most notably different, is that the reference file that forgers are attempting to match can be different from those on-line since adaptation can occur at different times. The results for the session error rates are shown in Fig. 7. The lines in the plot are interpolated from the experimental points. The similarity threshold required to obtain a zero session Type II error rate is in the neighborhood of 80 and the corresponding Session Type I error rate is 0.68%. The useability rates as a function of similarity threshold are displayed in Fig 8. Beyond 80 on the similarity scale we observe a marked increase in the U(100) and U(99) rates. This indicates that as the threshold is increased we begin to distinguish marginally successful users. It is their increase in Type I errors that is the dominant change that occurs with increasing similarity threshold.

Non-Adaptive Simulations

The next item we examine is how well our system does in a non-adaptive mode. We have simulated a system that allows three signature sessions. The problem of an overly consistent set of enroll signatures is handled by re-enrolling each user with an expanded set of signatures collected over a period of days. The expanded set consists of the original set of six signatures from the initial enroll session and the following six signatures collected during the early verify sessions. The session error rates as a function of similarity threshold are shown in Fig. 9. The crossover point, where the Type I and Type II rates are equal occurs at a threshold of 10 and

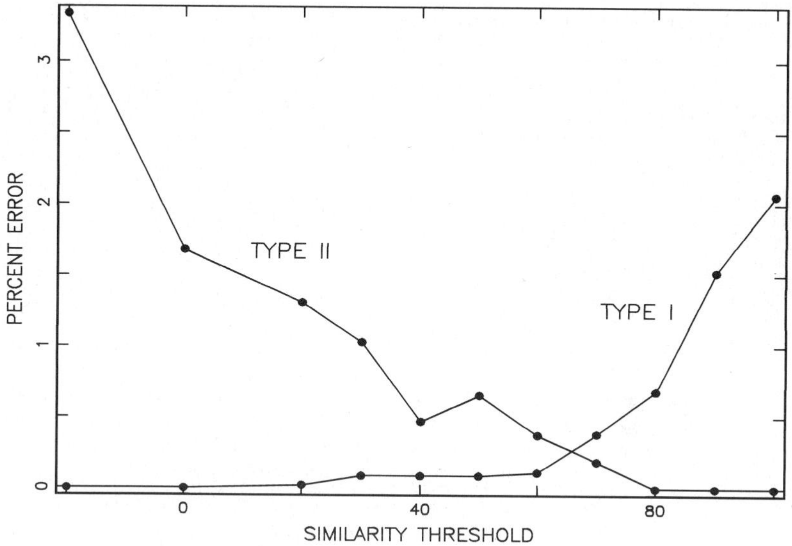

Figure 7. Simulated adaptive session error rates.

equals 0.75%. The curves interesting characteristics are the slopes of the forgery curve at low threshold settings and the verify curve at high thresholds. They indicate that the system tends to be more stable to variations in the forgery population than to those in the verify population.

Error Bounds

The uncertainty of the performance measures of personal identification systems is difficult to assess because they do not follow any standard statistical distributions. Successful forgeries are extremely rare and the number of events we observed is so small that little can be accomplished in determining their error bounds. The verify error rates offer more opportunity to establish bounds due to the higher number of events that occurred, but the use of parametric statistical methods must be avoided. We have used a randomization technique known as the bootstrap to analyze the Type I error rates. To determine a range of expected estimates of the user mean Type I session error rate a user population of equal size is randomly selected from the initial population with replication, the mean calculated, and the process repeated many times. Figure 10 shows the results from 32,000 iterations. The central 68% of the means are covered by the range 0.13% - 0.29% Type I session rate. To clarify: For any randomly selected sample population of 108 users, the mean Type I session error rate can be expected to fall within the range 0.13% - 0.29% 68% of the time.

One additional application of this randomization technique is directed at the dependence of the width of the Type I error rate on the number of users in the sample population. We randomly selected N users from the sample population, where N is less than the total sample population, and calculated the width of the distribution for 1000 iterations as described above. This process was then repeated 100 times to establish a mean and standard deviation of the width for this value of N. These studies show that there is little improvement in the width of the distribution beyond 50 users.

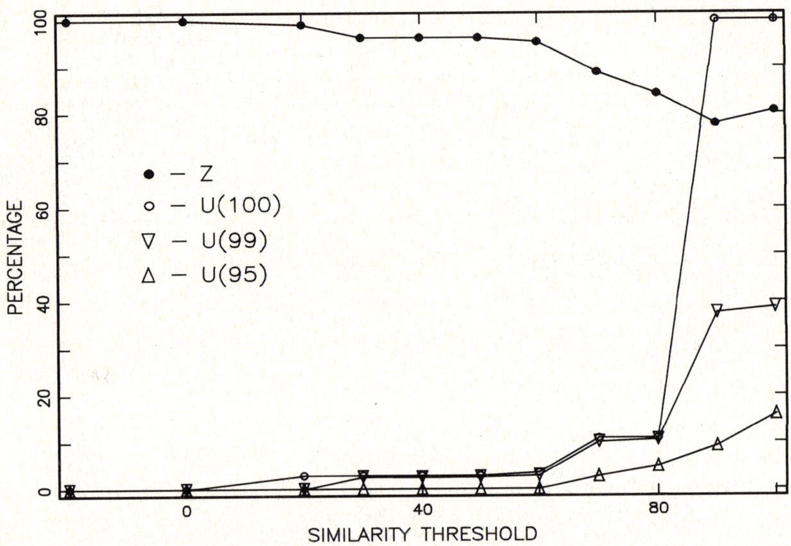

Figure 8. Simulated adaptive useability rates.

Pen Interchangeability

All implementations of a signature verification system require some level of pen interchangeability, ie. a user must be able to sign effectively with any pen. Pen interchangeability is considered in this section because it is as much an algorithm problem as it is a hardware problem. The pen converts the mechanical motions of signing into electrical signals via a set of transducers. These transducers can be characterized by a set of parameters which describe their response to various accelerations, forces and heat sources present when a person signs their name. If we had a model that described all of the effects on the pen during the signing process, and had a model which predicted the output from the pen for all of these effects it might be possible to predict pen interchangeability from measurable characteristics of each pen component and manufacturing step. This is clearly impossible considering the enormous variability of signature characteristics and the complexity of the pen.

We have chosen to address the pen interchangeability in three ways,

1. Mechanical imitation of the major pen forces combined with simulation studies of the algorithm.
2. The exchange of pens in a large test.
3. Comparison of similarity components for a pair of pens with a small group and the statistical analysis of the results.

Each of these techniques has both good and bad characteristics which will be discussed in the following sections but it is important to keep in mind that any set of manufactured pens will have variations which will effect the users' scores. The objective is to establish a design and a test procedure that will keep these variations within acceptable levels and still maintain a pen cost that is also acceptable.

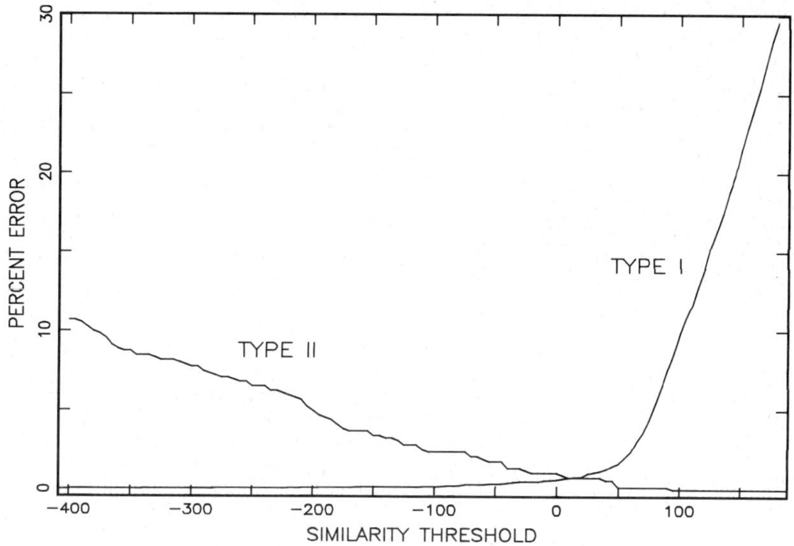

Figure 9. Simulated non-adaptive session error rates.

Mechanical Test Stand

A computer controlled test facility for the pen has been built. This test stand allows us to test pens after construction and to repeat these test after use and various aging tests. The test stand uses a commercial vibration stand to measure the response of the pen to acceleration in two orthogonal directions perpendicular to the pen axis. This measurements allows us to calculate the sensitivity of both accelerometers and angle between them. The pressure channel is tested by replacing the ink cartridge with a small mass and shaking the pen along its axis.

These three measurements are used to establish if a pen has been correctly assembled. However, the establishment of acceptability criteria of pens requires an understanding of how variations in these effect the performance of the system as a whole. The absolute sensitivity of the accelerometers does not enter the algorithm, both the correlation and coherence calculations (eq. 6,8) remove any variation in the absolute sensitivity by normalization. These equations are effected by variations in the relative sensitivities and the angle between the two accelerometers. It is difficult to try to evaluate these effects by examining the equations but it is easy to simulate the effects with the simulator and the data base. All that is necessary is to modify the data of the verify signatures and compare the performance to that obtained with unmodified data. A summary of some of these studies is shown in Fig. 11 along with the average measured values for the latest batch of 10 pens. The error rates shown in Fig. 11 are for a non-adaptive system. Adaptive simulations are much more time consuming to run and tend to mask pen variations. It is clear from these studies that accelerometer sensitivity match and orthogonality do not greatly effect the algorithm performance and the current design and test system are adequate for these parameters.

The test stand also measures the characteristics of the pressure channel, its absolute sensitivity and the corner frequency. These measurements insure that the pressure transducer is working correctly. The pressure calculations in the algorithm are normalized so that modest changes in

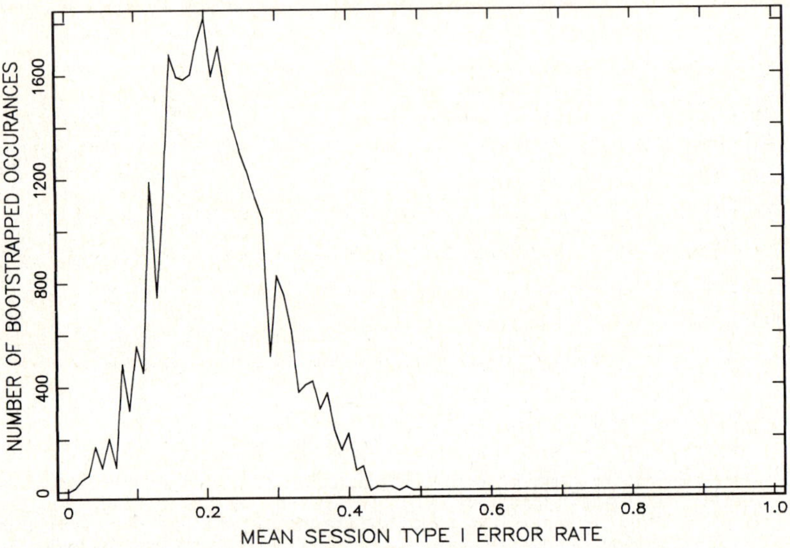

Figure 10. Bootstrapped distribution of user mean session Type I error rate

the sensitivity do not effect the scores. Simulation studies have also shown that the algorithm is not sensitive to pressure channel corner frequency.

Interchange Tests

The most direct way to test pen interchangeability is to take a large group of signers, have them enroll and sign with one pen, and then measure the change in performance when a new pen is introduced. We conducted such a study during a test of a non-adaptive signature verification system which occurred in June 1983. The test consisted of roughly 100 signers who signed twice a day for 5 weeks. The signatures were collected at three stations and the subjects signed while seated. The terminal interaction was preformed by the subject while a test monitor was in the room. There was no facility to cancel a signature a subject felt was not representative. As in the Charlotte experiment, the signers were motivated by a monetary prize per signature, but there was no prize for overall performance. The subjects were divided into three groups, and each group enrolled and signed with the same pen for several weeks. After this period the signers were allowed to use any of the three systems. The pens were secretly rotated on a weekly basis to get a uniform number of signatures with each pen per group without biasing the signers. The data was analyzed by calculating the average similarity components per group by pen, and the Signature Type I error rate. The algorithmic decision process of this system was the predecessor to the Charlotte system and in addition to not having the adaptation feature, made the pass-fail decision in a different way. The Type I error rates were dominated by a few signers who had trouble using the system which makes the error rates a poor measure of pen interchangeability in this experiment. Although the algorithm was different at the decision level the similarity components measured were nearly identical and those results should apply for the present system. This technique directly measures the change in Type I error rate and similarity components upon pen interchange. It does not depend upon any assumptions that the pen could be modeled by a set of parameters. In that sense it is a complete test of the overall design.

Accelerometer Parameter	Average for Manufactured Pens	Simulation Value	Type I Error Rate
Accelerometer Sensitivity Match	5.3%	0%	9.82%
		10%	10.13%
		20%	10.37%
Accelerometer Orthogonality	2.3°	2.5°	10.15%
		5.0°	10.19%

Figure 11. Test stand results and simulation studies for accelerometer parameters.

However, it is extremely time consuming and pen variations can be easily masked by the variability of the signers.

This kind of a test can only be done with a very small number of pens so that it is not possible to systematically study the effect of parameter changes on the scores. Although the error rates showed a systematic degradation, this was not reflected in the average component values. A possible explanation for this effect is that there were particular characteristics of a few individuals signatures which led to their poor performance under interchange, however, when we used this test data with the adaptive algorithm the problem signers disappeared. A pen interchange experiment was also performed in the Charlotte test by swapping the pens in the middle of the fourth week. Although pen differences tend to be masked by adaptation, an analysis of the system performance to look for any change in the error rate or the rate of adaptations following the interchange failed to indicate a measurable effect.

The limitations of the previous technique led us to develop a test which would allow us to test many different pens with varying characteristics in a short period of time. The test consists of roughly 20 volunteers who sign 12 times at one sitting, alternating between two pens. The scores from all pairs of signatures are calculated. The pairs fall into three groups, Pen A vs Pen A, Pen B vs Pen B, and Pen A vs Pen B. The average similarity components are calculated for the three groups. Unlike the large population test, this test does not directly measure an error rate but rather only the changes in the average similarity components. We can relate the change in the similarity components to a change in the Type I error rate by score simulations of the data base in which we reduce a particular similarity component and measure the change in Type I error rate. In the same sense as the Large Population test, this test is independent of a pen model but allows the systematic study of pen parameters to test the validity of a model.

This test was applied to the study of the transverse sensitivity of the pressure channel. The pressure channel should, ideally, not produce an output for forces perpendicular to the pen axis, however in practice there is a signal. The pressure sensor is the single most expensive component within the pen due to precise machining of the ceramic and multiple processing steps. The quality of the processing directly effects the size of transverse sensitivity, this makes it very important to establish a realistic tolerance on it or the pen will be forced to bear an unnecessary manufacturing cost. The transverse forces present while signing are difficult to measure and the transducer response is complicated by it's asymmetric response to these forces. It is therefore impractical to study this effect with a model and data simulation. We measure the transverse sensitivity of the pressure channel by replacing the ink cartridge with an 8 gram mass and apply a 10 Hz acceleration both parallel and perpendicular to the pen axis. The ratio of the maximum transverse (perpendicular) signal to the normal (parallel) signal at 10 Hz is the transverse sensitivity rejection (TSR) which is measured in dB. Most of the pens made from commercially poled PZT have TSR's of -12 dB to -25 dB. One pen showed an anomalously high TSR of +1.5 dB. This pen was atypical as the pressure transducer was a replacement. The original transducer had a TSR of -18 dB but was tested to destruction and then removed by machining. The new transducer was epoxied in place and gave the high value reported.

The pen chosen as the standard had a TSR of -30 dB. The transducer for this pen was poled and electroded at IBM but was of the same material used by the vendor supplied transducers. The experiment was repeated for each pen studied. The standard pen was not changed during the test. For each pen we calculated the pressure score components for each pair of signatures for each signer. It is interesting to compare the means of the cross term Pen_{AB} to the standard pen mean Pen_{BB} If the pens are "different" we expect the cross term to be substantially lower. To quantify this difference we calculated the average fractional score difference for each user.

$$\frac{Pen_{BB} - Pen_{AB}}{Pen_{BB}} \qquad [17]$$

The effect of the reduction in the pressure correlation and coherence similarity components on the Signature Type I error rate can be estimated by simulation of the algorithm. We reduced the pressure correlation and coherence similarity components and measure the change in the Type I error rate. These simulations were done with the non-adaptive system at a threshold of 10. The Signature Type I error rate at this setting is 9.55%. The results of these simulations is shown in Fig. 12. We chose the pens with higher TSR's for this test in order to establish an upper limit for acceptable pens. Clearly the pen with a TSR of +1.5 dB is unacceptable, however the remainder of the pens show only small increases in the predicted Type I error rate.

The acceptable level of pen interchangeability is dependent on the particular application, if signers are continually using different pens as would be the case in a point of sale application then the requirements are more stringent than an application like remote computer access where the users normally use their own pen. Adaptation also complicates the question, if the similarity measure is slightly lower with a new pen the system is likely to adapt, and create a new reference incorporating signatures from the new pen, effectively eliminating any effect. Interchangeability is also an economics question. In the case of TSR, if the acceptability criteria for pens set at -10 dB, rather than -5 dB, the pen cost will go up due to a lower yield but the pens will be more interchangeable.

Interchangeability is an area of study that requires an application dependent cost versus performance estimate. Only then can a realistic set of pen parameters be established. However, to date we have constructed more than 50 pens which met the minimum requirements of the pen test stand and none showed interchangeability problems in use.

System Integration and Conclusions

The software components in a Signature Verification system consist of: signature acquisition, a signature comparison and reference generation algorithm, enrollment and verification control, data base management, and an interface to pass the results to an application. We have two current prototype systems which demonstrate Signature Verification technology, one a stand alone IBM PC, the other a VM based system to control remote access of 'dial-up' terminals.

The stand alone system contained entirely within an IBM PC provides a convenient portable way to demonstrate the technology. The PC performs all the system functions of signature acquisition, user enrollment and verification, and data base management. A successful verification results in a cheerful tune to encourage the users. The software is written in PASCAL with part

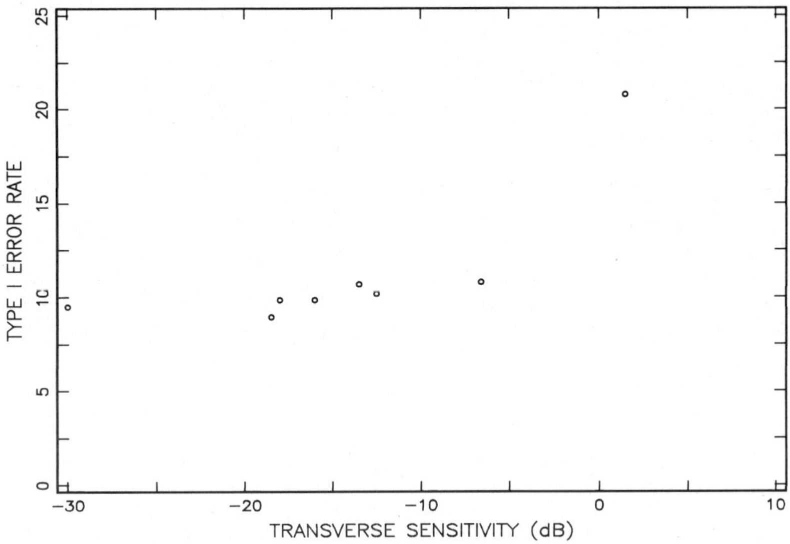

Figure 12. Type I signature error rate vs. TSR.

of the algorithm and acquisition code in ASSEMBLER and the 8087 coprocessor is used. The response time for a verification is typically 3-6 seconds and an enroll takes about 3 minutes.

We have also developed a system which uses signature verification to protect dial-up telephone access to the IBM VM network. The acquisition and control portions of the system are merged with a terminal access program developed at Yorktown called PCTERM (by Auslander, Harrison, Miller and Wegman). The signature verification algorithm and data base management is contained in a disconnected service machine which communicates with the terminal control program using the VMCF facility. The signature acquisition code has been merged with the PCTERM terminal control program in the PC. When a user dials a telephone number permanently connected to a special PCTERM service machine, a signature is requested. This signature is sent to a signature verification service machine for comparison to the users reference. The user is connected to the network only after the signature is accepted. This implementation has been further strengthened by building a signature acquisition card with DES encryption. Each card is personalized with a unique card ID and a secret DES key. The key is stored in a microprocessor on the card in a way which makes it inaccessible after manufacture. The host maintains a table of ID's and secret keys in a protected manner. When a session is requested, the card ID is sent to the host in the clear and the host encrypts a random session key using the appropriate secret key. The encrypted session key is sent to the PC. The microprocessor decrypts it to obtain the session key which is used to encrypt the signature before it is passed to the PC for transmission to the host. This protects against an eavesdropper either on the telephone line, or in the PC from acquiring a signature in a form that permits its reuse to gain access. We estimate the cost of this card to be about $190.

The primary reason for going to the effort of this encryption scheme is not to thwart someone with a telephone tap, but to prevent the owner of the PC from recording his signature and transmitting the recorded signature instead of generating a new one each time access is desired.

There is a real conflict between a system being user friendly and security, with the availability of programmable terminals and auto-dial modems, there is tendency for users to place all of the necessary phone numbers, access codes and passwords on their diskette. The effort needed to log on is then just the act of turning on the power to the PC. Our implementation of signature verification and encryption prevents this bypass of security in a way which we hope is not too offensive to the users.

Aknowledgements

Signature verification has been an IBM project for more than ten years. The technology we describe here is built on the work of many people, we have tried to reference specific contributions but much of the 'art' of signature verification was passed on to us in many conversations with Noel Herbst, C.N. Liu and Mike Martino. The pen design was greatly aided by Gene Komsa, he contributed to the design and invented most of the fixtures used to manufacture the prototype pens. We are grateful for his ideas and his craftsmanship. We would like to thank the AD-Tech group under Bill Rohland in Charlotte for their help in running the test described in this paper. We also take this opportunity to to thank the more than 500 IBM'ers who contributed their signatures and forgery attempts in our various tests over the past four years.

---

1 C.N. Liu and N.M. Herbst, "Automatic signature verification based on accelerometry." IBM Journal of Research and Development, Vol. 21, pp. 245-253, 1977.

2 A. Fejfar and J.W. Myers, "The testing of three automatic identity verification techniques for entry control." Final Proceedings of the Second Conference on Crime Countermeasures - Science and Engineering, 3A 09-3B 05, Oxford, 1977.

3 There are several companies that have announced products based on various personal identification technologies. They include: Palmguard Inc., 12810 S.W. Canyon Rd., Beaverton OR 97005. Fingermatrix Inc., 30 Virginia Road, North White Plains, NY 10603. Micropad Ltd., 10 Whittle Road, Wimborn Dorset BH21 7SD UK. EyeDentify, Portland OR. Sycon Inc., 3040 Scott Boulevard, Santa Clara, CA 95050.

4 H.D. Crane and J.S. Ostrem, "Automatic signature verification using a three-axis force-sensitive pen." IEEE Trans on Systems, Man and Cybernetics, Vol. SMC-13, No. 3, pp. 329-337, 1983.

5 D. Sykes, "Personal Identity Verification." Information Privacy, Vol. 1, No. 5, pp. 222-225, 1979.

6 C.N. Liu, N.M. Herbst and N.J. Anthony, "Automatic signature verification: System description and field test results." IEEE Trans. Syst. Man, Cybern., Vol. SMC-9, No. 1, pp. 35-38, 1979.

7 C.N. Liu and N.M. Herbst, "Signature verification method and apparatus utilizing both acceleration and pressure characteristics." U.S. Patent 4,128,829, 1978.

8 D. Botnick, "Automated signature to bow in '84 as current systems sharpen tech." Bank Systems and Equipment, Vol. 20, No. 8, pp. 95-104, 1983.

9 W.J. Hale and B.J. Paganini, "An automatic personal verification system based on signature writing habits." Proceedings of the 1980 Carnahan Conference on Crime Coutermeasures, University of Kentucky, Lexington, Ky, pp. 121-125, 1980.

10 Mike Martino, IBM Kingston, Private Communication.

11 N. M. Herbst and C. N. Liu, Automatic Signature Verification, in 'Computer Analysis and Perception' Editors: C. Y. Suen and R. DeMori. CRC Press, Boca Raton, FL 1982 pp83-105.

12 P. D. Welch, "The Use of the Fast Fourier Transform for the Estimation of Power Spectra", IEEE Trans Audio Electroacoustics, Vol. AU-15, June, 1970 pp70-73.

COMPUTER SECURITY
J.B. Grimson and H.-J. Kugler (Editors)
Elsevier Science Publishers B.V. (North-Holland)

EFT/POS NETWORK ARCHITECTURE

- A CANADIAN PERSPECTIVE

William J. Byrne

National Director - EFT/POS Networking

Telecom Canada

The subject of network and system security is a major consideration in the Telecom Canada approach to the definition of a Network Architecture designed to support the introduction of Electronic Funds Transfer services at the Retail Point of Sale (EFT/POS).

It is the contention of the design team that in addition to protecting Consumer interests that the participating Financial Retail and Technology providers will have to rely on integrated security systems in order to protect their considerable financial and reputational investment.

INTRODUCTION

By way of an introduction Electronic Funds Transfer Services which originate at the Point of Sale (EFT/POS) can be reviewed against two consumer services perspectives namely:

a) Financial transactions associated with the purchase of goods or services; where the transaction is initiated by means of a consumer held credit or debit card and accommodated as an extension of the services provided by Retail merchants.

b) Transactions associated with a consumers ability to access cash or personal financial services as offered by bone-fide Financial Institutions and usually accommodated via the provision of automatic teller or branch machines (ATM/ABM). These transactions re usually initiated by means of a debit card and are viewed as an extension of current personal banking services.

In a general sense current EFT/POS systems can also be viewed as a series of automated or manual operations directly related to the initiation, distribution and processing of financial transactions which originate within definitive point of sale (POS) environments, i.e....,

a) Methodology comprising technology and trained personnel equipped to accept credit and debit cards suitably embossed for use in imprinters and or supplied with a magnetic stripe (or Bar Code) encoded to identify the consumers primary account number (PAN).

b) Appropriate means of communicating inquiry and resultant authorization messages between the POS operator (card acceptor) and the card issuing Financial Institution.

c) Established procedures for payment or account reconciliation between systems participants.

d) Suitable manual and/or automated security procedures which are aimed at both protection of the business integrity of the system participants and the avoidance of embarrassment to the consumer at the point of sale.

When viewed in the context of generic EFT/POS networking systems these logical elements can also be expressed in terms of two distinct cycles i.e.,

a) A purchase authorization cycle whereby the financial standing of a consumer (card holder/account owner) who is requesting goods or services at the POS can be determined.

b) A payment or settlement cycle during which the appropriate Financial Institutions acting on behalf of their Retail Merchant clients can collectively reconcile all authorized transactions.

It can also be determined that the Purchase Authorization Cycle must be satisfied within a real time environment with the resultant authorized approvals initiating the Payment Cycle which in the collective opinion of qualified input can be satisfied in a non-real time manner (e.g. daily).

NETWORK ARCHITECTURE - STRUCTURE

The Telecom Canada position is to adopt the view that EFT/POS is primarily a consumer service which must be universally accommodated at the point of Sale and be supported by a comprehensive Inter-Financial Institution payment system.

The major building blocks proposed in reference to an accommodating architecture will therefore be designed to cover four segmented but operationally integrated environments i.e.,

a) The POS Environment, which is allocated the responsibility to provide suitable terminal access technologies in order to accommodate consumer entry to the EFT/POS system and to provide a means of initiating the payment cycle by periodically transmitting a transaction file to (an) appropriate Financial Institution(s).

The Telecom Canada EFT/POS architecture proposes that two logical levels be established to accommodate of these functions: i.e.

- an access level function to support the consumer interface (inquiry mode) and payment authorization services (purchase mode)

- a collector level function to support merchant payment reconciliation.

b) The Financial Environment, which is allocated the responsibility to provide appropriate authorization and payment services to the POS operators as as extension of the card base services provided to the consumer (card holder).

In terms of the EFT/POS architecture Telecom Canada proposed that the logical level of Authorization Server be introduced to satisfy the requirements of the purchase cycle.

It was perceived that F.I.'s could best support the activities of the Retail Merchant by providing a timely settlement of funds due and that this service could best be accommodated on an interexchange basis and supported by bi-lateral arrangements which could exist between members of the Financial Community.

In this context it was proposed that the logical level of Interbank Server be incorporated into the architectural model in order to satisfy the requirements of the payment cycle.

c) The Communications Environment, which is allocated the responsibility to provide the necessary level of inter-connection services designed to accommodate the EFT/POS requirement on a National basis.

d) The Security Environment, in which Telecom Canada proposes an integration of specific security measures designed to ensure the viability of a National EFT/POS Network Service. It was also proposed that the security measures would encompass System Access Control, Network Access Control and Terminal Security i.e.

SECURITY CONSIDERATIONS

To assist in the task of designing a security framework which would satisfy the EFT/POS requirement Telecom Canada design engineers were asked to map their perceived security design to cover three major areas of concern.

- Privacy

Which relates to the protection of information belonging to or concerning a consumer or a business entity. In the EFT/POS context this can be expressed as a need to preserve privacy with respect to the financial status of an individual or business entity.

In security terms it must be assured that in addition to protecting information held in manual files or computer data bases that financial messages are not mis-routed or intercepted and read while in transit.

- Physical Security

Can best be defined as the need to protect against unauthorized access and potential abuse of the system and network resources which can result in loss or disruption of service. These acts of abuse can range in scope from disgruntled or ex-employees to terrorism and organized crime.

Within the physical security framework we must also protect the EFT/POS system from the consequences of environmental damage e.g. fire, flood, power disruption etc.

- Systems Integrity

It is opportune to make the observation that all systems are somewhat open to an organized attack and in the EFT/POS context we can consider that an electronic message can be copied or altered relatively easily and that stolen or borrowed terminals or password files could precede a logical attack.

We must therefore ensure that appropriate security procedures are developed and introduced in order to

a) detect copies of genuine transaction messages

b) protect against messages having their contents altered in transit

c) detect messages which originate from unauthorized sources

d) detect suspect messages which appear to originate from bone-fide card/consumer/merchant access points

The Telecom Canada architecture documents recommended that the most effective methodology to support the desired level of transaction security was to introduce end-to-end auditable cryptographic protocols and also propose an integrated security design based on three major sub-divisions or responsibility. i.e.

- System Access Control

Which is designed to prevent unauthorized access to the Financial Institution computer environments and manual record files.

In order to associate a bone-fide card with a specific customer record or file and after determining that technologies such as electronic signatures, finger print or retina identification are operationally impractical the major card issuers have opted to utilize a system which is based on a unique card holder personal identification number (PIN) comprising four numerical digits.

y associating the PIN with a primary account number (PAN) the .I.'s address the requirement for

a) Message Authentication, which allows the card issuing organization to validate the message source (card holder), the message contents (transaction details against funds available) and intended destination (authorization point)

b) Message Referencing, which allows for message sequence checks, correct authenticator codes and time reference checks.

Most of the problems associated with these current security systems are fully recognized by the major card issuers, however their ability to implement an optimal security system is somewhat compromised by the inability of the consumer to be fully integrated into such a system (e.g. variable transaction keys).

This has led to a situation where there exists a perception that a logical attack is possible and this in turn imposes some responsibilities on the retail and networking participants to ensure that "Holes" do not exist which could be exploited in an ad-hoc or organized manner.

To accommodate this concern Telecom Canada proposed that a secondary level of security control be implemented namely,

- Network Access Control

  which is designed to ensure that only authorized retail and financial entities can access and exchange information via the EFT/POS communications routing environment.

  In this manner network access control would be responsible for the following functions,

  a) provide the necessary access and control functions which it is proposed could encompass access authorization, session control, format validation and in transit message integrity services.

  b) Activated control network routing as a distribution function.

  c) Provide logical interface functions to a central network and security management system in order to facilitate statistics collection, audit information and network access management functions.

To accommodate logical segmentation of the consumer access to authorization services functions and the need to relate the retail merchant to the inter-F.I. payment services Telecom Canada proposed that a further sub-division of network access control was applicable i.e.

- Point of Sale Access Control (PAC) which is designed to interface the POS environment to the communications level.

- Authorization Server Access Control (SAC) which is designed to interface the financial institution computer environment to the communications level services.

- Interbank Access Control (BAC) which is designed to accommodate automation of the payment process by accommodating specific interbank gateway access to the communications environment.

By introducing this hierarchy of access control and by further limiting the ability of each sub-division to initiate and accept sessions with other access control levels, Telecom Canada feels that the ability of the EFT/POS system to survive against the majority of perceived security violations is enhanced.

Terminal Security

It is generally acknowledged that the early versions of an EFT/POS network will have to accommodate an inherited base of POS terminals which would not satisfy the security requirement imposed by the system access control functions.

Telecom Canada proposed the concept of developing a Terminal Security Controller (TSC) which should be located as close to the non secure terminal population as possible.

It would therefore be the responsibility of the terminal security controller to participate in end to end security protocols with the individual providers of Financial Services.

The possibility of EFT/POS terminals being borrowed or stolen and probed for cryptographic key information which could lead to a logical attack on the system is a real consideration which must be addressed by the provider of POS services, however by combining terminal security, network access and system access control procedures in an integrated design Telecom Canada proposed that the consequences of such an act would be minimized.

CONCLUSION

The Telecom Canada Design Team recommended that EFT/POS should be viewed as a consumer service which must be accommodated at the point of sale with respect to enabling card based purchase services and be supported by a comprehensive Inter-Financial Institution payment system.

Based on this recommendation it was proposed that a National EFT/POS system should incorporate the concept of an Open Access System designed specifically to enable non-discriminatory access from Retail POS operations and be serviced by Card Issuing Financial Institutions.

In addition it was further recommended that a Distributed Gateway System should be developed in association with the Open Access System and be designed to support the evolution of an automated National Payment System.

From a security aspect it was also recommended that System Access Control as implemented by the associated Financial Institutions should be augmented by a concept of Network Access Control which would provide both access security features in addition to providing an application user distribution hierarchy.

Finally a number of major architecture levels were described in order that all systems participants could concentrate on providing specific expertise to the problems associated with design of an integrated system of this magnitude.

In conclusion therefore the following diagram therefore represents the Telecom Canada perception of a Logical Reference Model for a secure Canadian EFT/POS System.

LOGICAL REFERENCE MODEL FOR EFT/POS

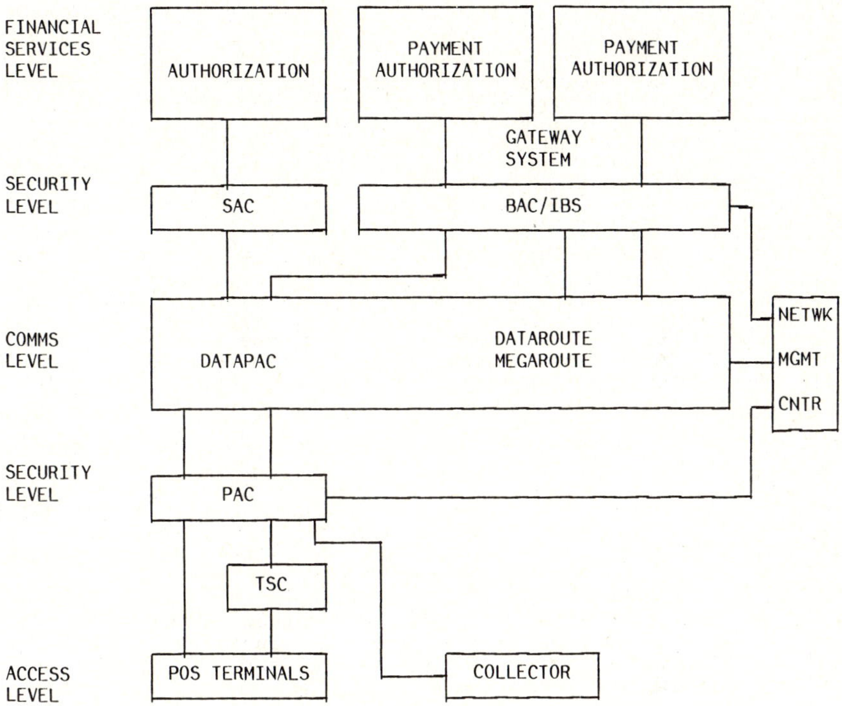

COMPUTER SECURITY
J.B. Grimson and H.-J. Kugler (Editors)
Elsevier Science Publishers B.V. (North-Holland)

DISASTER RECOVERY FOR ONLINE SYSTEMS

by Michael Nolan, Aer Lingus, Dublin, Ireland.

This paper examines the growth of computerisation in commercial air transportation, the growing business dependence on network online systems and the associated risks and potential losses. It further examines the available security and back-up options and also the contingency or disaster recovery options. It proposes a suitable disaster recovery plan both for the central system and the online network and goes through the process of planning, implementing and testing the plan.

Due to the great increase in worldwide air travel brought about by rising economies and the introduction of jet aircraft in the 60's, airlines reservations systems have grown from manual and semi-mechanical systems through IBM 1440 - IBM 360 or equivalent with worldwide online networks. What started as passenger and freight reservations only systems have now grown to be total business systems on which modern airlines are totally dependent. Typical airline online systems also host such functions as message switching both private and airline system to airline system, fare quotation and ticketing, airport departure control, flight information and planning, schedules control and planning, sales agency reporting and various passenger revenue and financial inputs.

The widespread functions are vital to the daily operation of the industry due to the uniquely perishable nature of the product-space on aircraft flights. Geographical spread means the system must be available 24 hours 365 days per year.

The required high level of availability demands redundancy and duplication in critical hardware, software and communicating links. The risks to the system are reasonably similar to other online systems, e.g. fire, impact, comms, failures, etc. but the financial consequences of system downtime are immediate and non-recoverable. Without immediate online confirmation of sales, passengers quickly switch to the competitors and, depending on routes and market share immediate losses of 7 - 20% of revenue follow. Without a viable disaster recovery plan an airline could quickly go out of business following a disaster to its online computer system.

Due to the immediate financial losses following a disaster, a viable disaster recovery plan must provide continuity of the system within a minimum time frame not exceeding 24 hours.

This stringent time constraint eliminates some common contingency back-up options, i.e. cold or relocatable computer centres. Warm or hot commercial stand-by centres may be suitable but may not be able to provide cost effective comms. links. This paper proposes that the most viable disaster recovery plan for an airline online system is to be hosted on a suitable airlines own system using the airlines common communications network "SITA". Planning for this involves maintaining a skelton of your schedules and routes, etc. on the chosen host system and the facility to load the last security dump of your database on to it.

The critical parts of the network using "SITA" can be software readdressed and rerouted to the host by arrangement. Arrangements have to be agreed with the local PTT to reroute or turn around local or private leased lines into the SITA network. This would only apply to less critical users that could sustain delays of several days.

Ongoing testing to maintain the compatability is required to ensure that in the event of a disaster, the back-up system is online to users with minimum delay and disruption.

BACKGROUND TO THE GROWTH OF AUTOMATION IN AVIATION

The economic revival of the 60's combined with the mass appeal of commercial jet transports brought about a boom in air travel, both leisure and business, worldwide. The industry found itself unable to cope adequately with the increasing workload of passenger reservations and associated operations and more and more turned to available automation to improve the service. The aviation industry was amongst the pioneers of online computer systems.

The manual systems of the 50's were slowly being replaced by the various types of mechanical tabulators, some using punched cards as visible records. This primitive equipment, by today's standards, could control flight inventories and produce daily passenger lists.

In the early 60's equipment came on the market with limited online capability which could show availability of seats on selected flights and update the inventory if a seat was sold or cancelled. The Bunker Ramo teleregister was one such system. Passenger name detail data was transmitted to the central site by low speed teletype and typically an IBM 1440 or similar was used to process the teletype punched output to produce passenger lists, status reports, etc. The up to date status of both systems needed to be reconciled on a daily basis.

These systems were already groaning under the travel business loads of the mid 60's. Concurrently IBM and the U.S. Dept. of Defence were developing a system called S.A.G.E. - "Semi Automatic Ground Environment System". This military defence system comprised a central site CPU with a front end communications processor that could accept data in real time via communications links from tracking devices. The systems demonstrated the feasibility of merging a network of computers and communications to provide solutions for complex real time applications. Building on this experience IBM and American Airlines in the U.S. developed a communications based reservations system that would satisfy the airline industry needs. The major improvement over the previous systems was that it not only controlled seat inventory but also processed passenger name data etc. It could also communicate directly with other airlines' computer systems and automatically request and confirm, buy or sell space on each others flights.

In 1969 the first airlines outside the U.S.A. began to implement IBMs new Airline Control Program (ACP) operating system running IPARS - the airline reservations application - typically on IBM 360-50 kit. These were the first CRT based systems bringing the remote offices and airports online with real time access to the central site mainframe database.

Through the 70's and 80's both the ACP software and the operating hardware have progressed to become a multi-function high performance worldwide system linking the airlines of the world. Similar compatible systems were developed by other manufacturers, notably UNIVAC.

The disaster recovery plans and philosophy presented here apply in principal to any medium sized airline preferably linked to the SITA system.

TYPICAL HARDWARE CONFIGURATION

This is an overview of the type of system that is used by a medium sized airline carrying up to 10 million passengers p.a. It comprises of a 3031-3033 type CPU with perhaps 6 to 8 MB storage.

DASD comprises of approximately 10 X 3350 type disks or storage of equivalent capacity.

Communications traffic is of two types, teletype low speed and high speed computer to computer traffic. 3705 and/or 1270 type front end communications controllers are used. Transaction logging and security dumps are done to tape.

Due to the critical uptime availability required - 24 hours per day, 365 days p.a. all critical hardware devices are duplicated. A "hot" standby CPU is usually available. This often is a development CPU or a mutual standby to perhaps an MVS batch or IMS system.

Disk modules are duplicated and updated online so that a mirror image is maintained on duplicated disks. Tape drives and communications controllers are also duplicated. Considerable planning is required to manage the switching options of the duplicated devices to the best effect.

Software wise the system supports both the live system and a test system. Almost all maintenance support and housekeeping functions can be done online so that planned downtime can be minimised to a few minutes per week. This duplication of devices and online support facilities ensures a fail-safe system with uptime performance in excess of 99% being achieved on an annual basis.

Response times, even to the remotest user are within two seconds due to the efficient assembler based software.

COMMUNICATIONS NETWORK

The worldwide nature of the air transport industry means that airports and offices on an airlines flight and sales network tend to be geographically spread out with an additional concentration in its domestic area. The communications network to link these users has become the vital part of the system. Besides the need for an airline to link its own users to its central system, interlining or passengers connecting from one airline to another means that airline to airline communications is also critical to the overall smooth running of the industry. SITA, the airlines' co-operative worldwide private communications network has evolved to meet these needs. The world's press, finance, meteorology systems, etc. have extensive communications networks but none match the global inter activity of SITA.

Typically an airline uses the SITA network on a per message cost basis for its lower activity users and for all inter-airline communications. For its busiest city pairs and perhaps domestic users private leased lines tend to be more economical. Critical users tend to be backed-up by either a SITA connection or an alternate private line.

An upcoming growth area is multi-access systems whereby Travel Agents, etc. can access several airlines or travel trade systems through the network.

Airlines also use the networks to multi-host smaller airlines who do not have a system of their own.

Typical networks cater for low speed teletype traffic and hight speed online or computer to computer traffic using various multiplexors, concentrators and front end 3705/1270 type processors.

TOTAL BUSINESS DEPENDENCE - THE RISKS AND POTENTIAL LOSSES

THE DR. BUDGET

The rapid growth in information handling, rising labour costs and reliable and cost effective data processing has lead to todays situation whereby many companies are totally dependent for their business survival on the integrity and continous availability of their computer systems.

The computer systems become the repository of data relating to trade or marketing secrets, passenger data, finance etc, often with no integrated paperwork to support it. The protection of this resource against unauthorised modification, distruction or disclosure is of paramount importance and of growing concern in business worldwide. There are also growing legal responsibilities to secure and insure the integrity of the data.

Airline Reservations, being a relatively modern business function has developed in conjunction with computerisation and lacks the traditional backing paperwork of other traditional functions.

The Online airline system totally controls the airline product - time and passenger/cargo space. The integrity and timely availability must be secured. In parallel with the development of the Reservations/Operational computer systems, airlines like most modern businesses have developed sophisticated batch and online database systems to handle Administration, Financial, Commercial, Technical and Personnel aspects. However, from the day to day survival aspect the reservations type systems are still the most critical and biggest loss potential.

A TYPICAL AIRLINE SYSTEM

The typical airline system handles some or all of the following functions, perhaps even for serveral hosted airlines also on the system.

1. Passenger Reservations and associated functions.
2. Cargo Reservations and associated functions.
3. Flight schedules and seat availability on airlines worldwide.
4. Hotel and car hire processing.
5. Fare quotation, flight ticketing and credit card authorisation.
6. Airport departure control, flight check-in and seat selection.
7. Flight Planning and Flight Information.
8. Schedules Control and Planning.
9. Sales agency reporting.
10. Direct reference information systems.

11. Data feedback to other systems.

12. Message switching including communications with other Computer Systems.

The efficiency of these systems has been well proved over the years and are now an indispensable part of the industry. A fall back to manual systems is just not possible to handle with current staff and expertise without causing massive delays and disruption and loss of business. The old manual ways are relics of a bygone age. Who now knows how to work out a manual flight plan or loadsheet? What agent can work through one hundred or so fares to pick the correct one? or phone up twenty hotels or car rental companies for a reservation during the high season?

TYPICAL EVERYDAY SECURITY PRECAUTIONS

Everyday computer security is reasonably well established and there is no great need to go into too much detail. There are plenty of good books available. As regards the airline system I have already mentioned the duplication of critical hardware devices - mirror image switchable disks, Stand-by CPU, duplicated Comms. controllers. In addition the facility would be protected by some physical access control devices, plus adequate fire, smoke and intruder alarms, 24 hour static guard, visitor reception facilities, battery and generator uninterruptable power supply and an excess capacity of stand alone or central air conditioning. Fire Control is typically a total flooding Halon type automatic system.

Software and Data wise the system is protected by Access Control (password control) limiting user access to limited facilities, dependent on their I.D. and pre-defined authority. Online captures and online updating of duplicated disks is standard. Checkpointing and transaction logging to tape is used. A vital records program of offsite storage is used.

WHAT ARE THE TYPICAL OR SPECIAL RISKS OR THREATS TO AIRLINE COMPUTER SYSTEMS?

In general the risks to the airline system are similar to those effecting any major business system but, the consequences of a disaster, due to the perishable nature of the product, can be extremely costly.

The building facility, hardware, software, database, Comms network and staff are vulnerable to the following threats in order of likelihood of occurrence - Human error, equipment failure, systems error, network failures, environmental power or essential services problems, theft or fraud, sabotage, fire or destruction. The risks can be summarised as the deliberate or accidental destruction, interruption, disclosure, removal or corruption of the resources. Volumes have been written identifying, analysing quantifying these risks and I do not think I need expand any more on this at the moment. I would warn about going into too much detail in risk analysis. Whilst your unprotected system will remain vulnerable you can waste months on an in-depth risk analysis and eventually may not be able to see the wood from the trees.

Suffice to say that a common-sense risk analysis must be performed to identify the risks particular to your installation as the starting point of any disaster recovery project.

HOW TO QUANTIFY THE POTENTIAL LOSSES

Having identified and examined the potential risks one must now identify the potential losses so as to develop a cost effective day to day security plan and a fallback disaster recovery plan. The day to day security plan must address the expected routing problems - Power losses, Head crashes, System recoveries, program or operational errors etc. The Disaster Recovery Plan must address all the unexpected risks with the ability to recover critical functions within the agreed timescale from any unforeseen disaster.

The potential losses can be estimated under some or all of the following headings:-

1. Loss of Physical assets: Buildings, Hardware etc.

2. Loss of Intangible Assets: Goodwill, Software etc.

3. Loss of Data and recovery costs

4. Liability Losses: Contractual, late payments penalties etc.

5. Personnel Losses: Death or Injury, or illness

6. Financial losses: Uncollected receivables, delayed cash flow Loss of Business, increased cost of working, Fraud etc.

Values must be calculated for all the potential losses. The following methods will be useful:

1. Do a complete asset inventory of Facilities, Contents and Services and calculate current and replacement values.

2. Examine the companies annual accounts - identify income or services that are computer dependent.

3. Talk to users. They know best the consequences, financial or otherwise following a computer disaster. This is a good opportunity to interest and involve the user in the recovery plans for the computer services he uses.

4. Talk to the Commercial and Marketing Managers, talk to the Economic Planners, talk to the DP Manager and the Insurance Manager.

   Typical losses that would result from a disaster to an airline system would include:

1. Immediate loss of Revenue as passengers and freight switch to airlines that can guarantee reservations.

2. Additional staffing to manually check-in passengers.

3. Additional staffing in Sales and Reservations to cope with frustrated potential customers.

4. Costly delays to flights due to passenger and freight congestion .

5. Uncontrollable load factors on flights.

6. Long term bookings losses as other airlines cannot process computer to computer bookings.

7. Long term loss of goodwill and credibility.
These are just the most obvious losses - It would take too much time to go into the full detail.

FUNDING THE DR PLAN - THE BUDGET

This exercise will give a feel for the potential losses involved. Some of the losses can be reduced or eliminated by extra security or precautions which I will talk about in a moment. Some losses may be so unlikely as to be not worth worrying about -e.g. Atomic bombs exploding on computer rooms and destroying the vital records storage site as well: Some losses can be insured against under such headings as Assets, Liabilities, Loss of business or Extra cost of working.

The desired end result should be reliable enough data to convince top management to make a policy decision on what level of security is acceptable and the funds to achieve this. Funding for everyday security is probably an ongoing cost so what is really needed is a commitment to fund the Disaster Recovery costs loosely based on the potential annual loss estimates.

This is always a difficulat challenge. Top management are reluctant to commit funds up front for something with no tangible results. In addition, because many types of losses are difficult or impossible to calculate, mostly due to the lack of data from any previous disasters the annual cost of the selected DR plan may exceed the estimated annual loss estimates. This difficulty in financing security means that the nest conceived DR plans have had to be modified by financial constraints - resulting in recovery time being adjusted, the criticallity of supported system functions re re-appraised and more risk being transferred to insurance. This type of compromise solution should be resisted. It may produce a "normal" or "Lip service" DR Plan.

This step of DR Budget funding is the stumbling block in DR projects in many organisations today.
Consider a typical scenario........
Say the estimated losses of a major disaster to the central site with total destruction of the Computer Room and Data Processing facilities comes to £6 million loss of physical assets and loss of business and increased cost of working costing £2 M for each month without a system. Without a viable DR plan already installed and tested and many people here could well be in this position, it would take a minimum of 3-4 months to get any type of system going again. In the meantime your business could have foundered altogether as the reality of a major computer disaster could be totally different from the estimated consequences. We just do not have an adequate history of previous computer disasters to learn from.

The business like approach would be to cover the physical losses by insurance and invoke DR plans to reduce the 3-4 months down time to as brief a period as will guarantee the survial of the business. Some loss of business and extra costs of working can also be covered by insurance but insurance recompense is of little use if the primary issue - survival of the business - has not been assured.

So how much money can one justify in security counter measures to prevent the non-physical losses incurred in such a disaster - £6 - £8 Million. The risk analysis theories are of little help. Typically they suggest working out the estimated frequency of such a disaster. For example if it happened every 100 years the annual loss expectancy would be £6 - £8 million divided by 100 or £60,000 - £80,000 per annum. Annual security budgets to counter the disaster of less than this figure would thus be cost justified. However this is a very untenable argument with little statistical back-up. Computer suites are usually well secured and from the actuarial point of view, there have not been enough disasters to form a trend. It is difficult to counter an argument that the estimated frequency could be totally different and this can destroy the budget funds. The financial top management will keep asking for a cheaper solution.

The only practical way to approach the problem is to look at the facts. If you have an inadequate or no DR plan at the moment - you could have a disaster tonight and it will cost the sample company £12 - £14 million and could destroy the company totally - who can tell?

The DR plan must be functionally as well as financially quantified. The critical functions to allow the company to survive must be provided for.

Therefore the calculated annual loss expectancy must be regarded as a "guestimate" at best and not a binding financial restriction. The most important aim is to be able to stand over a cost effective DR Plan that meets the mandatory criteria of the company and insures its business survival. In hindsight, in years to come it may be seen as overspending but nobody will deny the peace of mind in knowing that you had a secure recoverable system. People seldom begrudge the fire insurance premiums that they have paid for in years past. They are happy in the confidence that they were adequately protecting and fulfilling their managerial responsibilities.

THE DISASTER RECOVERY OPTIONS AVAILABLE AND WHICH ONE TO CHOOSE

For the purpose of this paper, I am assuming that although adequate security precautions are taken for everyday problems i.e. back-up CPU's, etc. - because of cabling limitations and operational efficiency, all the facilities are often within the one complex and could be all wiped out together in a disaster situation - "all eggs in one basket".

The other assumption is that the Company does not have another computer room or alternative facilities within the Company group. In other words, the Company has to go out to the commercial world to arrange disaster recovery back-up.

During the risk analysis phase of the project, the critical functions and critical timescales will have become apparent. This will allow top management to make the commercial decision - "X" critical functions must be recoverable within "Y" timescale. Secondary functions and timescales will also need to be identified and considered.

These terms of reference will to an extent define or limit the DR options available. As stated before, the operational and business survival of an airline demands some critical functions to be recoverable within 24 hours. This immediately rules out such options as cold start recovery centres, where hardware has to be procured and installed in a ready built empty computer room and also relocatable portable computer centres where the same problem applies. Some hardware, particularly in the Communications controller area, are custom built to the individual airlines specifications and long lead times would delay getting a replacement in a hurry during an emergency situation. This is not to say that cold or portable centres would not have a medium to long term role to play as part of the eventual restoration of normal DP services after the disaster. Partaking in a cold centre in Ireland, due to the limited number of members, can be expensive - up to £50,000 per annum. Portable centres are less expensive but have inherent delivery, assembly and site delays.

The next level of options to consider would be the general commercial "hot" start recovery centres where a compatible hardware configuration is quietly ticking over waiting to run your system in the event of a disaster. The system could fulfill the time criteria but to achieve the required airline type communications functionality in a cost effective way is a difficult problem. Again due to prolonged lead times, specialized airline type communications controllers and stand-by lines would have to be personally pre-installed. In addition to the annual retainer of perhaps £40,000 must be added, additional specialized communications capital costs of approximately £80,000, plus rentals for pre-installed lines of approximately £60,000 per annum. In addition, "hot" stand-by centres by their nature limit the occupation period to a few months so some medium term accommodation e.g. a portable computer room, might also be needed until the original DP facility is restored. From the airline point of view, the preferred system is a mutual or indeed one way back-up arrangement with another airline. This is reasonably similar to a bureau type back-up for say a batch system. The facility where-by one airline hosts one or more other airlines on its system is common-place and well proven. The advantages of a mutual back-up arrangement are obviously in cost savings but can lead to compatibility problems when one partner upgrades and the other does not.

For this paper I will only talk about a one way back-up hosting arrangement with another airline. This has the advantages of:-

1. Minimal upfront costs. I will get back to them later.

2. More likely to remain compatible than a "hot" general commercial system.

3. Ability to be operational within 24 hours - meets time criteria.

4. Problematic communications controllers should already be part of the host system.

5. Extensive access from your own users to the host through SITA connections.

6. Minimum re-training and maximum invisibility to users.

7. Proven procedures and technology.

8. Costs to activate system can be insured under "extra cost of working"

The disadvantages would include:-

1. Difficulty in finding suitable host to host all your critical functions.

2. Pre-payment and pre-installation of excess DASD capacity to cater for your needs on the host system.

3. The need to have all your critical users linked to SITA - they may currently be on private leased lines. So duplicate lines may be needed.

4. Commercial competitive positions may preclude you from going to the most suitable host.

As with any mutual or one-way back-up arrangement, this must be a legal contractual arrangement. A "gentlemans agreement" is useless for so serious and critical a project. In addition the host system needs to be pre-setup to receive your database which may also need to be tailored to suit the host.

IMPLEMENTATION OF THE DR PLAN:

At this stage, the following should have been examined and agreed with top management:

1) Survival Criteria - "X" critical functions to be operational in "Y" time.

2) Initial planning to wuantify losses and establish a budget.

3) Establish a working group to produce, get approval for, and document and implement the plan.

4) Provide for ongoing monitoring, testing and revision of the plan.

The working group or project team must be established under a project leader or co-ordinator.

The team should include DP Management, Systems and Programming, Communications Management, User Representatives,. Commerical, Marketing and Financial Planning Representatives. The Company's Internal Audit and Legal Office should also be involved.

Some companies may have sufficient expertise to lead this group. However, many specialist companies can provide short term security consultancy and project managers to assist in the preparation of the plan.

MAIN ELEMENTS OF THE PROJECT:

The major problem is to find another airline with sufficient compatibility and interest in the project. Whilst many airlines use IBM's ACP operating systems, the application software is often developed inhouse and could involve massive user retraining to be of any use. A thorough investigation must be done to best match up the critical functions required with what can be provided by the host. This will undoubtedly involve compromises and the original criteria must not be overlooked. Unsupported functions will need some alternative back-up plans. The chosen hosts software, whilst functionally suitable may have difference record layouts and programs will have to be developed to massage the latest version of the data base into record formats suitable for loading on to the host after a disaster. The host system will need to be pre-set up in advance with your schedules, routings, device addresses, etc. ready to receive the data. In addition, some retraining of users may be required. This brings us on to the hardward and communications problems.

The major problem is disk storage for your extra data on the host system. To achieve the required continuity with the 24 hour deadline sufficient DASD must be already available online to the host. There are many options on how this might be arranged, indeed the host may have already sufficient excess capacity to cater for you data.

As I say, there are various options. The worst situation would be that you would have to advance rent the additional DASD space required for the duration of the agreement. The DASD required will be much less than your normal configuration as only the data necessary for the supported critical functions is transferred to the host.

Communications: Compared to the DR problems of other business online systems, the fact that the airline industry has the co-operative SITA Communications Network makes it somewhat easier. It is assumed that the host system is on the SITA Network. This means that in the event of a disaster, all your users already on the SITA Network can be switched from your central site address to the new host address. This is achieved by a software trap at the nearest SITA node and is invisible to the user. As stated before, for cost reasons ones busiest and often most critical offices are often not on SITA but on private leased lines.

Depending on the local PTT, contingency arrangements can be made to turn around or switch some of the leased lines into the SITA Network as quickly as possible after a disaster. This arrangement would be unreliable to say the least and would cause problems due to line conditioning, etc. It would be much more prudent to install back-up links to SITA where required in the critical offices. This is a commercial decision.

Most of the problems have now been addressed and a fully functional test should be arranged with the host. The communications switching cannot be fully tested due to the continuous uptime of the live system, but can be proved to work. In parallel with this part of the project is the documentation of the DR plan. This is another subject well supported by publications so I will not go into it in detail. Suffice to say that a comprehensive DR plan documentation will include:-

1. Overview
2. Minimum Requirements
3. Emergency Classifications
4. Action to take in various situations
5. Notification + Call Out Lists
6. Constitutents of various DR teams
7. Activating Control Centre
8. Processing Alternatives
9. Activating Back-Up Recovery Plan
10. Assignments/Checklists
11. Hardware/Software Inventory
12. Vital Records
13. Testing/Updating
14. Interim Operations
15. Restoration to Normality

ONGOING SITUATION

Unlike the MVS batch and IMS type systems, Airline Res systems are not growing at such phenomenal rates so the basic compatability of the chosen DR plan will have a reasonably long life.

Periodic resting is required as well as periodic updating of the various tables on the host system that relate to your schedules route system etc.

An arrangement like this improves the overall security awareness of both host and oneself as any changes to functions etc. must consider the security back-up arrangement and continued compatibility.

In the event of a disaster the DR plan is activated according to the documented plan. The following is a summary of the key events.

1. Passenger bookings can continue to be processed by other airlines and by Travel Agents using multi-acces systems.

2. All traffic to the now inoperative system is held in queues by SITA by request.

3. The last security dump is retrieved from the vital records safe-keeping. The current transactions tape is retrieved from the Computer Room if possible.

4. The appropriate recovery team will fly to the Host centre, update the system if required and load the dump to the host system. SITA will intercept and re-address all traffic destined to the destroyed system to the new host system.

   When the recovery team are happy with the status of the new database they will request SITA to release the queues and the re-directed traffic. The system is now fully operational and the switch to a host system is invisible to the User.

   The DR plan should include how long this back-up arrangement should last, the intermediate accommodation plans and the eventual return to normal Data Processing.

I will briefly summarise the main points again:

1. How the business has grown with the help of Online systems

2. The major dependence on the system and potential losses

3. How to get the financial funding for the DR Plan

4. The DR options available and the preferred one

5. DR implementation project and documentation

6. Ongoing situation.

COMPUTER SECURITY
J.B. Grimson and H.-J. Kugler (Editors)
Elsevier Science Publishers B.V. (North-Holland)

SECURITY FOR SECURITY AGAINST COMPUTER INTRUSION

Donn B. Parker
SRI International
Menlo Park, California, U.S.A.
May, 1985

Confidentiality is a requirement that we face during our everyday work in information security. We must avoid the problem of the shoemaker's children running around in barefeet and practice what we preach. This topic of the security of security has never received sufficient attention in the information security field and is now more important because of the outsider computer intrusion problems caused by malicious hackers. This exposition may sound strong, but its purpose is to make a significant impression and motivate the information security practitioner. The broad issues of this topic will be presented followed by specific recommendations for security of security.

During the metamorphosis and advances in computer security during the past 15 years concern centered on how to secure a computer in a room in a building in a city. However, data communications changed the issues of security and we had to secure the computer and a computer network at many different sites. We started by dealing with data security consisting of security of data stored in computer media, and we advanced to the information security issues of today, which are far more comprehensive. Today's challenge is information and its security wherever it is in an entire organization and treating information as an organization asset. In the future, we will have to deal with such subjects as security of knowledge as artificial intelligence advances with expert systems, knowledge bases and robotry. We are advancing from data security to information security to knowledge security. How do we secure information that's inside of people's minds and the reflection of that information into knowledge bases inside computers?

Information security unfortunately has been in a progression that has advanced from an art form all the way to a supposed technology and engineering discipline, and the important aspect of developing a theory of information security has been all but ignored. We don't have a theory that has been sufficiently developed, and we've gone too fast in trying to apply art and transforming it into a technology. We are trying to do so in a vacuum caused by lack of the necessary theory that goes along with it. We're dealing today with microcomputers and global and local networks that have left information security far behind. We didn't know how to address this new technology because we have had no sound basis of invariant theory to deal with it. In the future, we're going to have to deal with voice data entry, voice data output, robot security, expert systems, portable computers, and automation of offices in the home. Cellular radio is going to make floppy diskettes obsolete as occurred with punch cards in the early 1980s. How are we going to deal with all of these new problems, when we do not have any basic, invariant theory on which to build?

There are only three invariant constituents of information security: people and forces as the sources of threats of loss and information that is the subject of threats. Everything else is changing. There are six invariant functions of security: avoidance of loss, deterrence of potential threat, prevention of loss, detection of acts after they occur, recovery from the losses, and finally the correction of vulnerabilities to reduce risk of repeat losses in the future.

All of these six functions can be performed with the application of a set of principles for effective safeguards. We know what many of them should be, but we need more. Now, the last major point here is that these six security functions should be performed within a set of principles and should be done in a secure manner. The rest of this presentation is now focused on the subject of performing security securely. It must always be assumed that the enemy knows as much as the security administrator. On the other hand, we do not wish to aid the enemy by revealing security information. We must keep these secrets as a part of security, applying the principles of least privilege and need-to-know. The military learned this a long time ago. In non-military environments and business environments, this concept is not as advanced as it should be.

There are two problems in dealing with security securely. One is passive and the other is active. The active problem is voluntary disclosure of secrets by trusted employees and experienced security staff. Information about security in computer environments is the most sensitive information in an organization. The controls are the keys to the kingdom. When the controls and lack of them are known to a potential enemy, risk of violation is greatly increased.

Voluntary disclosure is done in various ways such as at meetings and in conversations. It is alarming how much detailed information that technologist will tell strangers at a conference about their problems, vulnerabilities, the controls installed, how they work and so on. In World War II posters proclaimed "loose lips sink ships". In one encouraging counter-example, the first recommendation to a client was that they must maintain a confidentiality of their security activities. A low profile was important to avoid attack from malicious hackers by not revealing security information unless there was a sufficient need-to-know or benefit. Three weeks later, I called the client asking about progress in implementing our recommendations. The response was "I'm sorry we cannot discuss that with you. You are no longer in a confidential relationship with us." At least they implemented the first recommendation. I don't know about the rest of them, and I probably never will.

Among examples of problems is the reporting of losses to the authorities that poses a possible fundamental violation of security. Vulnerabilities, controls that may have been violated and the controls that may have worked become publicly revealed. Another area of great concern is response to mailed questionnaires. For example, one sent out by a company in England on resource access control software was very detailed. The questionnaire required the name of the company and address and asked such questions as specific product used, features used and not used, problems, and current vulnerabilities. Some recipients actually answered the questions, put their company name on it and returned it with no assurance of confidentiality, anonimity or assurance of integrity of the survey company. Telephone inquiries are equally dangerous. Unidentifiable voices call and ask details about security.

Many books on computer security recommend that security reviews should be done by a task force with someone from operations, another from the programming staff, and someone from systems programming combined with others. By following what these books advise violates the most fundamental concept of security. Somebody from computer operations is learning all about the vulnerabilities and the lack or presence of controls in the programming area. The programmer is learning about all the vulnerabilities in operations. This is not the way to maintain security in an organization. The task force can certainly be organized and the work carried out, but it must be done by dividing the group up so that the people involved in one area only deal with the security and vulnerabilities in that one area. They are not allowed to learn about vulnerabilities in other areas. That would be a basic breach of security.

Lack of controls of visitors and vendors who can pick up security information in sensitive areas is another problem. In many customer organizations these people have not signed confidentiality agreements. In one case I taught 17 Japanese businessmen in a seminar. I brought them to the USA, and by prior letter agreement I arranged for them to take tours to view the security of the computer centers in three banks. I was amazed that these 17 visitors from another country were shown every detail of all of the security. Of course, each of these people had two cameras and took pictures of everything. At the end of the tour, I asked them what the greatest common vulnerability was. They finally understood they were going back to their country with the detailed information of all the security of those three banking data centers.

Publications sent to computer users should not name the resource access control program being used. All they have to know is the limited amount of information of constraints and how they are to protect their data. Even revealing the name of the package is a violation of security and should not be done except where there is a benefit in doing so. Training programs and much information commonly revealed through terminals is another means of voluntarily giving information to a potential enemy.

The passive problem is involuntary revealing of security information. In this case the enemy actively obtains information by theft or observation. At one time, a computer security consultant in New York City had her hotel room robbed while she was out. She kept the complete set of detailed information about her client's security in a briefcase, and she dutifully kept it locked. The robbers seeing a locked briefcase, concluded there was something valuable in it; so they took it with them. She had to call her manager and, in tears, told him that the entire security of a large company had been compromised and that the information was no longer under her exclusive control. Two hours later, someone found the briefcase broken open in an alley next to the hotel, and it was returned to her. She called the office and said that everything was okay Of course, everything was not okay because it was unknown what had been done with that information while it was out of her control.

Espionage is another involuntary means of loss. A malicious hacker group recently used binoculars for what is euphemistically called shoulder surfing. They were looking through the windows of company offices, watching people key in passwords at terminals and then using that information to intrude on the company's computer system. Spoofing is another technique used by malicious hackers where they pose as trusted insiders by revealing knowledge of a small amount of technical information and convince victims that they should receive the rest of the information. They know the jargon and seek the details. This technique is also called social engineering and is another great vulnerability faced in business today.

Finally, the involuntary loss of exclusive custody is done by copying information about controls and taking security review reports identifying vulnerabilities that may be sitting on desks in unlocked offices. Malicious hackers engage in dumpster diving for obsolete reports thrown in waste baskets and emptied into waste containers behind buildings. These are the opportunities where an active enemy engages in seeking sensitive information.

A sensitivity test aids in identifying sensitive security information. (1) Is the information generally known? A fence around a building is obvious, and it is not harmful to reveal its presence. However, if detailed information about security is not generally known, it should not be freely given out. (2) Would the information give the enemy aid and comfort? What effect would information about the most serious vulnerability have if it were said to the worst enemy? Anything said at a conference must be assumed to be told to a criminal who is going to use it at the end of the conference.

If information passes the first two rules, then (3) is there a benefit received in return for revealing detailed security information to someone? That is, if information is revealed, will there be value in return? There are ways to exchange information in confidence on a beneficial basis to parties involved. (4) Can the source be anonymous? Surveys are often done anonymously; so it may be safe to respond to them. Finally, (5) can authorization be gained to disclose? Do not present a public talk or submit a report or paper on security without getting organizational approval. Make sure that informed consent is obtained to avoid taking the responsibility all by one's self.

Voluntary disclosure of sensitive information can be prevented. The methods may sound familiar because they are the safeguards recommended to all computer users but in a different context. Establish information policy and provide due notice of it, and make sure that people understand it. This applies especially to the people on the computer security staff. Promulgate a code of conduct. In some companies, it is difficult to accomplish this at large but can be done among security people on a limited scale. The code of conduct is the set of rules to maintain security of security. Rewards and penalties are necessary for a code of conduct. Without rewards and penalties, a code is only a set of guidelines.

Confidentiality agreements are needed. Many organizations require that consultants sign confidentiality agreements. If they don't require it, then the consultants should voluntarily submit a signed confidentiality statement to their clients. Avoid details in disclosures. Use of a resource access control package, passwords, and access attempt limits are reasonable to reveal, but the product name and the parameters specifying how many attempts are allowed should be secret. Hiring and termination of computer security specialists are more sensitive than for almost any other employee within the organization.

There is a social responsibility to report suspected crimes to the authorities, and if management does not do it, then security staff should be whistle blowers, put their jobs into jeopardy and report them. At the same time, we must weigh that action against the resulting violation of security by reporting suspected crimes to the authorities. The possible result may be a public relevation of vulnerabilities and the lack and presence of specific controls to the public. These may be conflicting principles and lead to difficult problems, but consider both sides of this issue before reporting losses. Make sure that legal counsel is involved in the decision.

Involuntary disclosure of information can also be prevented. One of the major efforts in computer security should be spoof-proofing of people in positions of trust by making them resistant to deception. Instruct equipment operators not to reveal information over the telephone without a procedure for positive identification of the caller. Spoof-proof people to avoid revealing details of their sensitive work in social settings.

Separation of duties in security work assignments is important as well as physical and logical protection from unauthorized access to information. In another area there are increasing numbers of security computer programs including risk analysis packages that can be run on mainframe computers shared with others. Consider using a micro- or minicomputer for this purpose isolated behind locked doors the way that military organizations do, because there is no adequately secure computer today for the high level of sensitive security information. Make sure that every copy of every document concerning security is numbered, logged, and controlled. Use shredders. I recommend that there be as many shredders as there are computer printers. Facetiously, one might like to see the paper coming out of the printer and going directly into the shredder. Few people need to know the name or location of the commercial company that provides remote data backup services. When traveling, don't put sensitive information into checked luggage, and lock it in the trunk of a car when driving and parking. Be careful when taking information away from protected facilities.

These are important and necessary precautions to maintain the security of security. The job that you save may be your own.

COMPUTER SECURITY
J.B. Grimson and H.-J. Kugler (Editors)
Elsevier Science Publishers B.V. (North-Holland)

HOW TO CONTROL MVS USER SUPERVISOR CALLS

R. Paans MSc[1] and Prof. dr. I.S. Herschberg[2]

Many computing centres install their own extensions to standard operating systems. These extensions, when processed in an authorized status, may seriously endanger system integrity. This paper, based on case studies over the past five years, spells out the risks run by computing centres under MVS installing home-grown user SuperVisor Calls. A set of design requirements is formulated with which these user SVCs must comply if they are to be considered secure. The latest developments in improving the security of some risky operations also are outlined.

1. Introduction

Controllability must be a primary aim of all EDP systems, implying at least reliability, efficiency and effectiveness of data-processing systems and implicitly also embracing the security of these systems. If the system is to process information reliably and efficiently, it will at least have to comply with some reasonable security requirements.

To the anger and sorrow of those entrusted with investigating th controllability, there are many lacunae in computer security or, to put it more strongly and more specifically, many centres suffer from permanent leaks in their security. To quote but one instance, Thomas [9] in his article on certifiability of systems, states that many systems are relatively reliable as delivered by the manufacturers but that the total security is badly damaged by local modifications, installed under the responsibility of local computing-centre management.

Following Thomas, we shall specialize in this article to systems operating under IBM's Multiple Virtual Storage (MVS) control program. This choice has not been dictated by the intrinsic insecurity of MVS, - on the contrary: MVS is rightly regarded to be one of the securest systems available for large commercial applications [7] - but by the pragmatic consideration that the vast majority of large computing centres *do* use MVS and are likely to continue to do so. Our choice is thus based on the relevance of MVS for the EDP world in which we happen to live.

The controllability of data-processing systems is a large area, of which we can hope to cover no more than a small part. The discussion will therefore be restricted to some aspects of non-standard SuperVisor Calls (the so called 'user SVCs') and an evaluation of these user SVCs such as should be done by anyone interested in their controllability. Moreover, we propose measures to counteract any security problem caused by the presence of user SVCs.

[1] Dunantstraat 1325, 2713 TR Zoetermeer, The Netherlands (during this research, Mr. Paans was with Delft University of Technology).

[2] Delft University of Technology, Department of Mathematics and Informatics, The Netherlands.

When discussing controllability and security of systems, one is confronted with a dilemma: indicating what has to be protected implies, however involuntarily, indicating the places in which a fraudulent person could well attack the system. On the one hand, one would like to keep the weak parts in the security secret in order to prevent that the less scrupulous will abuse this information for non-approved activities. On the other hand, it could well be put that those people already are aware of where to find the leaks, and that it is of major interest to inform those in charge of control about possible leaks in security. In the authors' view, the latter must prevail: in this paper, amongst others [1,2,6,7], they address EDP-auditors and computer controllers, primarily stressing a heightened awareness of the risks of user SVCs and, secondarily, aiming at eliminating these risks.

2. *What are user SVCs?*

In an MVS system, two classes of program are distinguished: the authorized and the unauthorized programs. In principle, *all* is allowed to authorized programs, whereas, equally in principle, unauthorized are allowed to do *nothing*. The first - authorized - class comprises the operating system, its subsystems (JES = Job Entry Subsystem, etc.), utilities for maintenance of disk space and others; the second class comprises almost exclusively user programs. Authorization, in the sense discussed, technically amounts to a relation (the intersection) among the specific authorities following:

supervisor mode. The program may use the privileged machine instructions (LPSW = Load Program Status Word, etc., which may influence the system's status or other users' status) as well as the problem-program mode instructions (the 'computing' instructions, etc.),
and/or

key<8. The program has authority to write in memory areas with a security key ('key in storage') less than 8, it being assumed that key=8 is the normal key for user areas and any lesser key refers to system areas,
and/or

APF-bit='1'. The Authorized Program Facility bit (APF-bit) indicates that a program has the authority to assign supervisor mode (which implies the use of all instructions) to itself and/or to obtain key<8 (which implies write authority for system areas).

By way of contrast, the absence of specific authority for programs in unauthorized state is technically determined by the union of the following conditions:

problem-program mode. The available instruction set is restricted to those *innocuous* instructions incapable, by their nature, of influencing the status of the system or of other users,
and

key=8. The program is only authorized to write in its own user areas and has, at the most, access to system areas for read only,
and

APF-bit='0'. The program is not allowed to switch to any other status.

Since many user programs, in fact a vast majority of them, will require the use of functions necessitating an authorized state, *ipso facto* denied to them, MVS provides a mechanism allowing user programs to request the system to execute these functions on their behalf. This mechanism consists, amongst others, of *SuperVisor Calls (SVCs)*. An SVC is, to put it crudely, a machine instruction capable of

```
user programs in unauthorized        || system programs in authorized
state, hence with:                   || state, hence with:
-  problem-program mode, AND         || -  supervisor mode, AND/OR
-  key=8, AND                        || -  key<8, AND/OR
-  APF-bit='0'                       || -  APF-bit='1'
-------------------------------------||--------------------------------

a user program wishes to perform     ||
I/O, it uses the instruction:        ||
  "SVC 0 (Execute Channel Program)"  ||
which, upon being executed, causes   ||
an SVC interrupt---------------------------> the SVC Interrupt Handler
                                     || obtains control in authorized
                                     || state; the Interrupt Handler
                                     || activates the EXCP routine
                                     || which, in the end, will
                                     || execute the privileged
                                     || instruction:
                                     ||   "SIO device  (Start I/O)"
                                     || effectively starting the I/O
                                     || for and on behalf of the user
               <-----------------------------
computer control is returned to the  ||
user in an unauthorized state        ||
-------------------------------------||--------------------------------
```

Figure 1. The authorization interface via an SVC: on request of an unauthorized user program, the system executes a function requiring authorization.

being executed by *any* program. A 1-byte code allows the caller to indicate the function requested. Execution results in an SVC interrupt, activating the SVC Interrupt Handler. This Handler, itself part of the control program, using authorized status, analyzes the caller's wishes and activates any system routines that might be necessary in order to execute the function called for. After completion of the operation, control is returned to the user program; it needs no comment that, when returning control, the user program is again in *un*authorized status.

A simple example may serve to clarify this mechanism: in Figure 1, a user program wishes access to a data set on disk. It is not, however, itself authorized to issue the privileged instruction Start I/O (SIO). Instead of SIO, one uses an SVC instruction with the 1-byte code zero (indicating the function EXCP = Execute Channel Program). Processing of this SVC activates the SVC Interrupt Handler, in turn activating the EXCP routine. The latter checks the user's request for any potential conflict in integrity and will, such conflicts being absent, in due time cause the SIO instruction to be executed on behalf of the user program calling it. This starts the I/O operation requested. After completion, control returns to the user program by intervention of the exit part of the SVC Interrupt Handler.

This mechanism provides a secure interface between unauthorized user programs on the one hand and the all-powerful system on the other hand. The 1-byte operand of the SVC instruction allows 256 codes to be specified for functions to be executed. As of this writing, codes 0 to 140 inclusive are used for standard SVCs supplied by IBM. SVCs in this range are completely secure to the best of our knowledge.

The range 200 to 255 inclusive is available for local functions implemented by the local system controller at his discretion. This allows the system controller to add his own routines to the system which, when installed, enjoy the same authorized status as those supplied by the manufacturer. These additional SVCs are termed, somewhat illogically, *user SVCs*. The terminology fails logically because it is not up to the user, but up to the staff controlling the computing centre to install these SVCs. A better terminology would be afforded by 'computing-centre SVCs', but in order not to increase the disarray in terminology, we shall continue to use the traditional appellation 'user SVC'

A slight amplification is in order on the subject of user SVCs: not all of them are developed purely locally, but many are supplied by software manufacturers as part of their packages. To quote but one example, IBM itself supplies (secure!) user SVCs for:
- System Log Display and Search Facility (SDSF),
- Information Management System (IMS),

and other packages.
It is characteristic of user SVCs that they are optional in the system, that they are specific to certain software packages, and that their code number (always in the 200 to 255 range) is not fixed but is determined locally by whoever is in control of the system.

In spite of this distinction, which is intrinsic to MVS, there is *no* distinction between standard SVCs and user SVCs. Both can be activated, quite legitimately, by an SVC instruction, simply by specifying its correct operand. This fact imposes a most exacting requirement on user SVCs: those installed under responsibility of computing-centre management should be *at least as secure* as the standard ones. It will be proved in the sequel that this is an imperative regularly infringed upon: user SVCs often constitutes an Achilles' heel to current systems.

3. A hacker's approach

In general, those in charge of evaluating the controllability of a system will work from the outside inwards. That is, they will start with an audit of *procedures* around the computer, work their way into whatever is stored in the computer's *peripheral* storage, possibly may inspect its *virtual* storage and so, in the long run, arrive at the SVCs and their implementation. The hacker, by way of contrast, usually works from the inside outwards [1,2,5]: he will attack the user SVCs by predilection in the first place and, having conquered those, will have easy access to the rest of virtual and peripheral memory, and will even be able to override any such procedural control as may have been installed. In the following, it is strongly urged that those responsible for controllability, say EDP-auditors, adopt the hackers' point of view [8]. It is argued that, in fact, they should 'think as a thief'.

Of course, a hacker will start by acquiring a rough knowledge of whatever is usual, procedurally, in a system. If he finds leaks in these procedures, these leaks will often provide him with a preliminary point of attack. At a deeper level, the hacker will also be interested in all local conventions, such as methods for identification of users, jobs, programs, data sets, structures of passwords, etc. Having obtained these, - which is an easy thing to do assuming that the hacker is a temporary or permanent user of his victim system - he will carefully probe the conventions, trying to break them while generating none or a minimal number of messages reporting attempts to violate security. The hacker is in favourable position because just a few messages will hardly impress most computing centres, which are swamped by the many thousands of messages passing the screens of the system controllers every hour. If, which is a rarity, all relevant information proves to be effectively guarded by those in control of the system, the hacker will concentrate on means which might be useful in disabling the security measures. It is evident that, at this stage, he will pry into the programs and constructs used by systems controllers and systems programmers in the execution of their duties, and which has often proved to afford almost unlimited possibilities to a hacker. If it should transpire that the computing centre has done its duty conscientiously, then the hacker will have to find other means in order to merit his title of hacker, or, as is more likely, he will have to give up his attempts altogether.

But let us assume that there are doubts about the conscientiousness of systems controllers and systems programmers, our hacker will then concentrate on the system's virtual storage including the SVC routines. In doing so, he will hardly pay any attention to standard SVCs because, in his opinion, what has proved to be secure against professional hackers during some twenty years (and this is how long the system and its predecessors have been in existence) is not likely to be easily penetrated by him. Even when he is gifted, it will require a substantial amount of time. Having removed these from the orbit of his intention, a hacker is all the more intent on investigating whatever has been added beyond the standard SVCs. As it happens, his investigation is as easy as it is usually fruitful: there is a generally accessible table (the SVCTABLE) in virtual memory containing the starting points of all SVC routines. Having obtained these, which he can do quite legitimately, it is a very easy matter to obtain these routines themselves on paper as a dump, or preferably, in disassembled form. If any user SVCs are present, the finding of leaks seems merely to depend on the puzzle-solving abilities of our hacker and, while persistence is a benefit and Lady Luck must not be altogether unfavourably disposed to him, with due persistence his efforts will be crowned with success in eight, or even nine, of ten computing centres that are exposed to his efforts.

Of course, in spite of the simplicity sketched here, the hacker is still confronted with the need to do a great deal of painstaking and time-requiring handiwork. His path, while clear, is far from smooth; but as we have indicated, in current installations the path may lead to the achievement of his aims: a complete mastery over the system and all it contains.

Those responsible for control have an equally arduous task ahead of them: they have to investigate the user SVCs, one by one, for potential leaks. While there is information available about those leaks (see Herschberg [1], Hoboken [2], Miller [5] and Paans [6,7]), and while it is true that such knowledge is generally available and documentation is accessible, few of those in charge of controllability are able to digest this information and realize the full impacts of such leaks. This being so, they are at a disadvantage relative to hackers, who are often fully familiar with the system and *have* access to what is to them completely readable documentation.

Our conclusions can be summarized in two points:

1. user SVCs and their penetrability are hard to evaluate for those in charge of system control;

2. it is equally hard for a system controller to hide these shortcomings from any would-be hacker.

4. User SVCs examined

We do not claim exhaustiveness in our analysis in the following six design requirements for user SVCs. Doubtlessly, it is possible to commit sins not to be found in the catalogue of malpractices to be avoided as given in the next subsections. However, the requirements listed below are realistic and transgressions against them have been found in actual systems currently installed in major installations, not, as one might believe in antiquity, but in the year 1984.

Design requirement 1. A user SVC may *never* provide the MODESET function.

Rationale. A user program being executed in problem-program mode does not have at its disposal a machine instruction allowing it to switch to supervisor mode, nor does it have an instruction permitting it to change the key for storage access from its usual value key=8 to a lower value. All instructions capable of causing such changes are contained in the set of privileged instructions not available, by a definition enforced by the hardware, to user programs.

In order to allow status changes for software in problem-program mode, MVS implements the MODESET SVC. It being an SVC makes it available to *any* program. When granted, execution of the SVC implies that the caller is given a new status, say supervisor mode and/or key=0. Internal checking within the MODESET-SVC routine makes sure that a user will not obtain the change of status unless he is authorized to do so. The criteria applied during this check are: the caller must be either in supervisor mode and/or key<8 and/or APF-bit='1'. If at least one of these criteria is met, the status change is granted, otherwise - and this will be the case for all illegal requests - the caller's program is terminated abnormally, that is, in effect, the caller is aborted.

The MODESET SVC is completely secure. The criteria applied are sufficient, and their verification can be guaranteed to be correct. Therefore, it is only authorized software that can use this SVC without the certainty of abortion. However, in the view of some systems programmers, the criteria applied are far too strict. Some of their shortcut ad-hoc constructs do not meet the criteria, but, unfortunately, still need the MODESET function in order to operate at all.

Some computing centres, unfortunately, have been misled into implementing a user SVC having the *functions* of the MODESET SVC but omitting to apply any checking at all [6]. The consequences are not hard to guess: not only are the ad-hoc constructs of the systems programmers allowed to use the MODESET function by issuing that user SVC, but this action has also, by implication and in practice, made this function available to *any and all* user programs. Such a user-SVC routine, often comprising no more than some ten machine instructions, creates a wide thoroughfare for computer fraud in all its guises.

Some forms of abuse of the MODESET-SVC routine are even subtler. In explanation: it is not even necessary for a user SVC to create its own code; it is sufficient to refer to some code already installed, in fact making the user SVC coincide, but for details, with a standard SVC. As an example, having come to light only a couple of years ago in a defense-related installation, we cite that a user had applied a modification in the SVCTABLE containing the starting points of the SVC routines. An entry, until then unused, in this table was suddenly found to contain the address of the MODESET-SVC routine, with a flag bit in the entry indicating that the MODESET-SVC routine should suppress its checking. This allowed the hacker 'in charge' to execute his fraudulent and system-modifying software in supervisor mode and with key=0, a hacker's dream of ultimate achievement. Systems programmers later found that they had been operating fully three months with a modified system without anyone in charge aware of the subversion.

Design requirement 2. A user SVC may not pass control to insecure routines or, equivalently, to any routines of uncertain security.

Rationale. An SVC-routine, once activated, is always processed in authorized status, viz. in supervisor mode and with key=0. Such a routine is automatically regarded as part of the control program. Jumps (the infamous GOTOs) to routines which are potentially insecure should be avoided at any price since the latter routines should only be processed in problem-program mode and with key=8.

This requirement too is often violated in practice by the nefarious activities of systems programmers, installing their own ad-hoc constructs which, while they do not meet security requirements, still are in need of supervisor mode and/or key=0. To quote yet another practical case, it has turned out that in a major commercial computing centre all systems had been provided for many years with a user-SVC routine consisting of a single instruction, reading: 'go to the address contained in register 1'. (The user calling any SVC may pass the address of a parameter list by inserting it into register 1.) The irresponsible systems programmer used this particular register to pass the address of his own ad-hoc construct instead of the address of a parameter list, effectively forcing the user SVC to pass control to the ad-hoc construct in supervisor mode and with key=0. It is not doubted here that the systems programmer in question was inspired by noble intentions when installing this particular user-SVC routine. The fact remains that he, at the same time, created a wide breach in the security to any and all callers, including hackers, because each SVC installed is available to any and all programs.

It is food for pessimistic thought that the existence of such a user SVC first came to light to one of the authors over lunch in a staff canteen. The revelation was implicit in one of the application programmers bragging about the unlimited possibilities for his own ad-hoc constructs provided to him by accidentally finding such a user SVC present in the system.

Design requirement 3. A user SVC should modify areas specified by its caller if and only if that caller has write authority for the areas specified.

Rationale. It may occur, in a systems programmer's approach, that his primary aim is not so much to obtain a new status for his own software, but that he wants merely to modify some memory areas rightfully belonging to the system. Such a desire, of course, runs contrary to the MVS security philosophy. Still, systems programmers are often tempted to introduce a so called *ZAP*-facility as a user SVC justifying it by the statement: 'it saves a great deal of programming effort in not being constrained by the security rules'.

In a major commercial computing centre, a user SVC has been found which had only one purpose, viz. to copy a number of bytes regardless of the security keys associated with source and destination areas. Before issuing this SVC, a caller has to build a list consisting of three fields: the address of the data to be copied, the address of the data to be overwritten, and the number of bytes to be copied. This user SVC was already in use for many years. It supported command processors requiring an authorized status but ran, in the foreground, under the *un*authorized Interactive System Productivity Facility (ISPF).

While installed with noble intentions, this user SVC introduces possibilities to abuse which are as limitless as they are trivial. To quote but one example, in many installations the passwords of all *active* users are available in 'fetch-protected' memory areas. A user SVC as described here allows these passwords to be copied by a hacker into his own user area and to be read there. Another, even more dangerous, possibility is that any and all user programs may abuse this user SVC to write into system areas in virtual memory, with results which are easier to contemplate with horror than to list exhaustively.

Design requirement 4. When returning any data in an area specified by a user, say in a parameter list, the user SVC should check whether the caller has write authority for the area about to be changed.

Rationale. Our fourth requirement, in fact, is nothing but a refinement of the third one. Whereas some user SVCs do not intentionally provide a true capability to move data regardless of security keys (such as is done by the 'ZAP'-SVCs), there may be some sloppiness in the writing of data into areas specified by the caller.

As a case in point, a disturbing error came to light two years ago in a user SVC that was part and parcel of a DB/DC system. It had the particular property that when the caller (deliberately) specified erroneous information in its parameter list and the address of that list was passed to the user SVC, the user-SVC routine would return a byte with the error code X'ØF' to an address specified in that parameter list. The user-SVC routine, however, failed to check whether that single byte, which it would modify, was within an area the user was *entitled* to modify. A hacker, discovering this manifestation of sloppiness by disassembling the routine, had the bright idea that he might well specify part of an instruction to the user SVC in order for it to return that particular byte (X'ØF') there. After deliberately offering erroneous information to the user SVC, the results were as expected by the hacker: the user SVC correctly determined that the information offered was incorrect and concluded that it had to write the error code X'ØF' at the address specified. By malicious intention, the hacker had specified an instruction of the access-control part of the operating system as destination for the error code. The result was disabling an important part of the access-control mechanism by converting a branch instruction into a null instruction.

Design requirement 5. A user SVC should never change the Authorized Program Facility bit (APF-bit) so as to allow an unauthorized caller to obtain an authorized state.

Rationale. It will be clear, after the preceding, that allowing a switch from an unauthorized status to an authorized status constitutes a severe threat to a system's integrity.

The background to this requirement is that occasionally it is necessary interactively to invoke load modules requiring authorization. For instance, while running the *un*authorized package Interactive System Productivity Facility (ISPF) in the foreground, with its full-screen editor and data-management support, this program provides the facility to compress a disk-resident library. In order to achieve this operation, a standard MVS utility - IEBCOPY - is invoked, which latter requires authorization because it uses a system area in virtual storage. According to MVS security rules, it is not permissible for an unauthorized program to invoke an authorized program. Unfortunately, in ISPF's salad days, many systems programmers had implemented a user SVC in order to bridge the authorization gap between ISPF and IEBCOPY. In order to achieve the compress operation in the foreground, one has to activate this user SVC which sets the APF-bit to '1' indicating authorization, thereafter to load and activate IEBCOPY in order to perform the compress operation in an authorized state, and then to activate the user SVC again which restores the original value of the APF-bit (always 'Ø', indicating the absence of authorization).

Hackers in many installations have used this user SVC and others in the same class by directly or indirectly invoking such an SVC from within user programs. In this way, a hacker can obtain the status APF-bit='1'. Another possibility of abuse is to apply multi-tasking or asynchronous error-recovery routines to run one's own malicious routines simultaneously with IEBCOPY. The impact of the APF-bit is address-space wide, hence all tasks, legitimately or illegitimately running in the same address space, are then allowed to change their status by issuing the MODESET SVC.

Design requirement 6. A user-SVC routine invoking load modules should only select those of warranted security.

Rationale. If a user-SVC routine invokes load modules found in virtual storage, such load modules may have been maliciously modified or loaded from a hacker's personalized libraries. Also, if a user-SVC routine invokes modules found in non-trusted libraries specified by the caller, such load modules cannot be relied upon. The use of such non-trusted load modules opens the way to abuses since a check of their security is no longer possible. Should it happen that a user SVC requires disk-resident load modules, such modules must be explicitly loaded within that user-SVC routine from a library the integrity of which is beyond doubt.

When trying to find a solution to the problem of compressing libraries in the foreground (see the rationale to requirement 5), many ingenious routines have been implemented. In practice, most of the user SVCs designed to bridge the authorization gap between ISPF and IEBCOPY, however ingenious, had one characteristic in common: they proved easy prey for hackers. This failure was primarily caused by an illicit transition in authorization, contrary to MVS security rules.

One of the mechanisms implemented to bridge the gap consisted of a user SVC which eliminated the danger of multi-tasking by blocking it and also rendered it impossible to invoke any asynchronous error-recovery routines. Only then was the APF-bit set to '1' and IEBCOPY was loaded thereafter. However, hackers discovered that the caller could also pre-load IEBCOPY and then could activate the user SVC, not without having extended IEBCOPY with his own hacking routine. The net result was that the user-SVC routine used the fraudulent pre-loaded copy of IEBCOPY and was persuaded to activate the hacking routine; this provides a classical example of a Trojan horse, though effective almost instantaneously.

5. Towards more secure solutions

Strict application of the design requirements listed above and of the general MVS security rules implies that one may obtain a secure system, but at the price of withholding certain functions such as an interactive compress of disk-resident libraries. Yet, interactive compress is a general computing-centre requirement because, by means of ad-hoc constructs, the majority of centres *do* now provide this service to their users. Hence, the wishes to have this facility implemented securely seem to be quite legitimate. Currently, IBM supplies two solutions: one applicable to all extant installations which may be seen as a temporary solution for the problems sketched, and the second to be considered as definitive but only applying to those having the extended architecture version of MVS (MVS/XA) installed.

The first solution is embodied in the user SVC delivered by IBM with version 2 of the Interactive System Productivity Facility (ISPF-2) but which is also applicable to its predecessors: SPF, ISPF and ISPF-1 [3]. This new user-SVC routine takes the precaution of causing all other tasks and asynchronous routines to quiesce before setting the APF-bit to '1'. It is only afterwards that IEBCOPY is loaded; moreover, this utility is loaded explicitly and from a trusted library. Though this user SVC violates our fifth design requirement, no hacker has been found able, as far as is known, to abuse this SVC. Unfortunately, this temporary solution conforms to Murphy's Law in that it may cause some problems due to inhibiting *all* error recovery, however innocuous, in its attempt to hobble all Trojan horses. As a consequence, in rare cases, error recovery during a compress operation may fail. Locally, we have developed an interface routine between ISPF and the ISPF-2 user SVC which is likely to eliminate the need for error recovery.

Even so, and in spite of being relatively simple, this locally developed interface constitutes a complicating factor in an already complex situation. Even with our extension, the ISPF-2 user SVC must be seen as a stopgap measure only.

A definitive solution is provided by the interactive Time Sharing Option extensions (TSO/E-XA) of MVS/XA, which affords a secure authorization interface [4]. The monitor program in charge of communication with the user and controlling the user software proved to be the weak link during authorization changes under the previous versions of TSO. With TSO/E-XA, the new policy has been introduced that whenever the need of a transition in authorization becomes apparent, the entire monitor program with all the user software working under it is temporarily deactivated. Thereafter, a second monitor program is built in a secure area. Should a compress operation be necessary, this second, trusted monitor explicitly loads IEBCOPY from a trusted library and provides all necessary error-recovery routines itself which are then the only ones to be active. The prior monitor program and the user software is re-activated only after completion of the authorized operation under control of the second monitor.

This authorization interface of TSO/E-XA also is available to all other unauthorized interactive programs requiring the activation of trusted, authorized routines. Hence, this interface avoids the need of implementing any user SVCs to bridge an authorization gap in the foreground.

The solution outlined here prevents any and all interaction between unauthorized user programs and authorization-requiring programs such as IEBCOPY, as we have pointed out, and makes all ad-hoc constructs bridging the authorization gap obsolete. In this solution, all sensitive operations are dissociated fully from the control of any user programs. This allows TSO/E-XA to perform the operation requested in a completely secure manner.

6. Conclusions

In summary, we have seen that the controllability of systems is often endangered, in the present state of the art and in the vast majority of installations, by ad-hoc constructs which take the form of so called user SVCs. The latter term is, we have seen, a misnomer since it only embraces SVCs that are installed by systems programmers under responsibility of computing-centre management. These user SVCs prove to be a rich hunting ground for the hacker: all those maintaining or certifying the controllability of systems are therefore required to give due attention to the traps lurking in them and to the possibility of exploiting these user SVCs for introducing Trojan horses or similar sources of mischief. It will well bear repeating that some 80% to 90% of installations exhibit this type of vulnerability, often without anybody in charge being aware of it. Examples reveal that many breaches in system security caused by user SVCs may go unnoticed for any length of time.

The problem addressed is far from trivial. The operational requirement of interactive compression of disk-resident libraries, implying activation of the authorized utility IEBCOPY, presents one example of a case in which an essentially insecure construction appeared to be necessary in order to provide the service at all. At a lower level, ad-hoc constructs applied, possibly with the best of intentions, by systems programmers provide many cases in the vast majority of installations. Of course, progress is being made in this field. The problem of interactive compress is now solved, at least in a temporary fashion as provided by the user SVC of ISPF-2 [3]; a permanent solution is delivered by TSO/E-XA available for MVS/XA systems [4].

Our recommendations include solving the interactive-compress problem by imposing, as soon as possible, at least the temporary solution offered. Furthermore, and more pressingly, we recommend investigating all ad-hoc constructs taking the form of user SVCs as to their penetrability.

Many a reader will be surprised at what is extant in his system. It must be stressed that the particular risk of a user SVC lies in the fact that *any and all* user programs may invoke them. If these constructs do take the form of a user SVC, they introduce exposure possibilities to any application program. Doing so, they eliminate the need for the unauthorized to penetrate in fancy form and easily spotted ways. All he has to do, while insecure SVCs remain installed, is simply to be aware of these SVCs and call them, quite legitimately, a fact which is extremely hard to spot since they are in no way distinguishable from quite legitimate SVC calls, hundreds or thousands of which are contained in any application program.

In addition, it has to be stressed that controlling information security is as important as the security tools themselves. Any access-control system only works effectively when applied in a well-controlled environment. In this context, a computing centre also has to consider the verification of the security aspects of user SVCs to be part of its standard security policy. This will result in a situation where a computing-centre manager may say: "Yes, we have user SVCs and we are still secure".

References

1 Herschberg, I S, and R Paans, The programmer's threat: cases and causes, in "Computer security: a global challenge" Proceedings of IFIP/Sec'84 Conference, J H Finch and E G Dougall (eds) (Sept 10-12, 1984) Toronto, ISBN 0-444-87618-9 North-Holland Publ, pp 77-90

2 Hoboken, W R C, The burglar's viewpoint, in "Computers & Security", Vol 3 No 4 (1984) pp 295-302

3 IBM, Interactive System Productivity Facility version 2, installation and customization, Program products 5665-317 and 5665-319, manual SC34-2143 (1984)

4 IBM, TSO Extensions (TSO/E) general information manual, Program product 5665-285, manual GC28-1061 (1984), p 16

5 Miller, J H, Characteristics of the computer environment that provide opportunities for crime, in "Computer security: a global challenge", see [1], pp 103-108

6 Paans, R, and A H J Bonnes, Surreptitious security violations in the MVS operating system, in "Computers & Security", Vol 2 No 2 (1983) pp 144-152

7 Paans, R, and I S Herschberg, A topology for secure MVS systems, in "Computer security: a global challenge", see [1], pp 137-147

8 Parker, D B, Human factor controls for information security, in "Security, IFIP/Sec'83" Proceedings of IFIP/Sec'83 Conference, V Fak (ed) (May 16-19, 1983) Stockholm, ISBN 0-444-86669-8 North-Holland Publ, pp 247-252

9 Thomas, R A C, and R Paans, Software certificering: utopie of werkelijkheid?, (in Dutch) in "Certificering van software", R Paans and M A Bongers (eds), ISBN 90-70621-15-0 (1984), available through the Dutch Association of Informatics (NGI) Amsterdam, pp 55-68

COMPUTER SECURITY
J.B. Grimson and H.-J. Kugler (Editors)
Elsevier Science Publishers B.V. (North-Holland)
IFIP, 1985

CONCEPTS OF PROTECTION IN THE IFIP WG 2.7 REFERENCE MODEL FOR COMMAND AND RESPONSE LANGUAGES

Hans-Jürgen Kugler

Department of Computer Science
University of Dublin, Trinity College
Dublin, Ireland

A generalised model for protection in command and response languages for object-oriented systems as incorporated in the IFIP WG 2.7 Reference Model is described. This paper discusses what protection aspects have been been included in the reference model without implicating decisions about the implementation of naming schemes and the representation of objects.

The general protection scheme relies on the typing structure as maintained by the command language system. Therefore the protection scheme can easily be integrated into specialised tailored user interfaces.

The objects and operations basic to the protection mechanism are discussed and it is described, what decisions a command language designer would have to make to derive a particular access control scheme from the model.

INTRODUCTION

Working Group 2.7 of the International Federation for Information Processing is concerned with issues related to Operating System Interfaces in general. It has so far concentrated on interfaces which take the form of Command and Response Languages and has developed a Reference Model for Command and Response Languages. This paper is only intended as an overview of the protection related aspects of the reference model. A more formal treatment can be found in [1], where the reference model is described in an object-oriented extension of the Vienna Development Method [2].

The IFIP WG 2.7 reference model defines a framework which can be used to develop command and response languages. To this effect it provides the designer of a specific command and response language with a "tool-kit". The reference model is intended to help to improve the quality and, where desirable, the conceptual uniformity of command and response languages by enabling the designer to express the semantics of the commands of a particular command and response language in terms of certain fundamental operations, which are precisely specified and are independent of the details of a particular language and specification.

With respect to protection the reference model similarly provides a framework only. This can be used by the designer of a specific command and response language to achieve consistency among various protection mechanisms which are to be implemented. The reference model indicates to the designer where a particular policy or implementation decision has to be made.

Overview of the Reference Model

A command and response language system is modelled as an object, which offers its users a variety of services which can be invoked by commands. Commands are accepted as input by the system and can cause the information stored by the system to be updated, or they can generate output in form of responses. These responses may provide information retrieved, or give other indications as to the state of the system.

The kind of information that can be stored by a system, and the transformations the user can invoke via commands depend directly on the kind of system commanded and the application in question. There are several concepts in command elaboration and response generation, however, which are common to all command and response languages.

The commands and responses must externally be represented in a form comprehensible to the (human) user, and internal to the system they must be unambiguously mapped to some of the fundamental operations. The part of the system transferring the commands in and the responses out is called the transmitter. The translation service tailored to the different users' specific needs is provided by the customiser. In the process of customisation the services of a helper may be needed to give advice to the user how to complete the instructions or understand the responses. The helper object is also directly available to the user to query the facilities provided by the system and its current state.

The meaning of the commands and the responses to be generated are determined on the basis of the context in which the command is issued or the response generated. The context is made up of a sequence of elementary contexts, each of which identifies a certain part of the object world as being accessible.

Each elementary context has a name manager and a protector associated with it. These identify objects named in commands and check the legality of the accesses requested. Object identification, sometimes also called name resolution, produces an object reference, which uniquely identifies an object in the bonded store, which models the universe of objects accessible from within the command and response language and maps object references to objects. Objects are entered into and retrieved from the Bonded Store by means of get and put operations. The processing of commands and responses is controlled by a CRLProcessor object.

CONCEPTS OF PROTECTION

Protection considerations are included in the reference model at various points, so that the designer can tailor the level of protection to the exact needs of the environment in which the command and response language is to be used.

Protection enables a user to shield own objects from accidentally being damaged, as well as protecting them from malicious damage by other users in the case of sharing.

Authentication

Known user objects model all information about a notional user of the system, including individual (human) users, inanimate user agents, and also relationships between users, such as user groups and projects, hierarchies etc. This information is persistent and includes information necessary to construct a suitable context for that known user. It should be noted that the (human) user, or user agent, is outside the command and response language system. This means that, even if the system can be called secure <1> in the sense of [3], the reliability of its protection will wholly depend on the degree of certainty with which the association between actual user and know user object can be established as being the intended one. The process of establishing and attempting to validate this association is called *authentication*. To authenticate an (actual) user who requires access to the command and response language system the *user manager* object needs to identify the user to find an appropriate known user object, and then verify that this is indeed the correct known user object for the actual user.

The known user objects need to specify user identification and user verification criteria. A user profile in the known user object contains information about the context to be established upon successful completion of authentication. More elaborate systems can require the user's history of connection to the system and a user pass (e.g. password, magnetic card, voice, image, thumbprint) to be used as well.

Depending on the protection requirements placed on the system authentication can be performed only once when access to the system is required first, on a timed continuous basis, or before permitting the execution of (certain selected) commands.

Object Access

After authentication users are permitted to issue commands and manipulate objects in accordance with their view of the system, as defined by the customiser and the object types tailored for their needs. The storage of those objects which can be manipulated by the users is modelled by a *store* object, which is an abstraction of the object storage of the underlying system, for example the filestore of an operating system, or the object management system of a programming environment. The store is defined as a mapping from object references to objects. The (unique) object references act as the handles required by the get and put operations for retrieval and storage.

If desired for a particular command language, the objects in the store could be made directly available to the CRLProcessor once the user has been authenticated. The level of protection in such a system would be extremely coarse, however. In the reference model the store is therefore bonded by not permitting the CRLProcessor to invoke operations on the store directly. If objects are to be retrieved or stored, the CRLProcessor needs to go through two steps, which in addition to customisation will check whether the required access is permitted :

(i) User chosen names must be mapped to object references.

(ii) The legality of the required access for the object identified by the object reference needs to be checked.

The first step is object identification and the second an extended form of access control.

The CRLProcessor elaborates commands in a context, which defines visibility and access information by the name manager and the protector objects contained in the elementary contexts forming the current context. Only the protector can invoke the get and put operations on the bonded store, which is thereby shielded from the user and the CRLProcessor.

Command Checking

A command object as derived by customisation consists of a sequence of Names, the first of which we shall assume to identify the operation requested. The remaining ones are assumed to identify the operands to that operation:

```
OperationName  OperandName1
               OperandName2
               ...
               OperandNamen
```

Note that all the operands and even the operation itself are objects to be manipulated through the command language. They are protected by potential visibility restrictions and protection, and can not directly be retrieved from the bonded store. The exact meaning of the command requested can be described as "execute the operation object denoted by 'OperationName' using the objects denoted by 'OperandName1' to 'OperandNamen' as operands". The checking of the command will now include all or some of the following:

(1) Check whether 'OperationName' denotes an object of the command language system which may be executed by this user.

(2) For each 'OperandNamei' check whether it denotes an object which this user may pass to the operation object derived under (1), at the specified parameter position.

Note the similarity of the checks indicated under (1) and (2). If we view "execute" as an operation that may be performed on an operation objects, then (1) is simply a special case of (2). We do, however, have to give "perform" a special meaning within the model, because otherwise the checking of whether "perform" should be possible on "execute" leads to an infinite regression.

Object Identification

Objects are identified by performing the ResolveName operation on a given name manager object. ResolveName takes a name and returns the appropriate object reference. Names can be structured and this is reflected by a directory structure accessible to the name manager, which maps components of names to directories or object references. Several such directory structures can be combined into a name manager, thus allowing name resolution to involve dynamic search lists. Within an elementary context only those objects can be accessed, which are referenced from within the name manager's directory structure.

The context consists of several elementary contexts, which can be used to structure the universe of objects in various views, which may even overlap. By narrowing and widening the context, and thus the number of objects which can be accessed, objects can be protected from being accessed altogether. For many command and response language applications this may actually be sufficient, since the context can be controlled down to individual command level <2>.

ACCESS CONTROL

Access control mechanisms allow dynamic control of what operations are permitted on what objects by evaluating protection information associated with object references. This evaluation takes place when the CRLProcessor invokes the access operation on the protector in the current context.

The protector consists of a set of protection domains, of which one is always designated as the current one. A protection domain is a mapping from object references to protection objects, which contain protection information about the particular object referenced. To facilitate the command language designer to develop coarser as well as finer access control schemes, the protection objects contain two kinds of information :

- o the type of the object referenced, and
- o a set of permissions.

Object Types

The objects the command and response language user can manipulate are divided into different classes called (CRL) types. The type of an object defines the operations which may be performed on an object of that type. Note that type abstraction, especially in the customiser, can be used to provide different users with views of the system which correspond to their actual needs <3>. This tailoring facility forms another aspect of of protection, for instance, by allowing sensitive information to be hidden. Tailoring aspects are discussed in more detail elsewhere (see also [6] and [7]).

Command languages are usually not statically typed and the type of an object (the view the user has of it) may actually change from context to context. Therefore type checking needs to be a dynamic operation performed at command elaboration. To accomplish this the protector uses the type information in the protection objects, which, by means of the current protection domain, are associated with the object references denoting the actual objects forming the command. The object reference identified by the first name in the original command must denote an object of an operation type, i.e. a type which includes execute among its operations. The execute operation requires an operation object as parameter. Similarly other operations must specify for all operands they require the type these operands must have.

The protector checks that all operands have an appropriate type to be allowed to be passed, at the position given, to that operation, which was denoted by the object reference identified by the operation name.

Access Rights

Access rights provide a finer grain of controlling the application of operations. Types simply define what operations are allowed in principle. Access rights control the actual subset of the operation which are currently allowed. Each type defines a set of tokens called principle access rights. In addition to specifying for each parameter which type the operand must have, the operation also specifies a set of access rights or tokens which must be possessed by the actual operands (see also [9] and [10]). For example, an operation implementing an 'Append' command on files could be specifies as :

```
proc Append ( FirstFile  : type FILE rights { MakeFront },
              LastFile   : type FILE rights { MakeBack },
              Result     : type FILE rights { OverWrite } )
```

where 'MakeFront', 'MakeBack' and 'OverWrite' are among the principal access rights of type FILE. A command denoting the invocation

```
Append ( bibliography, selfreference, trash )
```

would only be allowed - assuming correct typing, if 'bibliography' identified an object reference which held as part of its protection at least the access right 'MakeFront', 'selfreference' held at least 'MakeBack' and 'trash' held 'OverWrite'. Note that all these objects may have the conventional rights for reading from and writing to, which on its own would not be sufficient to properly control the execution of 'Append'.

Allow and Disallow operations on protection domains include or remove rights associated with a given object reference. Since the protector includes a set of protection domains, a number of different protection levels for various modes of operations can be constructed by the user. Switching the current protection domain can thus change the level of protection.

Permissions

Access rights unconditionally allow certain operations to be performed on objects. Sometimes it is required, however, to increase security by enabling some rights only when certain conditions are fulfilled. For example, rather than associating the right 'DoPayroll' with a database of employees, one might want to specify

```
employees : type        Database
            permissions { if LastFridayInMonth and
                              LaterThan( 18:00 )
                          then { DoPayroll }
                          else {}
                          end if,
                          ...
                        }.
```

The sole permission in the set associated with the employee database in this case allows 'DoPayroll' only if the specified context conditions are fulfilled at the time access is required. Permissions produce a set of access rights when they are evaluated by the protector (in current or some context specified otherwise). Permissions are a generalisation of access rights : each access right AR can be represented by the permission

```
if true then { AR } end if.
```

The protection objects associated with object references in the protection domains therefore contain a set of permissions, rather than a set of access rights.

Similarly the access control information associated with the parameter descriptions in the operations is generalised to a set of permissions.

When checking the legality of an invocation the protector evaluates each permission in the set of permissions which are in the protection currently associated with the object reference denoting the operand. Each permission evaluation returns a set of access rights (possibly empty). Let the union of the resulting sets of access rights be called 'GivenRights'.

The protector also evaluates all the permissions given in the operation description as required for an operand at this position. Let the union of the resulting sets of access rights be called 'RequiredRights'.

An operation invocation is considered <u>legal</u> only if the right to execute is contained in the 'GivenRights' of the operation, and for each operand 'GivenRights' is a superset of the corresponding 'RequiredRights'.

The command language designer can choose different schemes of conditions and their evaluation. By taking user and usage history into account in the permission conditions certain forms of information flow controls [3], e.g. security classes [11], can also be incorporated into the protection scheme, as well as user passes at object level, for instance.

SHARING AND ACCESS CONTROL

So far protection has been discussed only in connection with the execution of a command in a single user's context, i.e. protection as a means of avoiding accidental damage of objects. The bonded store is, however, meant to model the storage of the complete system. In the case of a multi-user system some users may see a certain subset of the objects stored, other users another. There may not even be users who see all of the objects, but many of these views of the object world will overlap - the sets of objects seen will not be disjoint. Sharing is absolutely essential for a multi-user system and will as a minimum include the underlying system software (and hardware).

In the command and response language reference model this is easily expressed by generalising the overlapping of object worlds which can already occur between different name managers for a single user. Different users may have different name managers in their respective contexts. The directory structures controlled by the name managers of different users may, however, contain entries referring to common object references, although in general these would have different names associated with them. As in the single user case, visibility of objects constitutes the first level of protection : only objects which can be seen can potentially be accessed.

A single user may have different protection information associated with the same object reference in different protection domains. In the same way different users will in general have different protection information associated with a shared object reference.

For each object there must be somebody who is "in charge" of it (or is being charged for it), i.e. there must be something like an owner. In the reference model this concept is called a registered holder. The registered holder is a known user object, which can represent an individual, a group, project or even another system in a loosely coupled network, for instance. The registered holder controls the accesses permitted to other users (the sharers) of the same object identified by a commonly know object reference. Initially the registered holder of an object is the known user object causing the creation of the object (and its subsequent storing in the bonded store).

The registered holder U of an object named N can use the Grant operation to allow user V certain permissions P on N by

    Grant (N, P, V) <4>.

Being the registered holder, U is in principle allowed to grant permissions, and the effect would be an inclusion of the appropriate protection information, together with the object reference which N identifies in U's current context, in a specific protection domain of V's, called the home protection domain. Although U can grant access in principle, V may not like this pollution the current context by foreign objects. Therefore the actual command language to be designed must allow for a protocol between U and V or it must allow V to state explicitly from whom shared objects will be accepted (especially since there may be charges involved).

Known user U might want to allow V to grant some or all received accesses to some other known user W. To accomplish this the type access right has a generic right RightToGrant, which is modelled a an operation which can be applied to a principal access right. If V receives as part of permission P the access right 'RightToGrant(AR)', then V can grant AR to W. In a specific language design this may actually be generalised to including information about a set of known users the access may be granted to.

Besides the 'RightToGrant' there is another special access right operation, called Transfer. 'Transfer(AR)' has the same effect as granting AR and the right to grant AR to all others, plus causing the removal of any AR right from the issuers context for the object reference under consideration. Granting can be done often, transferring only once. Those known users, who hold transfer rights for an object, are its registered holders. One can limit this to one registered holder by permitting only a complete rights transfer for an object at the same time.

CONCLUSION

The reference model for command and response languages is intended to offer the designer of a specific user interface a variety of options to achieve the desired degree of protection. For many command languages the protection mechanisms included may be too elaborate and the designer can leave out various parameters and options without fear for the overall consistency of the system.

Authentication and Protection

The object-oriented approach enables us to treat the the command and response language system itself as an object. Therefore one could have suggested to apply the same access control concepts to the overall system rather than introducing the special notion of authentication. The mechanisms of authentication are, as a matter of fact, expressible using the concept of protection domains and permissions. However, the protector inside the system has to rely fully in the integrity of the known user objects. To some degree this can actually be achieved, since known users are objects implemented and managed within the system, and therefore (reasonably) controllable.

Authentication is the link to the real world, it tries to validate the association of an actual user, a subject of the real world not under system control, to an object (the known user), which is under system control. Even if the workings of the protection system could be verified to be totally secure, the potential threat from the insecurity of the association of actual to known user would still exist.

In many systems it will therefore be necessary to include an authentication mechanism which is more elaborate than internal access control. The reference model retains authentication and protection of object access as two different concepts in order to emphasize this problem.

Object References

The concept of object references was not introduced in the reference model to recommend pointer-like implementations. It is a concept which links together visibility control, access control and object storage in such a way, that these parts are modular; thus emphasizing the tool-box aspect of the reference model. The get operation on the bonded store, once allowed, would the decrypt this information.

Object references could also be used to include a passive component into this otherwise active protection system. Rather than acting as mere handles for objects, the object references could represent an encrypted form of the decrypted form of the information stored in the object in denotes.

Acknowledgements

I am greatly indebted to all members of IFIP WG 2.7 for the many and prolific discussions during the development of the reference model. Special mention is due to David Beech, Christian Gram and Claus Unger for their comments on the many revisions of the protection concepts.

<1> A system is called secure, if all states which can be reached by applying commands are authorised, i.e. the issuer of the commands producing a state must have the rights to do so, if the state reached is to be called authorised. Ideally security should be a verifyable property of a system (see also [4] and [5]).

<2> Note that restricting the context for a command may in the extreme make only one operation and one object as operand available. In this case a very fine granularity of access control can already be achieved. It does seem, however, more natural to introduce access control as a separate concept which is available to the designer.

<3> Types in command and response languages are usually not static as the are in programming languages. They may evolve, for instance by adding new operations. To facilitate this more dynamic aspect of tailoring, type information is contained in objects of type type. These are also contained in the bonded store.

This notion of extensible types has also implications for sharing of objects (see [8]).

<4> Here is an interesting connection to tailoring. Different users may have different views of the same object, but nevertheless share it. In this case protection also has to ensure the integrity of these views.

REFERENCES

[1] Beech, D. and Kugler, H.-J. (Editors), The IFIP WG 2.7 Reference Model for Command and Response Languages, IFIP WG 2.7, (May 1985)

[2] Bjørner, D., Reference Model for the Meta-Language, in: Bjørner, D., Oest, O. (Editors), Towards a Formal Definition of Ada, Lecture Notes in Computer Science 98 (Springer, Berlin, 1980)

[3] Denning, D.E.R., Cryptography and Data Security, (Addison-Wesley, Reading, Mass., 1983)

[4] Neumann, P.G. et al., A Provably Secure Operating System: The System, Its Applications, and Proofs, Computer Science Lab. Report CSL-116, SRI International, Menlo Park, Calif. (May 1980)

[5] Popek, G.J., Farber, D.A., A Model for Verification of Data Security in Operating Systems, Comm. ACM Vol.21(9) (Sep. 1978) 737-749

[6] Kugler, H.-J., The KIWINET/NICOLA Approach: Tools for the Construction of User Interfaces, in: Beech, D. (Editor), Command Language Directions (North-Holland, Amsterdam, 1980)

[7] Kugler, H.-J. et al., The Construction of User Interfaces -Guide for Defining Abstract Machines-, Leeds University, Trinity College Dublin, Universität Dortmund (Nov. 1980)

[8] Kugler, H.-J., A Model of User-Oriented Protection in Command and Response Languages, Trinity College Dublin (Jan. 1985)

[9] Jones, A.K. and Liskov, B., A Language Extension for Controlling Access to Shared Data, IEEE Trans.Soft.Eng., SE-2 (4) (Dec. 1976) 227-285

[10] Jones, A.K. and Liskov, B., A Language Extension for Expressing Constraints on Data Access, CACM 21 (5) (May 1978) 358-367

[11] Cheheyl, M.H., Verifying Security, ACM Computing Surveys, Vol.13 (3) (Sep. 1981) 279-339

COMPUTER SECURITY
J.B. Grimson and H.-J. Kugler (Editors)
Elsevier Science Publishers B.V. (North-Holland)
IFIP, 1985

A FAULT AND INTRUSION-TOLERANT FILE SYSTEM

J.Fraga and D.Powell

Laboratoire d'Automatique et d'Analyse des Systemes du C.N.R.S.
7 avenue du Colonel Roche
31077 TOULOUSE Cedex
FRANCE

In this paper we introduce the notion of intrusion tolerance. The physical isolation between the system components and the resource redundancy are used in a distributed system in order to tolerate a certain number of intrusions without violating data security. In order to diminish the effect of an intrusion, we have used strategies which consist of reducing the significance of the information which is accessible to an intruder. With this aim, a file storage technique is presented : "fragmentation and scattering". This technique contributes to file secrecy and allows the recovery of accidental or intentional faults (service negation and unauthorized modifications). Another strategy considered in this paper concerns the access information (identifiers and keys). The use of voting techniques and of threshold schemes for these information items should allow an increase in their availability as well as a decrease in the risk of system violation in the presence of corrupted access mechanisms or access informations.

1. Introduction

The mechanisms and principles used to safeguard the security of information in distributed systems are very often based on the notion of avoiding intrusions. These mechanisms are designed to prevent security infringements such as malicious or accidental revelation of sensitive data or their unauthorized modification. However, the complexity and the characteristics of distributed systems (heterogeneity, physical distribution, the various control entities, etc.) make it difficult to avoid intrusions.

The access control mechanisms and authorization services which are designed on this basis are used in systems whose resources are accessible by means of a communication network. Access can be obtained either by presentation of the unique identifier of the requested resource or by that of the client. The degree of security of these resources is probabilistic since it depends on the difficulty of guessing their identifiers. Very often, these systems are extremely large geographically, so that physical protection of the different system elements is difficult. Under these circumstances, it is quite possible to corrupt a site or bypass a mechanism. Once that an intrusion has occurred, the intrusion-avoidance mechanisms are inoperative with respect to the minimization of the resulting security infringements.

Crytography is very often used in addition to the above mentioned mechanisms. However, the additional secrecy that crytography brings to the system is insufficient in order to exclude all possible security infringements resulting from an intrusion. However, the secrecy offered by cryptographical controls is again probabilistic; it depends on the relationship between the algorithmic power of the encryption/decryption system and the processing capacity of the intruder, as well as on the correctness of the key management entities.

Generally speaking, one finds in distributed systems a more-or-less unsolved conflict between the techniques used for data security and those used for reliability/availability. This conflict stems from the fact that the reduction of the number of access points to protected objects with the aim of limiting intrusion possibilities, causes equally a reduction of the objects' redundancy and thus their availability. This conflict is significant if one uses only the notion of intrusion avoidance.

Distributed systems make it possible to use a physical isolation between the different components of the system in order to reduce the effects of an intrusion. In a similar way to the techniques used for tolerating (accidental) physical faults, resource redundancy can enable operational continuity even in the presence of unauthorized modifications or of intentional faults (service negation attempts). By analogy, we propose the introduction of the notion of *intrusion-tolerance*.

A system which tolerates intrusions has to:
- tolerate a certain number of intrusions by minimizing their impact on data security,
- diminish the critical points with respect to data availability, which in general are the mechanisms used for the ensuring data security.

Two strategies have been considered in order to achieve these targets. The first strategy concerns the storage of files in the system. A file is stored by using a technique called "fragmentation and scattering":
- *fragmentation* consists of splitting and replicating a file; the results of these operations are elementary parts of the file called "fragments",
- *scattering* designates the operation whereby these fragments are distributed among a set of distributed archive servers.

The fragmentation and scattering of a file are carried out in such a way that intrusion into a site does not endanger the security of the data stored in the system.

Koga, Fukushima and Yoshihara have proposed a system of "distributed communication" which corresponds to the use of data fragmentation and scatter routing for secret messages in meshed networks [10]. In this case, messages are split into pieces and each piece is sent to its receiver by a different path. The same technique has been considered by Deswarte and Laprie in view of its application to the memorization of objects in a distributed system [6].

The implementation of a fragmentation and scattering strategy depends on the existence of a cryptographic system and mechanisms for access control and authentication in order to facilitate the retrieval and the sharing of fragmented objects.

The second strategy considered in this paper concerns the reduction in the system security reliance on file access information (names and keys). The use of voting techniques and of threshold schemes should permit an increase in their avaibility as well as a decreased risk of security infringement in the presence of corrupted access mechanisms or access information.

2. System description

The application of intrusion tolerance is being considered for a distributed system comprising a local area network of personal workstations (user sites) and specialized computers (service sites). The individual workstations correspond to the "physical areas" of their users. A user has full authority over the objects stored in his machine. The local operating systems of these machines are included within a network operation system (NOS) which use:

- a service support layer responsible for the implementation of the client/server model, i.e. for the definition of the syntax and the semantics of the "request" and the "responses" of the model,
- a layer called the distributed system kernel or inter-process communication layer, comprising a transport service and means for construction of the system's secrecy and security mechanisms. These means consist of a port service and cryptographic facilities (hardware and software).

We suppose that the transport service is of the datagram type. All messages are encyphered with redundancy in order to ensure message integrity and message uniqueness in time. The communication network failure-detection and recovery mechanisms are provided by the service support layers.

The system contains two sorts of specialized computers: archive sites (with mass storage devices) and security sites (figure 1). The <u>A</u> archive sites and the <u>S</u> security sites contribute to the formation of a confidential and dependable distributed file system. This distributed file system is essentially made up of four services: the file management service, the fragment service, the directory service and the authentication service. This organization and the use of physical isolation permit an increase in the availability and the security of the stored data.

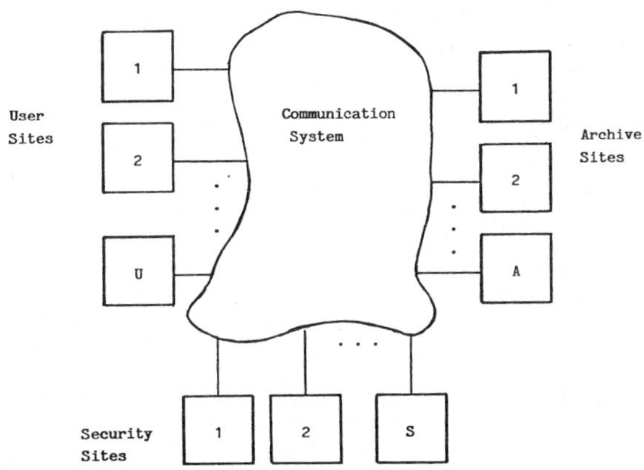

Figure 1: System environment

<u>File management service</u>: Every user site has a file server which supplies a well-defined file-management service interface. This service permits the storage or the retrieval of a file within the distributed file system. The file server uses the fragment service and the directory service in order to build the file structures. At the interface, file operations are: "open file", "close file", "create file", "erase file", "read file" and "write file". The more elementary file-access operations which are available to the user are executed locally by the host system (user site).

Fragment service: The fragment service is provided by the archive sites. The operations of these sites correspond to simple space allocations on the physical storage device and data (fragment) transfers between the storage device and the network. These fragment operations are only accessible to the file servers of the user sites. The archive site carries out an access control to the stored fragments. The presentation of the fragment names and their respective transformations into physical addresses constitute an access control mechanism of the capability type.

Directory service: The security sites supply the basis for the directory structures and for the file concurrency and access controls. The security sites form a replicated directory. Each file is identified in the distributed system by a "unique file identifier" (UFI). These identifiers are generated in the user sites. They correspond to integer numbers whose uniqueness is determined by a "site number" field and a "timestamp" field which respectively indicate the site and the date of file creation. The principal operation of the directory service is the transformation of the symbolic file names (visible to the users) into UFI's. This operation preceeds the opening of a file and is accompanied by the verification of the associated file access control list.

Authentication service: The security sites also perform a distributed authentication service. This service consists of assuring "confidential client/server associations" and the authentication of the system users. Each security site interacts with the user processes and the archive sites in complete independance of the other security sites of the system. The results of these interactions are submitted to a majority vote in the user sites and the archive sites. Under these circumstances, a corrupted or failed security site cannot interfere with the continuity and the security of the authentication and directory services.

Consistency in this concurrent and distributed environment is guaranteed by file operations designed as atomic operations. This is carried out by using a concurrency control mechanism and an "unchangeable versions" mechanism [14]. The concurrency control mechanism is decentralized and kept within the security sites. The lock granularity is the complete file. Locks are exclusive for the update mode (read/write) and shareable for the read mode. When a user demands the opening of a file, the user site has to obtain the majority of file-lock authorizations sent by the security servers. In a situation where the number of locks is insufficient, these locks are abandoned and the file service returns an exception code ("lock not granted") to the user. Whoever obtained the majority must obtain the remaining locks. The locks are maintained with a "session" in order to carry out the file operations. We define a "session" as the connection of the file management server to the archive services of the system for the file open period.

The "unchangeable versions" mechanism is established on the basis of the archive servers. A fragment-write operation (update) creates a new version of a fragment. A new version is only committed as the "current version" after the session has been cleared. The security servers are the "coordinators" of these commitments. They close the session at the moment of the close-file request. The security servers maintain a "session table" with the UFI's and the respective version numbers of the open files. This permits the results of a session to be undone in the event of, for example, a user site failure.

The access to a file is the result of the composition of the above mentioned services. At the moment of an open-file request, the file management server makes a request to open a session in all security sites. After the verification of the rights of the client process, these security sites release the parameters which permit the user sites to determine the file fragment names and their localization. The security servers open the session on each archive site, thus permitting the transfer of the UFI and of the access mode (the right) to the latter. Once the session is established, the exchanges between the user site and the archive sites can begin.

3. Fragmentation, replication and scattering of a file

During the storage procedure, a file is split into $\underline{N}$ fragments. Each fragment is then replicated into $\underline{R}$ replicas leading to a total of $\underline{M}$ = N.R file fragment replicas. The fragments and their replicas are scattered from the user site among the set of system archive sites.

3.1. Necessary conditions for fragmentation and scattering

The scattering of the $\underline{M}$ fragments among the $\underline{A}$ archive sites has to respect certain conditions connected with the number of archive sites:

a) The $\underline{R}$ replicas of the same fragment are stored in different archive sites; otherwise the availability of a file would be sub-optimal (availability condition).

b) The proportion of a file in a single archive site is given by the ratio T/N where T is the number of file fragments on a site. The information contained within the proportion T/N must not be sufficiently significant in order to permit the total or partial retrieval of the fragmented file (secrecy condition).

On the basis of condition (b), one obtains the relationship:

$$A.T \geq N.R \qquad (T/N \geq R/A) \qquad (1)$$

A.T being the available archive space for the N.R file fragment replicas.

3.2. Archiving matrix

File storage and retrieval are carried out by using an "archiving matrix" that consists of words of an m-out-of-n code where the values of the code weight and code length are $\underline{R}$ and $\underline{A}$ respectively. Therefore, the archiving matrix consists of $\underline{N}$ lines and $\underline{A}$ columns (figure 2).

Each file fragment is associated to a code word of the matrix. The "1"-valued bits of the code word associated with a fragment F_i (i=1..N) represent its $\underline{R}$ replicas. The archive sites allocated to these $\underline{R}$ replicas are determined by the numbers of the columns where the code-word bits are equal to "1". The column numbers (1..A) of the matrix correspond to a set of offset values d_{ij} (i=1..N and j=1..A) which are used in appropriate context tables to uniquely determine each archive site of the system.

R-out-of-A code
(R = 2 and A = 4)

File Fragments (N=6) => values of d_{ij}

	1	2	3	4
1	0	0	1	1
2	0	1	0	1
3	0	1	1	0
4	1	0	0	1
5	1	0	1	0
6	1	1	0	0

Figure 2: Archiving matrix

3.3. Fragmentation considerations

The implementation of a fragmentation and scattering technique has to consider two important aspects concerning file secrecy:

a) Fragmentation of a file is carried out in such a way that the establishment of links between the different parts of the file becomes as complex as possible (for the intruder). The value $\underline{N}$ is a measure of this complexity. As $\underline{N}$ becomes larger, it is more and more difficult to establish inter-fragment correlations.

b) The file's fragments are scattered as much as possible between the archive sites. We introduce two variables to measure the scattering of a file in the system:
   - dispersion D corresponds to the minimum number of archive sites to which one (the user or an intruder) has to gain access in order to be able to obtain a (copy of a) file,
   - concealment C represents the minimum number of archive sites to which one (an intruder) has to gain access in order to be sure to have a (copy of a) file.

Figure 3 shows the distinction between these two variables. On the example of figure 3a, the concealment $\underline{C}$ of the file corresponds to 3 as it is certain that if one gains access to any three archive sites then one obtains a copy of the file. The dispersion $\underline{D}$ in this case is equal to 2 as one can have a copy of the file by accessing two archive sites (sites 1 and 3 or sites 2 and 4). Figure 3b presents a scattering example in which the concealment $\underline{C}$ and the dispersion $\underline{D}$ of the file are both equal to 3.

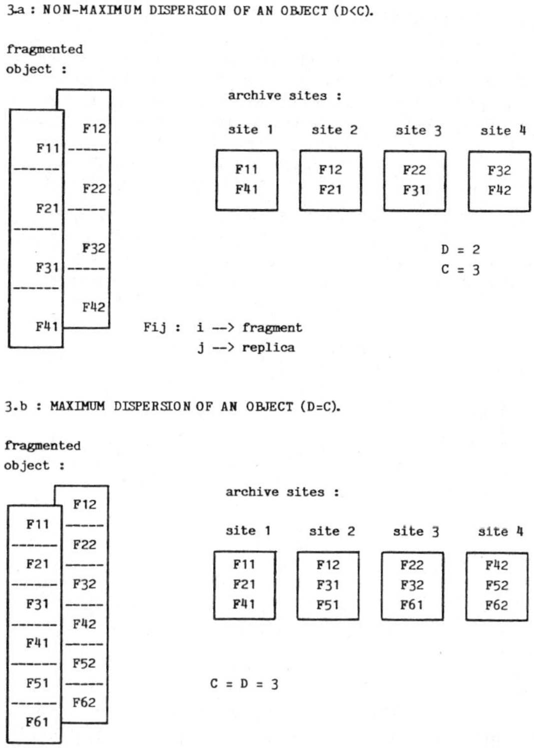

Figure 3: Illustration of object dispersion

These examples illustrate the scattering characteristics:

- The concealment of a file under conditions of fixed $\underline{A}$ and $\underline{R}$ is invariant and independent of $\underline{N}$.

  Proof: The $\underline{R}$ replicas of each fragment are on distinct sites: if the archive sites are divided into two subsets of ranks [A-(R-1)] and [R-1], the subset of rank [A-(R-1)] must contain at least one replica of each fragment (condition $\underline{a}$ of paragraph 3.1).

- The dispersion of an object depends on the fragmentation policy. However the dispersion is upper-bounded by the file concealment.

  We thus obtain: $D \leq C = [A-(R-1)]$ (2)

We have considered two possibilities for fragmenting a file. The first is called "saturated fragmentation" meaning that the archive matrix consists of the complete R-out-of-A code which results in that a file is split into $N = \binom{A}{R}$ fragments. The second possibility is referred to as "non-saturated fragmentation", meaning that the archive matrix consists of a subset of the possible R-out-of-A code-words: $N < \binom{A}{R}$ fragments.

3.3.1. Saturated fragmentation

If A and R are fixed, the maximum proportion (T/N) of a file on an archive site is constant whatever the fragmentation policy. However, saturated fragmentation corresponds to the maximum possible reduction in the size of the file fragments. In this case, the value of T corresponds to the maximum number of fragments on any archive site. Therefore, this corresponds to a greater complexity (for the intruder) to establish the correlations between the fragments of a file in one site.

The use of a complete R-out-of-A code permits the maximum dispersion of the file (D=C). The example of figure 3b corresponds to a saturated fragmentation policy for which the archive matrix consists of the complete 2-out-of-4 code.

3.3.1.1. Determination of the number of fragments in archive site for saturated fragmentation (T)

As far as saturated fragmentation is concerned, the number of file fragments which are not represented in a given archive site, corresponds to $\binom{A-1}{R}$. These are the fragments whose R replicas are distributed among the (A-1) remaining sites of the system. The number of fragments in an archive site is:

$$T = N - \binom{A-1}{R} = \binom{A-1}{R-1}.$$

For $N = \binom{A}{R}$ and $T = \binom{A-1}{R-1}$, condition (1) is satisfied with T/N =R/A.

3.3.1.2. Dispersion of a object

The determination of the minimum number of necessary archive sites in order to gain access to a copy of a scattered object is easily shown, if one supposes a set of successive accesses to the archive sites of the system. The contribution of the ith site, to which access has been gained, to the constitution of a file corresponds to $\binom{A-i}{R-1}$ fragments which are not represented in the i-1 sites of the former accesses. Therefore the N fragments of the object are obtained by D successive accesses, such that:

$$N = \sum_{i=1}^{D} \binom{A-i}{R-1}$$

The number D of sites necessary in order to be able to obtain a copy of each fragment, is given by:

$$D = \max i \quad \text{such as } \binom{A-i}{R-1} > 0 \qquad i=1,2,\ldots$$

let: $A - D = R - 1,$

then: $D = C = A - (R-1).$

In order to gain access to a complete file, at least A-(R-1) operating archive sites are necessary among those used for the storage of that file.

3.3.2. Non-saturated fragmentation

Saturated fragmentation presents a growing processing complexity with an increase in A (number of archive sites of the system). For example, in the case of R = A/2, the required processing is only feasible for A less than about 12 (for $A \geq 12$, R = A/2; $N \geq 729$).

In systems with a large number of archive sites, in order to diminish the effect of A on the processing, a non-saturated fragmentation has to be used, i.e. only a few words of the R-out-of-A code are used ($N < \binom{A}{R}$). The method which we have applied in this case is to choose a value of T such that $\binom{A-1}{R-1} > T \geq 1$. This fact, along with condition T/N=R/A implies a value of $N < \binom{A}{R}$. For these choices, the importance of N and T for the secrecy of the objects has to be considered.

The archive matrix derived from a subset of the words of an R-out-of-A code determines a non-maximum dispersion of a file (D<C):

$$A-(R-1) > D \geq N/T \qquad (3)$$

This implies that access to a file can be gained with a number of archive sites less than A-(R-1) (c.f. the example of figure 3.a uses a non-saturated fragmentation with an archive matrix consisting of 4 words of the 2-out-of-4 code).

3.3.3. Choice of redundancy and object concealment values.

In compliance with what has been explicited in equation (2), there is a conflict situation between the redundancy and the concealment of an object (C). A compromise has to be found between these variables in order to carry out fragmentation and scattering.

Several approaches are possible in order to establish acceptable redundancy and concealment conditions for a file:

a) the user determines the required concealment and the system, based on equation (2), maximizes the value of R,
b) the user determines the value of R and the system based on equation (2), maximizes the value of C,
c) the system uses average values for C and R (e.g. R = A/2 and C = A/2 + 1); in the case of saturated fragmentation, the value of N approaches the maximum value ($N=\binom{A}{A/2}$),
d) the user specifies values for both D and R; the system must choose a value of N:
   - for D + R - 1 = A, we have saturated fragmentation,
   - for D * R $\leq$ A, we have non-saturated fragmentation; where T = 1 and the archive volume could be more than the number of fragment replicas: in this case N = D.

In the field of local networks, we limit ourselves to a reasonable value for A: about ten mass storage devices. In this case, saturated fragmentation may be utilized with average redundancy and concealment (R = A/2 and C = D = A/2+1). Under these conditions, the system can tolerate A/2-1 corrupted or failed archive sites.

4. Description of the cryptographic controls

We use cryptography at several levels of this system. The cryptographic operations are available from a "cryptographic facility" placed at the kernel level of each system site. This facility contains a DES encryption algorithm and a key generator. The application and the operation of these cryptographic facilities are described in the following paragraphs.

4.1. Keys associated to a file.

When creating a file, it is associated during its whole lifetime to two random numbers KF and I, which are the "associated keys" of the file. In compliance with what will be described in paragraph 5, it is from these values that the localization and the access right for each fragment of the file, which is dispersed in the system, will be obtained.

These keys are generated locally by using the cryptographic facility of the user site. They are sensitive objects which means that the system has to supply a means of avoiding the release of a file key following an intrusion. Moreover, the system has to supply a means of making these objects available in the presence of partial failures of the system.

Threshold schemes have been designed in order to resolve the conflict problems between secrecy and availability. In a threshold scheme, a key KF is associated with a number n "image values" of KF: K_j $(j=1,2,\ldots,n)$, in such a way that:

- the knowledge of a precise number t $(t<n)$ of image values K_j permits the calculation of KF,
- the knowledge of less than t image values K_j is insufficient for the restoration of the key KF.

An efficient threshold scheme based on polynomial interpolation has been proposed by Shamir [13]. Asmuth and Bloom have created a scheme based on congruence classes [5]. Davida, Lipton and DeMillo [3] have proposed a scheme based on correcting codes.

We have not chosen any particular threshold scheme. However, the threshold scheme used in our system has to have $n = S$ (the number of security sites) and $t = S/2 + 1$. Under these circumstances, the image K_j is stored in the security site S_j $(j=1,2,\ldots,S)$ and replicas of that image are released at each "open" request for the corresponding file.

These conditions determine (a) that if an intruder obtains $S/2 - 1$ images of KF, the secrecy of the key KF is not endangered, and (b) that the restitution of the key is guaranteed even in the case of destruction of $S/2 - 1$ images of KF (sabotages or failures). The propositions mentioned here are also applicable to the key I.

4.2. Key and name management for the communication system

The kernel of the distributed system assures two services which are decisive for the security of the system: the port service and the key management service. These two services are combined in such a way that they simplify the secrecy and the authentication of transmitted messages.

For the IPC inter-machine services, the NOS uses the notion of a "port" as an access point to these services. Ports are objects protected by the kernel into which messages are placed or removed. Two rights are attached to each port: the receive right and the send right.

A port in this system is characterized by a receiving process (receive right) and a sending process (send right). This determines a unidirectional point-to-point connection which permits the authentication of messages received on the port (identification of the sending process). The send right can only be sent from the port allocation site to the sending process.

A cryptographic key KC, which is generated by the kernel at the moment of port allocation, is associated with every port. This key is used for the encryption of messages sent to the port and the decryption of messages received from the port. These keys are generated by the kernel during the port allocation.

The kernel of each site manages and protects for the local systems a (receive) table of reception ports (receive rights) and a (send) table of sending ports (send rights). These tables consist of "global representations" of ports (global port identifiers) and the keys associated with these ports. The associated key and the global representation of a port are designated by the host system by means a local name.

The security of transfers on the communication system depends on the establishment of what is called a "confidential association". A confidential association is a pair of ports which permits two processes to communicate. In this association, each process has the receive right for one of the ports and the send right for the other. In order to establish a confidential association, a user process has to allocate a port and send this port (the send right) to the destination process. The sending of a port corresponds to a procedure that called "port authentication". It consists of sending "association request" messages to the destination process by using the system security sites (authentication servers) as intermediaries. For these transfers one uses confidential associations between a (user or server) process and the security servers (these associations are described in paragraph 4.3).

For these transfers, the kernel of the local site uses a threshold scheme for the calculation of the KC_j images of the port associated key KC. The association requests are made up of the global representation of the port and one of the KC_j images. The messages are routed to the destination process, thus using various security servers. Such a procedure allows the reconstitution of the send right (reconstitution of the key KC by means of the threshold scheme) in the destination site, in the presence of $S/2 - 1$ failed or corrupted security sites.

The second process must send a port using the same procedure in order to complete the confidential association. The existence of these ports is limited to the duration of associations between the processes.

4.3. User log-in

A user of the system must possess a series of keys called "private keys" (KB_1, KB_2,...,KB_S). Each of the keys is used for the user's authentication with respect to one of the security servers of the system.

These authentications correspond to the establishment of the user's confidential associations with the system security servers.

Each KB_j is used to encrypt the send right (global representation and associated key) of the port allocated to the corresponding server S_j in the user site. The user's identifier and the encrypted send right are sent to a public port of server S_j in an "association request" message. The security server utilizes the identifier of the user to localize the key KB_j within an "identification table".

If the decryption of the port is considered correct, the server security carries out the allocation of a port and transmits the corresponding send right to the user port. This procedure applies to all security sites. The user is considered to be connected to the system when the number of confidential associations with the security servers is equal to or greater than the minimum number of servers necessary to ensure correct system operation (S/2+1). This limit number of confidential associations for the user connection leaves a margin for the loss or corruption of (S/2-1) user keys KB_j.

5. Overview of a fragmentation, replication and scattering procedure

The storage and retrieval of a file mainly depend on the determination of the storage locations (archive servers) and of the file fragment names. This is carried out in the user site by means of parameters released by the security sites. Without these parameters the reproduction of the access conditions to the file fragments is rather unlikely.

5.1. Storage of a file

The different steps that are necessary for storage of a file are as follows (figure 4).

(1) The user site must receive the UFI of the file and the images of associated keys (KF and I) from the security servers. These objects will be sent after the security sites have verifiered the user's access rights. The images allow the reconstitution of the keys KF and I.

(2) The object is divided into N fragments and an order number i is associated with each fragment N_i ($1 \leq i \leq N$).

(3) A random value "VA_i" (64 bits) is calculated for each fragment. This value is the result of the application of a one-way function (e.g. a hash one-way function [4], [15]) on a composition "g" of UFI, KF and of the order number i of the fragment:

$$VA_i = H(I, g(FUI, KF, i))$$

(4) The appropriate archive matrix for the value A is localized or calculated.

(5) The fragments N_i (i=1,2,...,N) are sorted according to their random values VA_i and each is associated with the corresponding code-word of the archive matrix.

(6) The d_{ij} values corresponding to N_i are determined as follows:

$$d_{ij} = a_j \qquad (j=1,2,\ldots,R)$$

where a_j ($1 \leq a_j \leq A$) is the column number of the jth bit at "1" of the code word associated to N_i in the archive matrix. These d_{ij} values are utilized during the scattering procedure, in order determine the receiving archive server of the R replicas of each fragment.

(7) The name of each fragment replica is formed by the concatenation of the UFI with the corresponding values of VA_i and d_{ij}. The "N.R" identifiers resulting from these concatenations constitute the fragment names $NAME_{ij}$. These names are utilized in the interactions between the user site and the archive servers. The requested archive-server operations are accepted if these names are present; the names are interpreted as "capabilities". The uniqueness of these names in the system is guaranteed by UFI.

(8) The fragments and their respective names $NAME_{ij}$ are sent to the archive sites by means of a transfer protocol called "scattering". The d_{ij} values are utilized in a scattering table (paragraph 5.2) in order to determine the port names of the archive servers in which the fragment groups will be stored.

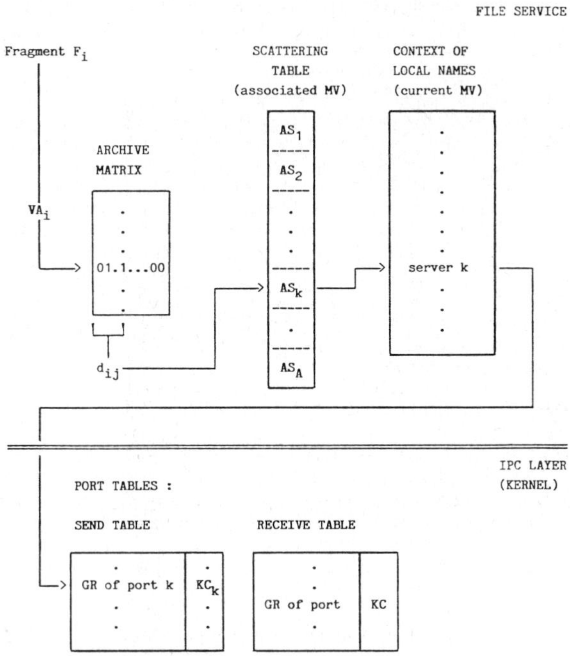

Figure 4: Outline of fragmentation, replication and scattering procedure

5.2. Retrieval of a file

Before a file can be reconstituted, the $NAME_{ij}$'s must first be recalculated in order to allow the access to the scattered fragments. The object retrieval algorithm must carry out steps 1 to 7, like the storage algorithm.

The fragment transfers depend on the strategy chosen for the detection and recovery of faults. Two techniques have been envisaged for the detection and recovery of faults and active intrusions (intentional faults):

a) Majority vote: The R replicas of each fragment are submitted to a vote. The content of one fragment corresponds at least to R/2+1 of its replicas. In this case, file reconstitution requires at least A-R/2+1 functioning archive sites. The system can tolerate R/2-1 failed or corrupted archive sites.
b) Fragment checkwords: The checkwords are utilized to verify the integrity of the fragments of an object. A checkword is calculated on the basis of the content of a fragment and an object version identifier (timestamp or version number).

We are considering the use of this second technique. The fragments are stored with their version identifier and their checkword in the archive sites. The utilization of version identifiers allows the detection of previous versions transmitted by failed or corrupted archive sites. The checkword algorithm that is used must have the property that it is rather unlikely for someone to construct a fragment that differs from a certified one but has the same checkword. The hash function proposed by Davies [4] can be used for the calculation of the checkwords.

The checkword method permits R-1 failed or corrupted archive sites to be tolerated. In order to facilitate the recovery of erroneous fragments, all fragments of a file are transferred to the user site during the reconstitution of the file.

In the user site, the fragments are collected in a matrix (NxR) where each line i consists of fragments whose names $NAME_{ij}$ contain the (random) value VA_i. Once this transfer has been achieved, the decoding procedure has to begin. The reconstitution of the file is carried out by taking at each line of the fragment matrix the first replica whose checkword and version identifier have been certified correct.

5.3. Reconfiguration of the system

It is very important to consider the variations undergone by the set of archive sites. These variations may be the temporary withdrawal of a failed site (decrease in A) or the reconnection of a repaired site or the addition of a new archive site (increase of A). In spite of these modifications, the system has to guarantee access to the files. The mechanisms concerning file access depend on the value of A. The variations of A are reflected in the archive matrix in the file system and the server name context in the local system. These variations require the memorization of information indicating the file system configuration at the moment of file storage, in order to allow the reconstitution of the conditions for futher accesses.

The notion of "Memory Vector" (MV) is introduced in order to give the constitution of the archive system at the give moment. Each archive server in this system is represented by a "server number" AS_j (j=1,2,...,A). The MV consists of the AS_j's of the archive sites present in the system, represented in increasing order:

$$MV = (AS_1, AS_2, \ldots, AS_A)$$

Each file stored in the system is connected with a MV: the "associated MV ". The associated MV supplies the configuration with which the file was last stored and so permits the reconstitution of its access conditions. The associated MV is stored in the security sites, together with the file access information (names and keys). The MVs coming from the security sites are also submitted to the voting technique. The associated MV is used by user sites in order to form the "scattering table". The offsets d_{ij} calculated from the archive matrix are used in conjunction with this table in order to determine a value of AS_j. The latter is used to indicate a port local name (figure 4).

The security servers are informed about the variations of the system and produce a "current MV" which gives the present configuration of the system. The connection or disconnection of an archive site and the update of the current MV's are carried out using an authentication protocol similar to that of the users (paragraph 5.2).

The current MV is turned into a file-associated MV at the request for 'write file' or 'create file'. The current MV is used for the update of local name contexts. It has to form the scattering table of the file being scattered. As far as 'read file' is concerned, the current MV and the associated MV have to be received by the user site; the first one for the update of the local name contexts and the second one for the reconstitution of the scattering table which has been used during the last file storage.

The value S (number of security sites) used by the protocols described in this paper, is a system invariant even if some security sites are deconnected. We consider that the value S chosen for the system gives sufficient redundancy conditions to the described protocols, permitting them to tolerate possible and temporary withdrawals of security sites.

6. Conclusions and future research

In this paper we have introduced the notion of intrusion tolerance. The physical isolation between the system components and the resource redundancy are used in a distributed system in order to tolerate a certain number of intrusions without violation of information security.

In order to minimize the effect of an intrusion, we have used two strategies which consist of reducing the significance of the information which is accessible to an intruder. With this aim, a file storage technique has been presented called "fragmentation and scattering". This technique contributes to file secrecy and permits the recovery of accidental or intentional errors (service negation and unauthorized modifications).

File fragmentation and scattering are carried out in such a way that it is difficult to establish a correlation between the file fragments which are present in a archive site.

Accesses to file fragments are carried out by the file service of the user site. These accesses are only possible by using parameters associated with the scattered object (UFI,KF,MV). These parameters are stored in the security sites using vote and threshold scheme techniques which allow an increase in their availability and a decrease in the risk of system violation in the presence of failed or corrupted security sites.

The authentication services of this system are carried out by security servers, separately maintained and implanted. Under these circumstances, system security is only compromised if the majority of these servers is corrupted.

The research presented in this paper will be continued within the framework of the SATURNE project (SATURATION NETWORK) (a joint LAAS-INRIA project) which has for aim the realization of a distributed system with fault and intrusion tolerance.

The present research will be enlarged in order to take into consideration:
- the use of an (unreliable) broadcast communication system,
- access to the protected object with a finer granularity than that of a complete file.

Acknowledgement

We extend our thanks to Yves Deswarte and Jean-Charles Fabre for their careful review and constructive criticism of draft versions of this paper.

REFERENCES

[1] Birrell A.D., Needham R.M. - **A universal file server.** IEEE Transactions on Software Engineering, Vol SE-6, No 56, pp.450-453, September 1980.

[2] Dannenberg R.B. - **Resource sharing in a network of personal computers.** Ph.D thesis, Carnegie-Mellon University, December 1982.

[3] Davida G.I., DeMillo R.I., Lipton R.J.- **Protecting shared cryptographic keys.** Proc. 1980 IEEE Symp. on Security and Privacy, pp.100-102, April 1980.

[4] Davies D.W. - **Protection.** Lecture notes 105, Computer Science, Springer-Verlag, pp.211-244, 1981.

[5] Denning D.E. - **Cryptography and data security.** Addison-Wesley. 1983.

[6] Deswarte Y., Laprie J.C. - **Distributed systems tolerating faults and intrusions.** LAAS Research Report LAAS No 84.023, April 1984 (in French).

[7] Fletcher J.G., Watson R.W. - **Service support in a network operating system.** Proc. COMPCON 80, pp.415-423, Spring 1980.

[8] Gudes E. - **The design of a cryptography based secure file system.** IEEE Transactions on Software Engineering, Vol SE-6, No 5, pp.411-420, September 1980.

[9] Jegado M. - **Recoverably aspects of a distributed file system.** Software-Practice and Experience, Vol 13, pp.33-43, 1983.

[10] Koda Y., Fukushima E., Yoshihara K. - **Error recoverable and securable data communication for computer network.** Proc. 12th IEEE Symp. Fault-Tolerant Computing, pp.79-84, 1982.

[11] Nassi I. - **The Liberty Net : an architectural overview.** Proc. COMPCON 82, pp.103-107, Fall 1982.

[12] Rashid R.F., Robertson G.G. - **Accent : a communication oriented network operating system kernel.** Proc. Eighth ACM Symp. Operating Systems Principles, pp.64-75, December 1981.

[13] Shamir A. - **How to share a secret.** Communications of the ACM, Vol 22, No 11, pp.612-613, November 1979.

[14] Tripathi A.R., Wang P.S. - **An objet oriented design model for reliable distributed systems.** Proc. Third Symp. on Reliability in Distributed Software and Database systems, pp.102-113, October 1983.

[15] Winternitz R.S. - **A secure one-way hash fonction built from DES.** Proc. IEEE Symp. on Security and Privacy, pp.88-90, April 1984.

COMPUTER SECURITY
J.B. Grimson and H.-J. Kugler (Editors)
Elsevier Science Publishers B.V. (North-Holland)
IFIP, 1985

SYSTEMS DESIGN AND DATA SECURITY STRATEGY

Thomas Osvald

The Vulnerability Board (SÅRB)
Department of defense
Stockholm, Sweden

Humans have a limited, intellectual and psychological ability to make complicated decisions or judgements based on a great number of entities or concepts. If these limits are unknown or ignored in systems design the result will be systems that are too complicated. Such systems cannot be intellectually controlled and therefore cannot be protected by conventional data protection measures. Some design principles that increase transparency and understanding are discussed.

SYSTEMS DESIGN AND DATA SECURITY STRATEGY

SÅRB - The Vulnerability Board - is a consultative body on matters of security and vulnerability in data processing. SÅRB was appointed by the Swedish Government in 1981 and will according to present planning conclude its work in 1985.

One of the Boards tasks is to increase the knowledge of factors contributing to vulnerability and to devise methods to cope with these factors. Among some 10-15 projects one is concerned with information system complexity as a vulnerability factor.

Wether we like it or not our society is rapidly becoming more complicated, not the least as a consequence of the extremely rapid development of information processing and data communication. Our times are also caracterized by increasingly large scale and long range decisions and effects. Unfortunately, this development does not correspond to a similar progress in our human ability to make wise decisions. It is therefore important that we recognize the limits of the human mind and our ability to understand and process complicated, long range decision problems. If complexity is not understood and kept within reasonable limits we will not be able to control developments and we will become slaves rather than masters of our information systems.

Characteristics of complex systems

What are the characteristics of excessively super-complex systems? One important symptom is that even experts find it hard or impossible to understand or comprehend the totality of such a system. The inability to comprehend is not an absolute criterion that does or does not exist but rather av vauge feeling - mainly of uncertainty. This basically goes back to the well-known fact that the human mind cannot deal with or keep track of more than about seven objects, entities or concepts at a time. Above that number, errors in the understanding and problem solving process increase disproportionately.

Why are such systems designed? I can think of three possible reasons. The first is a strategy error of systems development that may be called "revolutionary change" or "giant step approach". During the seventies some large, administrative government systems were re-designed i order to take advantage of new data processing and communication technology. At the same time, as part of a huge "total" project, organization and administration were redesigned - all in one giant revolutionary change. A better and more successful approach would have been - as it always is - to follow a step-by-step master plan where each step is based on previous experience and available resources.

The second reason is the sometimes uncontrolled, almost cancer-like growth of large administrative systems, without a master plan and without clear lines of authority and responsibility, in efforts to integrate and to exploit common data.

A third reason is the inability of systems designers to identify the problems of system complexity and our own inability to handle complex systems and to set a limit to growth and integration.

System complexity as a vulnerability problem

When does system complexity become av vulnerability problem? When we cannot intellectually understand and comprehend the system, we dare not change it because secondary effects cannot be foreseen, we can not replace it or even protect it because we do not know, in detail, what functions the total system performs.

Data processing was once almost exclusively used for tasks that previously were performed by humans. Today professionals tend to forget the skill they once handed over to computers. Furthermore, an increasing share of computer applications are exclusively designed for computers - they have never been, nor can they ever be performed by humans. Thus, more than ever before we have to depend on computer experts and systems documentation to be able to understand our systems.

Obviously an illdefined system may be compromised without our beeing able to notice it. Protecting an over complex system with conventional data protection measures is both impossible and useless, like protecting a rotten egg by padding it in soft cotton. System quality is thus a strategic data protection property.

Development of simple system

How can excess complexity be avoided? For a given application, obviously we must pay regard to the complexity problem during the design phase of a system. We must use system development methods and tools that take our human shortcomings into account.

Decision making limitations

Information systems are important tools for decision making. Information systems are designed through a series of decisions. Human decision making ability has severe limitations in perception as well as cognition or capacity for thinking and emotion. If we want to learn how to make better decisions we can (a) learn more about the decision making process, (b) develop better theoretical and technical aids such as decision models or information systems, (c) change the environment in which decisions are made and bring it more in line with human prerequisites.

In our society we have great and sometimes excessive confidence in theoretical and technical aids - also for complicated decision making. Many people argue, however, that the only realistic approach is to adapt decision making situations to the inherent human natural decision making ability such as it was created by biological evolution. We can never escape our biological inheritance. It is therefore better to adapt the environment according to the given conditions than to try to violate human nature.

Some findings of the research on human decision making process are particularly relevant in systems design.

Generally, it ought to be a true fact that the more information you have as a basis for a decision the better it is. This is true when the number of elements or factors that influence the decision and have to be taken into regard by the decisionmaker does not exceed 5-7. A decision maker cannot profit by an increase in the number of parameters. In fact some research findings indicate that more facts give poorer result. This is particularly remarkable since decision makers themselves believe that more information means better judgements and decisions when the contrary may thus be true.

Decisions are based on predictions or pure guesswork. There are some relevant observations on the human ability to predict (or guess).

- Humans make good predictions when probabilities are between 100 % and 1 %. Unfortunately, the rate of probability is very often less than 1 % in the most intresting and important decisions.

- We have ar tendency to ignore negative consequences for which the probability is small. "These things do not happen to me". From a psychological point of view this reaction is probably appropriate in our daily lives because it protects us form becoming apathetic which we might otherwise be if we realistically considered all possible threats to our health and our lives. But in the society, in designing an information system the decision maker has to reckon also with less probable or improbable incidents.

- Positive incidents are considered more probable than negative.

- The more remote in time an event is the less significance it has. Events that will take place in 20 years time are judged as approximately one third as important as the same event taking place today. A decision alternative that carries immediate benefits but long range drawbacks may thus seem more attractive than an alternative, from at rational viewpoint, better decision with immediate drawbacks but longrange benefits.

It is not difficult to imagine what consequences these tendencies may bring about in the long run for the vulnerability of a technological society.

Whith this background of self-knowledge about our imperfect ability to make complicated decisions and in view of the apparent risk that our decisions in spite of our self-knowledge will not be optimal we ought to be able to discuss some policies for systems design suited to reduce vulnerability.

Factor reduction

Knowing what we now do about limitations of human decision making capabilities it is obviously important to reduce the number of factors that the system designer must pay regard to in his design work. There are two obvious methods to reduce the number of factors.

One way is to enforce extensive standardization or modelling. The more complicated our world becomes the more important and necessary it is to utilize and set aside human creativity and decision making capability for the big problems. It should not be wasted on trivial problems and solutions. It is not true which some people argue, that we reduce the space or elbow-room for human creativity by adopting standards as long as these relate to trivial problems. It is just the other way round. By solving once and for all a number of trivial problems by way of adopting standard solutions - within our company, our country or internationally - we release creative resources that can be utilized for design problem solutions on a higher level. We make decisions capacity available in the bottom that can be used in the top of a decision hierarchy.

A well-known way to reduce the number of decision factors is modularization. At some point, when system modules or segments become too large, we risk losing comprehension and control. If we, on the other hand divide the system into too many, too small modules we may again lose control. There is probably an optimal module-size that may be established with the help of psychological expertise and which we might even establish as a standard. Large, complex systems might require hierarchally ordered modularization. A system module is characterized by having an absolutely clear-cut interface so that a module is interchangable for those who know the interface.

Flexibility

One of the problems of conventional, administrative, complex systems is that it is difficult or even impossible to change these systems in an orderly, controlled way. On the other hand there is a very rapid increase in the change rate in our society in general and a correspondingly increasing demand for flexibility of information systems. We are all aware of the soaring cost of software due to difficulties in correcting and upgrading as needs change over time. It is therefore more important than ever, or even necessary, to design flexible systems where easily replaceable program modules constitute incidental material with a high turnover rate. As a general rule I think it is constructive to consider the design of "new" systems as exceptions and the continuous administration and management of systems as the normal safe. Ease of maintenance or flexibility will become a prime design objective.

Traditionally systems design has meant the definition of processing rules, designing required output data and the collection and preparation of necessary inputdata. Design work is concentrated on the problem of formalizing processing rules and designing algorithms.

During the last few years it has become more and more obvious that the real problem is not to design the processing rules but rather to describe and handle the data that is the basis of data processing. From a technical point of view this means that we try to organize data processing not as a number of processing programs each with a separately defined data requirement but rather as a data base of commonly used data.

One of the reasons for this development is the growing awareness that system users must themselves make the design decisions, that users as a rule cannot be expected to program exept when very high level languages may be used and that users have a limited ability to define their own information requirements.

What we will have to accept is therefore that programs are for standard or non-recurrent use with an ever shorter life expectancy. On the other hand, data which is of course the raw material of information will not change as quickly as the processing rules. Data is therefore the resource that has to be cultivated, protected, tended, preserved and developed. This approach supports recent developments of systems design methods, such as 4th generation languages, IRM, data dictionary and database technique.

Transparency

A third important attribute of less complex and vulnerable systems is transparency. I must be possible - with a reasonable effort - for everybody concerned to learn and understand how the system functions. The first condition is then a good documentation. We all know from experience how difficult it is to have good documentation produced and even more diffucult to keep it up-to-date. With system and software developments where permanent system change is the rule it is presumably realistic to give up any hopes of having good, updated documentation produced with traditional, manual means. What we can do is to develop a documentation system and hierarchy suited to the new software and designsituation - maybe make it a standard - and require that handware and software vendors support and deliver effective automatic software documentaion aids.

The IRM-concept with data dictionaries and data base technique will focus interest dramatically on the problems of data quality (DQ). In an International standardization organization (ISO) draft international standard on information processing vocabulary on control, integrity and security DQ is defined as "The correctness, relevance, and accessability that make data appropriate for their use." In Sweden the nature and seriousness of this problem and the definition of DQ have been known for the last 10 years. Still, no efforts have been made neither in the government nor in the universities to increase our knowledge and improve DQ in our large administrative systems. We use e g more than 20 different income notions and no serious efforts have been made to bring about distinct definitions in spite of the fact that "income" is the basic data for control of taxes and charges that individuals have to pay and the benefits they are entitled to.

In short, it is a costly mess.

One reason may be that the work of defining data and analysing its quality is a time - consuming and rather unglamorous work. Another reason may be the multidisciplinary nature of the DQ issue. It does not come naturally to system designers to discuss data relevance.

COMPUTER SECURITY
J.B. Grimson and H.-J. Kugler (Editors)
Elsevier Science Publishers B.V. (North-Holland)

THE RELATIVE IMPACT MEASURE OF VULNERABILITY - A SYSTEM IN PRACTICE

Raimo Mäkilä
Sanoma Corporation
P.O. Box 240
00101 Helsinki
Finland

There has been a lack of practical procedures to assess and evaluate computer security risks. The Relative-Impact Measure of Vulnerability is a methodology to deal with these important tasks. This work is to introduce the basic structure of the methodology and a sample application. The method is found out to be easy enough to apply in real life, though numerical measures are used.

INTRODUCTION

The Relative Impact-Measure of Vulnerability (RIM) in a methodology to measure the relative impact on an organization of vulnerabilities of its computer system´s integrity. This computer risk assessment and evaluation procedure has been developed at SRI International.

The methodology has four basic steps:

1. Perpetrator analysis -- describing and quantifying the characteristics of people (potential perpetrators) who may threaten a computer system.

2. Target assessment -- assessing the relative impact of successful attacks on each of nine classes of targets, as well as measuring the relative attractiveness of the target classes to members of each perpetrator class.

3. Flaw identification and analysis -- determining the susceptibility of the computer system to various exploitable flaws and estimating the existence of exploitable paths linking perpetrator classes and target classes.

4. RIM - calculation -- combining the various measures to produce a non-dimensional relative impact measure for computer system vulnerability to integrity violation.

The methodology is further subdivided into a ten-step path that takes a person through a semistructured process to measure the impact. In this paper an authentic realization of the RIM-methodology is presented. The RIM-methodology has been applied to an administrative computer system in the following way:

PERPETRATOR ANALYSIS

The first task in perpetrator analysis is to consider the people, who are involved with the computer system. The people, who might be considered perpetrators, are then classified according as their ability to cause security problems. The perpetrator classes used were:

Class 1 (P_1) - No knowledge about the computer system
Class 2 (P_2) - Junior data-handling knowledge
Class 3 (P_3) - Senior data-handling knowledge
Class 4 (P_4) - Junior operations knowledge
Class 5 (P_5) - Senior operations knowledge
Class 6 (P_6) - Junior programming knowledge
Class 7 (P_7) - Senior programming knowledge
Class 8 (P_8) - Junior equipment knowledge
Class 9 (P_9) - Senior equipment knowledge
Class 10 (P_{10})- Special knowledge

The potential perpetrators were divided to the specified classes as shown in table 1.

	P_1	P_2	P_3	P_4	P_5	P_6	P_7	P_8	P_9	P_{10}	Total
External											
Vandals	3										3
Former employees	5		5				5				15
Building services	3										3
Clerical	180	20									200
Production	2										2
System related											
Users		124	30				12				166
Equipment Engineers								9	5		14
Application Programmers						7	20			3	30
System Programmers										9	9
Operations				8	12						20
Total number	193	144	35	8	12	7	37	9	5	12	462
Severity	10	60	90	110	140	120	150	30	20	300	
Proclivity	120	80	80	90	90	90	90	110	110	140	

TABLE 1
Perpetrator class transformation and severity and proclivity ratings.

The principal used in classifying different people to the perpetrator classes was the person's organizational position. In some cases a person's computer related skills presumed of transforming him to a more demanding class that his job would otherwise indicate.

Next step was to determine the severity rating for each perpetrator class. In this step, the relative severity is determined of the impact that would result should a member of one perpetrator class rather than another attack one of the system resources. The severity rating for each class was obtained by giving 300 severity points to the class that was considered the most dangerous in case of a system attack. After determining the most severe class, other classes' severity points were given in a relative manner. For example a member in class P_8 has 30 severity points. Severity points, obtained, are in table 1.

The final step in perpetrator analysis is to determine the proclivity of a perpetrator class to attack on any resource. This step attempts to measure the incentive or desire of one perpetrator class relative to another to commit an attack. A member in a perpetrator class was considered to have more proclivity to misuse the system if he was supposed to be more curious, or he would have more personal advantage than a member in another class. At first each class was given 100 points. After considering each classes deviation from the standard point rate, the final points were obtained. The proclivity ratings are shown in table 1.

TARGET ASSESSMENT

At this point of RIM-analysis nine different target classes were defined. A target class describes a way to misuse the computer system. For each target class there is a set of target elements that might be the specific objects under attack. Only the most important target elements were considered. The target classes used and their target elements were:

Target class	Objet of Attack	Target Elements
T_1	Programmatic change of data or programs	spool printing program, transaction file
T_2	Programmatic copy of data or programs	sensitive data files
T_3	Non-programmatic change of data or programs	input data
T_4	Non-programmatic copy of data or programs	paper prints of transaction files and data base files
T_5	Programmatic interruptions of service	booth control programs, application programs, data base
T_6	Non-programmatic interruption of service	same as T_5
T_7	Equipment mutilation	many pieces of important equipment
T_8	Theft of equipment or supplies	back up tapes, paper prints
T_9	Theft of service	no significance

TABLE 2

Target class characteristics and their target elements

In every target class each target element's importance was analysed by using a prefixed set of questions like: should the target element be compromised, how much effort would be required to undo the damage? What is the direct dollar loss? To what extent would continued business be affected? etc. For each question the answers were to be rough: small, moderate, large.

Finally in target assessment the relative ranking of the impact upon the organization that might result from attacks on various target elements is determined. A target class impact evaluation is based on the significance of single target elements, which have been already reviewed. In a case of an attack class T_3 was considered to have the most serious impact upon the organization. That impact was to describe 300 points. Other classes' impact was compared to the class T_7 and the relative impact ratings were obtained as shown in table 3.

T_1	T_2	T_3	T_4	T_5	T_6	T_7	T_8	T_9
50	50	50	100	150	10	300	200	0

TABLE 3

Each target class's relative impact upon the organization in a case of an attack

In target assessment the relative attractiveness of each target class to each perpetrator class is also evaluated. Attractiveness is defined to be the relative probability that a person in a perpetrator class will attack some target class rather than another, given that he will attack some target class. In practice the attractiveness measure was obtained by dividing the proclivity points of a perpetrator class to different target classes. The result is in table 4.

Proclivity	Perpetrator	T_1	T_2	T_3	T_4	T_5	T_6	T_7	T_8	T_9
120	P_1				100			7	15	
80	P_2			25	50			4	1	
80	P_3			25	45		5	4	1	
90	P_4	10	10	25	25	5	10	4	1	
90	P_5	12	12	23	23	6	9	4	1	
90	P_6	10	10	25	25	5	10	4	1	
90	P_7	15	15	20	20	7	8	4	1	
110	P_8	10	10	35	35		15	4	1	
110	P_9	10	10	35	35		15	4	1	
140	P_{10}	25	25	30	30	15	10	4	1	

TABLE 4

Each perpetrator class's relative attractiveness to attack a target element in a target class.

FLAW IDENTIFICATION AND ANALYSIS

In RIM-methodology a flaw has been defined as an error of omission or commission in the design, development, implementation, testing, or quality assurance of computer-based information systems or in the operation, administration and management, and/or audit practices of a computer facility that enables a person to perform an unauthorized activity. Five major categories of flaws were introduced: systems (operation and application), operational procedures, telecommunications, systems/user interface, industrial security. For each category a check list of possible flaws was provided.

Each flaw from the check list was analyzed and decided, if the flaw in case can exist in the system. For those flaws that might exist, the reviewer should determine the following subjective probability number: given that someone with the requisite skills and access seeks to exploit the flaw, what is the probability that the flaw exists in a form that will permit it to be successfully exploited? The probabilities were given relative to every other probability in the study. If a flaw was determined to exist, the perpetrator classes that could exploit the flaw by using some target classes were also determined. All these relative probabilities (f_i) were written in a table, where rows are perpetrator classes (P_i) and columns target classes (T_i). In this table are items which can contain several f_i values, because a perpetrator class P can exploit many flaws by using the same target class T.
The probabilities f_i are reduced to a single value F_{pt} using formula 1.

$$F_{pt} = 1 - \prod_{j=1}^{x} (1-f_j) \qquad (1)$$

F_{pt} is a relative probability that a perpetrator class P will exploit the flaws by using target class t.

Among the system related flaws the most significant ones were the ineffectiveness of the user authorization procedure, password procedures and the usefulness of the system log files. The most vulnerable operational procedures were input transaction and certain operation routines. Specially the operations staff's controls were determined inadequate. Considering the telecommunications and the industrial security the system was thought to be rather safe. The systems/user interface flaws were proceeded along with the systems flaws.

RIM-CALCULATION

The fourth step of the methodology brings together all of the individual measures of characteristics from the previous three steps and combines them to form the overall relative-impact measure (RIM).

The RIM-calculation started by forming the number RIM_{pt} using formula 2.

$$RIM_{pt} = N_p \cdot S_p \cdot F_{pt} \cdot A_{pt} \cdot I_t, \qquad (2)$$

where

N_p = the number of individuals in perpetrator class P,

S_p = the relative severity rating for perpetrator class P,

F_{pt} = the probability that a exploitable flaw can be found linking perpetrator class p to an element of target class p.

A_{pt} = the relative attractiveness of targets in target class t to individuals in perpetrator class p.

I_t = the relative impact upon the organization of a successful attack upon an element in target class t.

The figure RIM_{pt} can be considered to be perpetrator class´s p portion of the RIM-value, providing that the person tries to attack an element in class t. By summing up the values RIM_{pt} by the formula 3, the final RIM-value is obtained.

$$RIM = \sum_p \sum_t RIM_{pt} = \sum_p N_p \cdot S_p \cdot \sum_t F_{pt} \cdot A_{pt} \cdot I_t \quad (3)$$

Different perpetrator class´s and target class´s contribution to the RIM-value is calculated by formulas 4 and 5.

$$RIM_p = \sum_t RIM_{pt} \quad (4)$$

$$RIM_t = \sum_p RIM_{pt} \quad (5)$$

The most vulberable elements were found in target class T_4 (non-programmatic copy of data or programs). The most potential perpetrators were users and the most advanced programmers. Though the user class P_3 was the most dangerous, the few individuals in class P_{10} are clearly the biggest threat to the system. The perpetrator classes P_1, P_8 and P_9 had very little influences on the overall RIM-value.

CONCLUSIONS

The final RIM-value is of no value by itself. The most valuable results are the relative values RIM_{pt}, RIM_p and RIM_t, which can be compared within each group. Thus it is easy to point out the vulnerable system resources and the dangerous people among the system. On the other hand, after the RIM-values have once been calculated, the countermeasures to improve the safety of the system may be introduced. Then the RIM-value can be recalculated and the relative effectiveness of the countermeasures are evaluated. In addition the RIM-values can be used in intersystem comparisions.

RIM-methodology takes into account all the important resources of a computer system: people, system environment, possible flaws. The time required is about 10 one-hour interviews with system staff and about 2 days´ work to structure the RIM-model.

The RIM-methodology can be considered a versatile and practical way of dealing with computer security risks.

[1] Nielsen, N.R., et AL., Computer System Integrity: A Relative-Impact Measure of Vulnerability. SRI International, California 1978, 144 pp.

COMPUTER SECURITY
J.B. Grimson and H.-J. Kugler (Editors)
Elsevier Science Publishers B.V. (North-Holland)

SECURITY OF ELECTRONIC TRANSACTIONS

IVAN EKEBRINK

SKANDINAVISKA ENSKILDA BANKEN
STOCKHOLM
SWEDEN

New competitors, new services, increasing banking markets, new regulations and new techniques alter dramatically the use of computers within banks. From being book keeping tools they have become information processors and decisions makers. Information will in a near future be the most valuable part in the banks. This has increased vulnerability and threats in banking services. This paper will illustrate ways to lower threats in payment systems in the S-E-Bank.

INTRODUCTION

Human beings constitute the biggest risk factor - I mean here unintentional faults/errors. It is very important to think carefully before a system is installed.

At security conferences

- risk analysis
- capital protection
- data protection
- functional protection
- quality protection

are always talked about. This is a division of function and a vocabulary that we, as security experts, use and understand. But, when it is a question of informning the bank employee about the protection that has been installed and the responsibility that rests with him, this vocabulary cannot be used since different security measures interact and may provide protection for more than one type. The bank employee must understand why he/she should act in a certain way, e.g. have an opportunity, in retrospect, to supply customers with answers to questions such as how/when/why a transaction has been effected. In addition, the majority of protective measures protect the bank employee from being exposed to mistaken suspicion.

PAYMENTS SYSTEM

The Swedish banks have, over the years, developed and adapted a big range of services connected to the payment area. Example of such services are:

- efficient bank giro and postal giro systems
- integrated systems for domestic and international payments
- "automatic giro" including standing orders and direct debiting
- on-line teller terminals
- check truncation
- data clearing
- cash dispensers (ATM)
- teledata
- home banking
- point of sale systems (EFT-POS)

RISKS

Two types of risks are recountered in EDP systems: unintentional threats (everyday mistake and accidents) - by far the most common - and intentional threats (computer related crime).

The intentional threats to a payment system are of three broad categoris, fraud and theft, invasion of individual privacy and catastrophe. There are three components where payment systems are vulnerable: cards, terminals and communication link.

Three areas in information handling where protection is vital:

* delay, interruption, loss
* unauthorized usage
  - disclosure
  - modification
* substandard data quality
  - incorrect
  - out-of-date
  - incomplete

Has vulnerability increased through the use of terminalised computer systems?

The answer must be yes! The increased vulnerability can be

- organizational (poorly designed procedures)
- poor education (badly trained employees)
- unauthorised use of information through terminals
- key personnel

  etc

The S-E-Bank has protected itself against these risks in the following way.

ORGANIZATIONAL

All systems within the S-E-Bank requires segregation of duties also when terminals are installed and used. Segregation of duties is applied so that accountability for any significant event can be fixed to the level of a single individual. There are written rules, standards and instructions distributed from a central function in the bank. Procedure controls (internal controls) are demanded and the internal auditors checks that these controls are performed. The auditors also request full audit trail in all computer systems.

POOR EDUCATION

Before a system is implemented the user must have education and practice. It is important that security - actions and consciousness - is included in all internal courses.

TERMINALS

Why do the threats increase in terminalised systems?

There are many factors, but the main ones could be the following:

- Use of terminals creates a feeling of anonymity for the user
- The so called "time and space" factors are abolished
- A feeling of small risk for discovery
- Imperfect control structure

What can be done to lower the risks in terminalised systems?

Try to break the feeling of anonymity through a good and well administered access system.

Before a terminal is used within the S-E-Bank it has to be logged on to the system. For the log-on process "one time password" is sometime used.

There is also a "time out" function in the system. This means that the terminal will be disconnected if:

- it is left unattended a certain time
- too many faults have been made
- attempts to do something not permitted have been made
  etc

The control of access to systems and data has improved significantly by the proper use of access software. Such software provides the necessary authorisation and inforcement capabilities to effect the needed separation of responsibilities.

The access control system has four functions:

1. Identification of the user

2. Authentication, proving that the identification claim is valid

3. Authorisation, permission for an identified authenticated user to use a requested program or file

4. Logging of all transactions.

The method of identification may be through the use of card inserted into a reader attached to the system or the identification number may be keyed in on the terminal. The operator must then authenticate his/her identity with a password.

Authorisation is often overlooked but it is critical to real security; without it, we have a computer secured like a house. Once some one is inside he has access to everything therein.

The main requirement on the access control system is that it should

- control access to both hardware and software
- be simple to administrate
- give useful reports
- be transparent for the user.

It is not enough to buy "the best" access system and install it. After that you have no security. To build up and keep protection you must administrate the access system. This administration, which is critical to real security, must include

- someone responsible for the software in the computer
- someone responsible for determining who is permitted to have a password and to what system. Also keeping a list of all the users
- someone responsible for all access rules for the different files. The information has to be classified: for instance open, internal, limited, confidential or secret
- control that the access system is correctly used. One important thing is to analyse the different reports from the system:
  * list of trials not succeeded
  * changing passwords
  * "too many" passwords
  * "too many" authorisation rules for one user
  etc

In the S-E-Bank the password administration assigns a password to a user with instructions that he is to use his password for initial access, at which time he must then change his password. The password must be changed frequently. If a user forgets to change the password he will be reminded by the access system. If he still ignores to change, the system will delete him from the program/file which he has been allowed to use.

In the S-E-Bank we also try to bring back the "time and space" factor by connecting the physical identity of the terminal with the identity of the user. The personal identification number will first be checked if the number is registred as an employee of the bank. Next test will be if the person with this identification number is working at the branch/department where the terminal used is registered. If any of the tests is negative the connection will be broken.

Do allways use and analyze the reports from the access system and do not forget instruments like retrieval and retransmission within the system as a control device.

CARDS

Customers use of the card is connected with a PIN (Personal Identification Number). When the card could be used in different systems - where different values are involved - there is a great risk that the PIN becomes known by other people than the card owner. They could then "borrow" the card and withdraw big amounts from a bank account. Protections against such a situation are:

- different PIN for different systems
- no PIN at all for the "low-cost" system
- PIN in the bank system and ID-card and signature in the retailer system

Examples of threats to cardsystem are:

- copying the card
- steeling cards
- "looking over the shoulder" for PIN

Protections for these could be:

- The Watermark method by EMI, where a special reader reads track "0" for information that has been stored during the manufacturing process of the card. This is permanent information and cannot be changed.

- Distribution of cards and PIN should be done through different channels and at different times. The distribution system should be secure.

  It is important to inform the customer of the risk that card and PIN could be stolen. Keep them separated. The best is to try to remember the PIN without a notation anywhere.

- The customer keyboard should be protected against people who try to "look over the shoulder".

TELECOMMUNICATION

The amounts of money banks spend on telecommunication and data processing is enormous. It would be a mistake, however, to assume that the banks are relative newcomers to telecommunication. Telephone, telegraph and telex have long provided important communication channels for the banking community. The user of these channels has also built up a security thinking when communication is used. Examples of security arrangements are:

- Log-in procedures
- Assigning sequence numbers, in-put and out-put
- Sender identification
- Test key procedures

For control purposes we have the following:
- Transaction Journal
- Due from report
- Delivery confirmation
- Possibility to retrieve messages.

When building a transaction system based on a telecommunication network the following is important:

- Try to limit remote access. If possible give special time for each terminal.
- If dial up shall be used try to avoid any terminal from having direct access to the computer. If possible let the terminal request access and let the system (computer) call back to the terminal.
- Keep a log of all activity in the network. Do not forget to check the log.

In a "call-back" system, any incoming call supplies an identification which is associated with the dialing location. After the incoming call is received and disconnected, the identification is used to find the telephone number of that location. The dial-back is then initiated and the connection reestablished. It may be advisable to require additional identification before actual access to the bank system is permitted.

Then there is the protection of the telecommunication line. Here two techniques exist: complete encryption and the Seal Method. With complete encryption the message is scrambled (unreadable), while in the Seal Method additional information is sent with the message which is in clear.

The algorithm, used for encryption, must be regarded as known also to the "enemy" and the strength of the system is based on the secret key. The key therefore must be changed frequently in some cases for every transaction. The Data Encryption Standard - the DES algorithm - is recommended for use by financial institutes for line encryption.

A line encryption could easily be strengthened by having constant transmission on the line even when no message is sent, "dummy" transmission.

The use of line encryption requires a key management within the bank. The administration of the key management is a very important part of the security work.

The S.W.I.F.T. connection between the concentrator and the bank is protected through encryption. This is performed by a STERN a low-cost device offered through S.W.I.F.T. The STERN requires a very simple key-management procedure.

The Seal Method is an advanced cryptological program which has the effect of sealing every single bit of data in a data file or transmission by signing off with a sophisticated hash total. The transmitted data remains in plain text.

If any piece of data is changed without authorisation, a different hash total will show up when calculated in the computer. The key itself consists of one or more words of 35 digits which are a shared secret between sender and receiver.

The Seal Method can improve the security level in protecting payment information. It is also useful in a number of other applications, such as:

- External data exchange
- Remote data entry
- Double input check
- Distributed programs
- Maintainance responsibility for standard software
- In-house files
- Verification
- Storing accounting material
- Program libraries
- Back-up for databases
- Files kept on local and central computers.

KEY PERSONNEL

A bank must have a well defined and documented contingency plan, easy to understand and frequently tested. The plan should be tested regulary in order to ensure that it is complete, current and effective.

It is also important to analyse the staff situation within and around the data processing function. Within an organisation certain people are critical to the successful operating of a computerised information system. It is important to know who these individuals are and to arrange for reserves on all functions. These reserves need to get instruction and practice now and then to be able to take over if there should be an emergency.

RESPONSIBILITIES

Within the S-E-Bank, the principles of information protection is decided by the top management and documented in a policy statement. In addition to this policy statement, guildelines are published. These guidelines outline management and employee responsibilities together with minimum requirements, within different areas of security work.

The overall responsibility for information protection rests with the "security officer". He is a member of the top management in the bank.

The performance of information protection is the responsibility of line management, owners of information, users of information and employees. They have to follow the published guidelines.

The internal auditor is responsible for controlling existence and performance of security actions. All regular internal and external audits should include the protection of information.

CONCLUSIONS

How to lower the risk in a bank information system?

Require separation of duties and complete audit trail in all systems.

Staff must be well educated and trained.

When using terminals try to break the feeling of anonymity through a good and well administrated access system using all three functions: Identification, Authentication and Authorisation. Keep a log of all transactions at the terminal. Change the password frequently.

Try to bring back the "time and space" factor by connecting the physical identity of the terminal with the identity of the user.

Try to avoid dial-up connections, use two way connections instead.

Remember to use and analyze the reports from the access system and do not forget instruments like retrieval and retransmission within the system as a control device.

Use a secured distribution system for cards and PIN´s.

Let top management sign a policy statement concerning information protection and distribute the responsibility rules within the company.

Information security is a amalgam of organization, audit, physical security, computer techniques and management commitment.

COMPUTER SECURITY
J.B. Grimson and H.-J. Kugler (Editors)
Elsevier Science Publishers B.V. (North-Holland)

COMPUTER AND NETWORK SECURITY POLICY: A CHALLENGE TO ORGANIZATIONS

Louise Giovane Becker
ELGIN GROUP LTD.
Bethesda, Maryland

Computer-related resources are important organizational assets requiring appropriate safeguards. Consequently organizations attempting to implement a computer and network security program require a policy framework. This work discusses the elements of security policy and some of the prospects for improving security of computer and related networks. An effective means of formulating a security policy requires an increased awareness of problems and an organizational information architecture. This paper discusses security policy development within the framework of information resources management.

INTRODUCTION

The increased importance of automated information resources to organizations operational and management functions prompts concern with protection of these resources. The possible failure or misuse of these systems has serious consequence for organizations and, in some instances, society and the individual.
Computers and associated communications systems provides a unique opportunity to process, access and disseminate vast amounts of data. The proliferation of automated information systems gives impetus to consider effectively safeguarding these assets. The incalculable value to organizations of the computer-related resources and its importance in the economic viability of the concern makes it essential to formulate security policy to support organizational goals and objectives.

Computer and network security encompasses a wide range of activities associated with the life-cycle management of automated information resources and telecommunications systems.[1] These activities attempt to assure that these resources are maintained with adequate confidentiality, accuracy, integrity, and availability to achieve desired goals and objectives of the organization.[2] Safeguarding automated information resources is a complex and multifaceted activity. Achieving effective security is dependent on understanding the nature of threats and vulnerabilities as well as an appreciation of the tools and techniques that can protect the automated information resources. Furthermore, computer security implementation and associated policies are generally understood better if viewed within a comprehensive organizational information architecture and as part of an information resources management (IRM) approach.

This paper explores the potential of developing a computer security architecture and integrated formulation of associated policy. In this context policy relates to organizational behavior and action to obtain stated goals and objectives. Security policy is meant to provide a bridge between requirements and the eventual implementation of the appropriate security measures.

COMPUTER SECURITY IN PERSPECTIVE

Until relatively recently computer security was considered mainly an interest of the national security and defense communities. Consequently, leadership and support for computer and associated networks security was primarily the focus of that part of government. More recently both civilian government agencies and the private sector have taken an interest in protecting automated information systems. The realization that computer-related resources are vulnerable,especially sensitive data (financial, personal data, proprietary information, etc.), and that adequate security of these critical data must be provided is becoming more evident.

Certain developments and technological changes in automated information processing seems to diminishes differences between the needs of the national security communities for security and those of the private sector. At one time the stringent requirements of the defense and national security communities were believe to have little if any application to civilian and private sectors. With the proliferation of computer systems and associated networks in the private sector and the growth of sensitive applications there seems to be a greater interest in securing these systems. Consequently as the private sector seeks to obtain a higher level of security the distinction between security need of the private sector versus government seems to be less.

There is still a considerable difference in perspective and approach between the national security community and the private sector. In the national security communities concern centers on the threat from hostile forces while the civilian agencies and the private sector are generally more concerned with the threat from authorized personnel. Another difference between the these sectors is the labeling of information. Historically the military and national security community have implemented security based on a hierarchical classification of the data (e.g., confidentiality, secret, top secret). In addition, the military and related communities have depended on clearance procedures that assigns personnel a certain level of trust. These differences in approach and direction have caused some confusion in understanding the computer security problem.

Recent incidents of computer abuse and the increased awareness of the threats to automated information systems focuses attention on the need to safeguard computer-related resources. Moreover, media reports of unauthorized access of computer/communications systems by intruders, such as "computer hackers" has heighten concerns. Over the years incidents of computer-assisted crimes, sabotage of automated information resources, and misuse of the resources have focused attention on effective means to curtail abuses. Intentional and unintentional actions that result in errors, interruption of services, unwanted access to and manipulation of data, damage to equipment and information, hardware or software weakness, and failure in support systems (power sources and air conditioning) cause concern. The potential harm to computer-related resources from natural disasters, espionage, wiretapping and interception of emanations (electromagnetic radiation), further increases concern. In addition, there is a continuing danger posed by authorized and unauthorized persons who may gain access to systems and associated resources. In the opinion of some security experts the people problem remains the greatest threat to computerized resources.

Organizations have been slow in coming to understand the implications of the computer threats and vulnerabilities. A recent American Bar Association Task Force on Computer Crime survey indicates that the "controlling computer crime rests with private industry and individual users."[3] Many respondents to the ABA survey indicated that there was a "lack of awareness and concern by management and the public ... concerning computer crime".[4] The ABA concluded that [5]

> If the concerns expressed by a large number of the respondents are accurate, it would appear that the upper levels of corporate (and government) management may be underestimating both the potential magnitude and the probability of various types of computer crime. If this is so, public and private management may be implicitly or explicitly undervaluing the possible, or likely, losses from computer crime and, therefore, under investing in protective security measures.

Another issue addressed by the ABA is that there is a distinct difference in information technology development and responsive computer security technology.[6]

> ... from the comments provided by respondents to the Task Force survey. One is the apparent gap between computer technology generally and computer security technology. This gap, or lag, between the two seems to be increasing.

As organizations move toward protecting computer/communications resources they face a special challenge in identifying problems and implementing remedies. In addition they must allocate resources and order priorities effectively. Some organizations have difficulty in making the necessary investment in a computer security program; others find that even after they identify problems, limited resources and the lack of appropriate security tools prevents development of a comprehensive security program.

Organizations which have an information architecture or planned strategy with a well defined set of goals and objectives have been successful in formulating security policy and implementing a security program. Some find that the using information resources management approach can assist in addressing computer security problem. IRM permits the consideration of the computer security aspects in relationship to the overall organizational information architecture.[7] There is great validity to viewing the computer security an integral part of the total information process. Specifically the IRM approach or framework permits the [8]

- o the IRM group to concentrate on designing an information architecture that best supports organizational goals and objectives; group members are not distracted or otherwise influenced by operational activities.

- o the IRM group to best reconcile the wishes and needs of various groups, such as users and information handling service providers, in a manner consistent with management intentions.

Futhermore IRM approach provides a means of supporting the information security program by facilitating and understanding the framework of the conceptual model of the organization or an organizational information architecture.[9] This approach stimulates the development of a computer security architecture and the associated security policy. This processes benefits the organization by integrating the overall organizational information architecture with the security requirements.

LEGISLATIVE FRAMEWORK

Over the years both Federal and state legislatures have acted to protect information and penalize those that would abuse or misuse these resources. Currently over 35 states have a "computer crime" statutes and in 1984 the U.S. Congress enacted a Federal computer crime statute as well. Currently there are several bill in the Congress augmenting the computer crime law. There has been a continuing interest in protecting certain types of information and data. Certain statutes, (e.g., Census Act, Freedom of Information Act, Privacy Act of 1974, Right to Financial Privacy Act, Fair Credit Acts, as well as others) require protection of information.

More recently the Congress of the United States enacted the Counterfeit Access and Computer Fraud and Abuse Act. (Public Law 98-473). The new law provides penalties for abuse and misuse of government and bank computers. Another law enacted in 1984, the Small Business Computer Security and Education Act of 1984 (Public

Law 98-362). is directed at increasing awareness and fostering an understanding of computer security for the small business community. Interestingly the Act creates a Computer Security and Education Advisory Council composed of officials from government and the private sector.[10] This advisory group is designed to improve the small business community's awareness of computer threats and safeguards.

TOWARDS A COMPUTER SECURITY ARCHITECTURE

Creation of the computer security architecture is an important step towards achieving a cohesive program for protecting automated information resources. As has been mentioned the development of a security architecture should be linked to well defined set of organizational goals and objectives.

The security architecture aids in evolving appropriate strategies to cope with automated information systems vulnerabilities. Realistically the security architecture should provide a set of alternatives or options within the total organizational information architecture. The security architecture and the policy formulation activities are complementary activities and deserve to be carefully integrated. The two activities should be centrally coordinated or subject to a single oversight unit. Consequently formulation of organizational security policy may best be considered early-on and in conjunction with the security architecture. Subsequent modifications and changes should be coordinated within in the organization. The security architecture must be approached with an understanding of organizational goals and objectives.

Computer and information vulnerabilities are often recognized by those closest to the system. But experience indicates that those knowledgeable about security problems often have difficulty in getting management to come to the "something has to be done" stage. Organizations who develop a successful security strategy acknowledge that management involvement and support are essential to effective implementation of controls and safeguards.
Development of the policy and security architecture provides an important framework for management to assess and understand organizational requirements.

A first step in both policy development and security architecture planning is to identify intramural resources as well as those outside the organization that can facilitate the process. In addition, awareness training and educational resources should be made available when necessary. Identify individuals or elements within the organization which can contribute to the overall computer security strategy is important. In addition, outside resources should be identified to assist in formulating an appropriate team of people to work on the problem.

In order to assist in developing an effective security policy and implementation strategy it is essential that consideration be given to a re-examination of the organizational structure and responsibilities . In computer security policy this alignment of authority or responsibilities must be identified early on. In addition there is a need to provide a means to coordinate various elements within the organization. Appointing a center of accountability may or may not require changes in organizational structure or realignment of responsibilities but it should remain an option.

Surveying vulnerabilities or risk assessment is an important aspect of developing a computer security architecture and supportive policy. Risk assessment provides the organization a quantitative statement of potential problems to which the automated information process or operation may subjected. This process should provide an opportunity to identify threats and ultimately provide the basis for the selection of security measures. The risk assessment effort specifies the threshold of loss or destruction of the information resources. This enables organizations to fully evaluate the threat and possible remedies that should be applied.

Unfortunately in many organizations the risk assessment effort resembles the Queen's croquet game in Alice in Wonderland

-- where rule change accommodations are arbitrary.

There is a tendency towards retro-fitting remedies and controls. In general a reluctance to pinpoint responsibilities and wavering if not "gnashing of teeth" when controls must be placed. Since most organizations react only when confronted with a specific security problem they are seldom in a position to take appropriate action. A security architecture is meant to limit retro-fitting, identify controls, and facilitates changes.

SECURITY POLICY DEVELOPMENT

Establish a security policy is designed to assist in implementation of an effective security program. Consequently it is necessary to consider formulating policies that reflect the total organizational information architecture.

An information security policy might consider the following elements:

- o The security policy must be applicable to employees at all organizational levels and to vendors/contractors providing goods or services to the organization.

- o Responsibilities are identified at all levels of the organization

(senior managers, various levels of managers, planners, operators, proponents, users, and auditors)

- o Information systems security officer role and responsibilities should be defined and described.

- o Policies should be developed for all aspects of the system.

Policies must be developed that cover all aspects of the systems including some general aspects, systems and network elements, classification of information, contingency plans, physical security, insurance and any special audit requirements, personnel security, and contractors or others who would interact with the systems.

Organizations might consider the value of an information systems security advisory group or committee. Such a group should include the central officer responsible for computer and communications security, planners, controller, auditors,and various user and proponents of systems. The group can facilitate the exchange of information related to security policies, formulate or suggest policy and make recommendations for management consideration. In organizations having a well developed information resources management (IRM) program this information systems security advisory group might be a subset or task force of an overall information technology advisory function.

Special policies may be required to reflect specific organizational requirements. For example, organization's systems configuration that includes distributive processing or access to time-shared services may require different thresholds of reliability and integrity.

Classification or categorization of the data is needed if appropriate security measures are to be applied. The data categorization scheme may be simple as designating data either sensitive or non sensitive or it may be multi-level hierarchical scheme reflecting subtle variations of sensitivity. With either scheme it is essential that the categories be explicitly described in the security policy. In developing such schemes, an advisory group can be especially helpful if it is composed of representatives from the appropriate elements within the organizations. Once the categorization scheme is developed it may require periodic checks to determine if the data classification or categorization scheme is to be modified or adjusted. Changes to the classification scheme may be needed as new applications or data bases are included.

Another useful planning tool supportive of the information security strategy is the life cycle planning for information systems. This formalization of stages of the automated information system and associated networks development from inception to eventual replacement is useful in integrating the automated information resource security strategies and policies.

Involvement of systems user or proponent provides continuing review and sponsorship of an application or program. The user proponent or "owner" of the system provides control over direction and form of the information. The value of this arrangement in which the user is responsible for systems direction should not be dismissed lightly. The proponent or user can easily define the parameters of the system; this is extremely useful in appropriately securing the automated information resource.

PROSPECTS AND FUTURE DIRECTIONS

Over the years the concern regarding protecting of automated information resources continues to grow. As has been mentioned the possible abuse and misuse of computer related assets prompts consideration of a strategy to protect systems from threats and vulnerabilities. Although security technological innovations have not always kept pace with projected needs of computer and network users, organizations are finding that there is a considerable number of choices in selecting safeguards. In addition there is a growing body of literature indicating a wide range of approaches in the physical and administrative security arena.

A report, Computer Abuse and Misuse: An Assessment of Federal and State Initiatives, prepared for the Department of Defense addressed some of the key factors that may stimulate narrowing of the current security technology gap, including:[11]

- o The National Policy for Telecommunications and Automated Information Systems Security [NSDD-145] A new national policy in the United States that presents an opportunity to promote technological innovation.
- o Insurance requirements. and
- o Demands of the internal auditors for better controls.

As demands for computer safeguards increase it is believed that the market place may be stimulated to provide necessary security innovations. In the United States the new national policy is designed to encourage technology developers to identify markets stimulated by the growing needs of both government and the private sector for security technology.

One factor, with potential to stimulate security innovation is the requirement to appropriately secure automated resources for insurance or audit purposes. For example, organizations may obtain a lower premium rate for automated information systems that have the appropriate safeguards. These types of economic incentive may aid in developing a market for certain security innovations.

An incentive to stimulate the marketplace is demonstrations or prototypes of certain security features on existing or new systems. Sucessful "prototyping" or "implementation models" may encourage organizations to apply the new tools and techniques to their situation.

Another problem that deserves additional attention is assessing the lack of interest in applying some of the existing computer tools and techniques. There is very little accurate information on why certain tools or techniques in computer security are not applied. It is known that certain factors such as, the lack of awareness, costly initial investment, and the possible decrease in systems performance hampers implementation.-Nevertheless, it may be useful to quantify these problems so that decisionmakers may come to understand what factors hamper the implementation of certain security measures.

Organizations currently face a challenge in protecting information resources. There is a continuing need to explore fully those factors which will permit effective computer security tools and techniques to be fully used. As has been mentioned, there may be a need to develop prototypes so that organizations will have a better understanding of the applicability of certain measures and what policies will provide a viable framework for improving the security of automated resources.

FOOTNOTES

1.Relates to the planning, initiation, operation, and replacemtn phases of a system.

2. U.S. Library of Congress. Congressional Research Service. Computer Security: An Overview of National Concerns and Challenges. February 3, 1983. Authored by Louise Giovane Becker. Washington, 1983. p. 1.

3.American Bar Association. Section of Criminal Justice. Task Force on Computer Crime. Report on Computer Crime. June 1984. Washington, 1984. p. 42.

4.Ibid.

5.Ibid.

6.Ibid., p. 42-43.

7.Wood, Charles Cresson. Enhancing Information Security with the Information Resource Management Approach. Computer & Security 2, 1983:223-229.

8.Ibid., p. 225.

9.Ibid.

10.Becker, Louise Giovane. Computer Abuse and Misuse: An Assessment of Federal and State Legislative Initiatives. December 1984. P-1798. Alexandria, Virginia, institute for Defense Analyses, 1984. p.45.

11.Ibid., p. 6

COMPUTER SECURITY
J.B. Grimson and H.-J. Kugler (Editors)
Elsevier Science Publishers B.V. (North-Holland)

DEVELOPMENT AND ORGANIZATION OF THE AUDIT AND SECURITY FUNCTIONS

JOHN G. BEATSON

Manager, Audit & Security
Databank Systems Limited
Wellington
NEW ZEALAND

A vital aspect of any security programme is that of security management. Data security responsibilities should be delegated to a separate group and both the data security group and the internal audit department, must be adequately staffed to meet the requirements of the rapidly changing environment in which they are required to function. The wide range of potential involvement by both data security and audit personnel, demands that senior management know what they can expect from their audit department and have a way of determining whether they are in fact receiving the required information.

INTRODUCTION

The development of the audit and security functions are very much dependent upon the size of the organization and the importance placed upon those functions by senior management. Accordingly, some of the content of this paper will not be particularly relevant to every reader. It is however important, that each aspect described, is considered by management before making any final decision to waive a particular control.

DATA PROCESSING IN THE NEW ZEALAND BANKING INDUSTRY

Databank Systems Limited was established in 1966 by the Bank of New Zealand when two computer centres were opened in Wellington and Auckland. In the space of the two succeeding years, the remaining four banks joined as a consortium on a co-operative basis and resulted in a further four centres being established by 1969.

The co-operative concept proved vital in establishing a national computerised network providing services for the total banking system. Today, Databank Systems Limited has fifteen network centres linked to two central processing centres and provides data processing facilities for more than 1200 bank branches. Services are also provided to a large number of bureau customers, including other finance houses, legal partnerships and accounting organizations.

Facilities provided to the New Zealand banks, in addition to the traditional clearing house function and posting of transactions to customer accounts, also include terminal access to customer accounts for enquiry, maintenance and online capture of dollar-value transactions. EFT has been an integral part of the Databank development since the late 1960's when systems generating electronic payments were first introduced.

EFT today, incorporates various payment systems as well as Automatic Tellers and Point-of-Sale systems. Daily transaction volumes average three million, of which some 750,000 are electronically generated.

A most recent development is the introduction of videotex-based banking and information services for bank customers. This, with other EFT applications, ensures a continuation of Databank's position at the leading edge of worldwide banking technology.

The New Zealand Banking industry relies on its integrity to protect the individual and corporate organizations who are its customers. The decision to establish Databank Systems Limited was made in the knowledge that computer systems design could be made to create a secure environment - even greater that previous methods - to protect the individual customer.

Preventative security, protected by secrecy, is the keystone of systems integrity. However, Databank is continually searching for methods and techniques which can improve on the high level of security already imposed on the advanced and complex systems already in place.

Databank's security philosophy is that its security should satisfy three objectives:

- to ensure the continuity and confidentiality of our operation,
- to protect the capital investment in premises, equipment and environmental support systems, and
- to provide secure working conditions for staff;

These objectives are based on the premise that New Zealand's financial structure could be seriously impaired should any untoward incident occur to any equipment, building structure, systems or programming information, proprietary banking or commercial information held in our charge or to the personnel involved in any aspect of our entire operation.

In Databank, responsibility for the security function is shared between two departments. In the first instance, the Premises Department is responsible for all matters relating to physical security including access control, environmental aspects and co-ordination of external guard services. Remaining aspects of security, in effect all those relating to data security, together with the audit function, are the responsibility of the Audit & Security division.

ESTABLISHMENT OF THE AUDIT & SECURITY DIVISION

It was following a companywide review of security and effectiveness during 1980, that a new division was established with specific responsibility for audit and data security matters. At the time, that responsibility addressed:

- The establishment and review of standards for security (in conjunction with other divisions and banks) and monitoring compliance with those standards;
- Internal audit procedures in conjunction with the Company's external auditors, but excluding any financial audit activity;
- Continuing liaison with customers' audit functions.

The Audit & Security division reports directly to the Chief Executive Officer and has a direct link to the Board of Directors through membership of a board sub-committee known as the 'Systems Audit & Security Committee' (Figure 1).

The Systems Audit & Security Committee, on which the Board Chairman and Chief Executive Officer sit, recognises the directors' responsibility for the audit and security function and enables them to be more aware of the activities in those areas.

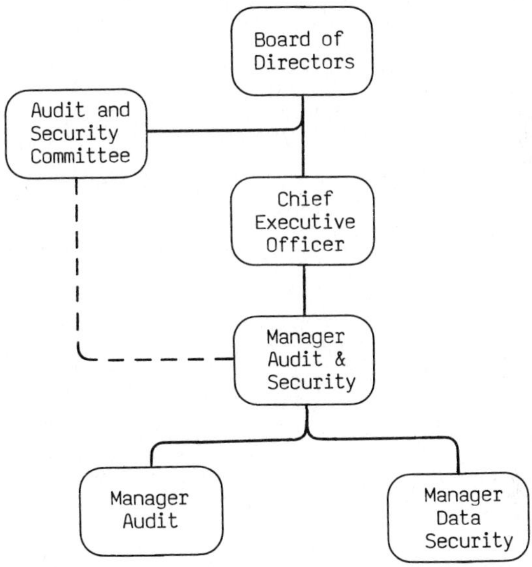

Figure 1 - Divisional Organization

The organizational position of the Audit & Security division, indicates the degree of commitment made by general management. The status of the division is sufficient to guarantee the accomplishment of its audit and security responsibilities, the free presentation of review findings and the prompt response to opinions and recommendations.

Decisions made in respect of the functions for which the division is responsible are binding on the people concerned unless over-riding directives are made by the Chief Executive Officer.

FUNCTIONS OF THE AUDIT & SECURITY DIVISION

The Audit & Security division is composed of two departments, Audit and Data Security, each with specific responsibilities which collectively address almost all areas of security concern. Activities carried out by the two departments are described in the course of the following paragraphs:

AUDIT

Application Reviews

Are the single largest activity carried out by our audit staff. Because of Databank's unique position, our own external auditors and those of our shareholder banks in particular, are dependent upon Databank internal auditors providing evidence that production systems are properly controlled and documented.

Reviews are primarily concerned with adherence to standards and the adequacy of controls in order to ensure maximum data integrity. Audit working papers undergo close review by audit management to ensure that standards are maintained.

Although we plan ahead over some three years, a schedule of application reviews for each fiscal year is compiled at the end of the preceding year and is ratified by the Systems Audit & Security Committee. If they wish, Bank auditors are able to contribute to the development of the schedule.

During the course of each review, extensive testing through the use of independent audit programs, is carried out in order to confirm the processing of the programs under review. At the conclusion of the review, a report is prepared for the Chief Executive Officer and conclusions and recommendations subsequently documented for the information of bank auditors.

New Systems Development

Is an area in which until recently, we have not been involved to any great extent. Databank is at the present time, however, redeveloping its entire banking system and a major move has been to have at least one auditor involved in each project team. The audit objective is to ensure that system controls are such that optimum control and data integrity will be maintained. It will of course be appreciated by the reader that it is also less expensive to incorporate controls during the development phase, rather than at a later stage.

Administrative Audits

Involve reviews of administrative, operational and security procedures in computer centres and Head Office departments. We schedule at least one visit, on a surprise basis, to each centre and department per annum; if considered necessary, an additional audit will be conducted in order to monitor action taken in response to an earlier audit. In the event of a management change, a special audit is undertaken to provide the new manager with an up-to-date audit appraisal.

As with application reviews, a report is prepared following each audit and distributed to management for review. On a monthly basis, audit reports are subject to discussion with the Chief Executive Officer and the Company's external auditors.

Financial Audits

Are a new activity commenced in 1985 and support the continuing evolution of the audit function and responsibilities. Aimed primarily at complementing the work of the Company's statutory auditors, it is our intention to address financial procedures on a more frequent basis.

Monitoring Processing Controls

Includes the investigation of problems which may arise during processing. Audit staff generally assist in resolving exception conditions and are required to approve any adjusting entries. Daily control reports are automatically produced within the Audit department and permit the regular monitoring of controls to ensure that no out-of-balance condition passes unnoticed by operational personnel.

Disaster/Recovery Audits

Are conducted periodically in order to test the adequacy of file backup procedures and the existence of backup files. Our objective is to provide management with assurance that in the event of a major disaster, we can recover promptly and continue processing with a minimum of difficulty.

Auditors are also involved in the periodic testing of contingency plans which are of the utmost importance to our entire operation as they are of course with most other major organizations, worldwide. The audit role is primarily to observe the 'test' in operation in order to identify any potential areas of concern.

A less significant aspect of the audit function, but nevertheless important, is the vetting of all updates to reference manuals describing the operation of application processing controls. Those manual pages are not distributed until approval has been given by an auditor.

DATA SECURITY

Protecting and Monitoring Computer Activity is a most important aspect of any Data Security function and in this respect, a number of specific activities are essential in ensuring maximum protection:

Security exception reports

Are produced daily from our major computer systems and identify users/tasks which have attempted to access data files without authorisation. The reports are the end product from a security system which is designed to control access to all information and resources including program libraries.

System logs

Provide a historical record of activity which has taken place on a computer during a given time period; usually 24 hours. We plan to review the logs on a random basis and look for unusual activity, including whether any programs are providing operators with the ability to bypass controls, whether the logs are complete, the presence of poor operating techniques and non-standard operator communication.

SMF (System Management Facility)

Provides information relating to computer activity and acts as a data gathering mechanism for Databank's Job Accounting system. Our auditors are able to monitor, inter alia, all jobs run during the time period under review, programs executed and data files accessed.

All System Changes are monitored in order to ensure that changes to existing production systems are properly authorised:

Program patching

Enables changes to be made to program code without changing the source code and thereby bypass normal control procedures. There exists a potential for introducing unauthorised changes to computer programs and necessitates very strict control measures to ensure that all changes are authorised.

Program Library Updates

Are periodically reviewed to ensure that all changes are authorised and follow normal control procedures. It is at this point that we take special interest in the continued adequacy of system controls.

Program source code changes

Made to sensitive programs are monitored with a view to identifying any possible unauthorised code which may have been included with other authorised changes. While not necessarily a simple task, we are able to identify all changes through the use of a source code compare facility and it is here that we seek to minimise the possibility of fraud occurring in the programming environment. It should be noted however that in practice, unintentional errors are a greater source of security risk than any intentional action.

Security Administration

The principle function within the sphere of security administration is that of the Data Security Administrator. Major tasks include the:

- Management of security software packages to control access to data and resources.
- Development and implementation of procedures for the use of data security software.
- Monitoring adherence to data security policies and investigation of any security breaches which are detected.

We also have responsibility for key management for all encryption devices installed on our terminal network. Procedures have had to be developed to ensure the orderly implementation of encryption devices (in conjunction with the Network Engineering Group) and proper control of physical keys and of course, the encryption keys themselves.

Security Audits

The department conducts security audits of the more technical applications, program products and the system programming environment. The various components of the operating system and peripheral systems are included in the audit programme.

Security Reviews

Based on the methodology used in 1980 but updated to reflect current technologies, security reviews are conducted in order to establish that no matters of concern have appeared since the previous review. As organizational and procedural matters are routinely addressed during administrative audits, recent security reviews have been limited to the more technical aspects and have included terminal, communications and physical security.

Security awareness

Of our staff is a major concern, and while responsibility rests very firmly with individual management, we see it being necessary to periodically present short seminars and supporting material. Our intention has been to ensure that all staff are constantly reminded of their responsibilities with respect to security in their work places.

In this regard we have used posters, stickers, an audio-visual and video presentations in addition to the periodic seminars. Where possible, we ensure that company publications have appropriate articles on security. A booklet on security for distribution to all staff, and particularly new entrants, is currently being produced.

Audit Services

Are provided in support of the work carried out by auditors - not only our own, but also, both the internal and the external auditors of our shareholder banks. The facility is available also to auditors of our non-banking customers.

The audit service provides a completely independent means for auditors to verify the integrity of data and adequacy of application controls.

Security Policy

The Audit & Security division is responsible for the definition and establishment of security policy. The division both initiates and receives proposals for new policies or amendments to existing policies.

After drafting, proposed policies are subject to review and acceptance by a Security Committee comprised of four other divisional managers and chaired by Manager Audit & Security. Policy statements finally determined by the committee must be agreed with the Chief Executive Officer and ratified by the Systems Audit & Security Committee of the Board of Directors.

The final step in the process of implementing security policy, is the formal publishing of the policy in a Security Policy Manual and the issuance of the necessary update pages over the signature of Manager Audit & Security. All departmental and computer centre managers are required to ensure that the new or amended policy is put into effect when required.

To some extent, the division is also involved with policy decisions relating to Physical Security; regular meetings with Premises management ensure that we are kept informed of and are able to comment on, and influence, any planned development and maintenance of physical facilities.

Education/Consultancy

A natural development has been to extend our activities into the field of education and consultancy in both Audit and Security. We have found that there has been and is a significant public demand for education in these subjects, and to this end, we have produced a variety of courses designed to meet specific needs, including:

Auditing EDP Systems
Audit Management
Computer Security

The more experienced staff have been engaged as consultants for specific projects and we have been host to a series of audit trainees from Indonesia who have undertaken 8-12 week practical EDP Audit courses in New Zealand. The audit courses mentioned above, have also been presented in Indonesia and Malaysia by our more experienced auditors.

Departmental Organization

Organizationally, both Audit and Data Security departments are structured in similar ways with the former being the more formally established at this time. The structure we have put in place is that shown in Figure 2.

Each audit team is headed by a senior auditor to whom report two audit analysts. These latter positions have supervisory responsibility for one or two systems auditors and/or assistant auditors. Each team is involved in similar activities.

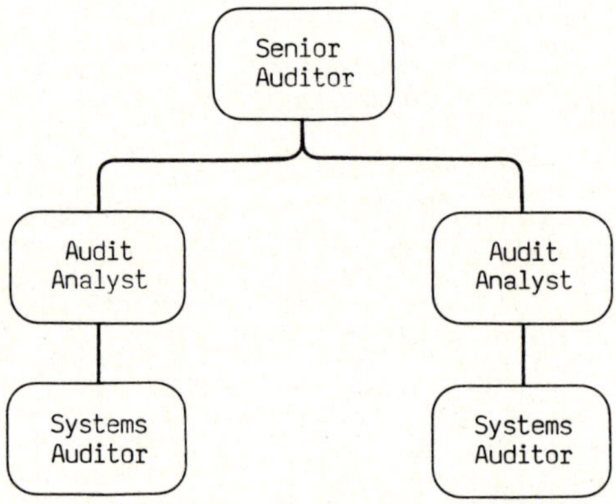

Figure 2.

In the Data Security department, although a similar staff structure is in place, position titles tend to differ, for example, there are Security Analysts or Data Security Officers rather than Audit Analysts, in order to more obviously relate the job title to the type of work undertaken. The Senior Auditors and the Data Security Administrator report directly to the Manager of their respective departments.

In establishing a departmental structure such as we have, it has been our prime objective to clearly identify career paths for Audit and/or Data Security staff while at the same time allowing us to attract more qualified personnel through higher salaries and wider benefits.

Skills Required

The continued development of the Databank Audit and Security functions has seen a parallel development in the skills required of personnel in the departments.

Desirably, but not essentially, audit staff should have a tertiary qualification in accountancy or business administration, as it is necessary for them to have an understanding of accounting controls. Most of our audit staff do have this type of academic qualification although two of our better auditors however, have none.

In today's rapidly changing technological environment it is becoming increasingly necessary for auditors to be proficient in data processing. Many auditors, particularly those who are perhaps more attuned to the financial environment, do not have the necessary aptitude to enable them to become conversant with terminology, let alone how it all works.

In the Databank case, I believe we will see an increasing number of auditors coming from technical environments, that is, systems analysts and programmers. Ideally that expertise will be combined with the accounting related tertiary qualification which is so desirable.

In the Data Security environment and particularly that of Security Administration, it is essential that personnel have an appropriate degree of technical and/or operational expertise. The tertiary qualification is not important or even necessary.

And what of the future

In recent years Databank has made significant moves to extend the scope of electronic banking in New Zealand. In this year of 1985 we have seen the introduction of a nationwide Point-of-Sale system and videotex-based banking services, which in due course will provide a home-banking facility.

As new processing technologies are introduced, Audit and Data Security personnel will be required to be familiar with, and review, systems using those technologies. New audit responsibilities coupled with advances in communications, computer and system technologies, will require specialist technical skills; those skills will need to be acquired.

Personnel will need to be well-educated and innovative; they must be able to develop new, untried ways of "proving" the integrity of computer applications. At least, they must know what measures should be in place to ensure maximum control and security of data.

Through the establishment of it Audit & Security Division, Databank has ensured that the audit and security functions within the company have the means to develop and be maintained as they should be, to meet the demands which will arise in the years which lie ahead.

COMPUTER SECURITY
J.B. Grimson and H.-J. Kugler (Editors)
Elsevier Science Publishers B.V. (North-Holland)

DP-Security: Attacks against Data Processing and preventive Measures

Hartmut Pohl
Cologne, Federal Republic of Germany

Attack-targets of penetrators into dp-systems are the organizational structure of governmental agencies or companies, the technical system with compromising emanation and cross-talking, manipulating hardware devices, software manipulation and communication lines wich may be intercepted, wire-tapped or dialled. Penetrators are employees (operators, programmers) with sufficient experience, extraneous employees with similar know-how (advisors, maintenance and cleaning people) and others who take notice of data more or less unintentionally. There are four attack-methods by-passing or overcoming the access-control-system: Using available or self-developed software without recording unauthorized activities, simulation of authorized users and garbage collection of remaining sensitive data of storages, devices or output. The only effective counter-measure against attacks is an automatic access-control-system which contains identification- and authentification-procedures and recording-procedures; records have to be analyzed.

0 Preliminary remarks

In the recent years security-problems in the area of data processing have been discussed intensively in government and industry of the Federal Republic of Germany. Some important articles of authors such as Cerny (1980) and Jahl (1984) have been published. With regard to the difficulty to develop "information-protection-systems" for the arising information and communication systems by the integration of data-, word-, speech- and picture-processing see Grochla (1983). The following paper concentrates on threats of data processing, which go beyond conventional aspects like natural hazards and assaults. This paper deals with the protection against unauthorized access to sensitive or classified data and their possible misuse. The following aspects are being discussed: Possible penetrators, targets of penetrators in information systems, attack-methods and counter-measures.

However conventional personal and material related measures, all aspects of data privacy and reliability problems are not dealt with here although they concern dp-security as well. The dp-technical measures discussed here could be used as anti-sabotage measures as well.

Acknowledgements: Because of the sensitive nature of this paper, some of the people to whom I am greatly indebted for their intellectual motivation and special inspiration cannot be explicitly thanked. Rather than ignoring anyones help, I have decided to give only five abbreviations in some order C.J., D.C., Dr. J.K., my o.s.o.b. Dr. G.P. and especially my recent Glw.

Manufacturers of data processing systems are now in a position to offer a certain amount of built-in security measures. Security is a function of hard- and software and their interaction. Provided that the hardware is capsulated and cannot be manipulated and maintenance activities are supervised totally, the level of security depends on how many security measures are built into the hardware itself or how close they are built around it. In any case built-in protection is more effective than add-on measures implemented later:

o Some weak spots discussed in the first chapter could be eliminated or rendered insignificant by a security-conscious design.
o Some attack-methods discussed in the third chapter would be less effective or even ineffective.
o Even the user is able to implement security by having the right design of software: Security measures should be considered already in the design-phase, in order to make them effective in the use and maintenance-phase of the software. In the future software-manufacturers therefore will develop tools to support the user in implementing software-security-measures.

To evaluate security measures in the area of data processing one would have

o to determine the possible, real and known threats;
o to discover the possible, real and known vulnerabilities and weak spots;
o to develop security requirements of dp-systems corrsponding to the required grade of protection.
o To determine security measures according to the security requirements and to include them in a check-list or a manual for the security officer of the company or governmental agency.
o To lay down procedures for the implementation of the recommended measures and to determine the tools (security-manual for the dp-section);
o to determine the costs;
o to evaluate the remaining residual risks.

1 Attack-targets

As the complex area of information processing offers a lot of possibilities for attacks, overall security needs a comprehensive approach.

1.1 The organizational structure of governmental agencies and companies

The organizational structure of the dp-section and the dp-using sections may facilitate penetration. To avoid this working procedures and interfaces have to be sufficiently defined with regard to users requesting information and those who process the data.

1.2 The technical system

In illustration No. 1 the possible attack-targets are shown.

1.2.1 Electrical and electromagnetic influences (indirect dangers)

Electrical equipment including electronic equipment has the property of compromising emanations. The devices radiate large quantities of electromagnetic energy as signals. This information or the data signals emanated may be intercepted and reproduced. Between communication lines cross-talking might occur. Data flowing on one line may be intercepted from another line.

1.2.2 DP-systems, equipment and devices

Central processing units and connected devices (peripheral devices and terminals) may be manipulated in a way that unauthorized access to data becomes possible (for instance the channel controller); the function of devices can be affected by activities from outside the building (EMP - Electromagnetic Pulse).

1.2.3 Software

Manipulating of available and/or use of self-developed programs with unauthorized capabilities makes unauthorized notice of data possible; see chapter 3 attack-methods.

1.2.4 Communication lines

Lines in open and closed networks linking facilities may become a target for interception and wire tapping. Hacker (see the movie "war games") penetrate data processing systems especially through dial-up lines. The target dp-system is dialled computer-assisted and possibly existing security measures will be overcome by computer- and program-controlled attacks in order to get at the stored sensitive data.

2 Penetrators

2.1 Employees

Employees from the data processing section and neighbouring sections often have sufficient know-how, qualification and experience to penetrate the dp-system. First there are the operators of all the equipment and devices; second the system-programmers are able to manipulate software-packages such as operating systems etc. Finally there are the programmers and the employees of the other sections.

2.2 Extraneous employees

Extraneous employees, which have similar knowledge and access-opportunities; such as maintenance personnel of the dp-system - of the hardware (manipulation, theft of data sets etc.), of the software (manipulation, inspection of entire files) and of the infrastructure (power lines, air conditioning, plumbing, communication lines etc.), cleaning personnel and in particular the organizational- and dp-advisors.

2.3 Others

Others who monitor the lines or receive the compromising emanation. "Crackers" as opposed to Hackers who only passively read data, agressively manipulate the data and are therefore much more dangerous. Others take notice of sensitive data more or less unintentionally for instance by getting access to output and listings from garbage (scavenging).

3 Attack methods

The access-control-system is the principal target of attacks against dp-systems. Penetrators want to by-pass, to overcome or to turn off the access-control-system in order to take notice of sensitive data. There are four methods of attacks.

3.1 Use of available programs for illicit purposes

In the dp-system existing programs such as firmware, operating systems, utilities and others can be used to get unauthorized notice; irrespective of the programs being stored or hardware implemented. There is a special risk by using stand-alone utilities (for instance the copy-function): Stand-alone programs do not need an operating system and are running without a supervisor with access-control-facility or any log-file! They may be started unnoticed after the break-down of the operating system.

Functions used to operating systems maintenance like SUPERZAP inserting bit-strings into the running system; with this routine the penetrator is able to manipulate the operating system and other programs without generating any protocol-information for the log-file.

3.2 Self-developed programs with unauthorized secondary capabilities

A program generated and documented in an authorized way may contain not-documented, unauthorized secondary capabilities (Trojan-Horse-method); sensitive data might be acquired through the unauthorized, not documented parts.

In addition there is the trap-door-method; a program with an unauthorized part is activated by a special trigger-signal from the penetrator for instance by a timer or a remote terminal etc.

3.3 Simulation of authorization

Unauthorized users may learn of sensitive data by using the password of an authorized user. The wired address of a device can be manipulated to an authorized computer-stored and controlled address.

The central dp-system can be simulated to get the logic and the access-control-information while communicating with a terminal; the next step is to use this information to simulate the terminal and penetrate the central dp-system; Sometimes this method is called modelling.

3.4 Garbage collection

This means all instances in which notice of sensitive data appears to be taken unintentionally; for instance by reading only logically deleted data and files in the main storage of a processing unit or other peripheral and external devices (tapes, discs etc.). Other means of acquired unintentional knowledge are reading copies or hardcopies like dumps and other output or more general data sets thrown away with any control and documentation and are analyzed out of the garbage (data leakage); this does not necessarily mean an act of intentional stealing.

4 Counter measures against attacks

There are two kinds of measures to protect against attacks.

- o person-related measures,
- o material-related measures.

Person-related measures will not be discussed in this paper. The organization of security tasks in the field of data processing is shown in illustration no. 2.

The material-related measures are subdivided into two parts

- o the traditional "lock and key" elements and the electrical and electromagnetic protection,
- o The logical measures furtheron called "dp-security-measures" are
  - organizational measures,
  - hardware-, software-configuration measures and
  - software measures.

The three dp-security-measures - the logical measures - will be explained.

- o Organizational measures: Optimizing interfaces and procedures in the dp-section and between ordering and data processing offices (for instance the data center) to establish a security level. That means compartmentation of sections and defining and establishing interfaces between sections in a necessary and sufficient way.

- o The hardware-/software-configuration has to be planned according to security aspects - for instance a special computer for data base handling and its connection with simplex-channels to avoid unauthorized access. This aspect is bordering the area of built-in security measures.

- o Software measures include measures to encode/decode data but especially it is the access-control-system; this includes all aspects of the control and protocol (log-file), recording all activities of or in the computer system (what does the user, using what program and what data, which peripheral devices etc.) and the evaluation of this protocol information, and finally the authorization- and password-management.

5 Final remarks

It is important to stress that those security-measures should be envisaged that are really required by the sensitivity-level of the data; those measures are not necessarily expensive.

6 Appendix

In the first part there are formulated principles of data security as a nation-wide policy on dp-security.

In the second part thare are six commandments of secure data processing for a dp-management not yet sensitive to security problems.

6.1 Principles of data security

1. Access-prevention of non-authorized people.
   The governmental or companys organization has to be structured in a form that authorized and non-authorized employees are seperated. The access of non-authorized persons has to be prevented.

2. Access-restrictions.
   Use of dp-systems by non-authorized personnel has to be prevented. Authorized persons are only allowed access to data which they are authorized and are allowed to handle these data in an authorized way.

3. Use-recording.
   All activities of the use of a dp-system have to be recorded: What data are handled at what time by whom and how (program-use). The records have to be evaluated and analyzed.

6.2 Six commandments of secure data processing

1 A sensitivity-level has to be fixed for all data similar to conventional document processing.

- o Accumulation and aggregation of data may require a higher sensitivity-level.
- o Parts of files may be rated more or less sensitive.
- o By connecting files of different systems combinations may be generated which may require a higher sensitivity-level.

Sensitive data have to be labeled.

2 Sections using data processing have to be organized in compartments. Service functions and security functions have to be seperated. Access of non-authorized persons has to be prevented.

3 Hardware- and software-configuration and the file-organization has to be checked under security-aspects.

4 Sensitive data must not be handled together with non-classified data in one data processing system: Seperate non-coupled dp-systems.

5 As a matter of principle sensitive data handling dp-systems must not be connected by lines of open or closed networks.

6 Access-control-system: Use of dp-systems by non-authorized persons has to be prevented. Authorized personnell is only allowed access to data to which it is authorized and has to handle these data in an authorized way. An automatic access-control-system contains:

- o Authorization-procedures that state: Who is authorized to handle what classified data and files, what programs are to be used in what authorized way and which devices (password-management). The user has to be identified and authentificated.

- o Recording all activities of and in the dp-system (which data are handled by whom with what programs and what devices) as well as a record of all data-sets including all provisional results; records have to be analyzed; attempts of unauthorized access have to be recorded and rejected.

References:

(1) Becker, L.G.: Computer Security - An Overview of national Concerns and Challenges. Congressional Research Service Report No. 83-135 SPR. Washington D.C., 1983

(2) Cerny, D.: DV-Sicherheit im rechnergestützten Führungsinformationssystem der Luftwaffe - Probleme und Forderungen. Truppenpraxis 8, 1980

(3) Der Bundesminister des Innern: Grundsätze zur Datensicherung in der Bundesverwaltung. Stand 2.9.1973

(4) Grochla, E.; Weber, H.; Albers, F.; Werhahn, Th.: Ein betriebliches Informationsschutzsystem - Notwendigkeit und Ansatzpunkt für eine Neuorientierung. Angewandte Informatik 5/1983

(5) Jahl, C.: Ehrliches Personal ist die sicherste Investition. Diebold Management Report Nr. 4/1984

(6) Weck, G.: Datensicherheit - Methoden, Maßnahmen und Auswirkungen des Schutzes von Informationen. Stuttgart, 1984

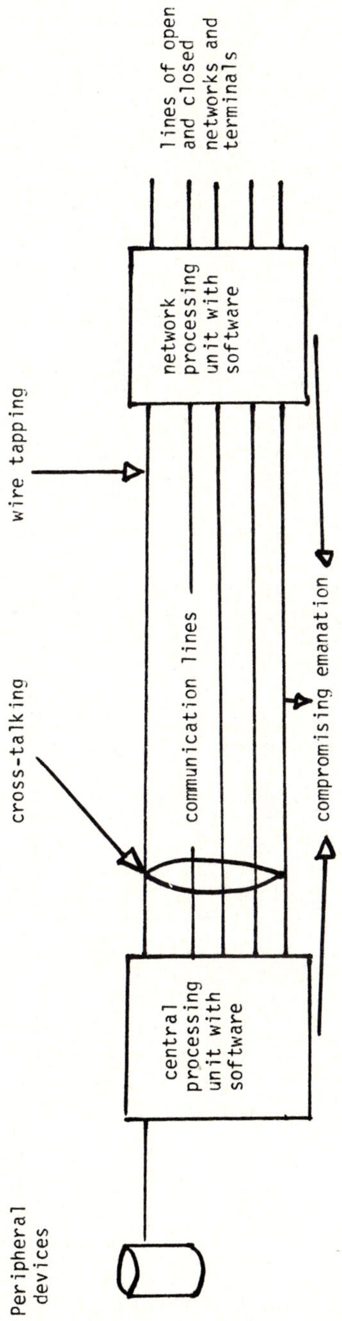

Illustration no. 1: Attack-targets of data processing systems

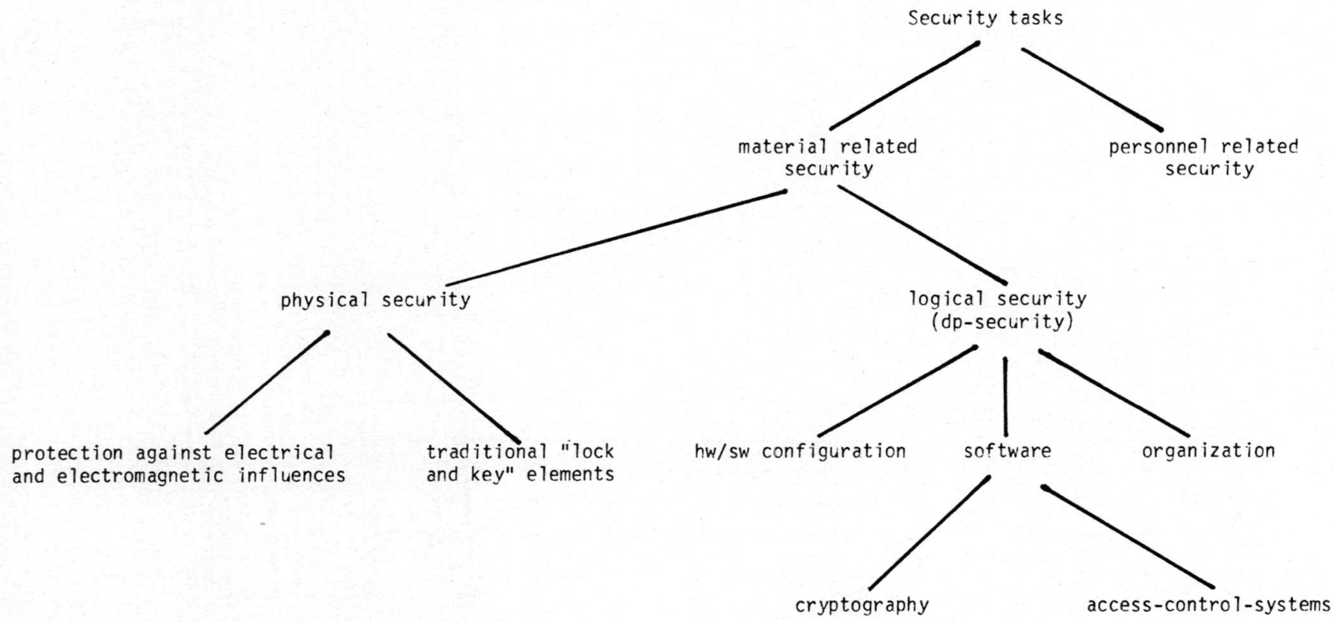

Illustration no. 2: Organization of security tasks in the area of data processing

COMPUTER SECURITY
J.B. Grimson and H.-J. Kugler (Editors)
Elsevier Science Publishers B.V. (North-Holland)

DECISION SUPPORT SYSTEMS — A NECESSITY FOR EFFECTIVE AUDITING OF CONTROLS

William T. Tener

TRW Information Services
Orange, California
U.S.A.

Automation in the corporate environment has produced a wealth of data that can be manipulated and analyzed. Audit scheduling practices inhibit the assurance that controls and effective security practices are present between audit engagements. This paper suggests that audit management utilize decision support systems, management information systems and management science models to identify and project deterioration of controls that can occur between audit engagements.

INTRODUCTION

Many of todays operational functions in the corporate environment have been transformed from mundane manual tasks to interactive sessions within an automated environment. The utilization of automation in the corporate context has produced a wealth of data that can be manipulated and analyzed to providing a supportive tool to the Audit Manager

Management information systems abound in companies, spurting forth reports and providing access to data that inundates operating units, creating a situation where this information is selectively or seldom utilized. Utilization of information on a selective basis can create a demise in the use of effective control practices.

Current auditing practices cite the need for risk assessment and the establishment of an audit schedule. Audits are performed at one to three year intervals. What happens to a function where the control practices deteriorate these assessment periods? The deterioration of controls, depending on where they reside, may generate security vulnerabilities.

I suggest that auditors should not be content with a yearly review of risk and selective audit criteria, but should tap this information resource on a constant basis ensuring the adequacy of controls. Audit management must begin to utilize established management information systems within their organization and the full capability of management science models. Utilization of these tools allow the auditor to evaluate control effectiveness in a consistent manner that will facilitate the utilization of decision support systems. Decision support systems can expedite the audit manager's decision regarding audit considerations and communicate those recommendations to management.

The decision support system is designed to be used in an environment of complex issues with large quantities of data. Audit managers can establish models utilizing existing data. From the analysis of this data, changes in the environment can be identified. Models can be interrogated, and the implications of anticipated changes in the environment can be investigated.

The primary benefit derived from the utilization of decision support systems, management information systems and management science models is the timely identification of deteriorating controls and the prediction of resulting impacts.

Effective security practices and control issues demand on-going monitoring and analysis of effectiveness in a dynamic environment. The challenge to Audit Managers is that they begin using these techniques to increase their effectiveness.

CURRENT SCHEDULING TECHNIQUES

Audit management is confronted with limited resources, a full audit program with additional audit assignments arising constantly. From these variables, management must determine the most effective utilization of resources while maintaining some form of assurance that control systems are in effect.

There are several scheduling techniques being utilized by the audit community. The approaches to audit scheduling range from a basis of experience or intuition to risk management. As we shall see these current techniques do not adequately ensure controls are in place and working during audit engagements.

Fixed term scheduling is established for audits on a repetitive basis, but risk analysis is not always a factor. Audits are routinely performed with a set program at time intervals ranging between one and three years. New audit assignments are difficult to integrate without modifying resource requirements.

Previous audit follow-up may be used in conjunction with the other scheduling procedures cited. This process is a measure used to ensure previous audit deficiencies have been corrected.

Post failure scheduling is a reactionary procedure to determine the cause and extent of security vulnerabilities or control failures.

The external audit firm may request that one or more audits be incorporated into the audit schedule. The likelihood of valuable results being encountered is minimal, otherwise the external audit firm would perform the audit.

Management or Corporate Audit Committee directives may define the audit schedule. This directive process detracts from the creativity that can be employed by the audit manager in establishing an audit schedule.

User requests may define portions of the audit schedule. The benefit of these audits can be minimal due to the audit being performed to enhance the users knowledge. Since neither party knows the state of affairs going into the audit, the results may be questionable.

Compliance audits are scheduled to test compliance to legislative and regulatory issues and/or adherence to corporate policies and procedures.

Improvement analysis in the areas of productivity or quality may determine the criteria for audit scheduling. The results that can be anticipated in this type of audit are predominantly connected with productivity and quality. Changes in operations to achieve these results may yield new security and control issues.

Risk analysis is based on the tendency of operations or systems to exhibit control or security problems. This form of scheduling is the closest approach to ensure that ongoing control and security measures are in effect, but may not be performed in time. ISSUES RESULTING FROM SCHEDULING TECHNIQUES

The utilization of these scheduling techniques may create four potentially non-rewarding situations or control issues due to the timing and selection of audits.

Undetected control degradation can occur due to lack of adequate monitoring. An inoperable control will provide an opportunity to perpetrate security violations.

Poor utilization of resources may exist without a guaranteed payback. Without some indication that significant audit findings will be derived, the value of the audit is questionable.

Security vulnerabilities may exist between audit engagements. The interaction of control processes may enable a security breach to occur.

The audit process may have questionable management support due to the issues cited, in addition to the difficulty of communicating the value of the audit process to senior management.

Table 1 shows the relationship of the scheduling process to the four issues cited. Two trends are apparent. Undetected control degradation and security vulnerabilities usually occur in the same scheduling process. Poor utilization of resources occurs in most of these scheduling processes. If the auditing process is to be considered beneficial by senior management then these four issues must be reconciled.

SCHEDULING PROCESS	RESULTING ISSUES			
	Control Degradation	Resource Utilization	Security Vulnerabilities	Management Support
Fixed Term Schedules	X	X	X	X
Previous Audit Follow-Up	X	X	X	
Post Audit Failure	X		X	
External Audit Firm	X	X	X	
Management Directive	X	X	X	
User Request	X	X	X	X
Compliance	X	X	X	
Improvement Analysis	X		X	
Risk Analysis	X	X	X	

DECISION SUPPORT SYSTEMS (DSS) OR MANAGEMENT INFORMATION SYSTEMS (MIS)

The advent of decision support systems occurred in the early 1970's with Michael S. Scott Morton. He characterized DSS as interactive computer based systems that aid decision makers utilizing data and models to solve semi-structured or unstructured problems. The time focus of DSS is present and future.

The forerunner of DSS was Management Information Systems (MIS). MIS provide reports and access to data. Access to data is initiated by retrieval systems usually in a data base environment. MIS involve structured information flows. The information is centered around specific business functions i.e., production, marketing, finance. MIS involves transaction processing and reporting with the objective of presenting information in a consistent manner. The time focus of MIS is in retrospect.

Management Science Models (MSM) involve structured tasks providing recommendations on optimal decisions or actions. The focus of these models is to derive better solutions in the current environment.

MIS and MSM can be key elements of a decision support system. Both emphasize large computer resource utilization in an off-line environment. DSS on the other hand emphasizes interactive utilization to expedite the decision process and communication of that decision within the organization.

Sprague and Watson proposed five design criteria for DSS. They are:

1. A set of models supporting decision making in various functional areas, and at various management levels.

2. Models devised as modules that can stand alone or be used in conjunction with one another to form more models.

3. A query language to interact with the data base.

4. Models with a mechanism to extract data from a data base.

5. Models with flexibility for modification to meet the requirement of a changing environment.

A DSS should have data management and modeling capability in a batch or interactive mode. Decision makers require the use of information produced either in batch or online processing.

The advantages of using a DSS are flexibility, user interaction and the fact a DSS is designed to process large amounts of data to derive complex decisions.

A DSS must handle constantly changing problems or decisions. The use and processing logic of these systems adapt to changing corporate decisions and the individuals using them.

User friendliness is achieved through a set of capabilities that allows user selection of decision making patterns. The form of cognitive style and assumptions utilized are user controlled.

The support provided to the user by DSS are:

- o Ad hoc query languages usually based on a data base management system

- o Financial and Statistical analysis routines

- o Planning model languages that can be used for interrogation and investigation of changes to the environment

- o Graphic display commands

- o Report preparation

The data base management, modeling management and user interface are intertwined yet interdependent. The DSS must be easy to use to meet organizational requirements at all levels. The DSS can improve decision making by improving the information source, providing best alternative solutions interrogated by sensitivity and risk analysis to enable the audit manager to understand the nature of the problem.

Experience in using decision support systems in the audit function, or for that matter, management information systems and management science models are rare indeed. Many auditors still exhibit a reluctance to use management science or mathematical models during the audit process. It may be for this reason that audit professionals have had problems exhibiting their functional value to senior management. Utilizing these tools could enhance the auditors credibility in the eyes of senior management.

My audit group is just beginning to design DSS in support of our audit process. Many of our operations are automated, which provides a data base of information relative to each operation. We are attempting to selectively interrogate these data bases to determine if controls are effective based on a mathematical model of each operation through trend analysis.

The audit scheduling process is based on an analysis of whether the controls are effective. Our audit schedule is always open for modification. A preliminary assumption is if one control is operating in a degraded mode, it can effect other controls providing the opportunity for a vulnerability. We believe DSS can determine the need for audits that will produce a payback and alleviate reviews on a fixed time frame. Some of the areas being investigated by us are:

- file maintenance and data base changes
- inquiry activity models by user identification
- error transaction models
- access control point activity models
- categorization and analysis of operational processes

By analyzing our current operating model to previously developed base models we can determine if our current statistics meet expectations. When these expectations aren't met, we must investigate the issues involved in creating the deviation. By utilizing risk analysis in this situation, we can establish the need for an on-site audit.

A DSS can analyze operational changes and audit recommendations to determine the impact to the organization and the models themselves. Since the system contains a fairly accurate representation of operations, recommended changes can be processed through the query language and interact with the models to produce various alternatives. The decision support system can assist in the derivation of optimal recommendations to the audit team.

> The financial analysis routines can be utilized in preparing departmental budgets, cash flows, returns and review pricing decisions. Distribution models can investigate locations, staffing and transportation decisions.

Decision support systems have been used in a variety of industries and functions. The usage of decision support systems can be advantageous to auditing as well.

ANALYSIS AND IMPLEMENTATION

The specific approach to implementation will vary whether your firm has a DSS group or not. If your company has such specialists they can work closely with the audit function using an iterative approach to refine the system. A corporate approach to DSS's may enable the sharing of systems. In the absence of a DSS group it is probably best to start with a DSS generation such as FOCUS, IFPS or Express. A key consideration is that an audit decision approach be utilized. The capabilities of the system must fit the auditors task and problem requirements. A second consideration is that the system be able to react quickly to changes in environmental conditions, audit styles and task definition.

Richard H. Sprague, Jr. & Eric D. Carlson suggest a four step analysis process to determine the criteria.

1. Identify the overall objective. The DSS must be user friendly to the audit department at all levels. The decision making style must fit the problems encountered by auditing. Since the audit environment is constantly changing the DSS must be capable of responding to an iterative design process.

2. Identify the general capabilities required. The system should be available to all auditors some of whom may be non-technical.

   The Audit Manager should identify the access requirements for data sources, and identify whether or not access is transactional. A decision must be made as to what data and operations are to be reviewed. Control points must be specified and analyzed in terms of risk, and if they are dependent or interdependent. The interdependency of control points must be analyzed to gain their impact of failure and risk significance.

   The problem-solving and decision-making capabilities must be identified to ensure the data is available in a way that will permit analysis and resolution. The problem-solving and decision-making capabilities must facilitate use by all levels of the audit group.

3. Identify the specific capabilities that are required to accomplish the general capabilities. There are three aspects to specific capabilities, dialog, data base and modeling:

   Dialog is essential to user friendliness. Specific capabilities include:

   - producing DSS output representation for user understanding
   - handling different user decision styles
   - handling different access devices (i.e., keyboard, mouse, audio)
   - supporting communication between users
   - maintenance of user activity or actions
   - supporting various degrees of user skills (i.e., prompting, help menus)

   Data base capabilities include such items as:

   - handling different data structure
   - retrieval and merging of data from different sources
   - data base management
   - informing the user of data availability and access method
   - storing data usage patterns
   - file maintenance

   Modeling capabilities should include at least the following:

   - stored routines and models
   - support to create new models
   - manipulation of models
   - modeling menus to show the user whats available
   - ability to retain and analyze modeling data

4. Identify the specific devices, hardware and software features that are required.

   Sprague and Carlson point out that the three general capability areas of data base, modeling and dialog must be integrated and available through the same mechanism. These three areas must be balanced in terms of efficiency and have the long-term goals of the system in mind.

SUMMARY

This four step analysis process includes phases which are beneficial in assessing the value of the DSS in the audit environment. This analysis gives the Audit Manager a good idea of long-range expectations during the beginning stage of the development life cycle. Decision support systems are expensive and require much more user involvement than other software development efforts. These systems are an extension of the user's decision process acting as a supportive tool.

The cost of these systems for auditing purposes can be reduced in many corporations due to the existence of operational data bases. Line management auditing can effectively utilize existing operational data to monitor controls and analyze operations. Although these two groups have different perspectives, the joint utilization of existing operational data and interaction may provide a more productive environment.

The decision support system changes the management of the audit function. Audit schedules are fluid based on the analysis of effective controls. The past perspective of annual audits are displaced by audit scheduling based on control degradation as shown by the DSS. Senior management is assured of valuable results from the audit. Prior to entering the audit we know we have a likely control issue. The time frame between audits is not set in a predetermined manner without the knowledge that controls may have been degraded, rather the DSS provides the visibility of control degradation as it's happening. The audit process validates our assumption and highlights the need for effective controls before further degradation of controls. This process provides management with a detective control and a known payback of rectifying control weaknesses and potential security vulnerabilities.

A word of caution must be interjected here. The DSS scheduling process should not eliminate all fixed-term audits where security vulnerabilities and control issues are considered high. The audit schedule should allow for the DSS process.

Audit Managers should utilize their organizational management information systems and the capabilities of management science models. The current auditing literature has not addressed this involvement for some time.

Operational management has been involved with MIS and MSM for at least a decade. It seems that it is long overdue for auditing practitioners to advance to this stage of development. The value and professional image of the audit function, in the eyes of senior management, should change. The audit function, itself, can be regarded as a decision support system.

I would suggest that auditors move to the utilization of a decision support system which incorporates the use of MIS and MSM. The utilization of decision support systems, management information systems and management science models when used by the auditor can not only present information on control effectiveness today, but project the impact of control usage in the future.

REFERENCES

1. D. P. Godier, "Automated Audit Risk Analysis," (The EDP Auditor, Vol. 11, 1984 21-28)

2. P. Gray, "Student Guide To IFIPS," (McGraw-Hill, 1983)

3. W. H. Gruber & G. Sonnemann, "Information Resource Management for Corporate Decision Support," AFIPS National Computer Conference, (1983) 409-413

4. C. Harrington, "Focal Points for DSS Effectiveness" AFIPS National Computer Conference (1983) 403-407

5. W. C. House, "Decision Support Systems, A Data Based, Model-Oriented, User-Developed Discipline," (Petrocelli Books, 1983)

6. D. T. Lee, "Database-Oriented Decision Support Systems," AFIPS National Computer Conference, (1983) 455-465

7. J. H. Mohr and P. Rucsh, "Fighting Computer Crime With Software Risk Analysis," Journal of Information Systems Management, Vol. 1, No. 2, Spring (1984)

8. R. H. Sprague, Jr. and E. D. Carlson, "Building Effective Decision Support Systems," (Prentice Hall, 1982)

9. M. D. Storslee and D. W. Breckel, "The PDQ Prioritizer, (The Internal Auditor," XL1:2, April 1984, 27-30)

10. "Systems Auditability & Control Study," Stanford Research Institute for the Institute of Internal Auditors, (1977)

11. "The Internal Auditor's Review of Organizational Control," The Institute of Internal Auditors, Research Committee Report 18, (1972)

12. R. Weber, "EDP Auditing, Conceptual Foundations & Practices," (McGraw Hill, 1982)

13. K. R. White and J. A. Xander, "Survey of Internal Auditing: Trends & Practices," The Institute of Internal Auditors, (1984)

14. L. F. Young, "A Corporate Strategy for Decision Support Systems," Journal of Information Systems Management, Vol. 1 No.1, Winter (1984) 58-62

COMPUTER SECURITY
J.B. Grimson and H.-J. Kugler (Editors)
Elsevier Science Publishers B.V. (North-Holland)

THE AUDIT, CONTROL AND SECURITY OF THE PROJECT LIFE CYCLE - PRE-IMPLEMENTATION STAGE

Roger T. Doswell

Senior Consultant The National Computing Centre Limited
Oxford Road, Manchester, M1 7ED, United Kingdom

This paper details the steps which should be adopted by the EDP Auditor when evaluating the Pre-Implementation stage of a proposed computer programming project. The paper is presented in the form of a checklist for delegates to be able to adapt and adopt for their particular organisations. It is based upon over ten years experience in the field of computor audit and has been used "in the field" by the author and his colleagues.

1. SYSTEM CONVERSION/TAKE-ON PLANS

a. Have the plans for the conversion and take-on of data from the existing systems been adequately defined and documented?

b. Do the procedures for the conversion and take-on of data from existing systems incorporate adequate controls? (e.g. to safeguard the confidentiality of the data/the reconciliation of accounts transferred).

c. Is the schedule for the conversion and take-on of data compatible with other aspects of the implementation programme?

d. Is responsibility for the conversion and take-on of data allocated to specific individuals within the project team?

2. PROGRAM AND SYSTEM TESTING

a. Does documentary evidence exist to show that all programs/modules received for system testing have been program tested adequately?

b. Do the contents of the system test primary data files cover an acceptable and comprehensive combination of data? (e.g. have all input message types been included?).

c. Are infrequently used system functions adequately simulated within the test data?

d. Is adequate provision made within the tests for invalid data and exception conditions?

e. Is adequate provision made within the tests to check for the system and program restart techniques used?

f. Have the expected results of each test been prepared and are these used for subsequent checking?

g. Does the method of result checking show that all functions within the system have been carried out satisfactorily?

h. Does the method of result checking show that all data used by the system has been correctly handled?

i. Does the method of result checking show that all calculations carried out within the system have been completed satisfactorily?

j. Does the method of result checking show that all logical paths within the programs have been tested by the data used?

k. Does Internal Audit, or the Project Team, intend to use a logic path analysis program prior to system implementation?

l. Has particular care been exercised by management to ensure that short-cuts to the completion of the system tests are not allowed?

m. Have the system test data and expected results been created and checked by persons who are independent of the programmers who are responsible for the system?

n. Do the methods used during the system tests ensure that all program/system errors identified are re-tested after correction?

o. Are the results of the system trials compared with previously obtained results output by existing methods?

p. Any special trials which need to take place outside the organisation's site, (e.g. at a computer manufacturers) should have the approval of Internal Audit. Are the programming team aware of this requirement?

q. Are the results of the two latest successful testing trials of each data item kept, together with the relevant details?

3. USER ACCEPTANCE TESTING

This section is designed to cover the degree of user involvement in system acceptance. Liaisons with other departments may well be necessary.

a. Determine the level of user involvement in the testing and acceptance of the system. (e.g. preparation of input and interpretation and approval of the results)

b. Is it appropriate, in your judgement? Comment accordingly.

c. Is the user satisfied that the system meets their requirements?

4. OPERATIONS ACCEPTANCE TESTING

a. Do the operational trials take place under conditions which simulate, as far as possible, the live environment, and under the control of operations personnel?

b. Is all supporting documentation available during these trials? (e.g. operating instructions, user manuals).

c. Do these trials allow for confirming the system and program restart facility?

d. Are all tests carried out under the control of Operations staff, independently of the systems development team?

e. Are all errors encountered during these trials evaluated and appropriate corrective action agreed before these tests are finalised?

f. Do these trials confirm that the back-up and recovery facilities provided with this system are adequate?

g. Is the level of operations involvement in the development of the system sufficient to ensure that a fully operable system is implemented?

5. RELEASE PROCEDURES

a. Have formal procedures been established for the conduct and control of the release of both new suites and individual programs/modules?

b. Is the release of programs to operations controlled by a central body specifically assigned to carry out this task?

c. Do the release procedures provide for different categories of release, and the activities related to each? (i.e. emergency, temporary, permanent).

d. Is the frequency of permanent releases established at pre-determined intervals?

e. Where amendments are introduced by the trouble shooters/ maintenance programmers as either emergency or temporary releases, are these satisfactorily authorised and the reasons for the changes documented?

f. Are all released programs uniquely identifiable?

g. Are temporary releases valid for one day only, subsequent uses being permitted only if renewal is authorised by the central release section?

h. Is there evidence of systems testing carried out prior to each release advised by the supporting documentation?

i. Where multiple admendments are introduced within a single program are these individually identified to the release control section by the supporting documentation?

j. Do the physical handover procedures for all amended programs call for:-

Details of where the source code file for the program is to be found?

Compatibility details?

Amended operating instructions?

6. ENHANCEMENT/MODIFICATION CONTROL PLANS

a. Does a formal control procedure exist for progressing design amendments, incorporating documentation and agreed procedures?

b. Does the detailed implementation plans include provision for the suspending of the design of each sub-system at a specified stage before implementation, and the formal accumulation of identified amendments until a later time?

c. In addition to (b), above, is provision made for the authorisation of amendments after the suspension date where the lack of such amendments would prejudice the implementation of the system?

7. FAULT REPORTING PLANS

a. Determine what plans have been made to cover fault reporting for any failure conditions likely to be encountered during processing.

b. Are these plans adequate in terms of the correct processing of all potential faults through to a satisfactory conclusion?

8. SOFTWARE AND OPERATIONS ENVIRONMENT

a. Identify the software and operating environment within which the application system is to be run.

b. Check that the software environment meets the organisation's control and security requirements.

c. Are you satisfied that the best use is being made of all security facilities available within the software?

d. Ensure that the operations environment meets the organisation's control and security requirements.

COMPUTER SECURITY
J.B. Grimson and H.-J. Kugler (Editors)
Elsevier Science Publishers B.V. (North-Holland)
IFIP, 1985

MULTIFUNCTION WORKSTATIONS AND MULTIDIMENSION ENVIRONMENTS

Eugenio Orlandi
Servizio Trattamento Informazioni e Modelli Organizzativi
ACEA - Azienda Comunale Elettricità ed Acque
Roma - Italy

Computer security is a successful, growing concept with several facets: integrity,vulnerability,privacy, confidentiality. Services and architecture that unite computers and telecommunications is also a continuously developing reality. This paper is an effort to propose a common framework for security engineering in a field where convergent technologies apparently require very different solutions in office information systems and data processing systems.

1. INTRODUCTION

The purpose of this paper is to present a unified approach to office automation and data processing security.

Office automation and data processing are only different operative dimensions of single workstations. Office activities and functionalities data processing procedures and transactions perform sequences of operations with different protection requirements on exclusive or shared information domains.

A distributed environment is made by several information domains. Each domain is partially about exclusive pertinence of its domain-owner and partially shared with other users. A domain-owner has to ensure the security level related to its necessities.

As far as security is concerned, an organization, represented by a conversational network, produces recovery/restart requirements and access policies. Authorization rules and rights propagation rules are interfaces between a set of subject resources and a set of object ones. Thus a relevant aspect of each security system is the implementation of an effective access-control system (privacy/confidentiality aspect of security). Moreover access-control is only an aspect of a diffused need of 'operation reversibility' (integrity aspect of security). Finally risk analisys and the evaluation of the probabilities of security-related events are the last components of the security concept (vulnerability aspect of security).

Hardware, system software, application software and a definition of security tailored on the organization's needs determine the security project pipeline.

A very general model to be customized, simplified or extended, is proposed as common framework and produces natural definitions of a security dictionary: memory and access control, EDP security administrator and EDP auditor. A binary (block) matrix carries the existence of relationships between subject and object resources.

The block structure depends on different possible levels of details in resource specification and allows a top-down approach.

The binary matrix is both a design and a verification methodology for protection systems. As design tool it models in-house developed security software.

A crucial part of designing access-control systems is an 'algorithm' which has some control on the current distribution of the access rights and manages their evolution.

As for access-control verification, the knowledge of how to manipulate authorization rules and rights propagation rules, a pre-requisite for an effective analysis of the system's security, is necessary.

The binary matrix model seems too static an approach: in fact each established system is expected to be affected by break-downs. Model extensions take into account the effects of dynamics on access-control systems.

By gathering additional information, it is possible to increase the modelling power of the binary matrix. Some generic relationships between subjects and objects can be specified as ownerships. Ancillary data structures, to be modified by primitive operations, bear ordering relationships. The resulting extended model seems suitable to modelling both access system evolution and recovery/restart requirements.

2. OFFICE AUTOMATION AND DATA PROCESSING SECURITY VERSUS SECURITY ENGINEERING

The objectives of computer security can be achieved by a project-like development methodology. In fact a security comprehensive plan can be managed as a project. It passes through the phases of feasibility study, analysis, design, implementation and administration. In small and medium size organizations, with normal requirements of data integrity and confidentiality, the figure of the computer security specialist, if there is one, is an additional workload for a single person (i.e. the internal auditor or the system software expert). In this case the adoption of standards may reduce the security project development time and make the selected measures more effective.

This paper, adopting a security comprehensive development methodology presents:

- an integrated view of information and processing requirements: there are no distinctions between office automation and data processing resources;
- a framework, a binary (block) matrix for a top-down approach to security; each block of the matrix can be regarded as a self-consistent sub-project to be treated by specific methodologies;
- an extension of the binary matrix that takes into account dynamic aspects of security policies and memory requirements necessary to ensure the data integrity.

The proposal does not make any distinction between office information systems (OIS) and data processing systems (DPS), both regarded as different responses to a unique need for information processing. In fact there are more similarities than differences. In DPS aspects such as (relative) stationary applications, centralized control and reduced multilevel hierarchy among subjects are prevalent, while OIS are more dynamic, distributed, with an articulate multilevel hierarchy and many more users classified in several dynamic roles. Fundamentally computers tend to store data, while OIS usually store the same data in a more valuable form such as processed information.

Scheduling a security project in conventional terms, there are three phases: initiation, development and administration. Each of these phases is described below:
Initiation phase. The first step is a clear definition of the security policies. Top-management, DP managers and security specialists must identify the level of security necessary to their organization. At the end of this phase, the security specialist produces a feasibility study.

Development phase. The development phase consists of a translation of the descriptive guidelines outlined in the feasibility study into prescriptive statements. The security specialist manages a continuous two-way flow of information with field specialists, collects internal and external knowledge and produces a static sub-model. Under the control of the security specialist, selected measures are adopted: software options are set, pieces of software are written and packages are installed.

Administration phase. Once installed the security measures have to be monitored. The continuous monitoring of security information outlines break-downs.

Because of its nature of distributed and part-time attended function, in small organizations, security administration in particular needs standard methodologies which introduce the field knowledge developed out of the organization (safeguards, field literature, packages), produce an efficient conversational sub-network linking security specialists, management and users and simulate the effects of dynamics on the system (grant/revocation of access rights, analysis of recovery/restart requirements).

3. THE ELEMENTS OF AN OFFICE INFORMATION/DATA PROCESSING UNIFIED ENVIRONMENT

An integrated OIS/DPS informal description, in natural language, states the following:

i) the concepts of subject resources, hereafter simply subjects, object resources, hereafter simply objects, and operations are assumed to be primitive;

ii) subjects and objects are only roles (meanings) assigned to entities defined by a selected level of details and picked up from a common pool of resources; once assigned, roles are fixed in certain sub-projects (blocks);

iii) there are relationships among subjects, for simplicity hierarchical ones; the existence of an organizational hierarchy does not affect the security hierarchy resulting from the authorization system;

iv) objects can be classified and characterized by memory requirements;

v) subjects may operate on objects: an operation is a privilege held by a subject to an object; an operation acts on data or activities;

vi) it is possible to imagine a unique information pool for each organization but the ownership on single sub-domains can have different forms: normally a subject is master of its local sub-domain and user of other sub-domains, regarded as its complementary domain;

vii) OIS and DPS are only different dimensions of a unique requirement of information; the existence of separate OIS and DPS environments is a sub-case of a more general model (normally $OIS \cap DPS \neq \varphi$ where φ is the null set).

Definition: a <u>compatibility matrix</u> is a binary matrix $H_{ij}(2)$

$$H_{ij}(2): S \times O \quad \{0,1\}$$

where S is the set of current subjects,

$$S = \{ s: s \in S, \text{ s produced by the conversational network} \}$$

O is the set of current objects,

$$O = \{ o: o \in O, \text{ o offered by the DP department} \}$$

and

$$x \begin{cases} 1 & \text{if any relationship between } s_i \text{ and } o_j \\ 0 & \text{otherwise} \end{cases}$$

The row s_i of the matrix is like a capability list for subject s_i; the column o_j is an access list for object o_j.

The compatibility matrix has the following peculiarities:

- its definition is a very general one; a first S-set and O-set partitioning (i) produces an initial matrix: its x_{ij} elements can be regarded as blocks; the block structure allows a top-down approach to security analysis and suggests different methodologies

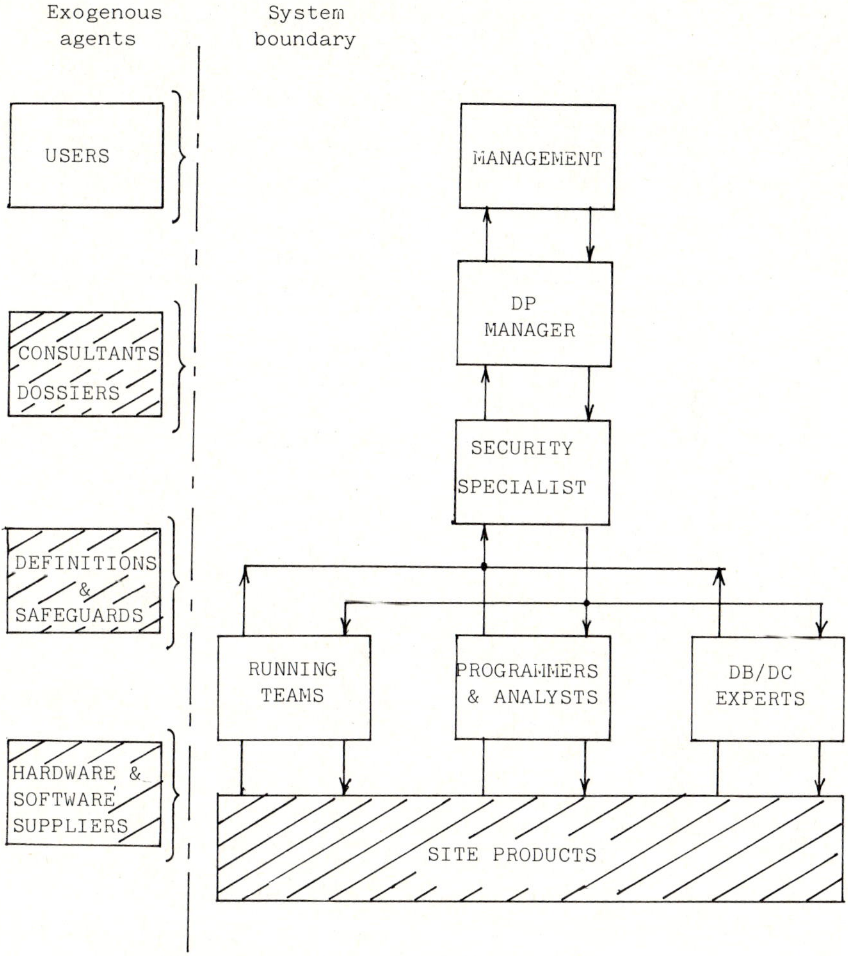

Figure 1
Schema of the a traditional conversational sub-network producing security-related managerial and committment acts. As a result of endogenous or exogenous events (the sub-network is an open system) each node can be source of break - downs. The shadowed areas are particularly suitable for an engineering approach.

for different security areas;

- the S-set and O-set are dynamic ones; a break-down in the conversational network (a new user or a new application) normally modifies the compatibility matrix.

The traditional partition in three major areas of security concern:

physical security, data security and operational security, with specific analysis methodologies is always less representative of a highly dynamic reality that joins computers and communications, hardware and software, office automation and data processing. Consequently a more general description is possible in terms of subject and object resources, where subjects and objects eventually change their roles, depending on the objectives of the analysis (see paragraph 7).

Definitions of subjects and objects (ii) are characteristics of each block in $H_{ij}(2)$. A subject can be defined by assigning to the right-hand member its ordinary, self-explicatory meaning

<subject> = <application-user> / <application>
<application-user> = <password> / <terminal>
<application> = <process>

An object is a logical or a physical entity that is of value to the organization; it can be defined

<object> = <software-resource> / <hardware-resource>
<hardware-resource> = <terminal>
<software-resource> = <file> / <data-item>

Each subject can also be an object if, among subjects, there is a relationship of 'ownership' (iii). A subject is an active agent, while an object is a passive element.

A capability (privilege) is the right of a subject to have access to a particular object with a particular set of operations (v). Possession of capability demonstrates the subject's right to have to access the object.

Definitions of subjects and objects are very broad; in terms of physical security, a badge-owner is a subject; electronic doors and compartmentalized areas are objects.

4. BLOCK STRUCTURE OF THE COMPATIBILITY MATRIX: CONSEQUENCES ON SECURITY ANALYSIS

On the common framework of the binary (block) matrix several methodologies can be developed. The matrix can
- degenerate into access lists and capability lists;
- increase its modeling power gathering additional information.

The block structure depends on different levels of details in specifying resources -degree of granularity- and allows a top-down approach.

During the macro-analysis the major areas of security concern are listed and translated into a $H_{ij}(2)$ tableau. Then each x_{ij} element can be detailed, i.e. time-sharing users represented in terms of logical-users, for shared terminals, or in terms of physical users, if terminals are dedicated to single applications.

Two sets of criteria identify the areas of security concern: cohesion and coupling. The traditional partition in physical security, data security and operational security, produces a tableau in which block-subsets of <subject, object> pairs have high cohesion and low-coupling. Then the complete freedom in defining subjects and objects helps tomanage fuzzy partitions (see paragraph 7).

Existing operating systems offer a complete set of different off-line and on-line operative 'dimensions': batch processing, real time, word processing, electronic mail and desk management. System software specialists may choose among several options and lockwards. The selection of options and lockwards has to be supported by methodologies describing the results of such selections in order to compare the selected measures and the security requirements.

The compatibility matrix is both a design and a verification methodology. As a design tool, it models in-house developed security software. As a verification tool, it tests security features of security packages and operating systems.

A macro-object, a catalog but also an electronic door or a terminal, can be used by a list of operators. A macro-subject, a password but also a badge-owner or a terminal, has some privileges on a class of objects. Restricting the rights of subjects to access objects is one of the cornerstones of computer security. Following information and processing requirements related to a certain level of detail, the S-set partition induces an O-set partition. The set partition helps to manage an m:n relationship between subjects and objects (see paragraph 7).

5. CONVERSATIONAL NETWORK AND COMPATIBILITY MATRIX

The compatibility matrix has too little modeling power. Each element $x_{ij} = 1$ only represents an 1:1 relationship between subjects and objects. A further step is to introduce time and correlate an instant of the conversational network to the compatibility matrix. In the following an organization is schematized by a conversational network which produces requests and corresponding engagements and where break-downs continuously appear. Break-downs produce a new network of managerial acts (requests) and committment acts (engagements). In this context the value of each act depends on the relationship existing between the source and the destination resources. A request can be fully accepted, conditionally accepted, modified or refused. When accepted, and formally correct, it produces an engagement to perform a certain action.

A possible way tomanage a security system design is to translate managerial acts into authorization rules, conditioned by constraints. The existence of authorization rules reflects the existence of a hierarchy among subjects.

Definition: a <u>direct operation</u>, DO, is a triple <S,A,O> where

S,A,O are domains: S is the subject resources domain, A is the domain of the possible operations, O is the object resources domain.

Definition: an <u>administrative operation</u>, AO, is a pair <S,G> where S is the subject resources domain and G = {AO,DO}. A direct operation specifies the rights of a subject on an object.

An administrative operation is a link between an algorithm (scheduler) that manages the binary matrix and the conversational network. Grant and revocation of direct operations and transferring grant privileges are administrative operations, AOs. Propagation of access rights is the consequence of authorization rules. Each DO needs an AO as legitimation source. For example, the statement: 'Mr. Brown may authorize Mr. Smith and assigns the right to modify file F1 to Mr. Smith' is transduced into the sequence

AO: <Brown, DO>
DO: <Smith, modify, file F1>

that, until revoked, enables a virtually infinite sequence of DO operations by Mr. Smith.

S,A,O are not simple domains. In particular an extension of the model takes into account the objects' type of permission and possible memory requirements (iv).

Definition: <u>memory</u> on its strong acceptance implies operation reversibility, while on its weak acceptance simply means access control.

A binary matrix is not sufficient to represent memory requirements. Thus the compatibility matrix is only a two-dimensional binary projection of a more complex data structure, able to record the object's history. The binary matrix merely extinguishes every conceptual difference between logical and physical access-control by specifying the <subject,object> coupling. Consequently an access-control system -physical as well logical- ensures only privacy and confidentiability. A three-dimensional structure, <subject,object, object's history> may ensure the integrity aspect of security.

Definition: a <u>DP security administrator</u> controls subject and object coupling for all the possible $\langle s_i, o_j \rangle$ pairs, where s_i, with i=1,2,..,I is a subset of subjects and o_j, with j=1,2,...,J, is a subset of objects.

Receiving as input authorization rules and rights propagation rules the security administrator produces an authorization system.
Definition: a <u>DP internal auditor</u> suggests which couples have to acquire the 3-D shape, properly defines the concept of history for each couple, controls all the sequences $U_{ikj} \langle s_{ik}, o_{jk} \rangle$ with K=1,2,...,K i=1,2,...,I and j=1,2,...,J realized by site procedures and representing information and processing requirements.

A DP internal auditor's current job is to introduce control and memory in ingenuous and memoryless computerized systems. A DP security auditor's job should be to define memory requirements for objects under his control and to consciously open certain objects to well identified subjects, on the basis of an authorization system.

The theory states that there is no algorithm which can decide the safety question for an arbitrary protection system, but the problem is decidable for a specific set of rules.

6. MANAGING DYNAMICS: THE COMPATIBILITY MATRIX AND ITS ANCILLARY DATA STRUCTURES

Theinstallation of a new software product, the development of a data transmission network, the delivering of a new dimension (i.e. word processing) to an existing workstation, affect an established security context.

Several events produce transformations on the binary matrix (v), such as

- creation, deletion, merging, splitting of subjects and/or objects;
- grant/revocation of access rights to subjects;
- variation of classification and/or memory requirements to objects.

The compatibility matrix merely reflects the existence of relationships between subjects and objects. Relationships between subjects and objects are m:n ones. By adding further hypotheses it is possible to characterize the problem better. For certain couples of $<$subject,object$>$ the generic relationship can be specified as an original relationship of ownership (vi).

Definition: an <u>ownership</u> is an 1:1 relationship between a subject and an object. A subject that owns an object, holds original privileges over the object.

This additional information can not be carried by a binary matrix. Moreover the introduction of symbolism in the matrix or of ancillary data structures helps tomanage the dynamics of the conversational network (subject and/or object insertion/deletion and grant/ revocation of privileges).

Definition: given a subject $s \in S$ and an object $o \in O$, a <u>bipartite graph</u> G(S,O) represents an ownership.

An owner may assign an access list (of subjects) to its objects. The rearrangment of all the access lists produces a set of capability lists.

The relationship between a subject and an object is operationally definied by specifying the rights which the subject has on the object. The legitimicy of every right comes from an original relationship of ownership of a certain subject to an object. Subsequently, administrative operations propagate the rights in the matrix.

Definition: an <u>authorization tree</u> represents an ordering relationship among subjects obtained by the S-set partition. The authorization tree reflects a hierarchical multilevel structure and realizes an access path, a discrete sequence of subjects along which access rights can propagate.

The dynamics of the subjects can be extended to objects as well. Definition: a <u>classification tree</u> represents an ordering relationship among objects obtained by the O-set partition.

The introduced ancillary data structures, ownership-bipartite graph, authorization tree and classification tree, respectively represent the existence of

- an original relation of ownership;
- an organizational hierarchy (relationship among subjects);
- an objects' classification (relationship among objects).

The authorization tree specifies the rights propagation rules among subjects. As a consequence of access rights, when necessary, objects must be protected by specifying memory requirements. Thus, memory requirements represent the objects' consistency rights, necessary to ensure a second level of protection against accidental errors and omissions of trusted users. Memory requirements are intended to preserve data integrity and must be specified at the object's creation. Memory functionalities can also be delegated by the object-owner to system software, such as DBMS, or periodical save/ restore procedures. Of course the identification of an authorization tree or of a classification tree is mainly concerned with the organization rather than the binary matrix. Unstructured S-set and O-set (flat set) represent degenerative cases of authorization and classification trees.

Memory requirements ensure the object's consistency after a sequence of operations. Lock/unlock primitives, before/after images, save/ restore of libraries and files are exemples of system and procedural responses tomemory requirements.

Nodes represent subjects in the authorization tree and arcs represent relations among them.

Each node must have a classification which is dominated by its predecessors. A node coding reflects the sequence path from the root to each node. Sometimes the authorization tree represents only a hierarchical dominance graph. For instance, top-managers can only assign the grant privilege to their subordinates, without having the execute privilege themselves, in order to ensure a clear division of responsabilities.

An AO has some effects on the ancillary data structures. As in the case of the authorization tree, AOs have to be translated by a software module in one of the following primitive operations:

INSERT (n,l)
DELETE (n)

and each insert/delete must be completed by the matrix rearrangment and the label distribution. An insert operation means a node division and the introduction of a connecting arc; n is the label of the split node, l is the capability list of the new node, specifying the node privileges (passive operations: read, append, write, execute). A delete operation means two nodes overlapping; n is the label of the node to be removed. In the restructuring phase, privileges have to be assigned to the new node and privileges held by a node to be deleted have to be examined. Insert/delete are active operations: they permit manipulation of other rights.

Definition: a <u>scheduler</u> is an algorithm which holds exclusive privileges on the compatibility matrix or on a certain block and its ancillary data structures. These privileges are primitive operations. Legitimation sources of primitive operations are AOs.

In its major realizations, a scheduler receives an AO from the conversational network or from object-owners, controls the legitimicy of AOs, simulates the effects of primitives, definitly accepts a primitive and consequently restructures the compatibility matrix.

In very simple cases, the scheduler is reduced to a checklist. While ancillary data structures are not necessary to a security analysis, the concept of scheduler -the software implementation of security requirements- is necessary. Different protection systems have different realizations of their schedulers. Schedulers can be block-bound or can interest the whole matrix. Moreover they can be distributed in different pieces of system software or in-house developed software. An AO specifying an insert primitive on the authorization tree must be completed by the subject's capability list. The scheduler controls the significance of the operating modes assigned to each node. An AO specifying a delete primitive on the authorization tree must be completed by the verification of its consequences on the bipartite ownership graph. If the result is the isolation of an object node, the delete primitive can be refused depending on the security policies.

7. SECURITY IN GENERAL COMPREHENSIVE OPERATING SYSTEM (GCOS) ENVIRONMENT AT ACEA (AZIENDA COMUNALE ELETTRICITA' ED ACQUE)

ACEA's software-resources security adopts standard file management supervisor (FMS) and integrated data store (IDS) facilities. Thus the proposed model is a key to read standard FMS and IDS security facilities.

The GCOS, general comprehensive operating system FMS provides a hierarchical cataloging structure: user master catalogs (UMCs) and level-n subcatalogs, where n=1,2,...,49.

The hierarchical structure facilitates access restrictions and resources control. Protection mechanism is assigned on a file-by-file basis by the file-owner. Each file has an owner, the macro-subject that knows the complete password-path to the file. The file-owner holds the modify privilege (M) that includes read (R), write (W), append (A), execute (E), recovery (REC), purge (P), lock (L) and create (C). 'Read' and 'write' mean what their name implies; 'append' is similar to 'read'; 'execute' means a subject may execute an object (only in time-sharing) but can not read or write it; 'recovery' allows write when a file is abort locked; 'purge' allows a file to be deleted; 'create' allows catalogs and files to be entered as subordinate to a certain catalog; 'lock' allows security lock to a file.

The owner may propagate some privileges to users external to the catalog (not-UMC users), by assigning:
- general permission (R, A, W, E, REC, P, L, C, M; default: none);
- specific permission, only to named users (default: none).
The exclude permission withdraws general permission for a named user, without giving him any specific permission. General and specific permission is the GCOS equivalent of 'enter r into' and 'delete r from' primitives, where r is a generic right. Passwords provide the protection mechanism. The existence of UMC passwords ensures a selective discrimination between UMC users and non-UMC ones. A non-UMC user can operate on a file only if he has permission and knows the file-password. File-passwords discriminate between UMC users, enabled to certain files, and other UMC users. Operationally the existence of file-passwords implies the delivering of such passwords to non-UMC users. Thus a correct file system design has to carefully discriminate between UMC users and non-UMC users, and among different policies for catalog and file passwords. Most of the ancillary authorization tree is external to the file system and interests the organizational hierarchy. Moreover an authorization tree is necessary for audit purposes, such as password management and division of responsabilities.

In this case the authorization tree model does not work as multilevel rights propagator: an owner creates an access list for each object, consequently the associated hierarchical tree does not propagate rights. The tree degenerates into a list (flat set) because of the irrelevance of every ordering relationship. Of course other ancillary data structures are possible: i.e. a simplified three-level tree, root/owner-level/subject-level, with a relevant subjects' redundancy (a subject can receive privileges from different owners). Even a hierarchical growth of sub-catalog levels does not reproduce the defined authorization tree: on the contrary each node is dominated by its successors, that know the full password-path, and such a growth has its limits in the password management. Then the file system design is a compromise between a reasonable number of UMCs and the sub-catalog levels in each UMC.

The ACEA on-line security sub-project has been developed referring to the standard security options offered by the General Remore Terminal Supervisor (GRTS), the Transaction Driven System (TDS) and its concepts (such as logical-ids; terminal-ids; authority codes) and a conceptual model in terms of <subject,object> . Here a unique entity can be alternatively regarded as a subject or an object, in different blocks or in different levels of details in the compatibility matrix, as in the case of terminals. Starting the analysis from the concept of a workstation, a subject is defined as

<subject> = <workstation>

and an object is defined as

object = < local computing facility> / <complementary facility>

A computing facility is local if the relationship between the subject and the object is an ownership, otherwise complementary (vii). Thus workstations (terminals) are defined as subjects

<subject> = <terminal>

while computing facilities, hereafter software products, are objects.

<object> = <software-product>

<software-product> = <real-time> / <time-sharing> / < personal computing option>

In particular, the ACEA real-time security, where terminals are dedicated to single applications, is based on

i) a system software patch to realize a one-to-one relationship between users (logical-identifiers and terminals (terminal-identifiers);
ii) a partition of transactions in groups, to fully utilize standard TDS facilities.

Point i) means <logical-id> = <terminal-id> . Each logical-id has an authority code. Then

<subject> = <authority-code>
<object> = <group-of-transactions>

where an authority code is a number used to specify authorized users of transactions. An authority code can be assigned to a set of logical-ids.

Point ii) requires the following steps

- partition of transactions in groups, on the basis of the transactions' confidentiality;
- construction of the logical-ids groups;
- a further subdivision of transactions: if subject s_i has access to only a part of an object o_j while s_h has access to all o_j and if $o_j = o_{j1} \cup o_{j2}$ and $o_{j1} \cap o_{j2} = \varphi$, where φ is the null set, then s_h is related to o_j ($s_h R o_j$) while $s_i R o_{j1}$.

As a result we have a binary matrix with <terminal, transaction> pairs without any row or column equal. In fact two or more equal columns (rows) mean a un-necessary transaction (terminal) partition.

8. CONCLUSION

In this paper a very general model to approach OIS and DPS security has been proposed. From the user's point of view, security can be described in terms of elements of sets, relationships among elements of each set, relationships between elements of different sets.

All these intrinsic characteristics are summarized in a common framework: a binary matrix.

Top-down analysis has been presented as a user's possible informing philosophy and reading-key of the compatibility matrix in the form of a block matrix. Each block can be developed as a sub-project.

Subsequently model extensions have been proposed to manage the system's dynamics and particular security requirements. Blocks can degenerate into flat sets or can require a more sophisticated description, in terms of ancillary data structures. Finally the theoretical model has been used to describe the ACEA security context.

REFERENCES

(1) Bellacicco, A.; Labella, A.; Le strutture matematiche dei dati, (Feltrinelli, Milano, 1979)
(2) Bussolati, U.; Martella, G.; Towards a New Approach to Secure Database Design, Computers & Security, 2 (1983) 49-62
(3) Fugini, M.G.; Martella, G.; Security Management in Office Information Systems, in: IFIP/Sec'84, Preprints (North-Holland, Amsterdam, 1984)
(4) Harrison, M.A.; Russo, W.L.; Ullmann, J.D.; Protection in Operating Systems, Communications ACM, 8 (1976) 461-471
(5) Landwehr, C.E.; Formal Models for Computer Security, Computing Surveys, 3 (1981) 247-278
(6) Montini, G.; Sirovich, F.; Access Control Models and Office Structures, in: IFIP/Sec'84, Preprints (North-Holland, Amsterdam, 1984)
(7) Parker, D.B.; Safeguards Selection Principles, Computers & Security, 3 (1984) 81-91
(8) Snyder, L.; Formal Models of Capability-Based Protection Systems, IEEE Transactions on Computers, 3 (1981) 172-181
(9) Warfield, J.N.; Binary Matrices in System Modeling, IEEE Transactions on Systems, Man, Cybernetics, 5 (1973)
(10) Wood, C.C.; Effective Information System Security with Password Controls, Computers & Security, 2 (1983) 5-10

COMPUTER SECURITY
J.B. Grimson and H.-J. Kugler (Editors)
Elsevier Science Publishers B.V. (North-Holland)

SECURITY FOR SMALL BUSINESS COMPUTERS

Peter P.C.H. Kingston & Martin Goulbourn

Kingston, Goulbourn & Associates Ltd.
160 Duncan Mill Road
Don Mills, Ontario
M3B 1Z5

Significantly more small businesses are becoming vulnerable because of their reliance on micro computers and the data that they are used to maintain. These businesses can not afford the prohibitive costs and time involved in securing and protecting large mainframe computers. The following is a practical approach to resolving these problems using an adaptation of traditional mainframe security and an application of common sense ideas.

Introduction

As the cost of computer hardware declines and the competitive pressure to have more efficient, cost-effective operations increases, more small businesses are acquiring micro computer technology. Whether this is in the form of micro-computers or word processing equipment, many smaller companies are seeking benefits that are now more readily available.

While wanting to enjoy the benefits that this technology can bring, most businesses do not fully appreciate how quickly they become dependent on this newly acquired equipment. This vulnerability can be quickly translated into financial losses that can be devastating. The equipment is usually easily replaceable if properly selected and can be covered by insurance; but the data may be hopelessly lost if adequate precautions have not been taken.

In a small office, prevention need not be expensive and need not require extensive procedures, excessive man-hours or be prohibitively complicated. Most safeguards are common sense or are an adaptation of ideas used to protect large mainframe computers. The following presentation is a practical approach to the solution of some of these exposures. The discussion is subdivided into these topical areas:

- Office Habits and Housekeeping
- Fire Protection
- Power Protection
- Backup & Recovery
- Disaster Recovery Planning

- Data Confidentiality
- Communications
- Insurance

Office Habits and Housekeeping

One of the easiest ways to secure a micro-computer is to put simple procedures in place that restrict access to it, secure the data that is used by it and protect the supporting environment.

Limit access to the physical equipment. Do not have it in an open area where everyone can see it. If possible, lock it up at night and on the weekends. Micro-computers are light weight and portable. It is very easy to remove one from an office.

If diskettes or cassette tapes are the medium used for storage, keep them in a secure place (e.g. locked in a desk) when they are not in active use. Do not leave diskettes or cassettes lying around on the desk where someone can pick them up.

For very sensititve information (e.g. payroll), use diskette for storage, even if a hard disk is available. Keep the diskette(s) separate from the other diskettes and keep them under lock and key. If your business is large enough to have several sensitive applications, a fire rated four drawer filing cabinet should be acquired (about $ 1500.00) to store diskettes, cassettes and valuable papers overnight.

The room in which the micro-computer or word processing equipment is kept should be as clean and free from fire hazards as possible. The room temperature should be in the range of 10 - 40 degrees C.

Don't allow eating or drinking in the immediate vicinity of the equipment. Smoking and other contaminents should be minimized as they can damage diskettes as well as the read/write mechanism. (An analogy between the read/write mechanism of a computer and a flying aircraft can be made. If the disk surface was a runway and the read/write head of a disk was made the size of a 747 airplane, it would be flying one meter off the surface of the runway. A large particle of dust or cigarette smoke would be at least a two meter high boulder by comparison.) Also an anti-static mat should be considered if the environment is dry or subject to static. A person with a static charge touching a diskette can destroy some of the magnetically recorded data. Likewise, a telephone should not be kept near diskettes as the magnetic field produced by the bell ringing may cause data loss of recorded information. Needless to say, properly grounded three-pronged electrical receptacles are essential - rewire any old outlets.

A log should be maintained of all files and all diskettes (or cassettes) with each diskette having an individual name. Never use a ball point pen to write on diskettes, as the point could damage the recording surface inside the protective envelope because of the pressure applied in the writing process. The log should be reviewed weekly to ensure that all files are listed properly and that all diskettes are present. The checking should periodically be done by someone other than the person responsible for maintaining the log. The log should be kept in a locked, secure place, separate from the diskettes (cassettes).

When an operator leaves the computer and the immediate area, the computer should be shut down and the diskettes put out of sight. This prevents casual access to the system by passers-by who may have no authority to view/change information.

An operator should save entered data to disk or tape approximately every 20 minutes in case of sudden power failures, fluctuations or interruptions due to static electricity.

All procedures should be written and maintained by the people responsible for operating the equipment. They may need assistance at the time of installation, but the responsibility must still be with the operating staff. These procedures should be reviewed regularly (at least annually) by someone other than the originator to ensure they are complete and accurate.

Fire Protection

It is recommended that a hand held (type ABC) fire extinquisher be conveniently available. There are Halon extinguishers that are available but some people are concerned with potential health risks. A minimum of paper should be kept in the room and all cartons or packing material not in use should be removed. If several terminals or small computers are kept in the same room an ionization type fire detector should be installed to sound an alarm both in the area and at the night watchman's desk.

Power Protection

Just as with large mainframes, power fluctuations and outages can cause serious damange to a microcomputer. There are a variety of devices available that provide protection against these problems. They fall into two categories:

- o surge protection
- o power outage protection

The former only provides protection against electrical power surges, known as spikes. They smooth out these types of fluctuations and do not allow them to penetrate to the computer system. They are relatively inexpensive but only protect against this one problem.

However, the second category of device protects against both power spikes and outages. They are based upon a battery principle and allow from 5 to 30 minutes of operation once external power has been eliminated. In most cases all that is required is enough time to shut down the system in an orderly manner.

There are a variety of warning devices available from an audible alarm to a message that prints on the screen and/or printer. These should be reviewed to identify the one that is most appropriate to the environment.

Back-up and Recovery

Cross-train staff in different functions to use the computer system. They should be required to use the system on a regular basis to maintain their knowledge. This provides personnel backup in case of sickness, accident and staff changes.

Duplicate diskettes to create a backup copy on a regular basis. This should be done after a review of the contents of each diskette to determine if the information should be retained. These backups should include both data and software. The backup copies of files should be kept off-site (e.g. at home) and a regular rotation of copies should be established. The procedures for generating backups should be documented.

All the copies should be logged and dated with reference to the original diskette (or cassette) name. A copy of the log should be kept off-site with the backup copies. A review of the process and the backup copies that are maintained should be done annually to ensure that the right information is retained and that obsolete information is discarded.

In the event that the recovery of a file or a diskette (cassette) is necessary, there should be written procedures identifying how the process works and who should be informed. A copy of these procedures should be stored with the backup copies. The recovery should be logged with the file name and the reason the original copy was destroyed. This log should be reviewed periodically to look for recurring problems that may be avoided.

Access to the backup copies of diskettes should be easy. There is no point in having data backed up if an authorized person cannot get access to it if and when required. However, this access should be limited to specific individuals who, through their function in the company, would require access to this data.

One of the most important aspects of having a recovery procedure is its testing and verification. Quite often weaknesses are uncovered that would have made the process unworkable in a live situation. These deficiencies can be corrected so that, when required, the recovery procedure can provide the protection it was intended to.

Disaster Recovery Planning

However small a computer system may be, there is an element of dependency on it. This dependency implies vulnerability. If a disaster were to befall your computer, how would you recover?

Would your critical records be lost? Would your company survive? Estimates have been made that up to 43% of businesses that experience a major fire go out of business due to loss of data. If you have followed the suggestions outlined earlier in this article, your computer records would be easily recoverable. However, your Disaster Recovery Plan should go further than just the retrieval of data. It should specify the responsibilities that different groups within the company will have, how vital equipment, including the computer, is going to be replaced and how to reassure your customers, suppliers and banker that you are still a viable operation.

These procedures should be documented and stored away from the office. They are of little use if they are destroyed by a fire in your office building. Discussions should be held with suppliers to establish their policy and timeframe for replacement of equipment and how it affects your plans. Other companies with equipment like yours should be contacted and the possibility of using their equipment (and vice versa) in an emergency, explored. This mutual backup arrangement should specify hours of access to the equipment and outline the facilities to be provided. Essential work should be identified to ensure that the workload can be handled in the time available (probably evenings) at the alternate location. If this isn't suitable, you may have to consider the possibility of keeping a duplicate, or slightly smaller system elsewhere (e.g. at home) in the event of an emergency. Potential problems should be identified, documented and solved as part of the plan's preparation. Also, insurance coverage should be reviewed and business interruption insurance investigated. The results of all this preparation should be reflected in the Disaster Recovery Plan.

As with the Recovery Procedure, the Disaster Recovery Plan should be tested and proven. Try running your programs on the other company's system. This process will uncover the weaknesses that need to be addressed. One company we worked with had to try it several times before all the components were remembered (special forms, programs, data, phone numbers of computers that we connected into.).

For small businesses, the Disaster Recovery Plan should be very concise and address the main functions that need to be maintained in order to keep the company going. Its preparation and testing can be done over a period of time and precautions built into the normal operating procedures that are followed daily. The procedures should be reviewed and tested once a year to ensure that they still work.

Data Confidentiality

How important is your data? Would it matter if a competitor saw it or if your customers realized others could obtain easy access to it? Some methods of restricted access have been mentioned earlier such as not leaving diskettes (cassettes) lying around. There are a few others that should be considered:

- use colour coded diskettes (cassettes) for specific data or for all data. In that way it is easy to identify when confidential data is being used and by whom.

- log all diskette usage and file generation. This provides an audit trail that could be followed in the event of problems.

- restrict the amount of work done at one time. When the unit of work is completed, put the diskettes and hardcopy out of sight.

- encrypt all data that is stored on diskettes. There are several software packages available that accomplish this task quite easily and efficiently.

- use access control software that requires identification and verification before an individual can do any work. These act in a similar way to those for large mainframes. While they may be less sophisticated, they easily thwart the casual offender who is not bent on mayhem.

- store diskettes in a fireproof vault or strongbox when they are not in use. Access to this storage facility should be controlled.

While some of the measures outlined above may be considered excessive and demanding, they are not. When integrated with a normal office routine they become accepted procedures and are viewed as necessary in the performance of the job.

Insurance

Regular office insurance can be easily upgraded to include the cost of replacing existing computer equipment. The cost is inexpensive and at least would accommodate the replacement of damaged equipment. It would not, however, address the cost of relocating to alternate premises, recovering data from backup and continuing business in the aftermath of a disaster.

Business interruption insurance covers this contingency. Depending upon the business, the cost to re-establish operations and the risk of a disaster, the cost of this insurance can vary considerably. It is a consideration that should at least be investigated to clarify its' validity as a viable option. Investigate more than one supplier as the variances in risk coverage and premium are significant and appear inconsistent in a competitive market.

Conclusion

Security in the data processing environment is as applicable to the small business as it is to the large corporation. Precautions can be taken that are easy to follow and provide the level of protection that is appropriate to the risk of loss of the facilities. The time required to recreate the data and the sensitivity of the information to inadvertant public disclosure must also be considered.

As more companies come to depend on computer technology and more people learn how to use data processing systems, the need for security and protection increases.

However, the effectiveness of such a program is dependent on management awareness and commitment. Point out to your management the risks that are present and the simple steps you would take to address them. Get them involved; provide sample company policies that they can issue as a framework for the procedures you want to implement. A top down approach works well in a microcomputer environment.

Good luck and hopefully the suggestions outlined here will allow your company to operate in a more secure environment.

COMPUTER SECURITY
J.B. Grimson and H.-J. Kugler (Editors)
Elsevier Science Publishers B.V. (North-Holland)

SECURITY IN THE AUTOMATED OFFICE

Robert R. Moeller

Alexander Grant & Company
Chicago, Illinois, U.S.A.

INTRODUCTION

The rapidly evolving automated office introduces a new set of security concerns that are somewhat different from either those of mainframe computer environments or from the traditional, manually oriented office. Fairly structured security controls exist in many mainframe computer environments, and less formal, but generally recognized, security controls exist in the typical, non-automated office. However, such security controls have neither been generally recognized nor implemented in the automated office.

This paper discusses some of the unique characteristics of office automation security. These concerns are discussed in the context of both computer and manual office security concerns. A method of security risk assessment is discussed as well as approaches to the selection of security controls. It will be suggested that security in the automated office should be a combination of computer related controls and traditional office procedures.

TRADITIONAL OFFICE SECURITY CONTROLS

The traditional office is one of papers, pencils, typewriters, and telephones. It has been with us for many years, and until recently, technological improvements to that office environment have been minimal. Rather informal, but well recognized, security controls have existed for that traditional office.

These are the controls of locked desks and information access limited to authorized persons recognized by sight. That is, it is necessary to ask a secretary or clerk to see a given document or to receive a bit of information. While this form of fairly casual security can be easily overcome, it has provided a level of information security for the traditional office. As organizations became larger, procedures such as authorizing signatures have often been required to gain access.

The individual attempting to gain unauthorized access was hampered by the physical mass of paper file and records. It has been pointed out that this very mass of paper files has been a security control (1). It can be difficult to gain unauthorized access to a document if one must first determine how it is filed and then must sort to a large mass of papers to retrieve it.

This type of security system that has existed in the traditional office also has some very structured access rules. For example, the managing director will pass critical, confidential dictation to an executive secretary for typing but would very much hesitate to pass that same dictation to the typing pool. This is because there is probably a greater perceived security concern that the information would fall into unauthorized hands. While these access rules would be defined through the mechanism of formal security clearances in a defense or government related office, they are usually much more informal in others. Despite this informality, they provide a level of information access control based on the organizational structure.

Other types of security controls have existed in this traditional office. These range from asset tags on physical equipment to office procedures requiring that key documents be locked in desks or files. Of course, it has always been fairly easy to overcome these controls. Just as passwords taped to computer terminals eliminate effective password access controls, desk keys stored in the desktop telephone directory eliminate the effectiveness of locked desks.

TRADITIONAL COMPUTER SECURITY CONTROLS

As mainframe computer systems came into increasing use for business data processing during the late 1960's, an evolving set of computer security controls began to develop. The audit community was, perhaps, the first to voice concerns about computer security. For example, Davis, in his 1968 book, Auditing & EDP (7), discusses such computer physical safeguards as fire protection and physical access controls. Similarly, publications such as the Canadian Institute of Chartered Accountant's Computer Control Guidelines (5) provide guidance in both computer physical and information security.

As telecommunications, distributed processing, and complex data base structures have been introduced to business data processing environments, computer security has evolved beyond locks on computer room doors. There are numerous guidance materials available to aid the data processing professional in modern computer security. Two examples of such are Parker's Computer Security Management (10) and Becker's Information Integrity (2). In addition, both the Calendar or Current Literature section of any issue of Computers & Security (6) indicate that there is considerable data processing professional interest in the subject.

The security system that has developed for the modern, more complex data processing environment is one of very structured access rules. Specialized software products are often used to drive these access control systems; examples are ACF-2 or TOP SECRET in large scale IBM environments. These systems require security specialists to define the rights to update or just access the various data elements found within a large information system. However, just as there can be security breaches within the informal system of the traditional office, they can also exist in this more structured data processing environment. This is because, among other things, proper attention may not be given defining access rules. Too many persons may be given "master passwords" allowing them rights to access numerous data elements, the access rules may be structured too loosely, or the system may just not be correctly implemented across all applications.

There is, however, a general data processing management awareness of security issues. Established security controls may vary from physical computer room locks and simple password systems to fairly sophisticated controls. While it certainly may be argued that data processing management has not properly evaluated all possible security risks and has not always established adequate controls, there is a level of management awareness of computer security issues. In addition, there is also a large body of guidance materials and tools available to allow for the implementation of an effective data security program.

THE AUTOMATED OFFICE

The term, "automated office," has probably been with us ever since the fairly widespeard introduction of word processing systems. However, the automated office of just word processing has been described (3) as an office environment of little more than just computer assisted typing. This is an automation of a clerical function where processes are similar across many organizations. The automated office of the future, however, may more properly consist of a set of tools which will impact professional and management personnel as well as clerical. These tools will tend to be unique depending upon both the industry and the relative functions and responsibilities of individuals in the office.

This automated office might be better described as one where there are fairly extensive word or text processing functions, where these devices are interconnected through some form of local area networking, and where there is fairly extensive use of microcomputers as local decision support tools and as intelligent terminals connected to mainframe devices. These data related functions, as well as those of voice and audio, will be combined into office workstations. While such devices have been frequently described (9), they have not yet fully reached the commercial marketplace.

This office workstation will probably be the key element to the evolving automated office. It will combine the functions of today's telephones, dictation systems, computer terminals, word processors, personal computers, and typewriters. Both the secretary and the manager level employee will be using a workstation device with compatable functions. This form of automated office will very much change basic procedures in the office. It will also introduce new security concerns.

SECURITY CONCERNS IN THE AUTOMATED OFFICE

Unfortunately, very little guidance material has been published in the area of office automation security. What little there is tends to be oriented to just word processing access control security. In a recent paper, Callagham (3) discusses even the limited published materials on word processing security. Other books (12) provide guidance for implementing the automated office, discuss such issues as organizational impacts, but give no mention of security. This can, perhaps, be explained because this automated office of integrated workstations has not yet fully developed. However, preliminary plans should now be made to design security procedures for that automated office.

Security in the automated office will be a combination of procedures commonly accepted for mainframe computer security and for the more traditional office. While it might be assumed that the introduction of computer-like equipment into the office will bring with it established computer security controls, there will be some unique aspects to the automated office as follows:

- Simplicity of Equipment. Office workstations will be designed to be relatively friendly and easy to use. A discussion of IBM's prototype "925" system (11), for example, pictures a fairly easy to use modular system. We can expect password access controls on such devices to be fairly rudimentary.

- Types of Data Handled. Historically, mainframe computer systems have contained such generally important data as accounting or inventory related records. Data in the traditional office may range from strategic plans to announcements of the upcoming plant summer outing. It is difficult to establish firm security rules over such a mixture of secure and not particularly critical data.

- Office Physical Facilities. Over time, larger mainframe computer security facilities have become more and more secure. The opposite is, perhaps, true for the typical office. The open landscaped office concept even eliminates the separate, individual offices where sensitive papers could once be easily locked and secured.

- Management Awareness. As has been mentioned, there is a large body of information covering computer physical security but not that much regarding office automation security. As a result, one would expect a lower level of management awareness.

In order to implement security controls in this unique environment of the automated office, there must be a marriage of the fairly established and recognized computer security controls with the more common sense security practices of the traditional, manual office.

PROTECTION GOALS AND CONTROL STRATEGIES

A first step to establishing a better awareness of security in the automated office is to establish a set of general protection goals which will be accepted by all levels of the office organization. One example of such a goal is the confidentiality of data and information. That is, access should be limited to only those with a legitimate need to know. Even though such data may only be recorded on magnetic media, it should be recorded in at least as confidential a manner as if it were in paper media.

Two related goals might be the integrity and availability of data and information. The goal of integrity means that there should be controls over office automation equipment such that data can not easily be modified by unauthorized persons as well as controls to ensure that such data has been entered in a correct and complete manner. The goal of availability means that office automation equipment should be implemented such that it can easily recover from any extended interruption in services. A fourth goal might be that of asset protection. There should be controls to prevent unauthorized access to and use of office automation equipment.

In addition to the protection goals, a set of general control strategies should be developed to address and achieve the protection goals. Initially, these control strategies might be stated in quite general terms as follows:

- Prevention. Controls should be established to prevent unauthorized or untrained persons from violating the confidentiality, integrity, and availability of data or information located on office automation systems.

- Detection. It is probably impractical if not impossible to build a totally secure office automation system. However, controls should be built into the system to detect any unauthorized accesses which had not been prevented by other controls.

- Recovery. In the event of an exposure to the integrity or availability of the office automation system, security controls should be designed such that there can be an orderly recovery of data or assets.

The above protection goals and control strategies are quite general and must be tailored to the given organization and the office automation technologies employed by that organization. For example, as general principles they would apply when implementing an office with one or two freestanding word processors or an office with an advanced, shared logic word processing system. However, they would be implemented quite differently in each of these situations. The shared logic system would have password and logging mechanisms that would allow a more data processing controls approach to security. Because of technological limitations, security for the freestanding systems would be more procedurally oriented.

OFFICE WORKSTATION SECURITY RISKS

We have discussed the integrated office workstation which will probably be a key element in the automated office. As mentioned, this device will combine functions of the word processor, personal computer, computer terminal, dictation system, and telephone. It will be implemented for both the secretary and the manager level employee.

We might first consider security for this device in terms of security over its word processing functions. These functions have evolved from the manual, paper environment of the secretary/typist where critical documents were kept in locked desk drawers and less critical ones in manual filing systems. Access controls were somewhat dependent upon the secretary/typist locking up key files and papers at the end of the day rather than leaving them by the typewriter. In many respects, the word processing operator should be instructed to follow similar manual procedures by locking diskettes up at night and the like. The similarities in such procedures should be emphasized.

By the very user-friendly nature of these workstations, they will not have particularly sophisticated access authorization systems. The organization must assess the risk of unauthorized persons accessing the system. If a concern, consideration might be given to implementing some form of encryption techniques. However, a better approach might be to keep critical files off of shared logic files and keep them on private files on the manager's workstation.

Such files could only be accessed through a special local area link from the private secretary's workstation. This might be accomplished through unique local area network links as has been described by Emery (9). Just as the organization manager would hesitate giving a critical, confidential document to the typing pool for security reasons, the same type of document should not be procedurally given to shared logic word processor system files.

The office automation workstation described here will also have the ability to do freestanding computing as well as to access mainframe systems. While many of the security risks associated with word processors are also valid here, there are also unique concerns due to their greater functionality. These risks should be avaluated in light of the office environment. That is, if the microcomputer is used to do all office accounting and payroll work, security risks are not unlike that associated with a larger, mainframe computer. However, if used to do little more than ad hoc analysis work or graphical financial reports, it becomes a tool not unlike other office productivity tools.

A similar analysis can be made regarding the communication links between workstations within the office and in related facilities. Communications security risks should be evaluated in the context of the particular office environment. If funds are being transferred through telecommunications systems, one might want to consider one of the more secure encryption schemes such as DES. If less critical traffic, a simpler form of encryption might be considered; while these can be broken by persons with crypanalysis skills, the casual person can not easily break them.

IMPLEMENTING OFFICE AUTOMATION SECURITY

After giving consideration to the general set of protection goals and the control strategies, the office automation manager should evaluate security risks within a given office environment. This evaluation should take into consideration the sensitivity of the information handled in that office, the probability of a security violation, and the cost of implementing various security controls.

Informal security controls, based on personal recognition and the like, have always existed in the traditional office. When introducing automation technologies, an attempt should be made to implement security controls which still give consideration to traditional procedures and control techniques. The result should be a set of security controls which is appropriate for the level of information sensitivity in the evolving automated office but which uses a subset of accepted mainframe computer security controls.

BIBLIOGRAPHY

1 Ball, Leslie D., "Managing Security in the Automated Office," AFIPS Automation Conference, Proceedings, March, 1981

2 Becker, Hal B., Information Integrity, McGraw-Hill, New York, 1983

3 Callagham, David R., "Securing the Distributed Word Processing Network," Computers & Security, Jan., 1983, pp 78-81

4 Chorafa, Dimitris, Office Automation: The Productivity Challange, Prentice-Hall, Englewood Cliffs, N.J., 1982

5 Computer Control Guidelines, The Canadian Institute of Chartered Accountants, Toronto, 1983

6 Computers & Security, North-Holland Publishing Co., Amsterdam

7 Davis, Gordon B., Auditing & EDP, American Institute of Certified Public Accountants, New York, 1968

8 Emery, James C., "Managerial and Economic Issues in Distributed Computing," Information Processing 77, IFIP World Computer Congress, Proceedings, 1977

9 Maekawa, Mamoru, Sakamura, Ken, Ishikawa, Chiaki, & Shimizu, Tohru, "Multimedia Machine," Information Processing 83, IFIP World Computer Congress, Proceedings, 1983

10 Parker, Donn B., Computer Security Management, Reston, VA, 1981

11 Selinger, Robert D., Patlach, A. M., & Carlson, Eric C., "The 925 Family of Office Workstations," Information Processing 83, IFIP World Computer Congress, Proceedings, 1983

12 Uhlig, Ronald P., Bair, James H., & Faber, David J., The Office of the Future, North-Holland, Amsterdam, 1979

COMPUTER SECURITY
J.B. Grimson and H.-J. Kugler (Editors)
Elsevier Science Publishers B.V. (North-Holland)

EDUCATING COMPUTER CRIME INVESTIGATORS

Philip M. Stanley,

Senior Lecturer,
School of Computing Sciences
New South Wales Institute of Technology,
P.O. Box 123, Broadway, 2007, Sydney, Australia.

The knowledge needs of Computer Crime Investigators and hence the education of programmes necessary, will vary for each class of investigator. For example, the Auditor will require more EDP knowledge. The Law Enforcement Officer will need both EDP and Audit Knowledge. The EDP expert will need knowledge in investigation techniques and audit. There is a need for a type of MBA course where people from different disciplines, emerge with a good knowledge of each others' capabilities. The contents of such a course are suggested, with reference to existing courses conducted by the FBI and RCMP.

THE NEED FOR INVESTIGATORS

The number of computers installed and in use in a wide variety of applications with fraud potential has increased exponentially over the past ten years[1]. Tried and tested batch processing has given way to on-line, real-time applications. Once the "black box" on which the auditor had to give an opinion of correctness was a physical device which he could see and touch, and had a finite number of personnel associated with its operation and use. Today, with the growth of network systems, satellite communications and microcomputers as terminals, there is an almost infinite number of persons and computers associated with the system, and hence of audit concern.

As simple propositions[2] (in order to establish the trends of computer crime it is advanced that:

1. Computer frauds will be related to the number of computers in use and the intensity of their use.

2. Computer fraud will be related to the number of people who have knowledge of computers and who have access to them.

3. Computer fraud will be related to the number of terminals which give access to computers.

As a further proposition it is advanced that the level of detection of computer oriented fraud will depend largely on the number of internal and external auditors who are competent in all aspects of EDP technology, and/or the number of competent investigators in this area. The deterrents to computer fraud will be increased controls in systems, the greater certainty of detection of attempts to subvert the systems and more rigorous investigations of detected computer fraud. As a further measure, analytic techniques such as financial ratios analysis, can be used to detect fraud as it is being committed.

INVESTIGATION OF COMPUTER CRIME

From my experience in working with Law Enforcement Officers over the past six years, I have found that a number of basic problems exist in the investigation of computer crime. These are as follows:

1. Evidentary problems
2. Competency of investigators
3. Complexity of the task
4. Volume/size of the task
5. Jurisdiction/law deficiencies
6. Terminology and definition difficulties.

It is often difficult for law enforcement officers to establish that a crime has been committed because of the transient nature of transactions and the lack of an audit/evidentary chain. Often the chain is destroyed before the investigation can commence due to the short retention periods and/or the delay in discovery. This was true of one fraud in particular where three months had elapsed before discovery, and although the identity of the culprit was reasonably certain, he could not be prosecuted. In such cases and others of this nature the case may have to be handed over to a private investigator. Proceeding from there is a delicate matter because of the laws of defamation and wrongful dismissal.

The competency of the investigator is another difficulty. The EDP world is a complex of different computer makes, model, programming languages and industry applications. No one person can know it all. To cover this difficulty I am currently engaged in creating a large matrix of computers (makes and models) and industries, with the name of the appropriate person expert in a computer/industry shown in each cell. This will permit the rapid identification of the appropriate person to bring into the investigation. At the present time, in New South Wales, (Australia), I have trained over 300 Law Enforcement Officers in basic computer knowledge, sufficient to co-ordinate and communicate with computer experts.

The complexity of the task of investigating a large computer fraud is considerable. In a large banking/credit union fraud, with hundreds of employees and terminals, a substantial investigation team is needed to resolve the problem quickly and restore operations to normal. The management of such a team, and the analysis of their findings is a task in need of a skilled project manager.

The volume/size of the task may interact with the complexity. The worst situation is a large fraud involving many transactions of considerable complexity. In general, the maximum use of the computer must be made in the investigation in both files interrogation and maintaining a data base of entities involved, such as people, places, dates, times, etc. The investigation team should have a person capable of quickly utilizing the computer as and where needed.

Jurisdiction problems will become a major difficulty in cases involving transborder data flows and satellite transmissions. The place that a crime is committed will determine the responsibity for investigation, and the fact that it is a crime in one country may not be so in another country. For example, in Australia, there is no crime involved in the "theft" of data, such as a mailing list. There is a need for an international standard on laws relating to computer systems used in transborder data flows [3].

There are still difficulties in determining what is a computer crime. Considerable debate has taken place on this matter, and I would suggest that it be resolved by calling it computer related crime. The test I would apply is as follows:

> If the crime could not have been committed both in method and magnitude without the presence of a computer then it is a computer related crime.

If the crime could have been committed without a computer, then it is a crime using the computer as a vehicle, not as part of the crime.

It is desirable to make this distinction for the purposes of analysis of modus operandi and types of computer crimes - in essence, to separate the wheat from the chaff. It is also desirable to have a simple distinction for the purpose of Police statistics. The more data gathered on actual cases, the more complete the picture of computer crime will become. From the training/education aspect, these cases can be used for case studies. I have a particularly good case study gleaned from an actual case in August 1984, involving the use of an Apple computer[4]. Such cases, suitably cleansed of names and sensitive data, supported by documents, disks, and videotape background material can be placed in an international clearing house for training, similar to the Harvard Case Studies Clearing House.

EDUCATION FOR COMPUTER CRIME INVESTIGATION

The primary requirement for an investigator is that he/she have an inquisitive mind, and not accept as fact the first answer given. Without this attribute, few investigators will succeed. They must be capable of dealing with incomplete data and making order and sense out of disarray. It must be appreciated that in computer fraud, at the upper level of operating systems and systems programmers we are dealing with persons of extremely high intelligence. While there is a world-wide worry about "hackers" breaking into systems, I am more concerned with those persons who are already inside the system and who know passwords and procedures (e.g. Rifkin). I have been involved in investigating such a case, and I found that while they are technically expert, they are not as capable in covering their other human frailties. The fraud that I am dreading is the one in which the computer is used to design the fraud, much as in the same way that computers are used to design computers. Beyond that, the AI (Artificial Intelligence) fraud will be the fraud of the century.

It should be possible to devise and validate a suitable aptitude test to determine investigator potential. I have used tests of this nature in assessing EDP systems skills, and they have been good indicators of reasoning ability and ultimate performance. While this aspect is useful for new recruits without a track record, it is preferable, if possible, to look at a track record - particularly in the case of Police personnel.

There are three major classes of expertise involved in a computer crime invesitgation involving money. These are:

- Law Enforcement Officers
- Auditors
- Computer Specialists

In terms of relevant skills, I would assess the pre-training situation as shown in Table 1.

Table 1 Pre-existing Skills (percent)

Expertise	Investigation	Audit	Computer
Law Enforcement	90	10	10
Auditors	50	90	10
Computer Experts	30	20	90

This will vary depending on background and prior experience, but for the investigator new to the area, this will serve as a basic scenario on which the education programme is based.

In Table 1 it is postulated that Law Enforcement Officers have a high level of investigation skills as they have participated in investigations, and are trained in gathering of evidence, preservation of the evidentary chain, interviewing of suspects (with warnings), maintenance of running sheets and analysis of suspects movements and associations by such means as matrices. The area with which they will not be familiar, and will need training, is the use of data base software to record names, places, dates, etc. for later advanced analysis. This is particularly useful in large cases. In brief they must be shown the advantages of moving to a computer for investigation of computer crime.

Auditors will need training in investigation skills in regard to the active search for deliberately false records and actions of malevolent intent. This will require a change in attitudes of the auditor, who has tended to adopt a passive role in audit (if no errors are found in the sample then it is all correct) to a more active attitude (it is suspect until it has been checked out fully). Training in this aspect will be best accomplished by formal lectures in investigation procedures and a series of case studies with embedded frauds [5].

Computer experts will need training in investigations. While they already possess skills in debugging programs and systems faults, they will need training in the human side of interviewing suspects and evaluating what has been said. They will need training also in basic investigation procedures and techniques.

In regard to audit skills, the Law Enforcement Officer will need training in what is done by the Auditor, audit techniques including statistical sampling, and the roles and responsibilities of external and internal auditors. There is a considerable misunderstanding by the non-audit community of what the audit of a system and the auditors certification implies. Without digressing, in many countries, the auditor is not responsible for fraud detection, contrary to popular belief[6]. This segment would be best presented by a practising auditor, with examples drawn from an actual audit of audit objectives, working papers, internal audit questionnaire, and techniques used.

The auditor is also in need of a skills upgrade for investigation purposes. He should be trained in the use of a generalised audit package and 4GL query language, preferably by hands-on experience. This will permit the handling of large amounts of data with computer assistance[7]. This is a complex area, and complicated by the variety of packages and the computers on which they will run. In the best case, the IBM mainframes (and look-alikes) are well provided with a number of packages. In the worst case some computer brands do not have a generalised audit package. In the micro area, there are few packages at all - I know of only two, both IBM PC oriented. There is a need for a standard "bare bones" utility, written in both COBOL and BASIC to handle interrogations of files on any and all mainframe and micro computers.

The EDP specialist has some basic skills in terms of controls, but must be educated in the role of audit, what it does, its techniques, and its function, both internal and external. He should be made aware of the problems of audit, especially in the interrogation of files and databases, ad hoc reports and other needs. In this aspect the training could be accomplished in an interactive manner, with the auditor as the poser of the problems, and the EDP specialist as the solver of them.

In regard to EDP and computer expertise, the Law Enforcement Officer will need a comprehensive course in computer basics. The major question to resolve is - should the course involve the learning of programming?

The FBI course, conducted for many years, and regarded as the pioneer in the field, includes a segment on RPG programming[8]. The RCMP (Royal Canadian Mounted Police) course has two weeks of COBOL programming[9]. The Australian Police course is planned to include a segment on BASIC programming.

The FBI course involves a large case study based on banking data obtained from a "live" banking operation. A number of frauds are built into the system and are required to be discovered by the participants. The RCMP course has a number of case studies involving frauds of increasing complexity. In both cases the participants need to be able to access files and produce reports, to assist in the investigation or to examine existing program code for code alteration.

The learning of programming is one of many ways of understanding what computers are and what they can do. In terms of cost/benefit in relation to time expended and knowledge obtained, COBOL and RPG are languages that are not readily taught to proficiency in a limited time. Having taught tertiary students in COBOL and BASIC, and to a lesser extent, RPG, I would suggest that if the objective is to learn programming for the purpose of writing ad hoc programs, BASIC is the language which gives the best cost/benefit in a limited time. If proficiency is needed in code examination in COBOL or RPG then this is probably best left to the EDP expert who will detect abnormalities a lot quicker and more adequately.

In respect of computer knowledge required by the auditor, the comprehensive computer awareness course conducted for law enforcement officers could be shared. The auditor is also interested in computer control procedures such as check digits, hash totals, batch totals, logging, balancing, etc., as well as security measures such as backup and restarts. The concepts of file based systems and data base systems using 4GL's are useful. The micro data base Dbase2 is a useful training tool to demonstrate the storage of facts and the selective retrieval and analysis. It is also useful in actual applications. The application of the Hollywood Police is particularly innovative[10].

The EDP expert can also benefit from further training in EDP, particularly in the area of comparative operating systems and data base systems. It is probable that a complex fraud will involve more than one computer of different brands, operating systems and different types of data base systems. A useful exercise for the EDP specialist is to identify the various makes, models and operating systems in use currently, and attempt to identify at least one person competent in each area from which help can be obtained if necessary. It would be advisable to have a microcomputer expert as well, as this type of computer is increasing rapidly in numbers and appearing in more computer related crimes, as the ARPA network penetration indicates that even the cheapest microcomputer can be used to break into a system[11]. An associate who is the internal auditor for a large American bank estimated that he spends almost half his time running to earth the attempts of children to get into the Bank's online system[12].

In identifying the areas of improvement in each of the three classes of investigators, appropriate courses can be devised with the objective of bringing skills up to levels sufficient to understand the dimensions of the problem and to communicate effectively to the appropriate specialist. Thus law enforcement officers will know enough about audit to assess if the audit should have discovered a certain fact, and to pass it on to the auditor for detailed examination. The auditor will know enough EDP to understand that if a cause of a program aberration cannot be established to pass it on to the EDP specialist for code examination. The EDP specialist will know enough about investigation to call the law enforcement officer before interviewing the suspects.

Each specialist in the investigation team will have an overlap with his associate - but no gaps. When they have been brought up to a relatively common standard of knowledge by individually tailored supplementary training courses, the next step is to provide them with a series of case studies for syndicate/team analysis.

In terms of educational philosphy, this approach follows closely that of the MBA (Master of Business Administration) course. In such a course persons of widely different undergraduate degrees are brought together. In the first year their weaknesses are rectified (accountants do more mathematics, engineers do accounting, etc.). In the second year, with all students at the same level, the course proceeds with a heavy emphasis on syndicate case study work in each of the subject areas. Much of the learning process occurs from the participants learning from each other by the observation of how each discipline views the problem, flavoured by their own background and experience.

Translating this approach to the education of computer crime investigators, the education programme would consist of two main phases:-

1. Specific training in any area necessary to bring the investigator up to a common base level of knowledge in the three major areas of - Investigation, Audit and EDP.

2. The team/syndicate approach to a series of graduated case studies concerned with the various aspects of computer crime.

In relation to the types of case studies, they should cover a range of the major commercial systems such as Accounts Receivable, Accounts Payable, Inventory and General Ledger as a basic starting point. Then movement can be made to industry specific frauds. Many frauds are the computer adaption of well tried manual frauds, and in all case studies this element should serve as the underlying base of analysis[13].

In relation to the construction of the case studies, they should consist of at least three types, as follows:

1. The structured case in which all the facts are given with the solution somewhere within, and which can be obtained by an orderly analysis of the facts.

2. The unstructured case in which all the facts are presented, but in need of reorganisaation and analysis, with the solution somewhere within.

3. The unstructured case in which all of the facts may or may not be present, and one in which a fraud or frauds may be present or not.

In such case studies each syndicate should be provided with a microcomputer of the IBM PC type and appropriate software. The case study can be contained on diskettes and supplemented by computer printouts. In terms of total effect, the case study should be as realistic as possible. Later case studies should move into the large mainframe area, with the syndicates having to work through the appropriate EDP Operations staff to get files and printouts.

Discerned trends of training in computer crime investigation by law enforcement authorities have indicated an attempt to train the one person to do it all. It is only by training integrated teams, as teams, that the more complex computer crimes will be unravelled.

In broad terms, computer crime exists in four main categories:-

1. Discovered crime for which a culprit has been identified.
2. Discovered crime for which a culprit has yet to be identified.

3. Undiscovered crime of which suspicions are held.
4. Undiscovered crime of which no suspicions are held.

Category 1 is the simplest but requires care in the preservation of evidence and the presentation of the case. This is another area of needed training, but involving prosecutors. There is little point in apprehending perpetrators if inept prosecution allows them to go free. Category 2 should be capable of being handled by persons trained in the manner previously put forward in this paper.

Category 3 and Category 4 will require further training in the detection of computer crime involving special techniques.

DETECTION OF COMPUTER CRIME

With many computer crimes the victim may be unaware that he/she has been defrauded, or may have a vague suspicion that all is not well. Comer supports this view in his statement that 30 percent of American bankruptcies are the result of fraud, and the average embezzlement continues for three and a half years before it is discovered, often by accident[14].

Fortunately research carried out by Altman offers an approach which is predictive of corporate bankruptcy - and as Comer suggests, 30 percent are fraudulently induced. Altman has identified five key ratios (and their coefficients)[15].

a. Working capital to total assets (.012)
b. Retained earnings to total assets (.014)
c. Earnings before interest and taxes to total assets (.033)
d. Market value of equity to book value of total debt (.006)
e. Sales to total assets (.010)

The procedure (briefly) is as follows.

- calculate the ratios as percentages
- multiply by their respective coefficients
- add the products
- compare the total of the products with the critical value (Z) of 1.8

Below a Z value of 1.8, bankruptcy is highly likely (and fraud as a cause is possible). Above 3.0, the organisation is healthy, and danger of bankruptcy is minimal. Between 1.8 and 3.0, bankruptcy (fraud) is possible. Such a test would serve as a good screening for fraud.

The use of the conventional financial ratios, and the comparison with industry averages and other interfirm comparisons is a useful diagnostic tool for possible fraud[16]. It must be faced that most of the data about the various assets of the organisation are kept on the computer, and that the computer crime usually involves the alteration of the computer record, with the removal of the same quantum of physical assets, such as cash or inventory. Another of a number of scenarios is the reduction of the amount owed by a debtor for money paid "under the table". The alteration of one account without the corresponding double entry will become apparent in the analysis of financial ratios, particularly if carried out in a network of related financial ratios. Comparisons on a one firm, multi year basis and a multi firm, one year basis will reveal unsuspected cases of manipulation.

Another technique which I have used to good advantage is regression analysis and curve fitting. This has good potential in screening large amounts of data quickly for fraud possibilities and which I would give instruction on in the advanced course. I will briefly outline two applications:-

a. The detection of money illegally removed from slot machines. In N.S.W, licensed clubs have slot machines as a major revenue source. I used a time sharing regression program to establish the degree of relationship between the number of members, amount of liquor consumed, money put into slot machines and signed-for prizes. The regression program gave me a regression formula with an index of determination and coefficients for each variable. Knowing three of the variables, the fourth could be estimated accurately. Clubs in which money was missing were found by printing out a list of estimated and actual takings, with those more than 20 percent under being investigated further. Nine clubs (out of 50 total) were found to be at fault.

b. The detection of brandy illegally removed from maturing casks. In the wine making district of Australia large quantities of brandy are stored for up to ten years for maturing. During that time the brandy evaporates through the wooden casks. In general terms it was postulated that the evaporation would show a linear relationship, i.e. the longer it was stored the greater the percentage loss. The data of the number of months stored, and percentage loss was entered into a curve fitting program for the 100 casks involved. The program fits the data for six different curves to determine the closest fit. The relationship was linear. Seven cases were beyond the 20 percent limit, with three of them outside the 95 percent confidence limits (also calculated by the program). These were investigated closely, and a further $10,000 duty paid.

I have used the microcomputer package LOTUS 123 in investigating an intricate operating system misdemeanour. The person caused certain confidential company information to be printed out publicly on two occasions. From a scrutiny of the operations log over the previous two months (fortunately kept) it was found that accesses had been made to the files in preparation for the action. Also after the event two more accesses were made to try and cover up. The attendances and times of the entire EDP staff were entered into LOTUS. It quickly produced a matrix of persons and dates/times from which the vast majority were eliminated as not being present on all dates and times when events had occurred. Only two possible persons were left. One is no longer employed.

The Costigan Royal Commission (Australia) used the computer extensively to handle a large and complex investigation into organised crime[17]. At the end of its four years term in had 20,594 files and 2,852,761 pages of data. A database was established with over 90,000 names. It was used to check for aliases and undisclosed associates. An accounting write-up program was provided to recreate accounts from source data. Some 4,845 accounts were recreated involving 1,500,915 entries. This provided a variety of accounts dissections and different time periods to be explored.

I am currently involved in a project to provide the same capabiltiy on a microcomputer such as the IBM PC XT. This will be accompanied by appropriate off-the-shelf software such as LOTUS 123 and DBASE3 to be used as a standard investigation aid kit which may be readily transportable to the site of the crime if necessary. It can also act as a rapid pull-down device to store data from a mainframe for later analysis.

The implications of these tools which are readily available are that investigators should be trained in their appropriate use. They are tools which can uncover crime not readily found by conventional means. There are more special purpose tools than I have described in this paper - including statistical sampling. The art lies in knowing when to use them and what the results obtained imply[18].

LESSONS OF EXPERIENCE

Computer crime investigation has a number of facets. First it is important to determine what has happened and its extent. This must be done quickly. If possible, obtain tapes of all programs and data disk contents, operating logs, library disks and other magnetic media records. This of itself may be a mammoth task and must be balanced with an assessment of the size of the problem. Preferably, use outside personnel in the taking of data, the analysis, and an outside data centre for processing. It is hard to know who is friend or enemy in the early stages of the investigation, and it is there that the trail is freshest.

Care must be taken to preserve the evidentary chain. It is frustrating to know the identity of the cuplrit, but not to be able to prove it because of careless handling of data. My usual approach is to copy all relevant records and files, return the copies to the organisation to carry on, and retain the originals, suitably identified. This avoids any arguments about whether the copy is a true copy of the original.

It must be remembered that people commit crimes and computers are usually honest. People have motives, and once the motive is found the person with the motive can be found. The crime requires motive, opportunity and competence. Each of these may be used to eliminate suspects. Only the criminal will have all three. The use of matrix methods, and/or data base retrieval on multiple keys can save a lot of manual checking. However before entering any data into the computer make sure that it is correct and has been verified. An error in a single fact, if computer analysis is used may be sufficient to cover up a possible lead. In analysis, print out the supporting data as well as the conclusions.

There is a considerable psychology involved in mounting an investigation. An open door should be maintained at all times for persons to volunteer views and information. Care should be taken to keep secret the results of any analyses and suspicions. For this reason off-site processing is preferable. Do not disclose any details discovered of the fraud, as knowledge of the method used may reveal the culprit from words dropped in conversation.

The criminal is in his/her home territory. They know the procedures and the weaknesses. The investigation team needs help from company personnel - often the internal auditor or EDP manager. However no one is above suspicion - a Tasmanian case involving a Bank's internal auditor bears this out. Where the investigation must proceed in a hostile environment, such as search and seizure, care must be taken in the planning to ensure all data is obtained at the one time - there may not be a second chance. Indemnity of the team members is necessary, particularly those who are not Law Enforcement officers against claims for negligence, etc., if data is lost or damaged in the seizure.

CONCLUSION

The many faces of computer crime have yet to be all seen. By appropriate training of investigation teams, these will be recognised eventually. However there is an immediate need to train as many investigators, possibly to an international standard, as the trends of EFTS and other large funds transactions have an international dimension. They must be allowed to get experience on reported crime, and then they will be ready to tackle the next task - of active discovery.

At the present time there is a scarity of investigators, and the cost of computer crime, impossible to estimate, must be increasing steadily. A figure of 2 billion dollars (Aust) for the U.K alone has been estimated [19].

REFERENCES

[1] Thornton, B. and Stanley, P.M., Computers in Australia - Usage and Effects, (Foundation for Australian Resources, 1984)

[2] Stanley, P.M., Computer Crime - Discovery, Investigation, Evidence and Proof, International EDP Auditors Conference, Singapore, Oct. 1983

[3] Bloombecker, Jay, International Computer Crime - Where Terrorism and Transborder Data Flows Meet, Computers and Security 1 (1982). pp.41-53

[4] Stanley, P.M., Unpublished - case concerns seizure of records held on Apple computer and print out of data.

[5] Stanley, P.M., A Tertiary Course for EDP Auditors, Australian EDP Auditors Association National Conference, 1982. Vol.2, p.205

[6] Lindley, L.J., London and General Bank Ltd., 2ch 166, 1985, as reported in Auditing, R.A. Irish, p.373

[7] Weiss, Ira R., Auditability of Software: a Survey of Techniques and Costs, The EDP Auditor Journal, Spring 1983, pp.29-35.

[8] Colvin, B., Computer Crime Investigators - a New Training Field, FBI Law Enforcement Bulletin, July 1979, (updated with a syllabus as at August 1984).

[9] R.C.M.P., Course Syllabus, 1981 (unpublished)

[10] Schnatmeier, V., Just the Facts RAM, P.O. Magazine, Nov. 1983, p.473 (Report of Police use to check prostitutes aliases).

[11] Sydney Morning Herald, April 23, 1984, p.6, Red Faces but the KGB was Innocent, (report on ARPA network penetration by children).

[12] Stanley, P.M., - unpublished, see also Computer Fraud and Security Bulletin - Pepsi Cola case - vol.3, No.3., pp.9-10. Elsevier International Bulletins.

[13] Allen, Brandt, The Biggest Computer Frauds - Lessons for CPS's, The Journal of Accountancy, May 1977, p.52.

[14] Comer, M.J., Corporate Fraud, (McGraw Hill (UK) 1980), p.49.

[15] Argenti, John, Corporate Collapse, (McGraw Hill (UK) 1980), p.49.

[16] Corey, D.S. and Rubin, R.S., Protect Your small Business from Impending Disaster, Microcomputing, Oct. 1982, p.45.

[17] Costigan, Frank, Q.C., Royal Commission on the Activities of the Federated Ship Painters and Dockers Union, Final Report Vol.2, 1984.

[18] Adams, D.L. and Mullarkey, J.F., A Survey of Audit Software, The Journal of Accountancy, Sept 1972, p.39.

[19] Computer World (Australia), 5th April, 1985, p.14.

COMPUTER SECURITY
J.B. Grimson and H.-J. Kugler (Editors)
Elsevier Science Publishers B.V. (North-Holland)

INFORMATION SECURITY IN THE FRAMEWORK OF THE INTERNATIONAL INFORMATION FLOW DEBATE - A BUSINESS VIEW -

H. van Tongeren

Senior Advisor, Information Protection
IBM Europe, Paris

Information Security is not only a technical, professional topic but also a societal issue. As such, it can be discussed as an important element of the International Information Flow debate and related to many of the issues raised in this debate. It has also become an issue in its own right. The international business community is involved in the discussions and has a clear position on the IIF issues in general as well as on the Information Security issue.

1. INTRODUCTION

Although Information Security is very much a technical, professional topic, it is important not to forget that it has become a societal issue also, on both the national and international level. As such, it can be discussed from many different points of view. In this paper, we will look at Information Security within the framework of the national and international "International Information Flows" debate.

2. INTERNATIONAL INFORMATION FLOWS

What is covered by this term "International Information Flows" (I I F)? We can try to answer in three points:.

. Firstly: it is a non-topic! That is to say: it is just an undefined label, a heading under which anybody can discuss any topic that is more or less related to data, information and information technology. Nevertheless, looking back at the debate during the last 10 years, we can at least discern the central themes:

. The debate started as a discussion of "Transborder Data Flows" (TDF or TBDF). As the terminology indicates, the discussion was inspired by the fact that information did not only cross national frontiers any longer in its classical forms such as documents, printed books, telexes, etc. but more and more in the form of digitized data through communication links of all kinds. Which raised governmental concerns about how to keep these flows under control, whether and how such flows should be subject to customs duty or be taxed, etc.

. Since some years, the discussion has shifted from "T D F" to "I I F", that is to say: from a concern about the form to concerns about the contents. As we will see, the principal concern of the I I F debate is: what will be the impact of the massive, worldwide flows of all kind of information?

3. I I F AND THE BUSINESS COMMUNITY

As my paper includes in its title "a business view", the next question has to be: why is the business community interested in this debate of a non-topic? Well, there are two main reasons:

. The first reason is a pragmatic one: the debate is there, so one can not disregard the discussion of many, sometimes important, issues, even when these are raised under this undefined label.

. The second reason is principal: the business community is convinced that there exists a vital need for an unrestricted transfer and exchange of information, of many different kinds, both within and across national borders. It wants, therefore, to make its voice heard in any discussion of the role and importance of international information flows in today's and tomorrow's world.

You may well ask whether anyone questions this need of an unrestricted exchange of information. Perhaps not as such. However, behind the question of worldwide information flows lies the whole world of new information technologies. And many of the issues discussed under the heading of I I F have arisen from uncertainties and concerns regarding the effect of those technologies on existing structures, be they economic, social or cultural.

Such concerns, whether well-founded or not, might tempt national governments or regional organizations to protect what they may perceive as threats to their national or regional interests. Such protection would probably be achieved through legislation or regulations. And what business has identified as the main, critical issue is that such legislation or regulations, trying to cope with the impact of information technology, may result in unwarranted barriers to I I F s.

4. I I F: ISSUE AREAS AND BUSINESS POSITIONS

After this long introduction, let us get to the heart of the matter. In order to discuss I I F, we should try to structure this whole area by grouping the many different issues that have been and are discussed under this undefined label. Although subjective, we feel rather comfortable with the following structure:

. Economic issues
. Telecommunications issues
. Privacy and Data Protection issues
. Other legal issues
. Cultural and social issues.

Let us consider shortly each of the main issue areas, look at some examples of issues and try to outline what in general is the position of the international business community.

o ECONOMIC ISSUES. Some examples of main issues:

. Economic sovereignty
. Employment
. Industrial competitiveness
. Trade aspects
. Economic development and developing countries.

There are two ways of looking at I I F and economic issues. Firstly: unrestricted I I F are essential to the growth and vitality of world economy. Secondly: unrestricted I I F may have a negative impact on governments' ability to plan and direct development. It will not surprise you that the international business community strongly believes in the positive effects of I I F s. Let me take some examples of business positions:

. Restrictions on I I F s will imperil their decisive role in worldwide trade and investment and, thus, harm countries' growth and prosperity.

. The exchange of data and information services should be carried out within the framework of the existing, open, multilateral trade system.

. I I F s offer developing countries an effective instrument to contribute to their development objectives.

A specific area of obvious importance to I I F:

o TELECOMMUNICATIONS ISSUES.

Also here, one approach is that an effective and efficient use of I I F s requires liberal access to and a free choice of a broad range of telecommunications services. Another approach is to regulate or constraint international communications for a number of reasons such as protecting national equipment and services industry or the revenue and employment provided by national monopolies. Examples of main issues are, therefore:

. Restrictions on transmission and equipment
. Discriminatory tariffs and standards.

In general, the international business community takes the following positions:

. National and international telecommunications facilities should be provided on a fair, competitive and non-discriminatory basis.

. All users are best served by a broad selection of telecommunications services.

A third and rather different area:

o PRIVACY AND DATA PROTECTION ISSUES

It is different because not concerned with economic but with human rights issues, such as:

. Individual citizens' freedom to receive and use information, including imparting it to others.

. Protection of personal privacy in its broadest sense.

. Guarantee that "personal data" is collected and used fairly and openly and that it is correct and relevant.

Such protection is achieved through many different channels, such as the Human Rights conventions of the United Nations and the Council of Europe, national Data Protection law and the international Data Protection instruments adopted by the OECD and the Council of Europe.

There may be conflicts between protection of personal data and I I F s, e.g. because many of these acts contain regulations pertaining to international flows of personal data. There are, however, other issues also as implied in the views of the business community, such as:

. Individuals' privacy protection interests have to be reconciled with the benefits derived from the use of personal information by society.

. Legislation in this area should recognize the variety of information needs of business and organizations.

. The legislation should cover both computerized and manually handled data.

. Inclusion of "legal persons" in privacy oriented legislation is inappropriate.

In addition to this special area of legislation, there is a wide variety of:

o OTHER LEGAL ISSUES.

This is an area that we will not discuss, but let me show some examples of issues:

. Confidentiality of business information
. Protection of intellectual property
. Trade documentation
. Liability
. Information security
. Extra-territorial effects.

We will come back to the principal issue of legislation and, of course, to the Information Security issue especially. But first, let us take a quick look at the last and very wide issue area:

o CULTURAL AND SOCIAL ISSUES.

The issues can be grouped under three main headings:

. Cultural identity
. Social integrity
. Vulnerability and national security.

The first issue relates to the concern that countries may be overwhelmed by "foreign" information products which might have a negative influence on national life styles and cultural structures and diversity. The second issue can be broadly characterized by the concern that the world is facing an "information revolution" which could change existing social structures as radically as did the "industrial revolution" last century. The last issue arises from the perception that modern society, e.g. the whole public sector administration, gets so dependent on complex and often integrated information systems, that it becomes too vulnerable to disruptions, which may result from a variety of causes.

It would take us too far to discuss all this in detail. Let me just cite some examples of the business view:

. The legitimate aspirations to maintain national identity, integrity and security should be recognized.

. Information technology should be seen, planned and used as an invaluable tool to support individual citizens' and nations' development.

. Balanced flows of information worldwide should be realized by creating local communications infrastructures, technical expertise and management experience.

. It is possible to control information systems and to minimize exposures through well planned information systems management, including information security procedures with back-up / recovery.

Which nicely leads us to our final topic:

5. INFORMATION SECURITY

In many of the I I F issues mentioned above, Information Security is an important element. It is a legal issue as it evokes the question in how far existing legislation, especially penal law, adequately covers all new criminal activities grouped under the label "computer-related crime"; it concerns the protection of personal data, it is clearly related to many of the telecommunications issues and it is obviously an element in the concerns about vulnerability and national security.

However, Information Security is also becoming a societal issue in its own right. For a number of reasons. In the first place, the information technology environment has changed: there is an ever increasing number of computer-literate users; there is a proliferation of terminals, intelligent workstations an PCs; systems and networks are more and more interconnected and can be accessed through dial-up. Secondly, the media have taken up this topic: stories of "break-ins" and "computer crime",

films like "war game" and "electric love", etc. And, thirdly, there is a growing number of publications, seminars and congresses dedicated to this issue. Finally, and perhaps most important, we have the definite impression that there is a growing awareness of the importance of information quality and information security.

And here we come back to the same critical issue that we identified before when speaking about I I F: also in the area of Information Security, governments as well as interested authorities like Data Inspectorates or professional groups such as Standards Organizations may react to this growing interest and awareness through all kinds of regulatory approaches. They might use updates of Data Protection law or administrative decrees issued by Data Inspectorates to define appropriate protection of personal data; government procurement rules could specify security requirements; national standards and / or certification procedures could be used to enforce specific security features.

Let me give you some of the business positions on the issue of Information Security:

. It is the responsibility of any information system owner to ensure adequate and appropriate information security.

. Only the information system owners can judge what is the required and appropriate level of security for their specific information system requirement.

. Any regulations relating to information security should not discourage innovation and new technological applications.

. If any guidelines on information security were to be issued, then they should describe what security should be achieved, not how it should be implemented.

. All technical security requirements for hard- or software as well as all technical security certification should, therefore, be avoided.

6. NEW LEGISLATION OR REGULATIONS - THE BUSINESS VIEW

All the above may have convinced you that in general it is the business view that unnecessary legislation or regulations are to be avoided, in all areas of I I F issues as well as in the specific area of Information Security. If so, you are absolutely right! I want to stress this point as one sometimes meet the bizarre argument of the "legal vacuum". That goes more or less as follows: "I I F s are internationally very little regulated; in order to guarantee unrestricted I I F s, it is necessary to issue regulations in order to fill this legal vacuum..." The argument is based on the fallacy that every imaginable area should be covered by regulations, because an interdependent world community of nations can not function effectively without rules and conventions.

The international business community does not share this fear of the legal void. Let me, therefore, round off this paper with the following summing up of this business view:

. New law, regulations and conventions only:
  - If significant harm is clearly demonstrable
  - If existing law or regulations are inadequate or inappropriate
  - If it does not result in unreasonable costs or delays.

. Voluntary codes to be preferred in order to:
  - ensure flexibility
  - avoid interference with growth and development.

. Insofar as possible, new law or regulations should be adopted within an internationally harmonized framework.

COMPUTER SECURITY
J.B. Grimson and H.-J. Kugler (Editors)
Elsevier Science Publishers B.V. (North-Holland)

PRODUCING RELIABLE, SECURE SOFTWARE

Gerald E. Murine
President
METRIQS, INCORPORATED
390 Oak Avenue, Suite G
Carlsbad, CA 92008
USA

The impact of adding additional code, complex design, and other measures to software to inhibit unauthorized use of software systems in turn directly impacts the reliability of the software itself. This paper examines the problem of measuring software reliability in computer security systems and suggests an approach to design in the reliability by making objective measures over the life cycle. The author presents some new concepts which will enable the software developers to measure not only the degree of security being built in the software but also its direct impact on reliability.

I. INTRODUCTION

Advances in computer software security techniques have in turn resulted in the creation of an environment whereby the reliability of the software may be adversely impacted. Additional logic required to inhibit unauthorized entry also produces additional potential situations for the software to malfunction. This, loosely translated, becomes labeled "unreliable" software, or software which fails to perform as expected (required). Under certain circumstances, this lack of reliability may discredit the built in security measures thereby resulting in both an unreliable and insecure system. This paper will address the problem of secure software's adverse effect on software reliability and will suggest some means of minimizing this effect. The approach will be to measure the software reliability throughout its life cycle and announce the necessity for incorporating preventive means when these measures imply some deterioration in either reliability or security. The measurement method we will use is called Software Metrics (SM) and has been shown to be successful as a predictive tool for software reliability. We will thus extend the subject of Software Security Metrics (SSM).

II. THE SOFTWARE SECURITY METRIC HIERARCHY

The Software Metric methodology assumes a three-tier deductive relationship between factor, criteria, and element. A factor is defined as a high-order management concern directly related to the issue under consideration--in this case, reliability. Software Security Metrics lists the following factors as relevant to software security.

- o INTEGRITY: The extent to which access to software or data by unauthorized persons can be controlled.
- o RELIABILITY: The extent to which unauthorized persons or data can cause a program to perform its intended function with required precision.
- o FLEXIBILITY: The effort required to modify an operational program.

Each of these factors in turn is measurable by assessing a set of software security attributes which define a characteristic of the software. Each member of the set is called a criteria. The criteria are direct reflections of the software itself and are measured individually by observing compliances of measurable events. (In the context of SSM, software is defined to include code, specifications and data). A criteria score is thus the ratio of compliance to event. The criteria for SSM are given in Table 1.

TABLE 1
SOFTWARE SECURITY CRITERIA DEFINITIONS

CRITERIA	DEFINITION
ACCESS AUDIT	Those attributes of the software that provide for an audit of the access to software and data.
ACCESS CONTROL	Those attributes of the software that provide for control of the access of software and data.
ACCURACY	Those attributes of the software that provide required precision in calculations and outputs.
SECURITY TRACEABILITY	Those security requirements of the software system that provide a thread from the system security requirements to the implementation with respect to software development and security environment.
DECEPTIVENESS	Those attributes of the software that provide explanation of the implementation of a dissimilar function.
SECURITY COMPLEXITY	Those attributes of the software that provide logical dependence of functions in the least predictable manner.
INCONSISTENCY	Those attributes of the software that provide random design and implementation techniques and notation.
PERTURBATED ERROR TOLERANCE	Those attributes of the software that provide continuity of operation under randomly controlled conditions.
SECURITY COMPLETENESS	Those attributes of the software that provide full implementation of the security requirements.
SPECIFICITY	Those attributes of the software that are specific to the functions performed.
COMPACTNESS	Those attributes of the software that limit expansion of data storage requirements or computational functions.
NOTATION COMPLEXITY	Those attributes of the software that disassociate the name of the function and its activity.

The association of criteria to factor is shown in table 2.

TABLE 2
SOFTWARE SECURITY CRITERIA VS. SOFTWARE SECURITY FACTOR

CRITERIA	FACTOR		
	INTEGRITY	RELIABILITY	FLEXIBILITY
ACCESS AUDIT	X		
ACCESS CONTROL	X		
SECURITY TRACEABILITY	X		
SECURITY COMPLETENESS	X		
ACCURACY		X	
PERTURBATED ERROR TOLERANCE		X	
SECURITY COMPLEXITY		X	
INCONSISTENCY		X	
SPECIFICITY			X
DECEPTIVENESS			X
COMPACTNESS			X
NOTATION COMPLEXITY			X

Finally, each criteria is measured by counting individual occurrences for specified attributes of the software. These attributes are called elements and their ratio of successes to events is called a metric.

III. RELIABILITY AS A SSM FACTOR

A first obstacle to overcome in measuring software reliability is obtaining a general acceptance of a definition for software reliability itself. Many engineers tend to prefer defining software reliability in a fashion similar to that used in hardware. This often implies some manner of deterioration of the software which is measurable by observing some average length of successful performance for a given period of time. Throughout this paper we will use the quality assurance definition produced by Dr. Barry Boehm for the National Bureau of Standards. Reliability is "the extent to which a program can be expected to perform its intended function with required precision." The criteria for the reliability factor are given in Table 3 as accuracy, error tolerance, consistency, and simplicity. This contrasts directly with the Software Security Metric (SSM) criteria of accuracy, perturbated error tolerance, inconsistency, and security complexity as defined above.

TABLE 3
SOFTWARE QUALITY CRITERIA VS. SOFTWARE QUALITY FACTOR

CRITERIA	FACTOR		
	INTEGRITY	RELIABILITY	FLEXIBILITY
ACCESS AUDIT	X		
ACCESS CONTROL	X		
ACCURACY		X	
ERROR TOLERANCE		X	
CONSISTENCY		X	
SIMPLICITY		X	
EXPANDABILITY			X
SELF-DESCRIPTIVENESS			X
GENERALITY			X
MODULARITY			X

Reliability will be increased if the same random number is used for both inconsistency and perturbated error tolerance; however, Integrity, when measured as a function of access audit and access control, suffers some impact. Security complexity tends to impact the quality factors of Maintainability and Testability, but does not heavily impact Reliability.

IV. SOFTWARE QUALITY VS. SECURITY FOR THE FACTOR OF RELIABILITY

A. RELIABILITY CRITERIA MEASUREMENTS

The criteria of Reliability as a software quality factor are defined as:

- o Accuracy: Those attributes of the software that provide the required precision in calculations and outputs.
- o Consistency: Those attributes of the software that provide uniform design and implementation techniques and notation.
- o Simplicity: Those attributes of the software that provide direct implementation of a function.
- o Error Tolerance: Those attributes of the software that provide continuity of operation under non-nominal conditions.

However, as we have seen above, only accuracy remains a criteria for Computer Security Reliability. The software quality criteria of consistency is replaced by the computer security criteria of inconsistency. Consistency is an attribute of the software providing uniform design, implementation techniques, and notation, whereby inconsistency is the measure of how little these characteristics may be predicted or assumed. In a similar comparison, the criteria of simplicity and error tolerance have their counterparts of security complexity and perturbated error tolerance, both of which may rely on some random deviations.

In the case of security complexity, some randomness of naming conventions for example, may be by class of substructure (function, subfunction, module, etc.) or may extend to an even higher level such as functional architecture or system. Transformation tables are required to re-construct these perturbations; however, no two transformations should be identical. The measure of the paired software quality Reliability criteria of simplicity is thus achievable by applying this inverse transformation.

Mathematically, if T_i is a tranformation on the jth security complexity subclass $\sigma_{i,j}$ of the ith class such that $T_r \neq T_s$ for all r, s; T_i^{-1} exists for all i security complexity classes C_i ; $\sigma_{i,j} \in \{C_i\}$; then the measure of Reliability criteria of simplicity S_i is given as:

$$S_i = \mu \left[\sum_{j=1}^{n} (\sigma_{i,j}) \right]$$ for n subclasses, and

$$C_i = \mu \left[\sum_{j=1}^{n} (T_i \, \sigma_{i,j}) \right]$$ for n subclasses of the ith class and

measure μ. Thus: $C_i = T_i \cdot S_i$,

$$T_i^{-1} \cdot C_i = T_i^{-1} \cdot T_i \cdot S_i = S_i$$

Hence: $$T_i^{-1} \cdot \mu \left[\left(\sum_{j=1}^{n} T_i \, \sigma_{i,j} \right) \right]$$

$$= \mu \left[\sum_{j=1}^{n} T_i^{-1} \cdot T_i \cdot \sigma_{i,j} \right]$$

$$= \mu \left[\sum_{j=1}^{n} (\sigma_{i,j}) \right] = S_i$$

and the total security complexity measure C_τ over m classes is:

$$C_\tau = \mu \left[\sum_{i=1}^{m} \sum_{j=1}^{n} (T_i \, \sigma_{i,j}) \right]$$

and the total quality criteria of simplicity, S_τ, is:

$$S_\tau = \mu \left[\sum_{i=1}^{m} \sum_{j=1}^{n} (\sigma_{i,j}) \right]$$

The Computer Security Reliability criteria of perturbated error tolerance may be constructed in a similar manner or, preferably, in a disassociated fashion. It is suggested that the software quality reliability criteria of error tolerance, being defined as "those attributes of the software that provide continuity of operation under non-nominal conditions", fluctuate either randomly by class or substructure and that this variance itself vary between successive applications. The later variance may be random, or as in the case with the criteria of security complexity, be defined over a fixed transformation. In this case, an error tolerance gate would randomly change within a class or substructure but the error tolerance between substructures would be defined by a fixed transformation.

Mathematically, if ${}_j\omega_\delta$ is a coefficient generated by some random time dependent function $\alpha(t,\delta)$, $\delta = g(t)$, $0 < (t,\delta)$, and if the pertubated error tolerance, P_i, is expressed as a linear combination of the Reliability criteria E_i of error tolerance elements, $\varepsilon_{i,j}$ defined over the ith class and j^{th} subclass, then we may select ${}_i\omega_\delta$ such that:

$$P_i = \mu \left[\sum_{j=1}^{\gamma} ({}_i\omega_\delta \quad \varepsilon_{i,j}) \right]$$, for the measure μ, where

$$E_i = \mu \left[\sum_{j=1}^{\gamma} (\varepsilon_{i,j}) \right]$$

If ${}_j\omega_\delta \in \{\alpha(t,\delta)\}$ such that ${}_j\omega_\delta^{-1}$ exists, the

$$P_i = \left[\sum_{j=1}^{n} ({}_j\omega_\delta) \right] E_i = W_i E_i \text{ where } W_i = \sum_{j=1}^{n} ({}_j\omega_\delta)$$

(for the j subclasses of class i) and $W_i^{-1} \in \{ {}_j\omega_\delta^{-1} \}$. Then W_i^{-1} exists and $E_i = W_i^{-1} W_i E_i$

$$= W_i^{-1} \left[\sum_{j=1}^{n} ({}_j\omega_\delta) \right] E_i$$

$$= W_i^{-1} \left[\sum_{j=1}^{n} ({}_i\omega_\delta) \right] \cdot \mu \left[\sum_{j=1}^{\gamma} (\varepsilon_{i,j}) \right]$$

$$= W^{-1} \cdot \mu \left[\sum_{j=1}^{\gamma} ({}_j\omega_\delta)(\varepsilon_{i,j}) \right]$$

$$= W_i^{-1} \quad P_i$$

Hence, the software reliability error tolerance measure may be preserved and calculated easily from the pertubated error tolerance error when stored as a time dependent vector; for example, if

$$[A] = \{ \omega^{-1} \} , [B] = \{ \sum_{j=1}^{n} ({}_i\omega_\delta)\} \text{ and}$$

$$[C] = \{ \mu \left[\sum_{j=1}^{\gamma} (\varepsilon_{i,j}) \right] \} \text{ then}$$

$$E_i = |A| \left[[B]\ [C]^T \right]$$

B. BEGINNING WITH THE SOFTWARE SECURITY PLAN (SSP)

Generally, Software Developers and Engineers have a plan (Software Development and Plan (SDP)); the Software Quality Engineers have a plan (Software Quality Assessment and Measurement Plan (SQAM Plan)) and Test personnel have documents (Test Plan, Test Procedures, etc). In order to assure that reliability is being built into a secure software system, Software Security Engineers should also have a plan. This plan, Software Security Plan (SSP) should describe the organization and procedures to be used by the contractor in managing the software security development activity. The SSP must include specific instructions for designing reliability into the secure system. As a minimum, the SSP should contain: introductory remarks relating the software development, quality security, and reliability; the organization of responsibilities for insuring reliability requirements and measurements are incorporated in the secure software; the approach for same; the facilities necessary for applying the quality assurance, configuration management, monitorings and control measures to be used to insure reliable secure software development, the schedule network plan, and resource allocation required which specifically addresses reliability measures for secure software; and the identification and abutment of risk items expected in including SSM criteria of accuracy, perturbated error tolerance, inconsistency, and security complexity in the reliability process. The SSP must be responsive to the Security Software Life Cycle.

It is the SSP which serves as a prerequisite for designing in reliability for secure software systems. This outline together with the measurement approach discussed above will provide visibility to the software development process in assuring both integrity and reliability.

---

[1] Boehm, B.W., Quantitative Evaluation of Software Quality, Proceedings 2nd International Conference on Software Engineering, pp. 592-605, October 1976.

[2] Murine, G.E., and Carpenter, C.L., Measuring Computer System Security Using Software Security Metrics, Second International Congress and Exhibition on Computer Security, Toronto, Ontario, Canada, IFIP/Sec '84, September, 1984.

[3] Murine, G.E., Applying Software Quality Metrics in the Requirements Analysis Phase of a Distributed System, Proceedings from Minnowbrook Conference, 1980.

[4] Murine, G.E., Improving Management Visibility Through The Use of Software Quality Metrics, Proceedings from IEEE Computer Society's Seventh International Computer Software & Application Conference, 1983.

COMPUTER SECURITY
J.B. Grimson and H.-J. Kugler (Editors)
Elsevier Science Publishers B.V. (North-Holland)

THE DEVELOPMENT OF A SPECIFICATION LANGUAGE FOR A COMPUTER SECURITY SYSTEM

Jan H.P. Eloff

Department of Computer Science
Rand Afrikaans University
P.O. Box 524
Johannesburg, 2000
South Africa

The primary goal of this paper is to define an initial step towards defining a 'systems grammar' based on the notion of formal languages which can be used as a 'tool' in the formal representation of computer security systems. Currently all modelling done on computer security systems are written-up as mathematical models. These mathematical models are usually based on the mathematics of relations amongst objects as opposed to the model described in this paper which is based on the theory of formal languages. The contents of this paper is aimed at people who are doing research on the logical aspects of computer security.

0. INTRODUCTION

Computer security can be seen as the protection of the organization's computer assets and the effectiveness of the installation to provide reliable and accurate service of a high standard. Functionally, computer security can be divided into physical and logical security. Physical security can be defined as the action that prevents physical harm to the resources of the computer system. Logical security is the protection of data and programs stored in the system.

As stated in the majority of the literature available, the three most basic requirements for a logical security system are:

- each reference made by a program must be checked to see if permitted
- the security system must be an isolated system, this feature will protect it from the interactions of any other systems
- the software security system must be proven correct.

A logical security system can be proven correct by one of the following alternatives:

- the code of the programs in the system can be proved correct,
- a prototype of the system i.e. a mathematical model can be proved correct,
- the system can be proved correct through excessive testing

In the current literature available all the prototypes of systems are represented as mathematical models. These mathematical models are mainly based on the mathematics of the relations amongst objects.

1. OBJECTIVES FOR THIS RESEARCH

The objective of this paper is to define an initial step towards defining a 'systems grammar' based on the notion of formal languages which can be used as a 'tool' when representing computer security systems formally.

These objectives can be diagrammatically stated as follows:

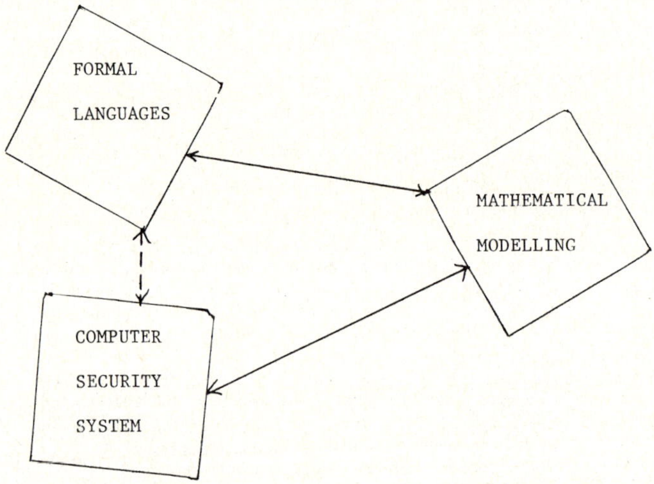

Thus, the three areas that play a major role in this research are:

i COMPUTER SECURITY
ii MATHEMATICAL MODELLING
iii FORMAL LANGUAGES

The objectives are to try to find an appropriate formal grammar/language which can be used to represent the elements as well as the relationships amongst these elements which form part of a computer security environment.

- The relation 'COMPUTER SECURITY SYSTEM - MATHEMATICAL MODEL' is very well defined in different mathematical models available today, e.g. the model developed by Bell & Lapadula.

- The relation 'FORMAL LANGUAGES - MATHEMATICAL MODEL' is well defined by the fact that the theory of formal languages is very strongly based on the theory of mathematics.

- The relation 'FORMAL LANGUAGES - COMPUTER SECURITY SYSTEM' is the stated objective of this paper.

The strategy followed to define the relation 'FORMAL LANGUAGES - COMPUTER SECURITY SYSTEM' was to define initially the 'logical' environment for a computer security system, i.e. all the elements that play a role as well as their interaction with each other. In addition we evaluate a mathematical model for this environment and define a formal grammar which will best represent this environment.

2. REQUIRED FEATURES FOR THE 'TO-BE DEVELOPED' GRAMMAR

The 'ideal' formal grammar to fulfill the requirements as set by the computer security environment can be summarized as having the following features:

2.1 Context sensitivity - this feature will implement the idea of a 'need-to-know' facility, i.e. a user should have a certain level of knowledge before he can gain access to a specifically protected object in the system.

2.2 Mapping - this is a common feature in all formal languages. This facility supports the idea of cryptography, i.e. the transformation of a readable message to a message in encoded form. Mapping will also contribute to the assignment of security classes and categories to the users in the system.

The mapping and context sensitivity features of a grammar support the idea of program pathing in our model. Program pathing allows for the dynamic allocation of a higher access authority under certain conditions.

2.3 'Numeric' - the to-be developed grammar must be able to interpret numeric constants, i.e. 3 must not only be seen as a symbol but also as a symbol with an attached numeric value.

The implementation of this facility will help us to compare symbols. Specifically in the security environment we want to compare security classifications of objects. We also need a 'numeric' facility to implement time indices (i.e. elements of a time set) which are needed to define a secure state of a system.

2.4 The to-be developed grammar must be able to control 'n' grammars, these grammars to be on a subordinate level. This will be the realisation of the concept of multiple users operating concurrently in a real system.

2.5 The to-be developed grammar must be able to test for the equivalence between strings, but also if possible test for the equivalence between a string and the contents of a cell (i.e. a variable). This feature will help us to do a test on the access rights of a user.

2.6 The to-be developed grammar must also be able to handle global and local symbols with not only rewriting capabilities but also doing assignments. This feature contributes to the implementation of concurrency in a multi-access data base environment.

2.7 Deadlock - the grammar must be able to handle the deadlock situation as we want to provide in the model for multiple users operating concurrently in a common data base environment.

3. M-SYSTEMS GRAMMAR

Let us call the grammar that will fit the previously mentioned features (§2) a M-Systems Grammar.

Existing formal languages were reviewed functionally. It turned out that no existing grammar is suitable to fit the requirements set in paragraph 2. However, the programmed, scattered context and permitting context grammars showed potential for further investigation. As part of the research done we showed that the pure programmed grammar provides a natural framework for representing concurrent usage of code.

As stated the idea is to keep the defined grammar as close as possible to the existing theory of the formal languages. The strongness of this concept indicated a path of migration to be followed while we were defining the 'ideal' grammar. The development of the M-Systems Grammar was as follows:

3.1 The programmed, scattered context and permitting context grammars will form the basis of the new M-Systems Grammar.

As the theory of formal languages are well proven, we want to keep the M-Systems Grammar as purely as possible, i.e. defined in the concepts of formal languages in the usual context. Thus our initial definition of the M-Systems Grammar will be without any deviation on the existing theory of formal languages. Let us refer to this version of the M-Systems Grammar as a Minimum M-Systems Grammar.

3.2 Defining the Minimum M-Systems Grammar.

The Minimum M-Systems Grammar is based purely on the three grammars mentioned previously. This grammar controls a number of grammars which will generate strings of symbols in parallel. The interdependency between the 'm' grammars on subordinate level will be controlled by a special set of symbols called the 'global' symbols.

The productions of the Minimum M-Systems Grammar can be divided into two groups: Firstly there is a set of productions specifically designed to manipulate the set of global symbols. Secondly there is a set of productions to manipulate the variables and terminals in the usual formal language sense.

The Minimum M-Systems Grammar can be seen as a 'high level grammar' as opposed to the programmed, scattered and permitting context grammars.

We will now give the formal definition of the Minimum M-Systems Grammar.

<u>Definition</u>: Minimum M-Systems Grammar

A Minimum M-Systems Grammar is a 6-tuple

$$G_{ME} = (\bigcup_{i=1}^{M} \{G_i\} , V_k , \bar{\bar{P}} , q , h , S)$$

where each G_i is a 4-tuple defined by

$$G_i = (V_{N_i} , V_{T_i} , P_i , \bar{B}_i)_{1 \leq i \leq M}$$

We will now discuss the meaning of each symbol:

$V_K = \{g_1 , g_2 , \ldots ,g_\ell\}_{\ell \in N}$ is a finite set of symbols called the <u>global symbols</u>.

Each G_i is a grammar defined as follows:

Each production in P_i has a unique label. q_i and h_i are mappings of production labels in P_i into the set of subsets of production labels in P_i. q_i and h_i can be different for each G_i. Let f be a label for a production in G_i. We will then refer to $q_i(f)$ and $h_i(f)$ respectively as the success and failure fields of f.

Let $q_i(f)$ be represented by $S(f_{i_1} , \ldots ,f_{i_r})$

and $h_i(f)$ be represented by $F(f_{j_1} , \ldots ,f_{j_t})$

i. V_{N_i} is the set of non terminal symbols:

$$V_{N_i} = V_K \cup V_{1_i} \cup V_{2_i}$$

V_K is the set of global symbols as defined above

where for every i:

V_{1_i} is a finite set of symbols, called the set of local symbols for G_i,

and

V_{2_i} is a finite set of symbols, called the set of own symbols for G_i.

$$V_{1_i} \cap V_{2_i} = \emptyset, \quad V_{1_i} \cap V_K = \emptyset \quad \text{and} \quad V_{2_i} \cap V_K = \emptyset$$

V_{1_j} may be different from V_{1_i} for $i \neq j$, but need not be. The same applies for V_{2_i} and V_{2_j}, $i \neq j$.

Let $\bar{V}_1 = \{V_{1_1}, V_{1_2}, V_{1_3}, \ldots, V_{1_N}\}$

and $\bar{V}_2 = \{V_{2_1}, V_{2_2}, V_{2_3}, \ldots, V_{2_N}\}$

$\bar{V}_1$ is the total set of local symbols for all G_i,
$\bar{V}_2$ is the total set of own symbols for all G_i.

ii. V_{T_i} is the set of terminal symbols for grammar G_i and $V_{N_i} \cap V_{T_i} = \emptyset$

iii. $P_i = P'_i \cup \bar{P}_i$ where

(a) P'_i is a set of productions specifically designed to manipulate the sets of local and global symbols. Every production in P'_i is of the form:

$$(f_i)\ A \to B \qquad S(f_j) \quad F(f_r)$$

with $A \in (V_K \cup V_{1_i})$ and $B \in (V_K \cup V_{1_i})^*$

The application of the above production is the same as for a production of class P_{1_i} as discussed further on.

(b) $\bar{P}_i$ is a set of productions to manipulate the variables and terminals in the usual formal language sense. $\bar{P}_i$ consists of two classes of productions namely P_{1_i} and P_{2_i} :

i.e. $\bar{P}_i = P_{1_i} \cup P_{2_i}$

Productions in P_{1_i} are pure programmed grammar productions of the form:

$$(f_i) \quad X \to R \qquad\qquad S(f_j) \quad F(f_r)$$

where

$$X \in V_{2_i} \text{ , } R \in (V_{2_i} \cup V_{T_i})^*$$

An application of a production of class P_{1_i} to a string U has the following meaning: If X is present in U it can be substituted with R and the follow-up production will be selected from $S(f_i)$ or, if X is not present in U, no substitution will take place and the follow-up production will be selected from $F(f_i)$.

Productions in P_{2_i} are of the form:

$$(f_i) \; T \to R|U:\emptyset| \qquad S(f_j) \quad F(f_R)$$

where

$$T \in V_{2_i} \text{ , } R \in (V_{2_i} \cup V_{T_i})^* \text{ and } U \subseteq V_{N_i}$$

A production of class P_{2_i} is used as follows:

If T appears in a string W and all symbols of U appears somewhere in W, then T is replaced by R and the follow-up production is selected from $S(f_i)$, otherwise the follow-up production is selected from $F(f_i)$.

Note that the production above is actually a permitting context production. Note further that this production can be simulated by a series of pure programmed grammar productions. This form of the production is therefore only used as a shorthand notation.

(iv) B_{i_ℓ} is an initial symbol of G_i and $B_{i_\ell} = \not{C}_i C_i S_i$

where

$\not{C}_i \in V_K$ (i.e. a global symbol)

$C_i \in \bar{V}_1$ (i.e. a local symbol)

$S_i \in \bar{V}_2$ (i.e. a variable)

B_{i_ℓ} is thus a <u>specific</u> initial symbol for a <u>specific</u> grammar G_i.

Let $\bar{B}_i = \{B_{i_1},\ldots,B_{i_r}\}$ i.e. $\bar{B}_i$ is the set of initial symbols for G_i,

and $\bar{B}_j = \{B_{j_1},\ldots,B_{j_s}\}$ for $i \neq j$ Then $\bar{B}_i \cap \bar{B}_j$ need not be empty.

We have now defined the elements of the grammar G_i.

Initially we defined the Minimum M-Systems Grammar G_{ME} as:

$$G_{ME} = \left(\bigcup_{i=1}^{M} \{G_i\} , V_k , \bar{\bar{P}} , q , h , S \right)$$

The first two elements have already been explained.

$\bar{\bar{P}}$ is a single production of the form:

$$S \rightarrow B_{(i_1)_\ell} \, B_{(j_2)_k} \cdots B_{(z_m)_s} \qquad i,j,k,l,m,s,z \in \mathbb{N} \; (\mathbb{N} \text{ is Natural Numbers}) \qquad \ldots\ldots.(i)$$

where

S is the start symbol of G_{ME}, and

$B_{(i_1)_\ell}$ is a start symbol of G_i, and

<u>NOTE</u>: Both B_{i_ℓ} and $B_{(i_1)_\ell}$ represents the same start symbol for G_i. However, take notice that $B_{(i_1)_\ell}$ contains information on the position of this starting symbol in the string of starting symbols as generated by S (as

in (i) above). Therefore $B_{(i_j)\ell}$ will represent the ℓ'th start symbol for grammar G_i in the j'th position in the string of starting symbols as generated by S.

This completes the definition of a Minimum M-Systems Grammar.

The concepts implemented in the Minimum M-Systems Grammar which were originally set out in our set of required features are:

- context sensitivity,
- mapping,
- global and local symbols,
- parallelism.

3.3 Define The M-Systems Grammar

The M-Systems Grammar is based on the Minimum M-Systems Grammar with a few additional features. Most important is the implementation of the concept of a 'variable' in a grammar, as stated in our set of required features. This concept will help us in testing for security classes of objects in a computer security environment.

Seven classes of productions are defined where the majority of these classes provide for the handling of 'variables', i.e. a symbol which is the name of a cell which again contains a symbol.

The M-Systems Grammar can be seen as a 'high level grammar' as opposed to the Minimum M-Systems grammar.

This M-Systems Grammar is a deviation from the existing theory of formal languages and cannot be defined as purely as the Minimum M-Systems Grammar. However it inherits all aspects of the Minimum M-Systems Grammar and for that reason it also inherits all aspects of the programmed, scattered context and permitting context grammars.

3.4 Define An Enhanced M-Systems Grammar

The previously defined M-Systems Grammar contains most of the required features of the 'to-be developed'grammar. However we are still unable to make comparisons between numeric values.

The highlight of this enhancement to the M-Systems Grammar is to implement a 'numeric' concept in a grammar. This is implemented through a special set of symbols called the 'counting' symbols.

This enhanched M-Systems Grammar contains all of the required features as set out in paragraph 2 as well as some features to qualify as a pseudo programming language. Examples of programming constucts that can be provided, are:

- IF --- THEN constuct
- DO --- WHILE construct
- basic assignments eg. A = A + 1

NOTE - the formal definitions of the 'M-Systems Grammar' and the 'Enhanced M-Systems Grammar' are not given in this paper. These two grammars are based on the Minimum M-Systems Grammar as defined in this paper. This concludes our definition of the M-Systems Grammar.

4. CONCLUSIONS

The Enhanced M-Systems Grammar is an enhancement as well as a deviation on the existing theory of formal languages.

This grammar serves as a 'formal tool' which can be utilized for the modeling of a computer security system. The unique benefit is that this 'formal tool' is based on the theory of formal languages which can be accepted as mathematically correct.

This 'formal tool' has more benefits as opposed to a mathematical model as it contains pure computer related features, e.g. it inherits strong programmability features.

This 'formal tool' can also be seen as a control structure through which many of the concepts used in operating systems theory can be represented, concepts like:

- concurrent processes,
- deadlock,
- locking and unlocking of records.

This 'formal tool' also contains certain features that will contribute to the definition of expert systems. These systems are becoming an important part in the 'logical' aspects of computer security.

5. REFERENCES

(1) Bell, Elliot D. et al, Secure Computer Systems: A Mathematical Model Volume II (Mitre Corporation, Nov 1973).

(2) Eloff, J.H.P., Computer Security with special reference to the software aspect, M.Sc Dissertation, Rand Afrikaans University, South Africa (1980).

(3) Eloff, J.H.P., Selection Process for Security Packages, Computers & Security, Volume 2, Number 3, (1983) 256 - 260.

(4) Eloff, J.H.P., Selection Process for Security Packages, in: Finch, J.H. and Dougall, E.G. (eds.), Computer Security: A Global Challenge, Elsevier Science Publications B.V. (North Holland) IFIP, 1984.

(5) Eloff, J.H.P., The Development of a Specification Language for a Computer Security System, Ph.D. Thesis, Rand Afrikaans University, South Africa, (1984).

(6) Lipton, R.J., & Budd, T.A., On classes of Protection Systems Foundations of Secure Computation, (Academic Press 1978) 281 - 296.

(7) Nicolas, J., Logic for Improving Integrity Checking in Relational Data Bases, Acta Information, Volume 18, (1982) 227 - 253.

(8) Salomaa, A., Formal Languages (Academic Press 1973).

(9) Von Solms, S.H., Random Context Array Grammars, Proceedings of IFIP Congress 80, (North Holland 1980) 59 - 64.

Introduction

Recently a multinational bank (henceforth the Bank) was faced with a difficult choice: develop bank-wide technical standards for encryption or allow various applications and systems groups to proceed with separate encryption implementation plans, resulting in various incompatible encryption technologies. A number of these Bank encryption implementation projects were already underway; meanwhile, the banking community was in the process of developing encryption standards. If the Bank did not establish internal encryption standards, the costs of retrofitting various systems to a new standard would be prohibitive. On the other hand, if the Bank did establish standards, they would need to be revised to comply with soon-to-be-issued industry standards. Additionally, Bank management knew a marketing advantage could be gained by providing financial services more secure than those of the competition. Therefore, the Bank decided to have the Systems Engineering Division's Information Security Department develop in-house standards -- something that few financial institutions have done.

This paper describes the project management considerations related to the development of these encryption standards. The project is particularly noteworthy because it was the first technical information systems security standard for the Bank. Accordingly, the author -- who was project manager -- offers perspective and advice to readers who may be involved in similar efforts.

Assessing the Need for Technical Standards

When it comes to information security problems, many organizations refuse to admit that serious systems exposures exist. At the Bank, most system-related managers were acquainted with both a majority of the threat types and the common control measures applicable to their systems. Accordingly, little management awareness raising was needed. The managers were also familiar with the Foreign Corrupt Practices Act and other personal liability laws, which helped to ensure their cooperation. In many organizations, however, managers are not aware of the true exposures; they are familiar only with the superficial exposures described in newspapers. If such is the case, management's awareness must be raised via films, articles, speeches, and/or (heaven forbid) severe internal losses before a technical systems security standards effort can be launched.

The Information Security Department had to assign a priority to the many yet-to-be-done "high priority" tasks. To gather information required for this priority setting effort, the department interviewed senior managers in data user, data custodian, and data owner departments. Besides publicizing the existence of the newly-formed Information Security Department, these interviews allowed the department to obtain firsthand an indication of which projects management thought were most important.

After obtaining suggestions to immediately address over ninety specific large-scale projects, the department manager examined in detail the sequence of projects that would allow the group to cover the most ground in the least time and with the fewest resources. The suggested projects were categorized into three groups: policies/standards, systems/ networks, and applications. Then a CPM (Critical Path Method) chart was prepared to indicate the dependencies between these projects. CPM analysis revealed that encrytion standards needed to be prepared before systems security work could begin on a high-speed front-end switching computer, on an in-branch customer-selected Personal Identification Numbers (PIN) system, and on other projects.

The following potential benefits also justified the encryption standards project:

- The speed of secure applications development would be increased (a particularly important concern for a large Bank competing in the newly deregulated American financial services marketplace).

- The standards would ensure an adequate level of security thoughout all systems, thereby substantially reducing requirements for EDP Audit and Information Security Department resources.

- The standards would describe an explicit target operating environment that could be used in systems development and planning efforts (e.g., network and database design).

- Inconsistent implementations of encryption technology, which could unnecessarily hamper the appropriate movement of data between computers and networks, would be avoided. This was particularly appealing because the Bank seemed to have at least one of every type of computer ever sold, and accordingly faced the problem of making these often-incompatible machines communicate with each other.

- The standards would support integrated cross-system controls, such as the use of a super-fast front-end switching computer to handle communications line encryption for all connected mainframe hosts. That is, this project would support a wider security perspective, rather than the too-often-found "band-aid" approach of addressing only one system and one threat type at a time.

- The standards would allow systems developers and others to avoid duplication of effort where they would reinvent something that another group within the Bank had already created.

- The standards would facilitate bargaining for vendor concessions, such as volume discounts and research and development on special customized gear.

The Bank employs thousands of people, and many different departments would ultimately be affected by the encryption standards. To assure that the standards addressed their needs, it was decided that many of these departments should be involved in the development effort. Accordingly, extensive interviews with people who had a vested interest in the project were conducted at the time of project inception. People who had expertise in encryption, managed a systems development project that would be affected, managed a department that would be affected operationally, or who otherwise had an interest in the project, were consulted. The intent of these interviews was to obtain support from people who might oppose the standards, to refine the project scope and objectives, to get a sense for the work done to-date throughout the Bank, to identify the major players, and to screen people who might later serve on an encryption standards working committee. The two weeks spent discussing the project with over forty-five people turned out to be a very worthwhile investment that later paid off in goodwill and cooperation.

Specifying Project Objectives and Scope

Explicit statements of the project's objectives and scope were carefully developed before release to people outside the Information Security Department. Because this was the first systems standard to be developed by the department, it was clear that the reputation and credibility of the department depended in part on the project's success.

The overall scope of the project involved the provision of implementation specifics needed to protect, via encryption, all sensitive digitized computerized text and graphics. Certain digitized representations of text and graphics that were not used extensively at the Bank, such as videotex (Prestel), were considered outside the scope of the project. The project did address encryption implementation specifics for such matters as computer resource access control, user and process authentication, protection of proprietary software, detection of message replay, detection of message and file/database errors, detection of unauthorized data modification or deletion, and prevention against unauthorized disclosure of sensitive data. More esoteric uses of encryption, such as providing user autonomy and preventing traffic analysis, were not included because there was no demonstrable short-term need for them in the Bank's operating environment. Voice encryption (scrambling) was also deliberately excluded from the project scope because the technology is substantively different from that used for digital data encryption.

To temporarily stop development efforts that were soon to involve or already involved encryption, a memorandum describing the project scope, objectives, and expected results was sent to concerned management and technical staff. Addressing those who wished to continue with encryption-related projects independently of the encryption standards working committee, a special memo was prepared for project managers in charge of encryption-related efforts. The memo explicitly requested that the project managers defer any efforts to implement encryption devices or software until the Bank-wide encryption standards document was issued (an anticipated four month period). The project managers were asked to temporarily refrain from entering into new binding agreements with encryption vendors. Other tactics, for example, telephone calls from senior managers, were also used. Be it good luck or genuine compliance with these requests, no major encryption-related implementation work proceeded and no major encryption vendor commitments were made during the development of the draft encryption standards document.

To ensure that all who should know were notified of the project, a brief article was included in the Bank's internal newspaper. This article gave a definition of encryption, a list of ways that encryption can be used, and a list of the members of the encrytion standards working committee. Paraphrased below is a broad project objectives statement that was provided in the article:

> The mission of the effort is to provide an approach that will permit management to focus and redirect encryption efforts throughout the Bank. This approach will foster cost-effective encryption implementations that are consistent with information security policies, standards, and practices of both the Bank and the banking industry. Additionally, the approach will facilitate and speed the deployment of encryption technology in a way that is in the best long-run interests of the Bank.
>
> Focusing on computer- and communications-system resident data, the project working committee will create a document that is a current "how to" guide for evaluating the need for, designing, implementing, and operating, encryption systems. The document is intended to have the specificity and enforceability of a Bank-wide technical standard.

Targeted Encryption Environment

One of the innovative and most helpful approaches the encryption standards working committee used was developed early in the project. The committee described the target environment toward which the Bank was to move. Documenting the target environment assisted the working committee in characterizing the directions to be taken by external encryption standards-making bodies and also in determinating appropriate directions for the Bank to follow. This target environment included end-to-end (originating point to destination point) encryption protection for sensitive data, secure and rapid movement of data among Bank computers, gateways to external networks and other organizations, and user-friendly and largely user-transparent encryption commands. An important part of this target environment was the automatic secure handling of data on the basis of its sensitivity (confidential, secret, etc.) rather than on the capabilities of the systems handling the data.

Specification of the migration path from the Bank's present systems to this target environment was an important part of the standards document. For instance, as an interim measure, link-by-link encryption is expected to be used; eventually, this will be overlaid by or replaced by end-to-end encryption.

To ensure that the encryption standards document would remain current regardless of the almost constant developments in the computer and data communications fields, the committee decided to refer to generic hardware and software types rather than a specific products. It was decided that a separate purchasing group would determine whether specific products were in compliance with the standards document.

Consistency with External Standards

Over the last few years, considerable work has been done on encryption standards, particularly for financial systems. Because considerable work remains to be done (for instance in retail financial application system encryption key management), many financial institutions are reluctant to purchase encryption gear or software, much less establish technical encryption standards.

The Bank is an innovative offeror of Electronic Funds Transfer (EFT) services. To allow the Bank to proceed with financial service systems development and enhancement efforts, it was imperative that encryption standards be compiled and adhered to. Accordingly, the it was decided that internal encryption standards would comply with all existing industry and other relevant standards, and would remain as flexible as possible so that compliance with new external standards could be achieved with minimal rework and additional expense. It was also decided that, to the extent possible, the encryption standards document would chart the directions of the external standards-making bodies and would dictate standards consistent with those directions.

The working committee furthermore determined that a precedence relationship between the external standards-making bodies should be established. In this way, if/when a conflict between the standards of different bodies existed, it could be readily resolved (all technical issues aside). The committee decided that, except for systems already installed, all implementations of encryption must comply with the standards issued by all the following organizations: (1) the Bank (standards developed in-house or adopted), (2) American Bankers Association, (3) American National Standards Institute, (4) U.S. Department of Commerce - National Bureau of Standards, and (5) the International Standards Organization. Thus if a conflict of encryption standards existed, compliance must be first with Bank standards, and then with the organization listed below it, etc. The higher an organization on this list, the greater the force of the standard issued by that organization.

Information Systems Security Organizational Structure

Ahead of most financial institutions in the information security area, the Bank has been concerned about systems security for many years. Five years prior to project inception, it established a corporate (Bank-wide) information systems security department. The corporate group, in turn, spawned information security coordinators in each of the Bank's major divisions. Through membership on an Information Security Council, these coordinators shared information on effective approaches to security, and also arranged for an information systems security manual to be prepared, published, and adopted as a Bank-wide standard. The primary duty of these part-time coordinators was to apply the policies and procedures documented in this manual. Unfortunately, the manual contained but two references to encryption, and gave no specific technical guidance for appropriate encryption implementations. Because most of the coordinators were bankers, rather than systems experts, they could not rely on their own expertise to bridge the gap between what was available and what was needed.

One of the first steps in the encryption standards project was to obtain the support and approval of the Information Security Council. Certain systems executives, however, disputed the legitimacy and jurisdiction of the council. To ensure they had no objections to the encryption standards project, prior to commencing activities, the working committee obtained these executives' support and approval for the project.

The Information Security Department had been recently established to provide the entire Bank with technical information systems security consulting and research services. On the other hand, the corporate information security department, largely administrative and political in nature, had been established for many years. Some employees therefore considered the corporate department the appropriate group to develop and coordinate Bank-wide systems security standards. Accordingly, extensive consultation with and heavy reliance on the vice president in charge of the corporate group were important throughout the project. Although not originally chosen as a member of the working committee, the vice president of the corporate group expressed such a great interest in the project that she soon was made a member.

When the encryption standards project got underway, no specific group was responsible for Bank-wide technical systems standards -- security related or otherwise. In some sense, the encryption standards project made evident the need for a subsequently-created corporate systems standards board and supporting corporate systems standards administration group. At the time, the best that could be done expediently was to appoint as the locus of Bank-wide systems standards activities a Systems Engineering Division group that specialized in systems development methodology standards and other project management standards. To allow systems security consultants to focus on other matters, responsibility for the text editing, publishing, periodic updating (after technical consultation), and distribution of the encryption standards document was delegated to this group.

Selecting the Project Team

A working committee was appointed to create the encryption standards document so as to foster inter-departmental and inter-divisional cooperation, reduce the chance that the standards would be perceived as applicable to only one division, and better distribute the work load. Members of the working committee were selected on the basis of their encryption expertise, their position at the Bank (particularly in terms of representing interested groups), and their group-oriented personal working style. The committee was kept small (eight members) to avoid troublesome coordination and communication problems. Ultimately, the participants included a senior technical consultant from a branch automation project, a project manager from a customer-selected PIN project, a senior technical consultant from a systems procurement group, a wholesale banking standards-and-policy group vice president, and a front-end switch development project senior technical consultant.

All the working committee members served in a part-time capacity. Those who had frequent travel commitments or other problems in attending appointed alternates. A written assurance of the committee members' participation was requested from their managers (or, in the case of higher level managers, from the committee member directly). Although not all members submitted written assurances, the act of requesting itself was effective in eliciting oral commitments of participation.

Length of the Standards Document

One of the objectives of the project was to document in one place all the encryption implementation information necessary for a staff-member. Although other standards documents were referenced, their contents were summarized sufficiently so that a staff-member need not figure out the different terminologies used, read the referenced standards documents, or make major decisions about what such external standards mean in light of Bank operations. The working committee considerably condensed the external standards documents, but the resulting document was still quite long. In addition, because no other authoritative Bank documents treated encryption in more than a cursory way, the working committee felt that considerable tutorial material should be included with the standards document. A lengthy standards document also resulted because guidelines and implementation details were covered in addition to standards. To provide a quick reference for those who already knew about encyrption, an appendix to the document presented the standards in a checklist format.

Standards Document Design Choices

At the onset of the project, the issue was raised of how best to document and distribute the encryption standards. Initially, to a large extent because that is how all systems security pronouncements had been done, it was thought that the encryption standards would appropriately be a more detailed section of the information security manual. This notion was quickly dispensed with when it was realized that the manual was approximately 180 pages of high-level policies and procedures, whereas the encryption standard would probably be of about equal length and would be considerably more detailed. A separate encryption standards document accordingly was required. To address the confusion that might result from having several documents referring to encryption, the separate encryption standards document was to be cross-referenced in the systems security manual and vice versa.

Because the intended audience was so broadly defined (systems designers, users, EDP auditors, systems programmers, etc.), the committee decided that the sections of the document should become progressively more technical. Although some redundancy was thereby introduced, it was agreed that each of the identified types of readers should be able to start from the beginning of the document and learn enough about the topic to understand what they are required to do. The sequence of sections was as follows: management letter about the applicability of the document, checklist of steps that must be followed to be in compliance with the standards, table of contents, introduction, conceptual description of encryption, glossary, background, available organizational resources, benefits of encryption, risk-analysis/risk-acceptance, encryption policies, principles of encryption system design, encryption function placement (in the ISO/OSI layer model), why these standards should be used, encryption algorithms and modes, key management, operational procedures, physical security, message authentication codes, and various technical and reference-related appendices (including a detailed standards checklist).

Some Project Management Tools

In developing the standards document, the Information Security Department obtained copies of all possibly relevant internal and external documents. This enabled the department to create an encryption library that could be used by systems developers and other Bank personnel (many of the documents in this library were subsequently listed in the Bank's systems library's card catalog).

Many people were involved in the generation and revision of the various documents that eventually were combined in the encryption standards document. To organize these efforts, a list of current documents was created and maintained. This list showed current document title, word processor reference number, control number, author, and most recent revision date. Because most of the working committee members had access to WANG word processing systems, or access to a bridge to a WANG system, it was decided that all exchanges of data between working committee member departments would be done via WANG-readable eight-inch floppy diskettes.

The working committe held regular meetings. Before each meeting, a detailed agenda was distributed. The agenda indicated who was responsible for each section of the meeting. At each meeting the participants received a schedule showing: to-be-completed tasks, dependent tasks, deliverables, expected start and completion dates, and committee members responsible for each referenced task. Besides being helpful in obtaining adherence to deadlines, the schedule was an invaluable communication tool.

Enforcement Mechanisms

Because no organizational structure existed for the promulgation of Bank-wide systems standards, enforcement of the encryption standards was of considerable concern to the working committee. To limit the scope of committee member involvement, enforcement responsibility was assigned to the EDP Auditing Department and the Information Security Department.

The first test of the new standards came after their formal approval by the executive vice president in charge of Systems Engineering and while the standard was being prepared for formal publication. A European systems development group of the Bank proposed to use an algorithm (the SWIFT STEN) other than the one mandated by the encryption standards document (the U.S. National Bureau of Standards' Data Encryption Standard). Just before the European group prepared its proposal for a secure international telecommunications network, the Information Security Department had established an agreement with the Systems Engineering procurement group. The procurement group agreed to send all major hardware and/or software purchase requests that obviously involved information security to the Information Security Department for review. Thus the Information Security Department received a copy of the European funding proposal before any major commitment with a vendor was made. The European group was informed that its proposed system was not in compliance with the newly established encryption standards. If the European project had not been caught, the Bank might have spent considerably more than it needed to, because many bridges and converters would be required to allow systems using different algroithms to securely exchange data.

The encryption standards are also to be enforced through the systems development methodology standards, with which all major systems development efforts must comply. A recently approved modification to the systems development methodology requires that systems developers explicitly consider security at certain stages of the systems development life cycle. At those stages, either EDP Auditing or Information Security is to review the proposed encryption implementation for compliance. Another important part of the requirement in the systems development methodology is that designers of new encryption implementations must review all expected current and near-term future interfaces and determine whether or not the the proposed system is compatible with such systems -- from an encryption standpoint (key management, algorithms, modes of operation, etc.).

Obtaining Approval

Besides a presentation to the executive vice president in charge of Systems Engineering and his direct reports, a final presentation was also made to the Information Security Council. Separate comment and approval sheets were provided for all managers and coordinators who attended the presentations. It was requested that these sheets be returned within three weeks. These comment and approval sheets were an effective way of determining who had officially approved the standard and with whom follow-up was needed. Fortunately, no major modifications were called for at this stage; had they been, reapproval of a large number of other people would have been necessary.

Before the management review associated with these final presentations, the Information Security Department had solicited technical comments on the final draft document from ninety-five staffmembers who had a vested interest in the project results. To ensure timely completion of the project, a three-week technical review and comment period was strictly enforced. An error was made, however, in assuming that non-receipt of comments from technical reviewers was equivalent to approval. Later, several of the technical reviewers denied ever having received a draft encryption standards document. A better approach would have been to require return of a comment and approval sheet, even if no comments other than "approve" were in order.

To enhance the attractiveness of the draft encryption standards document to the executive vice president in charge of Systems Engineering, his staff, and the members of the Information Security Council, expert opinions on the draft document were provided by two external consultants. One of the consultants was an employee of the vendor that supplied most of the Bank's systems equipment, and the other was in private management consulting practice. Because these consultants were well known in the cryptography community, and because they approved of the document (albeit with minor modifications that were included), management had significant assurance that the directions outlined in the standards document were appropriate and in the best interests of the Bank.

Defining Next Steps

To ensure appropriate use of the standards document, the Information Security Department provided management with a list of appropriate next steps to be addressed by non-committee Bank staff. These included formalizing encryption-related organizational structures and responsibilities so that, for instance, there would be one point of contact for encryption consulting assistance and one for encryption vendors. Other steps included: modifying other documents (such as the information security manual) to recognize and cross-reference the encryption standards document, publicizing the encryption standards document, and developing an umbrella architecture for providing integrated encryption protection for a number of financial services.

Conclusion

While this paper deals explicitly with the development of an in-house encryption standard, the philosophies and the specific steps employed are equally relevant to the development of other systems security technical standards. For example, a standard dealing with the deployment of and use of security modules (protected hardware devices that securely store sensitive data and programs) could be so addressed.

Organizations cannot afford to continue to allow uncontrolled and uncoordinated control implementations to jeopardize the future security, cost-effectiveness, and interoperability of their systems. Explicit systems control standards should be created, adopted, and enforced.

COMPUTER SECURITY
J.B. Grimson and H.-J. Kugler (Editors)
Elsevier Science Publishers B.V. (North-Holland)

THE FORMIDABLE - IF NOT INSURMOUNTABLE - ORGANISATIONAL PROBLEMS OF DISASTER RECOVERY PLANNING

Victor Lane

North East London Polytechnic
U.K.

John Step

Head of Audit Consortium
East Sussex & West Kent
Health Authorities, U.K.

The ideas presented in the paper are based upon the authors' practical experience of (1) designing information systems in many organisations and (2) developing and implementing contingency plans. The paper discusses the organisational problems which obstruct the development of recovery plans and attempts to identify the source of company motivation for recovery planning. To indicate the difficulties a methodology for contingency planning is outlined and this is compared with practical experience of implementing a plan within a large public utility with significant computing expertise. In the past, a great deal of attention has been given to the technical aspects of contingency planning and consequently less attention has been directed to organisational problems. There is evidence that a majority of users do not have disaster recovery plans. The problems are not of cost or because of the technical complexity of the problem. Reasons must be found elsewhere. The paper attempts to identify the reasons for this. On this basis, attempts can be made to overcome the problems in order that disaster recovery planning can take its rightful place in organisational priorities.

1. INTRODUCTION

A recent study of one thousand four hundred minicomputer and mainframe computer installations in the United Kingdom, indicated that approximately fifty per cent had no disaster recovery plan. Related to this statistic, the paper attempts to show the influence of technical, organisational, operational and financial factors in order to identify ways of improving the situation. The majority of disaster recovery literature stressses the need for management involvement in recovery planning. Similar suggestions are made with respect to the analysis and design of information systems. Since systems design and recovery planning are carried out in not dissimilar environments, it is to be expected that it is assumed that the management involvement in the two situations is similar. This is not the case and the comparison is grossly misleading. To understate the degree of management commitment required for disaster recovery planning, or to equate the commitment to that in systems design is a clear recipe for failure. Based upon experience of implementing a recovery plan for a large public utility, the authors believe that the development of a recovery plan is:-

(1) not technically difficult

(2) not costly in terms of normal data processing budgets.

Therefore the reasons for enterprises not instituting disaster recovery plans must be of an organisational or a social nature. The paper discusses the nature of the problems, in addition to showing how recovery planning can be developed in organisations and within the development the role played by users, computer personnel and computer consultants.

2. A THEORETICAL APPROACH TO CONTINGENCY PLANNING

A methodology for developing and implementing a security policy for an organisation is to:-

(1) Analysis risks in order to provide a basis for developing a security policy.

(2) Select cost effective security safeguards to reduce exposure to losses

(3) Implement appropriate security safeguards

(4) Develop contingency plans for (a) back-up operation (b) disaster recovery and (c) emergencies.

(5) Train personnel.

(6) Plan and conduct security audits.

(7) Adjust security safeguards and contingency plans (Lane, 1985 and NBS, 1974).

Within this approach, there is need for a procedure, as illustrated in Figure 1, for identifying and implementing defence mechanisms.

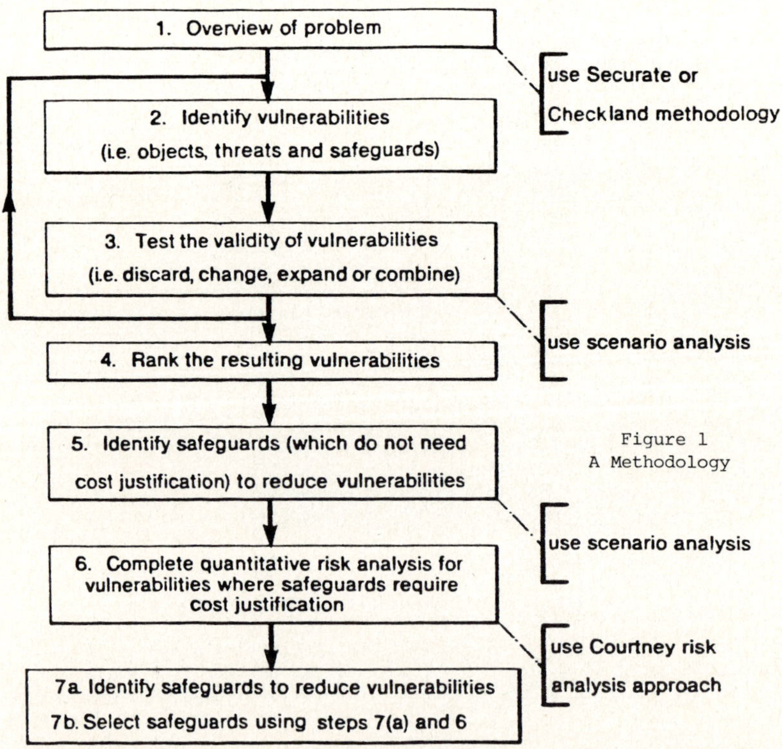

Figure 1
A Methodology

In the above approach, the steps which specifically relate to contingency planning are (4), (6) and (7). It is outside the scope of this paper to describe the detail of the tasks which are involved in these steps in an investigation of an organisation to design and implement a contingency plan. Nevertheless, although the work in preparing a contingency plan is well documented, it is not to be assumed that it is simple to apply in practice and parts of the investigation which are influenced by organisational and social factors are extremely complex.

A contingency is an unscheduled interruption of computing services which requires measures outside of the day-to-day routine operating procedures. A contingency can vary from a trivial event, like a minor interruption of the electricity supply, to a disaster such as flood or fire. Other contingencies may result from explosion, failure of hardware, software faults, breakdown of air conditioning and industrial action of computing personnel directly and indirectly employed. Despite all the precautions of full and rigorous security procedures, it is impossible to eliminate risk and eventually something is bound to go wrong. Therefore the purpose of contingency planning is to ensure that swift action can be taken to achieve recovery with minimum loss if computing services are disrupted.

When an incident occurs the minimum of difficulty will be experienced if there are documented, realistic and reasoned procedures which have been rehearsed. It is impossible to make plans for all eventualities but overall the contingency plan must provide for:-

(1) standby procedures of operation for times during which normal services are disrupted

(2) recovery procedures after the cause of the disruption has been identified and corrected

(3) personnel responsibilities to achieve (1) and (2) above (Broadbent, 1979 and Friedman, 1982).

The first and possibly the most important feature of a contingency plan is to define responsibilities in the event of an incident. Consequently, there is a coordinator or manager who takes control and decides what actions to take. Since actions include delegation of responsibility to members of an approved recovery team, the coordinator must have access to names, telephone numbers and addresses in order to contact the team members. The plan is not likely to be sufficiently detailed for many eventualities. Therefore, the coordinator must have confidence in the team in order for him to delegate quickly without going into detail.

Other features of a contingency plan are:-

- mutual back-up arrangements with other institutions

- lists of jobs which are important and jobs which can be suspended

- manual fall-back systems for operation during short duration stoppages

- membership of a disaster protection scheme.

Organisations are often of the opinion that in the event of a major disaster computer hardware would be relatively easy to replace but that a computer room and its necessary support facilities would take considerably longer to obtain. Therefore they enter into a contract with a company who provide an empty room with ancillary services in time of need. Irrespective of how well documented a contingency plan is, it is essential that parts of the plan are rehearsed before a real disaster occurs. This will ensure that it is practical and workable and that staff know what is expected of them. Organisations with well conceived contingency plans have tested their plans by simply closing the door of their normal computer centre and instructing staff outside of the centre to operate emergency services. Trials such as these usually highlight large gaps in the contingency plan. Problems occur because of simple things like inadequate supply of preprinted forms or out-of-date user instructions and operations manuals. All aspects of a contingency plan must be reviewed and updated from time to time and in addition they must be rehearsed occasionally.

One essential updating requirement relates to new information systems. The contingency needs of each new application system should form part of the design process and therefore be part of the system specification and the clerical procedures manual.

3. A REAL-LIFE CASE STUDY OF DEVELOPING A DISASTER RECOVERY PLAN IN AN ONLINE SYSTEM ENVIRONMENT

This section of the paper relates to the development of a disaster recovery plan for a large public sector organisation.

Disasters are major contingencies which occur because of the destruction of all, or virtually all, computer processing capability. In the case of this public sector organisation, an investigation showed that a computer centre disaster would impact upon:-

(1) the billing of 1½ million customers

(2) the payment of creditors and

(3) the paying of wages and salaries to 4,000 employees.

The impetus for the recovery plan came from a routine audit of safety and security which indicated that the arrangements for dealing with a disaster or a major security breach, were inadequate. Consequently, a group of four, consisting of computer operations manager, computer integrity officer, security officer and auditor, examined the problem. The group first identified the major threats to computing services and the essential elements of a plan. The next decision was whether the plan should be developed by:-

- company employees or
- consultants.

It was decided to use company employees and the group quickly looked at the two major contingency areas, namely standby and recovery. In producing an outline plan for recovery, the shape and scope of the overall plan quickly became clear. It was found that a large proportion of the fundamental studies were of a non-computer nature and therefore the work could be carried out by the non-computer members of the group. This is consistent with the ideas of Schweitzer (1982). In order that the group could assess the impact of any breakdown and to be aware of priorities, all major users were met and encouraged to participate.

3.1. A DISASTER RECOVERY PLAN

The disaster recovery plan is in the form of:-

(1) detailed instructions - instructions to a number of nominated individuals setting out the circumstances under which and the manner in which the plan may be activated.

(2) lists of nominations for (a) a recovery coordinator (b) logistics controllers (c) hardware controllers (d) software controllers and (e) public relations officer.

The recovery coordinator - as the title would suggest - convenes the controllers, coordinates their activities and liaises with senior management. The logistics controllers' duties are to ensure that all support services (e.g. electricity, transport and clerical services) are available so that the technical controllers can concentrate their efforts on their own specialisations. The hardware controllers assess the damage to hardware, the likely period of breakdown and arrange for long-term recovery. The software controllers carry out similar duties to the hardware controllers except that they concentrate upon system and application software. The public relations officer is there to deflect all enquiries away from the other team members.

The investigations focussed attention on the crucial role of the computer and led to a close consideration of the relative virtues of different standby arrangements. The principal methods are:-

(1) sharing a remote site with other companies

(2) participating in a scheme to install a prefabricated computer building on a company site and

(3) reciprocal backup arrangements with other companies using compatible hardware.

Reciprocal backup arrangements and sharing a remote site were both found to be inappropriate.

4. COMPARISON OF ACTUAL EXPERIENCE OF DEVELOPING A CONTINGENCY PLAN WITH THEORETICAL APPROACH

The theory of developing a contingency plan or a disaster recovery plan emphasises techniques such as risk analysis. These are important and valuable but relatively straightforward to use. The more difficult areas occur because organisations are people oriented and any major change, like the implementation of a disaster recovery plan, must consider the intricate sets of relationships involved therein. It is the authors' firm belief that it is organisational factors, and not technical factors, which prevent organisations from developing disaster recovery plans - this is highlighted in a recent report (Datapro, 1985) which shows that less than half of organisations surveyed have a recovery scheme and a quarter do not intend to develop a plan. This topic is discussed further in section 5.

4.1. MACHINE BACKUP

The methods of providing computer standby arrangements as listed in section 3.1. above are not all practical in the 1980s. The authors had experience in the early 1970s of agreeing reciprocal arrangements with companies using compatible hardware but nowadays realistic, workable arrangements are very much more difficult to negotiate despite the fact that companies use more powerful computers - perhaps this is because organisations have correspondingly bigger workloads. Therefore it is often necessary to join a consortium to gain access to the use of a prefabricated computer building for erection of a company site. The basis of this approach is that it is easier to obtain a backup machine from the computer manufacturer than it is to obtain time of another company's computer for a significant period.

4.2. EXTERNAL SECURITY CONSULTANTS AND A DETAILED RECOVERY PLAN

Consultants can be used to advantage in many situations. However, with disaster planning it is felt that there are significant benefits in using company personnel. Of course, there are problems in producing the plan in-house, but the result is a considerably more detailed plan than that which could be produced by a consultant. In addition, staff become knowledgeable about the plan and therefore are better equipped to operate the plan if the need should arise and to maintain and modify it. It has been suggested that a plan is unlikely to be sufficiently detailed for a real life contingency and that the recovery coordinator will need to be able to tell staff what is required of them according to the particular disaster (Norman, 1983). Our experience has shown that a detailed plan is possible because in many situations there are only a small number of critical applications (Lane, 1979).

4.3. DISASTER REHEARSALS

Information systems are subject to change and as a result disaster recovery plans can become out-of-date. Therefore rehearsals are essential (1) to keep plans up-to-date and (2) to ensure that plans are workable.

In practice, it is found that this is a highly suspect area. It is not unusual for companies to invest significant resources in developing a recovery plan but to be unwilling to commit resources to the testing and rehearsing of the programme.

5. INSURMOUNTABLE ORGANISATIONAL OBSTACLES?

Reference was made in section 4 to a recent survey of computer installations which found that some fifty per cent had no disaster recovery plans. Companies employ chief executives, computer managers and auditors generally with wide knowledge and experience. Why should experienced senior management ignore recovery planning? Is it because there is no need to prepare or are there other factors which create this state of affairs? Organisations are complex systems and within them there are many forces at work - some encouraging and others discouraging individual members of staff from becoming involved with recovery planning. Nevertheless there are certain people in each organisation who could be expected to give impetus to the work of evolving a disaster plan. They include:-

- chief executive
- computer manager
- computer operations manager
- systems development manager and
- auditor.

Therefore, in the next section, the following questions are considered:-

(1) why do senior managers in organisations not initiate disaster

recovery plans?

(2) in situations where plans are prepared, are they maintained?

(3) can professional computer staff in organisations do more to encourage organisations to create disaster recovery plans?

(4) do auditors have sufficient organisational influence to bring about change?

5.1. SENIOR MANAGEMENT

It is obvious that recovery planning requires the support of the most senior management i.e. the chief executive. All of the literature refers to the need for a company policy. But if there is no company policy, is this to be assumed to be a conscious decision or is it simply one of the areas on which the company has not come to a decision? Although senior managers spend time responding to immediate problems, they also spend considerable time on long and medium term planning, i.e. on requirements like contingency planning. They respond to those items which they consider will be important in the future. It is apparent that they believe that there is no danger or that the danger relates to other companies. If disaster recovery planning is important, computer scientists are not communicating the message to the important people i.e. the decision makers of companies.

5.2. NO RESOURCES FOR REHEARSALS

From experience of developing information systems and contingency plans, the authors are aware that it is difficult for organisations to have continuing interest in a system or plan once the first working system has been evolved. The situation with contingency planning is more difficult than with an information system because senior management are required to have an interest:-

- over a long term
- in something which probably has no short-term payback
- in something which possibly has no payback at all.

Therefore it is not surprising that once the initial investment is made they hope and in many cases believe and act as though their efforts are completed. Consequently testing and rehearsals receive little support and without those features a plan can be worthless. For example, the recovery plan outlined in section 3 above included details of telephone numbers of personnel who hold keys for access to backup electricity supply. Therefore, if the plan is not kept up-to-date with respect to telephone numbers major problems may occur in emergency. This is a relatively small change to plan details and yet it is not easy to guarantee that such changes can be provided for. It needs little imagination to appreciate the problems which can ensue from computer software changes.

5.3. THE COMPUTER PROFESSIONALS HAVE LITTLE TO OFFER

Computer personnel are often accused of being wedded to their discipline rather than to business objectives. If this is true then it is apparent that they are unlikely to identify with a major task which :-

- involves lots of work
- has no visible return and

- does not have the support of senior personnel of the company.

However a more significant factor is that of the computer centre being under continual pressure from users to produce software. Therefore, the efforts of the computer staff are more likely to be directed towards applications than recovery planning and even if a plan is developed it is always difficult to commit personnel to recovery rehearsals when there are pressures from users for 'action' - even though rehearsals are fundamental to disaster recovery and can be justified on company objectives, if not on departmental needs. In the day-to-day pressures too many attitudes are parochial and what is needed is the person with the company view and the organisational power to see that the needs are matched by realistic action - responsibility of this type is outside of the domain of the computer department staff and can only be met by the chief executive or a senior colleague of the chief executive.

Auditors may have sufficient power to influence company priorities and consequently help initiate contingency planning. However, the role they can play must not be exaggerated when considered against the pivotal position of the chief executive. In addition, the internal auditor may not have expertise in computing and in some organisations there may be no internal auditor. (In the UK, the external auditor is not required by law to initiate developments such as disaster recovery planning).

6. CONCLUSIONS

The paper identifies the need for a logically developed approach to disaster recovery planning which recognises the presence of organisational difficulties. It is common for advocates of recovery planning to explain the techniques involved in contingency planning (such as risk analysis) and to call for management commitment and involvement. The request for management involvement is generally not given significant emphasis because it is posed in the same way as the request for management involvement in design of information systems. In information systems design a nominal commitment of management may be sufficient, provided that there is enthusiasm of computer professionals and users; and after implementation, users provide the motivation for additional development. In recovery planning, there is no substitute for management commitment.

The paper compares practical experience of developing disaster recovery plans with a theoretical approach to show that:-

- the cost of devising a recovery plan is small in terms of data processing budgets

- the techniques involved in contingency planning are relatively straightforward.

Since it is technically straightforward and inexpensive, it is difficult to believe that in a study (Datapro, 1985) of 1,400 users of minicomputers and mainframe computers:-

- slightly in excess of 50% of users had no disaster recovery plan and

- approximately 35% of minicomputer users and 25% of mainframe computer users had no intentions to develop a plan.

These figures can only reflect the low priority which senior management give to recovery planning compared with other organisational activities. This conclusion is supported by the experience within the development outlined in section 3 where senior management were unenthusiastic about the production of a contingency plan and within other organisations of which the authors have knowledge where responsibility for the task is set at an inappropriately junior level. The management commitment for disaster recovery planning is fundamentally different from that required in information system design. For effective development of a recovery plan management commitment is imperative. Without this, a plan cannot evolve and there will be insufficient resources to finance rehearsals.

In addition, the case study based on an actual, realworld development of a contingency plan, illustrates that disaster recovery planning:-

- is not difficult technically
- can be done by company staff without the assistance of external consultants
- requires analysis studies to be undertaken by non-computer personnel and
- requires user participation through user forum (Lane, 1980).

An understanding of organisational behaviour is necessary if we are to help organisations to commit adequate resources for the development and operation of disaster recovery plans. If we believe this type of plan is critical, then the main thrust of security awareness and education must be directed to the most senior managers, ideally the chief executive.

REFERENCES

[1] Broadbent, D., Contingency planning, (NCC, Manchester, 1979).

[2] Datapro, British user ratings of computer systems, (Datapro, CH-1164 Burchillon, Switzerland, 1985).

[3] Friedman, S., Contingency and disaster planning. Computers and Security, 1, No. 1 (1982) 34-40.

[4] Franz, C.R. and Robey, D., An investigation of user led system design: rational and political perspectives, Comms. ACM, 27, No. 12 (1984) 1202-1209.

[5] Lane, V.P., The communications and management implications of distributed computing (Proceedings of Euro-IFIP, London, 1980).

[6] Lane, V.P. and Wright, F.G., Human resources systematically applied to ensure computer security (Proceedings of the 2nd European Conference on Informatics, Venice, 1979).

[7] Lane, V.P., Security of computer based information systems (Macmillan, London, 1985).

[8] National Bureau of Standards, Guidelines for automatic data processing physical security and risk management (FIPS PUB 31, Washington, D.C.,(1974).

[9] Norman, A.R.D., Computer Insecurity (Chapman and Hall, London, 1983).

[10] Schweitzer, J.A., Managing Information security - a program for the electronic age (Butterworth, London, 1982).

COMPUTER SECURITY
J.B. Grimson and H.-J. Kugler (Editors)
Elsevier Science Publishers B.V. (North-Holland)

HOW TO USE THE DES SAFELY

Donald W. Davies
Data Security Consultant
Sunbury-on-Thames
Middlesex UK

Among the ciphers which are in the public domain, the Data Encryption Standard must have been studied more intensely than any other. Since it is widely used for encipherment and authentication of financial messages, its security is a matter of public concern. As with all ciphers, advances in knowledge and technology can reduce its strength, so that its use then requires more care. This paper reviews what is known about the DES and the precautions needed to use it safely. No guarantee of security can ever be given, since an unsuspected weakness might exist, either in the algorithm or the way it is used. We do not consider, in this paper, the protocols employed in systems incorporating the DES and these need at least as much care as the cipher itself.

CHARACTERISTICS OF THE DATA ENCRYPTION STANDARD

The paper begins with a summary of the known regular properties of the DES, then discusses the question of its key size in relation to today's technology. The effect, on its strength, of message redundancy and repeated encipherment of the same plain text are described, then the recommended method of multiple encipherment (now contained in a draft ANSI standard) is described. Some conclusions are reached in the final section of the paper.

A satisfactory cipher should produce a result which is not detectably different from random, whether regarded as a function of the plain text or the key. Any regularity in the function can be regarded as a weakness but, with the knowledge of the regularities which exist, the algorithm can still be used safely. None of the known regularities of the DES should be regarded as advantageous, but collectively they do not limit its application very much.

The first of these regularities is the complementation property, namely:

$$\text{If } y = Ek(x) \text{ then } \overline{y} = E\overline{k}(\overline{x})$$

In this notation, x, y and k are the complements of $\overline{x}$, $\overline{y}$ and $\overline{k}$ in which each bit is inverted. This property arises from the structure of the algorithm, in particular, the way that the key enters in a linear fashion. The non-linear part, the substitutions or S boxes, are contained between two exclusive OR operations. It is hard to imagine that the property could have been introduced unintentionally, and it has been claimed that it helps in verifying the value of distributed keys, but there are better ways of verifying keys which do not need this property. Under special circumstances, it reduces the effective size of key by one bit when searching through all keys. It would have been better to have avoided this property when DES was designed. If complementation enters into any aspect of the design of a secure system around DES, this property must be checked to see if it introduces weaknesses.

A second form of regularity is the existence of special keys called 'weak keys', 'semi-weak keys' or 'periodic keys'. They all derive from the extremely simple method of producing the 16 sub-keys from the 56-bit key of the DES, using two shift registers of 28 bit length. Any pattern of bits in these registers which is periodic can cause special key properties and the relevant periods are sub-multiples of 28, namely, 1, 2, 4, 7, and 14.

The keys of period 1 are produced with all zeros or all ones in the two shift registers. There are four weak keys, for which the DES is an involution, encipherment and decipherment being the same function. Keys with period 2 include also the 'alternate' patterns 0101.. and 1010.. and these include the twelve semi-weak keys which comprise 6 pairs having the property that encipherment by one of the pair is the same as decipherment by another. In effect, these are very small sub-groups within the totality of DES operations. The other periodic keys do not have any known properties of this simple kind but keys of period 4 can be shown to reduce the complexity of the DES operation. The reduced form of the cipher is similar to that of a DES with 8 rounds instead of 16. There are 240 of these keys of period 4.

The weak and semi-weak keys could be a danger in multiple encipherment. Where session keys are chosen at random, the probability of obtaining one of these 16 special values is so low that no attacker will be able to wait for their occurrence. On the other hand, where keys are chosen for an important, long term use, particularly where multiple encipherment is used, a test should be made for weak or semi-weak keys and these values rejected. It may also be desirable to reject keys of period 4, but this is not usually done.

The structure of the DES can be represented as shown in Figure 1, which shows two rounds of operation with sub-keys k_i and k_{i+1} in which E is the expansion permutation, S represents the substitutions in the S boxes and P is the 32-bit permutation of that name in the DES specification. Marc Davio and others (1) have shown how this representation can be transformed, in two steps, into the

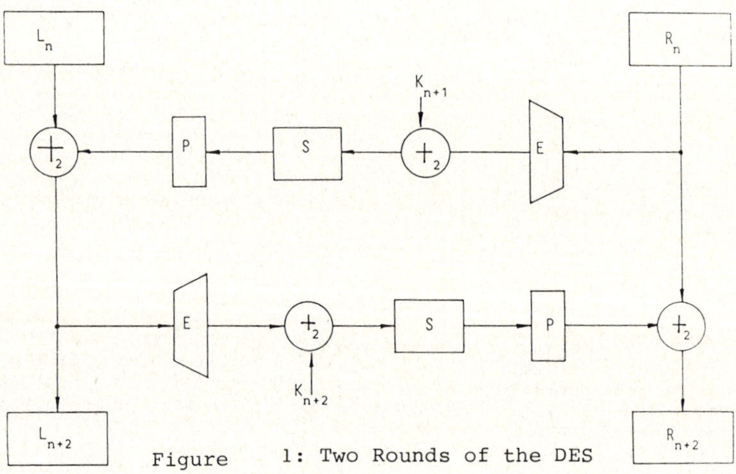

Figure 1: Two Rounds of the DES

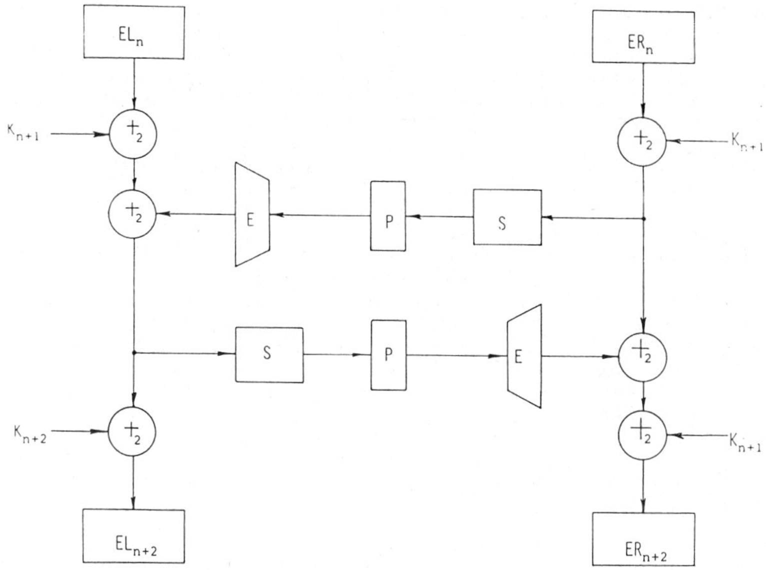

Figure 2: Transformation by Moving the Operations

arrangement shown in Figure 2 in which the operations S, P and E are combined and the modulo 2 addition of the sub-keys is brought into the main part of the ladder network. In this arrangement, two rounds of the SPE operation are combined into a function F of 96 bits which is applied to the DES variables between each modulo 2 addition of key data. The 48 bit variables ER and EL are redundant, they are the 32-bit variables RN expanded but because the sub-keys do not have this redundancy, the function F really does operate on 96 bit variables.

Using this modified representation of the DES, the action of the periodic keys can be seen in a new light. Figure 3 shows the DES algorithm (less the initial and final permutations) with the XOR functions of the 1, 2 or 4 different subkey values for weak, semi-weak and period 4 keys respectively. The keys of period 4 produce a simplified structure, indicating that it may be worthwhile to eliminate them in sensitive applications.

THE KEY SIZE OF DES

In the early controversy about security of DES, the limited key size of 56 bits was emphasised. A method of key searching was proposed, using one million devices, each capable of testing one million keys per second. Such a machine would enable keys to be found by searching in less than one day, given corresponding plain and cipher text blocks. The cost of the machine was itself a matter of controversy but the figure in the region of $US10,000,000 would be realistic. Few users of DES would regard this as a significant risk because the cost would be beyond that of the largest criminal organisation imaginable. Subsequent improvements in technology have affected the estimate mainly by producing lower cost devices with the same potential speed and low power consumption, rather than by large improvements in the speed itself.

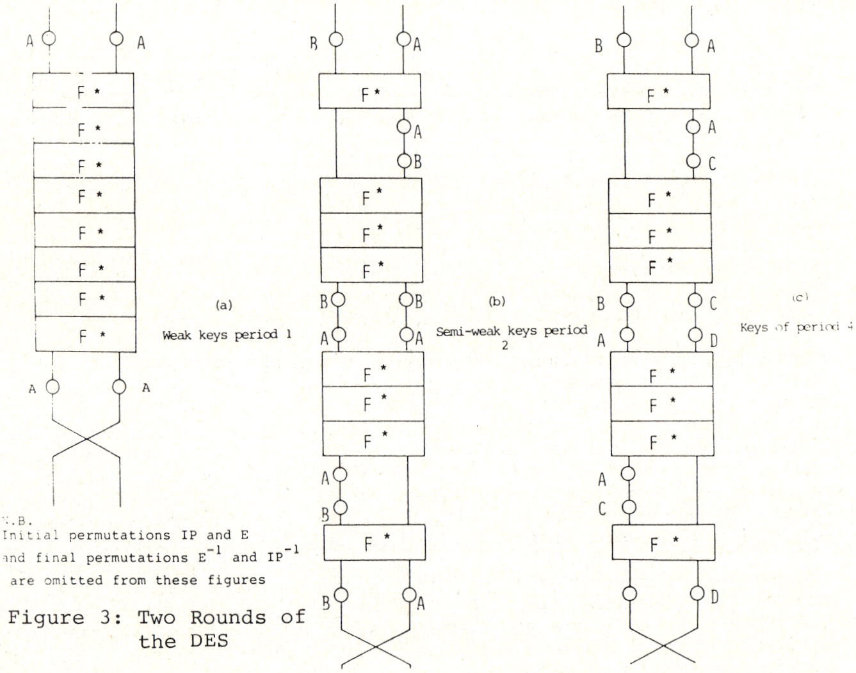

N.B.
Initial permutations IP and E and final permutations E^{-1} and IP^{-1} are omitted from these figures

Figure 3: Two Rounds of the DES

Progress in technology has not been so rapid as was predicted at the time, but it would be reasonable to assume that a machine to break the DES in approximately in one day by searching would now cost $1,000,000 and that the development problems are less, because of the lower power requirements and the improvement in design techniques for large scale integration.

The estimate of the present strength of DES should be based on particular applications, not necessarily the 'one day' scenario. If, for example, a useful attack could be made in 100 days then the same cost estimate would reduce to $10,000, which is within the means of many criminal organisations. However, the need for development work and the design, development and manufacture of special chips would increase this figure perhaps to $100,000 but might leave it within the bounds of possibility.

The 'one hundred day' scenario applies when a key is used for a corresponding length of time. For example, a master key used to encipher session keys would be attackable if the messages containing session keys have enough redundancy for the search to be possible. This question is explored in the next section. It does not matter that the session keys themselves are out of date long before the analysis has succeeded, since the target of the attack is the master key,, knowledge of which enables future session keys to be discovered. Single encipherment by DES may not be sufficient where master keys of this longevity are employed.

MESSAGE REDUNDANCY

The analysis of attacks on a cipher by key searching are usually expressed in terms of known plain text and this fails if the plain text is a random number such as a key. However, the search can be based on any type of redundancy in the plain text. The formats employed for automatic key distribution usually provide this redundancy.

A particular case is the use of electronic code book mode for encipherment of session keys being distributed. According to the Federal Information Processing Standard and the corresponding ANSI Standard, the key should have odd parity in each of its octets. The draft ISO standard does not make this requirement but treats the relevant binary digit in each octet as a spare digit. If the parity condition is applied to every session key, it becomes possible to test deciphered values for comformity to this property.

Given a cipher text, it can be subjected to a search by decipherment running over the entire range of 56 keys and will produce a pseudo-random set of 64 bit numbers among which the true session key value is hidden. The parity property will eliminate all but one value in 256. Given the cipher text for a different session key, the field can be reduced by the same factor again, so that after 8 session key cipher texts have been used, the probable remaining number of candidate keys is one. If a unique key has been found, it must be the correct one but supposing that a few values were obtained, then one more session key cipher text would suffice to eliminate the remaining false values. If key values are normally distributed in this way, it becomes plausible that a searching machine with this property of testing for octet parity will be constructed. The extra effort in the multiple searches is very small because they are applied to such a small proportion of cases. Instead of storing the matches from the first search, it is better to test them at once with all alternative cipher text values.

We might conclude that the use of parity in the key variable is undesirable. This requirement was removed from the ISO draft standard because there were suggestions that the spare bits could be used for other purposes. Other uses for these bits and special formats for key distribution messages also provide redundancy which could be exploited. Instead of trying to remove redundancy from the messages, it is probably better to employ stronger cipher techniques.

REPEATED ENCIPHERMENT OF THE SAME PLAIN TEXTS

A general rule in cryptography is not to send exactly the same plain text under different ciphers or with different keys. The usual reason given for this rule is that if one cipher is successfully attacked, it provides known plain text for attacking the other. In the case of DES, there is an additional risk which we will now examine.

Suppose that the same plain text is enciphered under a number of different keys with the DES algorithm, and that an enemy can obtain each cipher text, how many cipher texts of this kind are needed before the information exists to find the plain text? In this question, we are supposing that an exceptionally large amount of processing and storage capability is available, which is similar to the assumptions underlying the 'unicity distance' defined by Shannon. Therefore, we can consider a calculation which would be difficult to carry out but which tells us how many cipher texts are needed before the plain text is, in principle, obtainable.

Imagine that, for each cipher text, we explore all the possible keys, running over 56 bits and list the corresponding plain texts. Among these will be the plain text we want, occurring, with high probably, only once because only one in 256 of the possible 64 bit words is including in the list. Similar lists can be made from each of the cipher texts and after enough lists have been obtained, only one of the 64 bit values will be common to all the lists, which will be the plain text that we seek. It can easily be seen that with 8 lists of this kind, the expectation of the number of words they all have in common is one. Using 8 such lists, there is a likelihood that we shall find two results, the correct plain text and one that has passed the test by accident. Certainly, if 9 different encipherments are given and we make 9 lists, it is highly probable that only one common value will emerge and this must be the correct plain text. From the various lists, we can also find the key values if we need these.

Therefore, we have a new kind of unicity distance. Instead of continuing encipherment of different plain texts with the same key until it becomes possible to determine that key, we continue encipherment of one plain text with different keys until it becomes possible to determine that plain text. In our case, we need consider no redunancy of plain text or key to achieve this result. It arises because the length of DES key is 8 bits less than the length of plain text block.

The calculation is heavy, but is similar to the kind of calculation envisaged in the 'meet in the middle' attack (2) which is regarded as a weakness of double encipherment. The process consists of sorting each list into order, then merging the lists with a note on each entry of which list it comes from. By examining the clusters of identical entries, the one represented in each list can be found. If we assume that a DES search is feasible, the main extra requirement which this method imposes is for a very large random access store.

MULTIPLE ENCIPHERMENT

If or when we reach the stage that DES encipherment is insecure because of its short key length, multiple DES encipherment with different keys may enable the algorithm to be used safely. But it would be wrong to assume that this provides the same effectiveness as a cipher with 112 bit key since it has been shown (2) that such an encipherment can be attacked by the 'meet in the middle' method using an amount of computation not much greater than the attack on single encipherment but with a capability for storage of lists of 2^{56} items.

The method proposed to overcome this limitation is now part of the key management standard for wholesale financial transactions produced by ANSI as X9.17. Figure 4 shows the form of encipherment and decipherment used in this standard. The two keys KL and KR are regarded as the left and right hand parts of a key variable K* of 128 bits. The notation used to express this method of encipherment and decipherment is:

$$y = \text{ede } K^*(x) \qquad x = \text{ded } K^*(y)$$

which corresponds to the relationship:

$$y = EKL(DKR(EKL(x))) \qquad x = DKL(EKR(DKL(y)))$$

The reason for this structure is that it can be made compatible with single encipherment using key K by setting KL = KR = K.

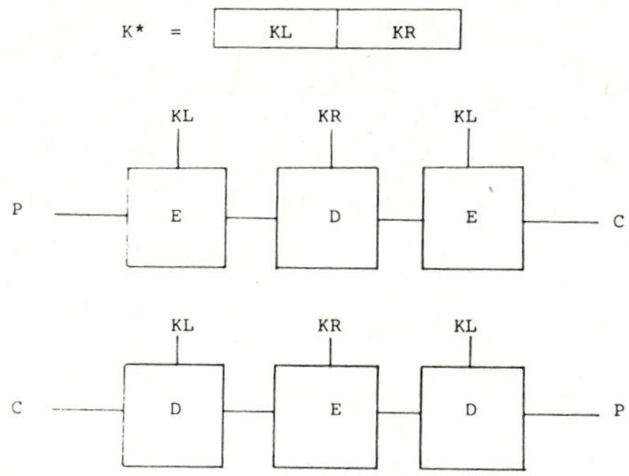

Figure 4: Treble Encipherment with Two DES Keys

The proposed attack on double encipherment by 'meet in the middle' uses an amount of storage which is at present unrealistic. Nevertheless, storage technology is advancing more rapidly than processing technology, so a standard which looks to the future must envisage this kind of attack. It depends on having known plain text and is not, it seems, amenable to the use of plain text redundancy.

An objection has been raised (2) to the security of the treble encipherment method but this depends on using a chosen plain text attack to search through an entire 56 bit key space and is so far from being a plausible attack that it is usually discounted. However, the security of the method is no more guaranteed than that of DES itself and some internal property on DES could, if we are unlucky, reduce the extra margin of safety it gives. In particular, if the DES cipher functions formed a group, any multiple encipherment method would be unproductive. This question has been studied (3) and the evidence is strongly against DES having the group property, which would have weakened it also it in many other ways.

CONCLUSIONS

The information generally available about the DES suggests a number of precautions in its use. These precautions help to avoid known problems but cannot guarantee security because many other factors influence the security of a system and we cannot be sure that there are no unsuspected problems in the use of the DES.

Weak and semi-weak keys should be avoided at higher levels in a key hierarchy, for keys with a long life or wherever multiple encipherment is used. There is an indication that a third category of keys (those of period 4) should also be avoided, but the existence of a risk is still uncertain for these keys. The complementation property should be considered when the security of key management scheme is examined, and methods based on complementary key values avoided, in general.

The same plaintext should not be subjected to encipherment by DES using a number of different keys. Where it is convenient, the spare bits of DES key variables should be chosen at random, rather than given the conventional values for odd parity of octets. This accords with the draft ISO standard for DEA1 but not with FIPS46 or the ANSI standard for DES, X3.92 - 1981.

Master keys having a life of the order of 100 days or more can be attacked by exhaustive search if the data they encipher have easily exploitable redundancy. In these circumstances, treble encipherment using two DES keys, as described in ANSI draft X9.17, is recommended.

REFERENCES

1. Davio, M., Desmedt, Y., Fosseprez, M., Govaerts, R., Hulsbosch, J., Neutjens, P.P., Piret, P., Quisquatier, J.J., and Wouters, P., 'Analytical Characteristics of the DES', Proceedings of CRYPTO'83, Plenum Press, 1984

2. Hellman, M.E. and Merkle, R.C., 'On the Security of Multiple Encryption', Comm. ACM 24 No. 7, 465 - 467 (July 1981)

3. Kaliski, B.S., Rivest, R.L., and Sherman, A.T., 'Is the Data Encryption Standard a Group?', Proc. EUROCRYPT'85 (Linz) to be published by Springer.

COMPUTER SECURITY
J.B. Grimson and H.-J. Kugler (Editors)
Elsevier Science Publishers B.V. (North-Holland)
IFIP, 1985

EMERGING PRIVACY ISSUES

Willis H. Ware

The Rand Corporation
Santa Monica, California
U.S.A.

Because of the essential nature of information in the affairs of society, governments, and institutions, computer- and communications-based systems are creating new aspects of personal privacy threats. This paper examines emergent privacy issues (e.g., those related to electronic mail and internetting of systems), and relates them to security requirements and to difficulties of designing laws. It suggests a possible legal environment to accommodate problems to be faced.

INTRODUCTION

I want to speak broadly about privacy issues this morning. I would like to suggest new aspects of it and also to try out some ideas because there are themes not now in the public debate that I believe must be surfaced. Certainly I must relate privacy concerns to security as we will face it ahead and to any law that we may wish to create. Of necessity, I will present the discussion in the United States context; I do not know the European situation well enough, especially to illustrate points from time to time.

I do want to treat this presentation in the nature of a conference keynote. I will try to suggest things that the conference might wish to talk about; hopefully, I can plant seeds in the minds of conferees. But I will raise more issues and questions than I can provide answers.

Privacy Now

First of all, what is privacy as we know it in our professional world of informatics? Historically, it has dealt with information about people, and the way such information is used to make decisions about them, primarily in regard to a determination of entitlements, rights, or privileges a given person might have. As such, the thrust of privacy concern has been to assure that such information is accurate and complete for the intended use, and that its use would be confined to that intended at the time the information was provided by the individual to the record keeper. The issue as it has developed over the last 15 years is sometimes called information privacy or record-keeping privacy.

In the United States the first records of concern were those related to personal credit. As other law has been implemented, there have of course been many compromises between the strict ideal situation and practical reality. For example, United States law is generally easy to circumvent with regard to the intended use of information, or "routine use" as it is called in the 1974 Privacy Act. Federal agencies find it quite simple to use information initially collected for one purpose for some other purposes later.

The thrust of United States privacy law has been predominantly to assure the proper use of information by authorized users; organizations who hold information are responsible for assuring that it is used for its intended use and for assuring its accuracy. In general, the protection is that of a "Code of Fair Information Practices," the details of which were conceived in early 1973 and presented to government officials in July of the same year. The law has given only minor attention to the risk of information falling into unauthorized hands as a result of system penetrations or compromises, malfunctions, design flaws, or poor operating procedures. It does not address the possibility that information will be pilfered from systems and used to the disservice of an individual.

Regrettably, computer security is only addressed indirectly in United States law; agencies are simply directed to protect information but the threat against information is not even specified. United States law does, through its routine use provisions, concern itself with the improper transfer of information from one record keeper to another; such a transfer would be a form of use by unauthorized recipients.

The law is quite different, of course, in other countries not only in the details of protection afforded individuals but in regard to implementation of the law and its ongoing oversight. For example, in Europe the general arrangement is a Data Protection Board or an entity of similar name; there is usually a federal official in charge of the situation. A record system often must apply for permission to exist, and there is an agreed upon set of rules governing its behavior. The Board often is a body through which an individual can seek remedial action against the record keeper. In the United States, there is only loose oversight by the Office of Management and Budget supplemented by an annual report to the Congress about how the law has worked in the past year; there is no official in overall charge of privacy.

A United States citizen must be prepared to take a lot of after-the-fact action to protect his rights. There is a real minimum of a priori protection assured to him, but he is helped somewhat by consumer protection agencies which play some role in supporting the individual. Basically, he is on his own most of the time.

Privacy Ahead

Privacy ahead will have additional dimensions. It will retain its record-keeping aspect; but much information will be collected, explicitly or otherwise, about individuals that is not intended for decisionmaking in the usual sense and could be used to harm or to put an individual or group at a disadvantage. But as I hope to show you in this discussion, privacy in the years ahead will be much more complex than the relatively straightforward issues that have been faced in record keeping--complexity in terms of the number of organizations involved, in terms of the intricacy of the information flows, and in terms of the difficulty of conceiving appropriate legal safeguards. It is not at all certain that the practices and law which have been developed for present privacy protection can work for new situations.

EXPECTATIONS

I would like to suggest several basic attributes of the privacy situation, as I see it developing. In a sense, they can form a framework for identifying potential privacy invasions and infractions.

Over calendar time, perhaps over a lifetime or even more than one generation, people build up expectations about the behavior of the environment in which they are immersed, and with which they must interact. So to speak, people come to understand how something--like the banking system--works and derive a set of expectations about how it will respond to an action by an individual. They also learn how to exploit its characteristics for personal advantage and to utilize anomalies that might exist, e.g., to use the cash float for personal funds managment. This is especially true of record-keeping or communication systems, which can be seen simply as the technological embodiments of the basic information processes that make one's personal life, society, government, and all of commerce and industry function.

Often the expectations transcend simple operational details and include protections of information that an individual perceives as important to himself, or that society and its processes have deemed important for the overall good. Such broader expectations arise from past experiences with systems and organizations, from specific instances of system behavior, from the legislative framework, from administrative rulings, or even from judicial processes and case law decisions. Moreover, the totality of one's expectations stem not only from his own life experience but also from the many decades of past history.

However, information technology has, in recent years, maintained a very rapid rate of progress with the consequence that computer and communication-based information systems have proliferated rapidly, introduced many new consumer services and products, many new uses of information and new information services. Such systems have pervaded societal institutions--government, industry, education, transportation, entertainment, travel, medicine, health care delivery, etc. In some, possibly many, instances the onrush of technology has abruptly changed the actual workings of systems and organizations, often invisibly to the individual. Commonly, laws fail to keep up with technology changes or are easily end-run or circumvented.

As one might expect, people will carry their expectations forward to the new environment, not realizing that some or all of them may no longer be valid or may have even been destroyed completely. People can therefore be at risk in new ways not foreseen or lose some right, privilege, or legal standing but not know it. Let me offer some examples.

Electronic Mail

Historically, individual or business correspondence has been assured that it will have the protection of a sealed envelope from sender to recipient. Such protection has been written into law, and the exceptions to it were carefully stipulated and controlled. For example, a legal process must take place before a sealed envelope can be opened although the so-called mail cover is easier to implement. Moreover, we implicitly pay for the protection through the additional cost of first-class service that allows an envelope to be sealed. International agreements have also existed to extend sealed-envelope protection across national borders.

Electronic mail does not provide end-to-end protection of similar nature. From the time a sender creates a message, either at his own electronic terminal or by delivering it to a commercial service, until it is seen by the recipient, the material is in electronic forms that are readily interceptable and readable by anyone with the necessary equipment. Thus, the casual extrapolation of experiences based on the traditional mail system to an electronic era results in expectations that are not valid, cannot be fulfilled, and are not perceived realistically by individuals and even organizations.

There is a confused legal situation as well in the United States. Since electronic mail services, be they private, commercially offered by the traditional communication carriers or by independent vendors, utilize the common telecommunications network of the country, they fall under the jurisdiction of the United States Communications Act of 1934 while such mail is in electronic transit. Such electronic mail services also use computer systems owned perhaps by government, perhaps by an individual, or perhaps by a commercial company. Information in the custody of one of them might be subject to the Privacy Act of 1974, to other privacy law in the 50 states, to various telecommunications regulatory rulings, or even to no law. If a particular electronic mail service uses the United States Postal Service as its delivery means, and some do, then various postal statutes come into play.

What historically had been a conceptually simple situation has become a mishmash. So long as mail was the sole province of the Postal Service and involved the delivery of physical objects, legal protection could be assured. The Postal Service even had the authority to extend its obligations and responsibilities to contractors that might work for it. The arrangement though was the culmination of 300 years of evolution of a national mail system. What has been one postal service operating under a prescribed set of laws with delineated protections, all of which led to widespread public understanding and expectations about the system, has become a jumble of technological, legal, organizational, jurisdictional and not well-perceived fragments. For example, a commercial vendor of electronic mail services has no authority whatsoever to compel telecommunications carriers to provide protection against electronic eavesdropping. In another instance, an administrative ruling originally created for telegraphic service has been applied to compel six months storage of electronic mailgrams.

Telephone Systems

Over the years, the United States has had one national telephone system whose implicit authority resulted in standardization of equipment, operational procedures, functional capabilities, and service. Foreign attachments to the system were prohibited, and various laws (the Wiretap Act, for example) and administrative rulings (for example, by state Public Utility Commissions) established details of protection for not only the conversations when en route through the telephone network but also for the billing records. Given the forced breakup of the AT&T, post-divestiture as it is called, many of the prior characteristics remain true but important differences have appeared. Among others, a very aggressive and innovative consumer electronics industry has produced a wide variety of devices that anyone can buy, attach, and use, subject only to prescribed technical rules by the Federal Communications Commission which regulates telecommunications.

The expectations of the past may or may not carry forward; and to the extent that they do not, individuals and even organizations are likely not to realize the change either in exposure of conversations to potential eavesdropping or in protection of billing/accounting records.

A technically obvious and recently publicized example of the abrupt shattering of historical expectations is that of the cordless telephone, ones whose handset communicates with the desktop part by radio. Since it uses radio transmissions, whose reception is well understood and for which appropriate equipment is readily available, the possibility of unauthorized access to conversations has increased sharply, and there are instances of interception of telephone calls with ordinary FM radio receivers by law enforcement authorities. No longer does the Wiretap Act seem applicable; its name is even wrong. In fact, the 1934 Communications Act would seemingly apply, but it allows reception of radio transmissions freely as long as the information gained is not passed to a third party. No longer does a state Public Utilities Commission have total control of the telephony situation because the Federal Communications Commission at the national level is in charge of overseeing use of the electromagnetic spectrum.

An individual has developed an expectation of privacy for his voice conversations because he knows through media treatment and other sources about wiretaps and various laws to control them. He is very likely to extend that same expectation to data transmissions because he reasons that the same "telephone system" is used in either case, but the United States Wiretap Act specifically applies only to aural conversations. Largely unpublicized but equally interceptable are systems such as cellular telephones, mobile telephones, and the recently introduced AirFone in commercial aircraft.

PRIVACY ALERTING

Our discussion so far vividly illustrates how easily privacy issues can emerge or be latent and be completely unnoticed. Individuals might not notice; organizations, even a responsible one that originates some computer-based or communications system, might not notice. Government is the least likely to notice, and even less likely to take remedial or preventive steps unless a major cause celebre has developed. Thus there are major unresolved questions:

- Who is responsible for identifying and flagging new privacy issues?

- Who is responsible for alerting society?

There is no absolute answer to such questions, but I will note that the technologists initially were strong voices in the United States and still are. More recently, there are groups within the legal community that are actively supporting the general cause of privacy and, importantly, introducing privacy concerns into law curricula in significant ways. The issue is also being addressed in the legal professional societies, but in only a few places.

Information specialists and technologists clearly will have an ongoing role, largely because they will be most perceptive of the ways in which information can leak into unauthorized hands. Consumer groups will clearly play a role. Governments are not liklely to play a role in the alerting process because democracies tend to be reactive. They address problems after they have arisen; normally they do not take preventive steps to deter a problem a priori.

SMALL VERSUS LARGE

Next, a closely related issue which I would like to call privacy in the small vs. privacy in the large. It revolves around the volume, or total amount, of some kind of information that can be related to an individual. It is easily illustrated in terms of the ubiquitous telephone number.

A lawyer will argue that an individual can have no expectation of privacy with regard to a telephone number because he is compelled to provide it in order to complete a call. In terms of the language in the Privacy Act of the United States, it would be called a routine use of a telephone number, as would many other things such as listing in the directory, doing statistical traffic analysis, and billing. In the small, one has to agree.

However, in the large, I would argue that the expectation is quite different because the totality of the numbers that one calls over time is very revealing of lifestyle, of one's friends, of the organizations that he does business with, of perhaps his travels, and possibly also of events. While the latter might not be illegal or criminal, they might nonetheless be ones that a person does not wish to have publicly visible; for example, social interactions with persons of like sex.

The expectation in the large would be that the so-called billing or accounting records should be protected against access by unauthorized parties. Indeed this is so because such records are generally protected either by law or by administrative ruling, especially against access by law enforcement authorities.

The point extends to many other categories of information, for example travel arrangements. One trip reveals little, generally, but a year's worth of trips and other reservations might be very valuable information in some circumstances.

NETWORKING

Let us try a different issue that arises from technology advances. At one point in time a computer-based information system served its specific population of users, and in fact most are still of that nature. Privacy concerns centered around the system, its set of users, the organization that owned the system, and the manner in which information was used. To the extent that sharing among systems occurred, it has generally been of small volume and by relatively slow means; for example, exchange of magnetic tapes.

Modern communications technology has made it possible for computers to communicate with one another on a second-by-second basis or to exchange large volumes of information through all-electrical connections. Networking, as it is called, is common within many systems already; for example, computers in the authorization system that supports bank credit cards automatically dial one another periodically to update records and even whole databases. But networking across systems which are not in the same company or even in the same community of companies is beginning, but is not yet commonplace. Let me clarify what I have in mind.

Many large corporations operate extensive networks for their internal affairs; I do not mean them. Many business communities operate networks that include a large number of corporations. The financial community is an obvious one. Banking is networked worldwide and the privacy concerns can be addressed collectively for the whole community, subject only to the details of transborder dataflows and the variation from country to country. I do not mean such community-of-interest networks.

I do mean situations such as the following example.

A Retail Example

It has become popular in the United States for large grocery markets--the supermarkets--to use automated checkout stands. The most recent ones scan special codes on merchandise with a laser device, and consult a database in the attached computer for price and other information. To the extent that such a device functions like a traditional cash register, it is not a problem. It calculates the bill and provides an itemized receipt. It may also do inventory control for the market, and it may automatically produce orders for restocking of merchandise, but such information is impersonal and not related to individuals by name.

However, it is popular in the United States to pay for groceries with a bank check, and there is a lot of concern about bad ones, those without funds behind them. A specialized industry has arisen to verify checks offered in payment not only for retail markets but anywhere. Basically such a system keeps track of individuals who pass bad checks, of delinquent accounts, and of account numbers that correspond to lost or stolen checks. Obviously, it is a system with positive social value. There is no question that such an automated scheme is a wise business approach, and there is no question that it is good for the consumer as well because the losses from bad checks will be passed on to the consumer in the price structure.

Thus, we find that the automated checkout stands have been electrically internetted to the automated check-verification systems. The latter serve a large number of retail outlets either by permanently connected or dial-up telephone connections. It is an instance in which a large number of organizations in one business community--the retail business--individually internet to a few systems in another business community that provide services nationwide.

Incidentally, note that a local retailer's system could, if he wished, also capture information about the individual. If the check verification system is to work, some identifier must be entered from the same keyboard that is used to ring up purchases; typically it is the number on one's driving license. The retailer can buy a mailing list from the Department of Motor Vehicles in his state, or he might opt to enter the name and address directly since these data elements are commonly also on the check.

For those stores that accept bank cards, there can be a corresponding automated interface to the bank card authorization system. The debit card is coming into use in the United States, as it is also in Europe. Inevitably there will be an automated interface from check-out stands directly in one's bank.

Systems such as in this example which internet across functional lines, or across business communities, are the ones that I do have in mind.

Obviously we do not want to make laws that try to control information use in the retail market area. Even if we unwisely did, would the grocer or the retailer who connects his payment system to a check verification or debit card system, appreciate the privacy consequences? To him, it would be a sound business decision, not an informational privacy matter. Even if there were privacy restrictions governing retail records and even if he diligently obeyed them within his own establishment, would he think to ask what the "other system" to which he is connected might do with the information he forwards to it? Is he even in a technical position to notice the point? And even if he were, the business advantage would probably overwhelm any privacy considerations.

The salient point is that networking per se, even though in the best of business or other motivations, can inadvertently transgress on privacy protections. The risks can become significant because so much information about the individual is, or can be, aggregated in one place. We should also notice that networking can circumvent security protections that might be present in a system. To the extent that the business sector becomes extensively networked in the functional sense that I have noted, then the privacy problem becomes increasingly difficult to deal with under law; and the system security problem becomes more and more like the one faced by the military and defense establishments.

BYPRODUCT COLLECTION

Here is another broad aspect of the future. Much information about people will be collected as a byproduct of a transaction; the debit card is a good example. As an individual moves through his daily life, his bank will have been contacted many times to record a payment for some expenditure. At minimum, his pattern of spending will be captured in the bank records. The bank in its own interest and protection will more than likely time and date every transaction, not only for audit purposes but also to resolve errors. By combining such information with the names of the merchants from whom he has purchased, his physical whereabouts can be ascertained.

Let us suppose that banks aggressively move into new directions of business. Throughout the world, the telephone system is becoming heavily computerized. The mere presence of a large very capable computer, whose power can be extended far beyond simple telephony needs at modest marginal costs, will, and already has in the United

States, lead the telephone companies to offer general data services to subscribers. Many banks, major ones at least, have large computer installations. Why should they not go into the business of offering general accounting services to smaller retail merchants? If a bank were to do so, the precise details of every purchase would also be in the bank computer records, in addition to what is already there. The details of an individual's life have become distressingly centralized on one set of records.

The exchange of information between the merchant and the bank is for the purpose of a payment transaction, a legitimate business motive. One cannot argue about capturing the information necessary to make the electronic funds transfer from payor to payee; nor can one argue that it must be retained for some period of calendar time to resolve possible errors and to provide for audit reviews. The risk comes when additional information gets into, or can be related to, the basic record; for example, information such as mailing addresses, or purchase records, if a bank happens to be in such a line of business.

APPROACHES TO PROTECTION

Let us pause for a moment with these last two aspects--internetting and byproduct collection--to try out some ideas for doing something about providing privacy in such an environment.

There will be no way that we can prohibit a retailer from connecting himself to other services, such as a check verification service; nor will we be able to prohibit a bank from getting into other lines of business. The United States is in an age of deregulation which means that a lot of historical prohibitions about how businesses work will vanish; and it already is beginning in banking. What could we do?

Legal

We might seek a law that provides an umbrella of protection over (say) retail customer records. If we were bolder, we might try for a law that extended the protection to other systems with which the retailer might interconnect. Or we might try to imagine reasonable interconnections of systems, based on probable business relationships, and try to address combinations of business records in law. The United States Privacy Protection Study Commission adopted this last view. It suggested, for example, that insurance companies plus their various supporting organizations be treated as a single entity for privacy purposes. Even if we were successful in doing this once or twice, we would soon find ourselves in a never-ending sequence of new laws as technology and business applications of it create a steady stream of new systems and interconnections.

Technical

We could ask a technologist how to address the problem. He would probably observe that the basic amount of information necessary to conduct the essential transaction would have to be collected and that's that. It would be analagous to the single telephone number; the expectation of privacy for the minimum data necessary to complete the transaction would be nil. But he would also observe that we ought to install good computer security safeguards in order to protect even the minimum data relevant to each transaction against unauthorized access; and we ought to make sure that authorized users of the information are identified in automated audit trails and be governed by strict security-oriented procedures and management oversight. In short, he would advise us to do the computer security job comprehensively and properly.

On reflection, he would probably notice another thing. He would observe that the privacy risk escalates if we allow collateral information not necessary for the basic transaction to be blended, accidentally or intentionally, into the records. Pursuing such an idea, he might suggest to us that mailing addresses be kept completely separate from the financial transaction information and never allowed to mix with it. Somewhere deep within a computer would be a carefully protected table that would link financial data to mailing information solely for the purpose of preparing billing statements. Such a table would have extensive error controls to assure that wrong data elements could not be linked; and access to it for the purpose of updating would be carefully limited to a few trusted persons.

Going one step further, he might propose that all records be treated in the spirit of the anonymous Swiss bank account. Wherever data might exist that could create a potential privacy risk, all identifiers associated with the data would be anonymous. Sooner or later, though, data would have to be aggregated for collateral purposes such as mailing of statements; but in every such instance, the system would consult its carefully controlled tables to aggregate anonymously identified data elements for legitimate business needs.

His line of argument would be that privacy protection would be assured by means of a very elegant set of technical security safeguards which will assure that all sensitive information has only anonymous system-assigned identifiers, and that all relationships among such data will be governed by carefully controlled and protected tables to which only trusted individuals will have access. Correspondingly, the software processes that would work with such tables to aggregate anonymous data elements into complete records will similarly be carefully designed, checked, maintained, and controlled by trusted individuals. In fact, the anonymity might start even with the collection of data incident to a transaction. An individual might carry one of the so-called "smart cards" whose internal electronics can transmit in encrypted form the anonymous identifier that only the internal protected tables can associate with a specific individual.

Such a suggestion has merit because it effectively centralizes all the potentially trouble-making software processes and the control of access to sensitive data in a set of tables and some associated software. It would be quite unlike today's systems which generally put all manner of data together in one set of records--the popular integrated data base--and generally distribute the security problem throughout the system, especially throughout all manner of software.

But there is a very serious other side. In the name of privacy we would attempt to dictate the general architecture of systems that process sensitive data. I do not know how one would write such a law, nor do I know how one would oversee its enforcement.

FILE MATCHING

Let us come back to the central theme and press onward, but this time we will give the example first and identify the issue afterward.

It has become popular in the United States to match computer files from different agencies in an effort to identify individuals that in some way are in defiance of the law. For example, tax information files can reveal whether an individual earns too much income to qualify for public welfare assistance. In each case, the files of interest are ones that were collected for some quite specific purpose but the routine use provision of United States law did not include matching with unrelated files. In each case the underlying payoff to society was deemed positive and not in question. As one might anticipate, the results from early attempts were very much in question; and there were many indviduals improperly accused of wrongful actions. Guidelines were developed within the government for the conduct of matches by its agencies, and more recent attempts have been more palatable, although the economic return from the effort has often been questioned as being far too small to have justified the privacy exposure or potential harm to individuals.

Whatever one may think about the desirability of computer matching, it does raise an interesting privacy issue. Files from different sources are very likely not to be consistent with regard to individual identification. Names will have been spelled differently; addresses may have changed; errors may have occurred. At least in the United States, there is no universal personal identifier that makes matching a certainty. Hence, in the "hit list" resulting from matching two files there will inevitably be many individuals who are present only because the computer process could only guess that records in the two files pertained to the same person. Later, manual processing will resolve the ambiguity and clear the innocent; but for a time at least, one can be under suspicion not because of a reasonable expectation of a wrong having been committed, but because of "noisy" computer data and the software matching processes that try to deal with it. We are not talking, of course, about the legitimate hits from the match; such individuals have in fact crossed the law and deserve the consequences.

Such an approach is certainly inconsistent with the usual legal attitude that would be much more careful about making even an implied accusation without decent evidence of wrongdoing. From a privacy point of view, there has been an invasion of privacy for some people on the hit list even though there has not been any subsequent negative or harmful action. Is this a privacy dimension that we must be concerned with? Perhaps not in the computer matching process as it is now practiced, but suppose that one's mere presence on a hit list is retained and used later for other purposes; suppose it becomes the basis of what lawyers call "fishing" through facts in the expectation of finding something wrong. Combine "invasion of privacy without action" with the earlier comments about internetting of systems, and one may have a very important issue a decade or so from now.

OFFICE AUTOMATION

Let us think about the office environment and its automation, combined with the expectation issue raised earlier. It will raise a rather different connotation of privacy.

In the traditional office of personal desks, file cabinets, and their contents, there is an expectation of private ownership. It extends especially to the contents of one's desk and to lesser things such as the contents of a rolodex or mailing list. An individual will often feel uneasy entering another's desk even though the relationship between the two may be a well-established one between an individual and his secretary or colleague. It is almost as though the established tradition of the sanctity of a personal home and belongings has been extended to one's workplace; one does not enter without having been invited.

Whether it is a feeling of personal turfdom as with a home or the fact that one has himself created the letters and memos in files, whether it is an emotional question or even biologically based, it is clear that such expectations of privacy against physical invasion of things which are regarded as personally owned exist and are strong. It is not clear that they are well founded or even essential, nor is it clear whether such expectations will pass over time; but in an automated office environment, ownership of things--notably on-line files--is likely to be shared.

Ownership

There is also the question of who owns information stored in a computer. United States law has held that the organization owning the computer also owns its contents. Such a position is quite inconsistent with the normal view that the contents of one's desk are generally not open to prying by corporate eyes. The same question of ownership becomes exceedingly important in the case of electronic mail systems, especially if the system provides such mail services to the general public. There has already been a major incident with regard to a government-owned computer and the electronic mail in it.

One would anticipate that such an expectation of _ownership privacy_ would be important for the ready acceptance of office automation systems and their electronic mail features by an organization. It would seem a good principle that office systems should generally meet the same expectations of the paper office, or at minimum, not drastically offend the a priori expectations based on decades of being embedded in a traditional office.

PRIVACY AND SECURITY

It is time now to relate such privacy issues to computer security. Privacy of course relates generally to information about people and how it is used. It may be used to deny access to some entitlement or privilege; it can be used to seriously harm, such as destroying an individual's credit status. It can be used to annoy as with unwanted mailings or solicitations that depend on information lists obtained from records collected for other purposes. It can relate to ownership of information and one's personal feelings about such ownership.

In whatever dimension though, if information is to be used for legally or socially accepted purposes and not for spurious purposes, it must be protected against loss, modification, or theft, and access to it must be controlled. In the last aspect, "access" could be by individuals or it could be by another computer-based system. Safeguards for such protection and for access control are collectively the body of knowledge that we generally call "computer security." Clearly, if privacy protection is to be provided with high confidence, computer security safeguards must be in place first.

I would not pretend for a moment that our systems today are well-off from the view of computer security, but at least the principles of doing the job are rather well understood. There is a growing body of expertise that can deal with it, and significant research is under way on many of the technical parts. We have come to understand that comprehensive computer security will require attention to physical protections, hardware safeguards, software safeguards, safeguards for communication, personnel control, proper procedures, and attentive management oversight. There are ways to do risk assessment, and to decide what safeguards are appropriate. For the organization that wants to install security safeguards and that is willing to make the necessary investment, we do know how to install system-wide safeguards for many kinds of installations. In particular, we know how to do the computer security job for a system that involves one or a connected set of processing centers and serves a user population indigenous to the system, and that is under a common--or at least coordinated--management structure. We even know how to take care of a cohesive community that is willing to work together. The financial community is such an example.

When we introduce internetting, the situation is much less promising. Especially will it be troublesome if the systems were not intended originally to communicate, or if the systems are to share only specified parts of records with one another. Especially will it be troublesome if the systems are under unrelated managements, or parts of different federal agencies or corporations, or under the regulatory purview of different laws. Quite aside from the managerial or legal aspects, or the distribution of liability among internetted systems, or of even knowing whether all systems are complying with desired privacy and security guidelines, there are major unsolved technical problems related to providing <u>network-wide</u> <u>security</u> safeguards.

LEGAL FRAMEWORK

Let us look now at the legal part of the matter. For an information environment that

- o will be extensively internetted,
- o will collect much information about people as a byproduct of other transactions,
- o will abruptly and perhaps invisibly negate expectations of privacy and ownership as technological advances are made, or

- o can induce differing expectations depending upon "small vs. large," and

- o may incur invasions of privacy without subsequent immediate action,

what legal framework can we imagine that will embrace a future of such diverse and complex structure? What philosophical legal approach will accommodate a future of the kind we anticipate?

Traditionally, privacy law in the United States has given the individual the right to compel proper behavior of an agency, and it has been targeted on a specific body of records. He can require the correction of a record, and the dissemination of the correction to all who received the erroneous record; he can require the deletion of some information; he can compel an agency to abide by its "routine use" public position. Beyond that, the individual has no standing for action. Can we adopt such an approach in trying to deal with the privacy problems of the future? Can a "code of fair information practices" be conceived and implemented in a law that will span all the aspects of privacy concerns that we can foresee? Will a "targeted approach" ever be able to keep up with the problem?

Traditionally, Europe has adopted what I shall call "positive control." A Data Protection Board or an equivalent organization monitors record-keeping organizations for compliance with law, and plays a very definite proactive role in establishing the conduct of the record keepers. Can such a regulatory body be extrapolated to deal with our projected future? Could it possibly attempt to license beforehand all the possible informational linkages that business, industry, and government might conceive? Would it even be acceptable for such a Board to intrude itself so deeply into non-governmental affairs in the private sector? Might not the problem be so huge that it would overwhelm even the best-intentioned positive control effort?

A third possibility is that we tell the individual that it is all his problem. We could take the position that the formal institutions of government cannot help because the future is too complicated, and that we cannot design appropriate law that will afford privacy protection but at the same time not be intrusive and excessively binding on the conduct of a country's affairs. If we go such a way, how do we assure that individuals are well enough informed to be alert to problems and to know what legal remedies are available?

As another option, can we conceive an umbrella approach in which one law is meant to apply to many and diverse organizations that deal with information about people? Or do we use an area-specific approach, as the United States has? The latter has a separate and different law for credit, for education, for federal agencies at large, for census data, and for tax information. The European approach approximates an umbrella aproach; the United States, a targeted approach. Incidentally, the latter is likely to stay that way simply because of the difficulty in establishing a constituency for broadly based action.

Or we could try some combination of them, plus others that have yet to be innovated. To date, we all have drifted forward--the United States on its approach and Europe on its. We have not had a significant dialogue on the underlying question of which, if either, is appropriate for the future. We probably need to inaugurate such a public debate promptly.

Information Representation

However we decide the general legal approach and however we design the laws, there is an important trap to avoid; it has to do with the information representation issue that has troubled the protection of things under copyright. Whatever personal information we decide to legally protect must be assured of its protection whether it is stored in a computer, written on a magnetic tape, in transit over a communications channel, or printed on paper; and it must be so internationally. As far as I know, privacy law has not stumbled in this regard, but it could happen. For example, some years ago the United States Congress created a wiretap law which applies only to aural information. It has not been illegal so far to intercept data communications, but any technical specialist will tell you that one cannot decide from looking at a stream of digital information whether it is a data communication or a voice conversation that happens to be represented in digitized form. We will have to be cautious in the design of law to avoid creating circumstances readily circumvented by technology. So to speak, the protection embodied in the law will have to be indifferent to technology.

THE WORLD AHEAD

Where does that leave us, as we look toward the future and try to imagine what new privacy issues will emerge and how we will deal with them? First, note that information is a very universal commodity; all organizations and all people must use it to achieve purposeful behavior. Therefore, the world will increasingly be stiched together more and more intimately by its information threads. Technically, this will mean extensive data communications and internetting of systems. Databases will not be confined to textual information; they can also include audio and video that can be searched, combined, or displayed as readily as text and perhaps combined with it. Internationally it means continuing attention to transborder data flow issues. For each company it will mean ongoing and increased attention not only to computer but also to system and network security safeguards.

The privacy and security problems that will arise are likely to be basically the same for all countries that have about the same stage of technological advancement. The developing countries will encounter the problems later on; but on the other hand, technology exporting countries will drive the issue, and the developing countries may see the problems much sooner than might be anticipated. International business communities (for example, banking) will tend to spread any privacy or security problem worldwide but such communities will also be very important focal points for achieving action.

Solutions though are likely to be country dependent. Many years ago Dr. Claes-Goran Kallner, the first chairman of Sweden's Data Privacy Board, cautioned me that privacy solutions that might work for Sweden would not necessarily work for the United States, simply because of the difference in geographical size. I was not to appreciate his observation about the importance of scale factor until my understanding of the privacy issue in the United States matured some years later. Size does make a difference.

Solutions will also be country dependent because of cultural heritages. European countries are accustomed to population registers, to personal identifiers, and to federal-level record-keeping procedures over the population. The United States is very resistant to all such federal intrusions into the life of the individual.

Technical Issues

There are new and tough technical problems before us. For example, if it were to prove desirable to legally constrain the kinds of information--or even specific data elements--that could be electrically exchanged among systems, we have technical problems in the commercial world that have been faced only in the military and defense world. If we became convinced that the only way to handle commingled sensitive data in a system would be to keep it anonymous in the file but aggregate it with high-confidence software processes, we have a whole new dimension of computer security for which we would need not only new technical solutions, but also ways in which to specify to vendors and to systems implementers how their hardware and software should function. In a sense, we would have imposed a very new and quite different functional requirement, even architectural requirement, on vendors in behalf of privacy.

In that regard though, the complaint would be one of "too expensive"; the position would be that "we cannot afford the computing power to implement such an involved scheme." To such a position I hold a personal view that I think is pertinent. The cost of computing power has been declining dramatically for decades; we have exploited it to enhance the level of automation in the information infrastructure that supports our countries, societies, and governments. We must now be equally diligent in using computer power to assure ourselves that a creeping information-intrusiveness does not occur.

Personal Impact

The evermore extensive record keeping and the drive for automation in behalf of efficiency and economic operation throughout all parts of society and a country are gradually tightening the processes of society. We do not enjoy options that were available to individuals only a few decades ago. It is virtually impossible to be personally anonymous without forsaking the standard of living and privileges of a our modern world; one would have to withdraw completely from society. Even our personal money management is impacted; not only is the money float in our personal accounts gradually diminishing but banks decline to make funds available until several days after deposit. In the extensive information infrastructure that modern countries and society must have to function, we cannot allow the analog of environmental pollution to develop.

We must concern ourselves in an ongoing basis with the use of information and its protection. But what about the individual? Where will he stand? In the end, it is he that privacy really concerns, and it is he that loses if we, who are the attentive professionals in this area, are careless or irresponsible.

PRIVACY LAW AHEAD

As I look toward the future of not only countries but also a world of highly internetted information systems, each complex in itself, but which transcend national borders, federal agencies, governments, corporate boundaries, and boundaries of business communities, I cannot imagine a single legal construct that can accommodate the situation. Laws of today that were constructed for monolithic situations will not be satisfactory for systems and combinations of systems that transcend jurisdictional boundaries.

For those bodies of information that are now covered by extant law, we should let well enough alone other than to plug loopholes and revise the protections. Whether we have achieved the law with a targeted approach or an umbrella approach really does not matter, so long as the transborder question can be handled. There will be some new bodies of information about people that will deserve a specific law; for example, electronic mail is presently under consideration in the United States. There will be some business communities that can be treated as a single entity.

But what about all those other circumstances and situations? What about all the opportunities for connecting systems together and for exchanging information about people for whatever purpose, but which might never put a large enough group of people at risk to get federal or even state attention? What about expectations--the reality of present socially accepted systems vs. the consequences of technological advances? Or expectations in the small vs. in the large?

PERSONAL RESPONSIBILITY

My view is coming to be that there will be a large part of the privacy issue for which the individual will have to take care of himself. Major parts can be handled by law as they are identified, but the individual will have to be on his own for a lot of things. That may be fine, but he will need a basis for remedial action when necessary. One approach might be a form of insurance, perhaps required of all businesses just as are business licenses. It could even be insurance at the federal level, just as a United States agency now insures savings account deposits. Alternatively, we could provide the individual with a legal basis for remedy. For example, we could give him standing to bring civil suit and recover damages. Such a course is a little tricky because it might be hard to show damages related to information misuse. If that is a viable possibility, hopefully legislators can design appropriate law. However, let us not overlook the international aspect in an era of internetting. It will be perfectly possible for the misuse of information to occur in a country other than one's residence or other than the one in which he happens to be at the moment. We will have the problem of harmonizing privacy protections worldwide.

If he is to take care of himself, the individual will also need to be well informed about information matters, because many things that might concern him will probably not be particularly visible. I have no insightful suggestions beyond the usual ones--consumer protection groups, government publications, activist information professionals everywhere, appropriate educational content throughout curricula at all levels, and certainly proper content in the curricula for technical people so that they understand how to build the right kind of systems and can also conceive new technical ideas.

On balance though, it would appear that a combination of approaches can make a very livable world from the information privacy point of view. It does not look hopeless to me; there are ideas. It may not be easy, but there are several principles that can be helpful. Moreover, we have not really begun to think about privacy in the very broad perspective that I suggested this morning. How to get there from here though is quite a different matter, and a topic for another occasion.

COMPUTER SECURITY
J.B. Grimson and H.-J. Kugler (Editors)
Elsevier Science Publishers B.V. (North-Holland)

COMPUTER ASSISTED REDUCTION OF VULNERABILITY OF DATA CENTERS

Björn T Cronhjort
Ericsson Information Systems AB, Sweden

Antero Mustonen
Oy Wärtsilä Ab Helsinki Shipyard, Finland

CONTENTS

1 SUMMARY

2 INTRODUCTION

3 DIFFERENT METHODS FOR THE EVALUATION OF EDP RISKS
3.1 Check Lists
3.2 Quantitative Risk Evaluation Methods
3.3 Scenario Based Method, Evaluation of the SBA Method
3.4 Qualitative Risk Analysis

4 EXPERT SYSTEMS
4.1 What is an Expert System?
4.2 The Structure of the Expert System
4.3 Expert Systems as a Means of Risk Management

5 APPLICATION OF AN EXPERT SYSTEM TO THE GENERAL RISK ANALYSIS
5.1 The Basis of the System
5.2 The Structure of the Knowledge Base
5.3 Risk Calculation
5.4 Control Mechanisms

6 AREAS OF APPLICATION IN AIR-CONDITIONING AND ELECTRICITY SYSTEM DESIGN

7 SUPPORT SYSTEM FOR THE EDP OPERATOR

8 OTHER APPLICATIONS

9 CONCLUSIONS

1 SUMMARY

As an introduction, some published methods for the analysis of vulnerability of information processing activities are presented and discussed. Based on the survey, the authors proceed to suggest an expert systems approach for the evaluation of EDP risks, and for risk control. A methodology based on the Dempster-Shafer Theory of Evidence is proposed, and the essential principles for the implementation of such an expert system are outlined. The proposed system could be used both for planning new computer centers, and for improving security in existing computer centers. It is suggested that further work could be pursued through a new Working Group of IFIP/TC11.

2 INTRODUCTION

Several different methods of controlling EDP risks can be found in the literature. A problem common to all these methods is, however, that they are difficult to adapt. For example, it is impossible to put quantitative methods of risk calculation into practice in service center surroundings. On the other hand, there are no aids for planning new computer centers with respect to risk control. Another essential problem is the lack of means for controlling disturbances and other risk factors in daily operation.

There is an extensive literature dealing with EDP risks and measures for controlling them. The problem is that the information is scattered and difficult to find. A special problem is the consideration of local conditions. Many computer center risks are due to lack of information, there is for example no knowledge of how to act in a critical situation.

The above mentioned considerations lead us to propose expert systems for controlling risks. An expert system is a method of collecting and structuring knowledge for several users. We feel that such an expert system could quite easily be compiled for performing vulnerability analyses and drafting security plans. The greatest benefit would be gained through the accumulation of existing knowledge and through the variability of the knowledge base (Haye 83 and Nego 85).

The introduction of security measures for controlling data risks seems to constitute a special problem. It is hard to convince management of the profitability of the often very large investments needed to improve security. This is also the weak point of the analysis methods found in the literature. They do not take into account how decisions are made in reality. An expert system, that would allow simulation of the occurrence of different risk factors, could be very helpful as an aid in the decision-making.

3 DIFFERENT METHODS FOR THE EVALUATION OF EDP RISKS

3.1 Check Lists

A traditional way of controlling EDP risks is to use check lists, which point out possible risk factors and present solutions. The most complete check list, consisting of several hundred pages, has been presented by Kraus (Krau 80). There are, however, some problems connected with this method:

- The lists are very extensive, which makes the management and application of knowledge more difficult.
- Local conditions, such as vulnerability factors, EDP systems solutions and dependency on EDP, are not considered in the lists.
- The lists cannot be used for testing the security level of different data center alternatives owing to too many details.
- The lists do not provide synthesized information about the security level, which information would be needed for the decisions. The same applies to the cost influence of different security solutions.

The latest published catalogue of check lists (Aald 85) also includes a scoring system for evaluation of the security level.

These check lists do, however, provide a good starting point when the expert systems are being compiled.

In his book, Parker (Park 81) suggests that the risk factors are listed and analyzed according to three categories:

- situations that have occurred in the system
- situations that have occurred elsewhere
- general check lists

As an alternative, we have suggested a method where the organisation and its surroundings form the basis from which risks and vulnerability factor suggestions are automatically being derived. If necessary, control questions would be asked by the system, and the answers to the risk suggestions and control questions would lead either to a more thorough investigation of that risk area, or would mean moving to other risk areas, i.e. moving on to different levels of the knowledge base tree structure. Thus the accuracy of the investigation can be optimized according to the needs of the organisation in question.

3.2 Quantitative Risk Evaluation Methods

A quantitative calculation method can be used if there is no historical material available (Perr 81). The probabilities are thus based on estimates. The method is suitable for large systems or for planning physical security (fire protection etc.). If the real probabilities are known, they can also be used. This method was originally presented in the 1960s by Robert Courtney.

The computer facilities, systems, etc. which are vulnerable to risks should be grouped according to their size, and it should be determined which part of the system is at risk. The loss may be complete or partial.

The probability of a risk is estimated by giving the frequency of occurrence in powers of ten (once a day, once every ten days, once every 100 days).

The risks (E is expected monetary loss per year, i.e. annual loss expectancy) can be calculated from the formula:

$$E = 1/3 \times 10^{(P+V-3)}$$

where V = 1 if the loss is 10 \$, 2 if 100 \$, etc., and P = 1 if the risk occurs once every 300 years, 2 if once every 30 years, etc.

It is to be noted that the same target area or activity can be exposed to several different risk factors.

This method is the most widely known of those in use, and it provides a systematical means of evaluating risks. It can, however, be criticized for the following reasons:

- There is a logarithmic relation between the occurrence frequencies and the value of the losses, which is not mathematically justified.
- The seeming accuracy of the method can be misleading.
- The method gives an annual estimate of the losses. This can be misleading if the probability is small but the value of the loss is high.

Subjective risk evaluation is based on one or several persons giving a probability estimate of the risk factors. There are three ways to do this:

First, the risk evaluation result can be derived from the formula

$$E_V = \frac{a + 4 \times b + c}{6}, \text{ where:}$$

E_V = expected value of the frequency (e.g. frequency per year)
a = pessimistic estimate
b = probable estimate
c = optimistic estimate

a, b and c are given e.g. per year.

Second, this method can be generalized for any number of estimates.

$$E_v = \frac{a + K \times m + b}{K + 2}$$

where K = 4 and m is the arithmetic average of the probability estimates when a and b have been deducted.

Third, by the scoring matrix approach:

The risk evaluation result can be derived from the formula

$$\sum_{F=1}^{n} (WF_F \times S_F)$$

where F is the number of the vulnerability factor influencing the risk, WF is a weight factor and S is an estimated score of how the factor influences the risk. From this formula a so called severity index can be determined for the threat. After this the occurrence frequency of the threat is estimated. These two can be studied graphically so that the severity index is represented by the x-axis and the occurrence frequency by the y-axis.

The advantage of the scoring matrix method is mainly that it makes it necessary to analyze the factors contributing to threat occurrence.

The drawback of the method lies in the fact that the severity index is influenced by the number of vulnerability factors. Thus it is difficult to compare the indexes because they are not normalized.

3.3 Scenario Based Method, Evaluation of the SBA Method

The SBA method is based on a scenario analysis of possible risk factors. This analysis is carried out by the users of the EDP systems and the risk management experts (SBA 83). The method as such does not take account of the existing knowledge of EDP risks and the control of them and does not assist the users to make the right decisions. This method requires experts to be consulted. The end result is a great number of forms which are almost independent of each other, and which present possible but not necessarily probable EDP risks instead of quantitative information.

Some of the drawbacks of the method are:

- It is not suitable for small or medium-size companies owing to its extensiveness.
- It contains forms and questions which cannot always be answered as assumed, because certain questions require extensive investigations, especially in large organisations.
- The risks may be analyzed subjectively and superficially if outside experts are not consulted.

- It does not include a feedback function for finding the right risk control methods. In our opinion it is a disadvantage that the SBA users are not forced to go deeply into the risk control methods, instead the security measures may be chosen very casually and without coordination. The method should form a logically coherent system that considers the mutual dependency of the risk factors, offers risk control solutions when the risks have been identified, and takes account of the mutual dependency of the risk control methods.

On the other hand, the great advantage of SBA lies in the fact that it is user-oriented and that it emphasizes the importance of risk control.

3.4 Qualitative Risk Analysis

At the IFIP/SEC 84, Smith and Lim (Smit 84) presented a very interesting risk analysis method. The solution is based on the fuzzy set theory. The vulnerability is determined with the help of a set of about 1000 questions organised in a certain way. The questions can be answered by yes or no or on a linguistic scale of five degrees (very high-very low). Based on the answers, the scores measuring vulnerability and risks are calculated for every target area.

The advantages of this method are:

- The check lists are easy to use.
- The analysis can be carried out rapidly.
- A summary of the vulnerability is obtained quickly and easily.

The problem is, however, that this solution mainly aims at automating the use of the check lists so that they can be used for analyzing the security level of existing computer centers etc. It would be quite difficult to use the method as an aid in the planning of new computer centers, because it does not consider layout solutions, except on a very rough scale.

4 EXPERT SYSTEMS

4.1 What is an Expert System?

An expert system is a knowledge based system which, due to its knowledge base and conclusive ability, is able to solve problems that are considered to require considerable human expertise.

The following is characteristic of an expert system (Haye 83 and Nego 85):

1. High intelligence and a large amount of knowledge. The systems can solve very difficult problems, in some cases even better than the best human experts.

2. Highly developed interface. For example, it is possible to communicate with the systems in a limited natural language much the same way as with human experts.

3. Ability to give reasons for its actions. The systems have meta knowledge and comprehend their own knowledge. For example, it is possible to ask a system why it asked a certain question or why it arrived at a certain result.

4. Ability to process heuristic and uncertain information.

5. Gradual increasing of knowledge as new information is accumulated into the knowledge base.

6. Ability to handle descriptions and problems presented in the form of symbols.

4.2 The Structure of the Expert System

The expert system consists of the following basic components:

1. Knowledge base/source
2. Inference engine/procedure
3. Working memory, global database
4. Interface

The knowledge base contains the facts, beliefs and heuristic IF-THEN rules needed to solve the problem. The facts consist of generally accepted basic knowledge of the area. The beliefs and heuristic rules consist of knowledge that the experts have acquired by experience. Knowledge of this kind is usually not found in textbooks and the experts often use it unconsciously. The extent and quality of the knowledge base determines the quality of the whole system.

The inference engine is a control mechanism by which the knowledge base is used. In contrast to the knowledge base, it does not contain specific knowledge. The knowledge base can be updated without changing the inference engine. The function of the inference engine is usually quite straightforward. For example, the operation algorithm may simply be based on the application of the IF-THEN rules to the knowledge base, until some end condition has been fulfilled or all alternatives have been scanned.

With the help of IF-THEN rules the inference can be data controlled. The information contained in the THEN part can only be used by rules with corresponding information in the IF part. If the system cannot independently apply some promising rule or solve some part of a problem, it has to seek outside information and may ask the user a question.

In order for the systems to be able to justify their conclusions and actions, e.g. the questions HOW and WHY, it is usually required of the inference chains, the IF-THEN rules and the conclusions that they can be easily followed and printed out. The working memory contains information about the different stages of problem solving, previous conclusions and input data.

The most important general techniques and formalisms developed for the presentation and handling of knowledge are:

1. Logic. In systems based on artificial intelligence, the first order predicate logic is the most commonly used. The Prolog language, for example, is based directly on this predicate logic. The great advantage of formalisms based on logic is that they usually ensure correct system structures and conclusions, in contrast to other methods.

2. The production system is the most important way of presenting knowledge. The basic idea is to associate conditions with measures by using rules of CONDITION-MEASURE type:

   IF Condition THEN Measure

3. Frame. By using frames, generic objects and structures can be defined in slightly the same way as when using records in databases. The frames are often arranged as a conceptual hierarchy, where the subconcepts take over the characteristics of the higher concepts, cf. object oriented programming. Complicated side effects and procedural attachments can be defined for the updating etc. of the frames.

4. Semantic nets. In the semantic nets, concepts and their relations and associations are presented in the form of a net. The advantage of this formalism is that it gives a clear picture and that the concepts are directly connected to each other by the arcs of the net. Thus the concept associations are easy to find and can be used for controlling the inference function.

The most common method of solving problems used in the expert systems is the search method. The problem is presented as a set of states and operations, by which it is possible to move from one state to another. All possible states and the movements between them form or tune the net-like search space of the problem area.

The solving of a problem in a search space means searching for an operation sequence by which it is possible to move from the initial state of the problem to the goal.

Roughly, the search involves application of the knowledge base rules in order to move from the initial state of the working memory and arrive at a desired goal.

4.3 Expert Systems as a Means of Risk Management

It should be possible to apply risk control methods to the following situations:

- When planning new computer centers, data systems, etc.

- When analyzing existing computer centers and suggesting measures to be taken

- For simulation of risk factors and their consequences, cf. scenario method

- For daily operation control and supervision

- For controlling operation during breakdown and recovery

The characteristics of a good set of methods are:

- Local conditions, risks, dependency on EDP, etc., can be applied to the model.

- The target area can be described using the concepts of the method, which are then analyzed.

- The calculation of risks can be carried out using different qualitative or quantitative methods.

- Based on identified risks, the method suggests measures that are to be taken.

- The system should be hierarchical and applicable on both a rough and an exact level.

Considering the above, the authors have chosen to propose an expert system type of an approach for managing EDP risks. In practice, the method would consist of several different components:

- General risk analysis and selection of security systems
- Dimensioning and selection of computer room layout and structures
- Dimensioning and planning of air-conditioning and electricity
- Instructions for supervisory and alarm measures triggered by heating, water, ventilation, electricity, burglar system alarms etc.
- Measures to be taken by EDP operators etc. when disturbances occur in the computer room
- Service management

5 APPLICATION OF AN EXPERT SYSTEM TO THE GENERAL RISK ANALYSIS

5.1 The Basis of the System

The system should enable the evaluation of the security measures which are applied to data, documents, programs/systems, equipment and facilities, user security and protection of security systems. From this point of view it should be possible both to analyze existing computer centers and to plan a new one. Here the concept "computer center" is used in a broad sense. It may consist of several decentralized computer centers and it also includes the user areas where there is EDP equipment or where data is stored.

Due to this, we need a set of concepts by which we can describe both the physical and the functional structure of a computer center. The physical structure includes the surroundings of the computer center, the rooms, and different connections between these. The structure should be described topologically so that different solutions and the possibility of risks spreading can be analyzed. It should be possible to join both the physical and the functional structure definitions.

The description of the computer center layout should be hierarchical so that the risks can be studied on different levels of accuracy. The basic concepts of the model are:

1. Surroundings
   - area
   - site
2. Zone
   - room
   - unit
3. Access
   - personal access
   - transports
   - communications
   - ducts and other networks
4. Characteristics of the room
   - size
   - surrounding structures
5. Relation room/room
   - adjacent
   - above
   - below
   - access from one room to another (direction)
6. Relation room/surroundings
   - adjacent
   - access to the room (doors, windows, etc.)
7. Access control
   - access control
   - locks
   - structures
   - fire dampers
   - passwords
   - enciphering etc.

This definition is based on the so called perimeter security control concept which, by the way, can be applied on both physical rooms and data systems.

To each zone/room should be added the targets to be protected and the vulnerability factors and security measures for each zone/room. The same applies to the surroundings.

It should be possible for the users of the system to copy the relevant parts of the description. This means that there should be a frame into which the data is inserted. The system presents a tentative list of vulnerability factors and security measures for each zone/room. This list is corrected and completed, and the user can then duplicate it for similar zones or rooms. Thus the analysis can be carried out rapidly.

Some typical questions are:

- If vulnerability factor X occurs in area Y, what are the risks?
- In what areas are the largest risks most likely to occur?
- How does security measure X improve the security level?
- What are the costs of a certain security solution?
- How do risks, e.g. fire, spread and how can their effects be limited?

The aim of the expert system should be:

a) to analyze the vulnerability factors behind the risks
b) to suggest solutions
c) to combine the measures into a suitable system
d) to look for "loopholes"
e) to achieve an overall security level within given cost limits

The prevailing conditions should be taken into account when the risks are being analyzed, see figure 1. Based on this, the expert system should suggest only relevant risks, so that the user does not have to go through too much material.

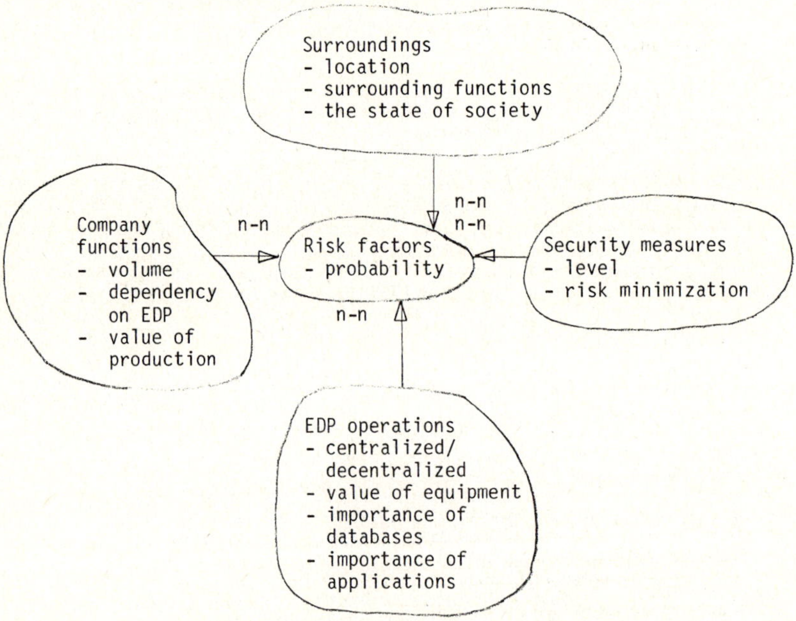

Figure 1: Factors that influence vulnerability. The notation n-n means for example that one security measure can influence several risk factors, and several security measures can be needed to limit one risk factor.

5.2 The Structure of the Knowledge Base

The expert system developed for computer equipment fault analysis provides a useful analogy when the knowledge base for risk analysis is being developed (Davi 83).

The knowledge base consists of a hierarchy of levels:

Level 1	describes	the physical structure and layout of the computer center
" 2	"	data processing functions in different rooms
" 3	"	data processing equipment in different rooms
" 4	"	the personnel working in different rooms
" 5	"	documents, programs and data stored in different rooms
" 6	"	security measures that have been taken or are possible
" 7	"	the vulnerability factors on the different levels

An example of the hierarchy representing the physical structure and layout is shown in figure 2 below.

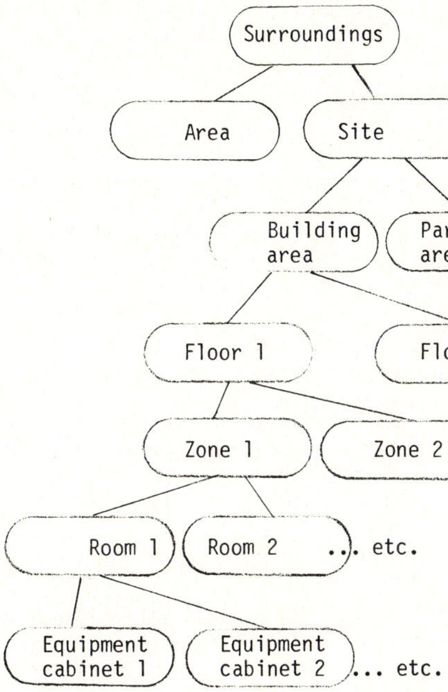

Figure 2: The hierarchy of the physical description

Within each room, equipment units that are to be separately protected can be defined. Such units are e.g. modem cabinets, distribution centers for electricity, etc.

The aim of the hierarchical structure is to enable the description to be made at different levels of accuracy, e.g. for each room or zone.

The hierarchical description is complemented by a so called connection description consisting of two parts. One part describes how the rooms are located in relation to each other and the physical protection between them, and the other describes the access from one room to another and the access control solutions, as shown in figure 3.

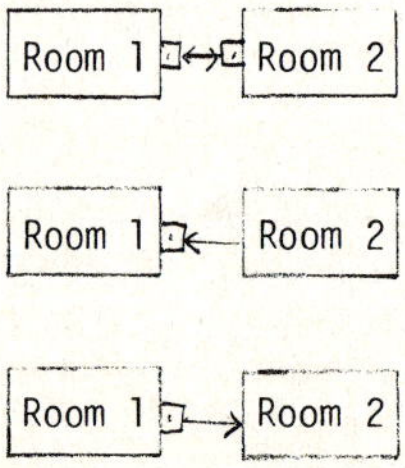

Figure 3: Access from one room to another is controlled by various control points, such as locks, access control devices, fire dampers, etc.

By access we mean every possible communication, such as persons, information, air-conditioning, etc., between the rooms. Due to this, the rooms are provided with a number of control points. The connection between the rooms can be one-way or two-way and there are different means of supervising the communication, for example each door is a control point. Each type of control has its own set of rules, e.g. the access control is based on rights of access, which are presented by means of production rules.

The authors propose that the knowledge base should be presented as a semantic net. A semantic net seems to be quite suitable for a problem area of this kind, where the knowledge is of structural type (Mylo 83 and Barr 81).

The basic relations are:

- INSTANCE-OF
- PART-OF and
- IS-A

By means of the INSTANCE-OF relation, the objects are connected to their types, e.g. flood is an INSTANCE-OF risk caused by nature. The PART-OF relation joins the different parts of the object to the object, e.g. as when the components of a data system are joined to the system itself. By means of the IS-A relation, each object class is connected to concepts on a higher level. Besides the above mentioned relations, we propose that two more relations should be used, which are connected to the specific problem area.

Thus, in the knowledge base, the access from one room to another is described by the relation called "Access":

Relation: $Room_X$ Acc_{ij} $Room_Y$

where i is the type of access, e.g. access in both directions, access control unit in use, etc., and j is the group of persons who have access to room Y from room X.

In a similar way, the relation "Access" determines the rights of each group of personnel to use the facilities or data systems:

Relation: Group of personnel$_X$ Acc$_i$ System component$_Y$

where i is the type of access right. The system component is usually some part of the system situated in some room.

The physical protection level between rooms or between rooms and surroundings is determined by the relation called "Shield" (Blai 71):

Relation: Room$_X$ Shi$_i$ Room$_Y$

or

Relation: Room$_X$ Shi$_i$ Surroundings$_Y$

where i is the protection level between the rooms, e.g. fire wall A120, fire door A60, etc. The same relation can also be used for defining which rooms are adjacent.

The relation "Shield" can also be applied to rooms situated on different floors. In that case the rooms above/below can be defined.

The structure of the knowledge base presented above enables an analysis of the perimeter security control. Another typical analysis question would be how the data of a system have been protected during the different processing phases, who has access to the rooms where data is being processed, etc.

In the same way the physical protective measures can be analyzed. A typical question would be: There is considerable risk of fire in room X, do the surrounding constructions fulfill the requirements of the fire protection class?

A search in the knowledge base can also be determined by means of a semantic net (Barr 81). In the above described case this would mean that we define what relations room X should have and compare them to the structure of the knowledge base.

5.3 Risk Calculation

A general risk analysis should contain a method of some kind for calculating the pay-off of installing security measures. The company's ability to assume risks, which can be concluded from the company description, should also be considered. It should therefore be possible to use the analysis method in a case where the expected value of the annual losses is the same, but the value of the losses and the probabilities are different (Raif 70), and to get different risk values depending on the company's ability to assume risks (figure 4).

Example:

Fire: P (Probability) = once in a thousand years
L (Loss) = 10 million $

Water damage: P = once a year
L = 10.000 $

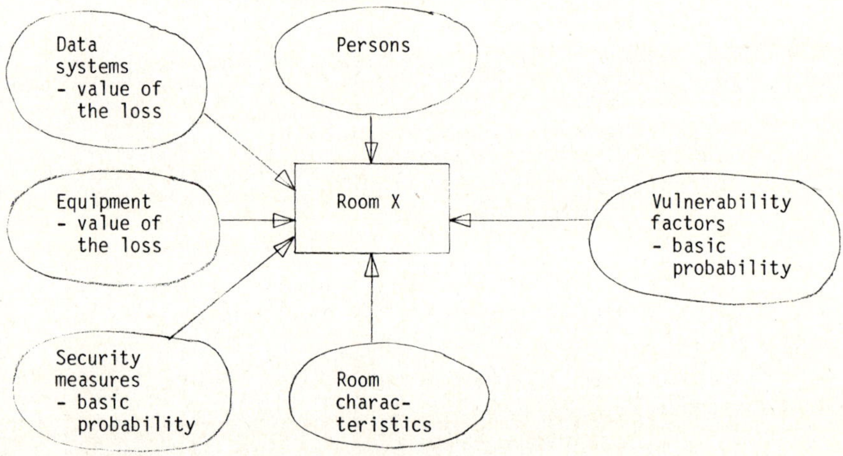

Figure 4: Basic concepts of the risk calculation method

The authors propose the risk evaluation to be based on the Dempster-Shafer Theory of Evidence (Buch 84). For each risk factor the size of the risk is determined by means of so called belief functions. The possible occurrence of a risk, e.g. monetary loss through the occurrence of fire, is a hypothesis, and the probability of the occurrence is increased (MB = Measure of Belief) by so called vulnerability factors and decreased (MD = Measure of Disbelief) by different security measures. These factors and measures are so called singleton hypotheses, which are grouped hierarchically. For each risk factor we thus obtain a hierarchical hypothesis tree, the base of which consists of the hypothesis of risk occurrence/non-occurrence. This tree structure makes it possible to study the risk factors at different levels of accuracy.

The hypotheses which form the set of hypotheses (θ) should be mutually exclusive and exhaustive. The latter requirement is fulfilled by adding the branches "Other vulnerability factors" and "Other security measures" to both of the main branches of the tree structure, and the remaining probability should be allocated to these added branches. This model also means that the user can freely add new vulnerability factors and/or security measures to the hypothesis tree depending on the case in question. An example of a hypothesis tree is shown in figure 5.

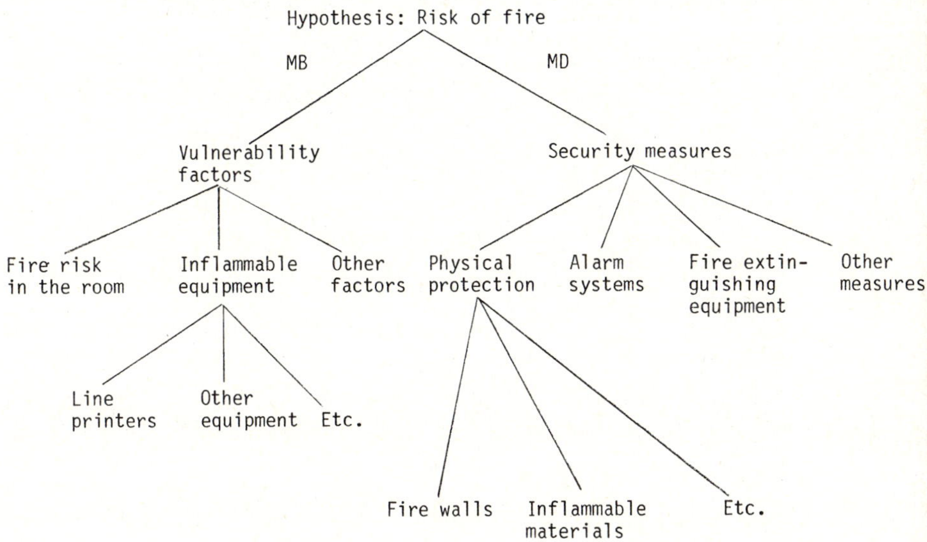

Figure 5: Risk evaluation according to the Theory of Evidence. The hypotheses form a tree structure. The tree consists of two main branches, on the left side the vulnerability factors, which increase the probability of a risk (MB), and on the right side the security measures, which decrease the probability of the risk (MD).

Each singleton hypothesis is given a so called basic probability expressed in numbers within the interval [0.1] or as a linguistic value within the interval [very low, very high]. The latter is changed to a basic probability value with the help of a table. The basic probability is = 0, if a vulnerability factor has no influence or a security measure is not employed. The basic probability is determined by means of so called triggering rules of each hypothesis, i.e. the user has to answer a number of test questions.

Every branch of the tree in figure 4 also represents a hypothesis. This means that the above mentioned triggering rules are also applicable on the upper levels. These rules may differ from the rules used on the singleton hypothesis level. The probabilities for these combined hypotheses are determined correspondingly. Hereby all required subsets of the singleton hypotheses which form the combined hypothesis are taken into account.

Furthermore, in each main branch of the tree the sum of the basic probabilities of all the subsets (2^{θ}), which are made up of singleton hypotheses, should be = 1. In this respect the Theory of Evidence differs from the conventional probability theory. This is due to the fact that a hypothesis on a higher level, e.g. inflammable equipment as a cause of fire with the probability X, may contain other vulnerability factors than those explicitly defined on a lower level, e.g. in the above case equipment cabinets, electricity supply, etc.

By means of the belief function we can determine a measure of belief or disbelief (MB or MD) for every subset X of the set of hypotheses θ. This value is the sum of the basic probabilities of all the singleton hypotheses and the basic probabilities of all the subsets belonging to X.

We have here on one hand hypotheses which support the possibility of a risk occurring, and on the other hand hypotheses which support risk negation. Thus we get two values for the main branches of the hypothesis tree, the first describing the belief that the risk will occur (MB) and the second that it will not occur (MD).

Dempster's Combination Rule enables the calculation of the net influence of two belief functions (Bel 1 $\oplus$ Bel 2). This makes it possible to study the influence of new risk decreasing measures, when we know the possible values of the losses.

The costs of the security measures can now be compared to a value which is determined as follows:

$$(MB \oplus MD) \times \text{values that can be lost}$$

In the tree structure the security measures are arranged as shown in figure 6.

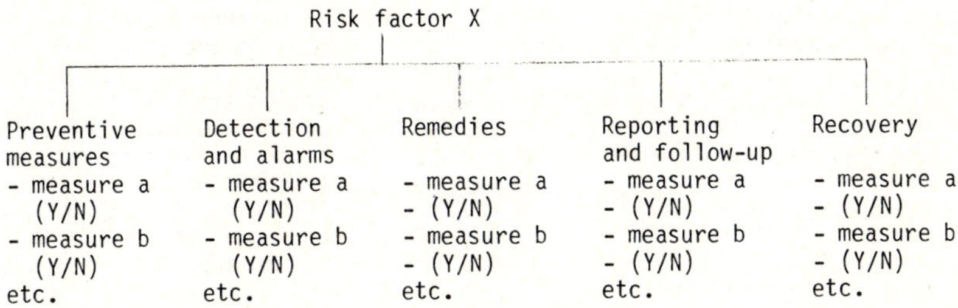

Figure 6: Classification of security measures. For each measure the basic probability is determined. Y/N (Yes/No) indicates whether the security measure has been carried out or not.

The vulnerability factors are structured as shown in figure 7.

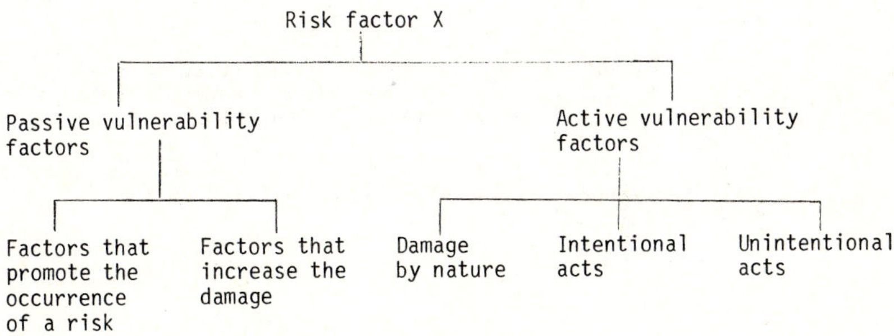

Figure 7: Classification of vulnerability factors

Figure 8 shows how the consequences of the risk factors are calculated. The risk occurrence hypothesis is divided into components according to the figure.

Example:

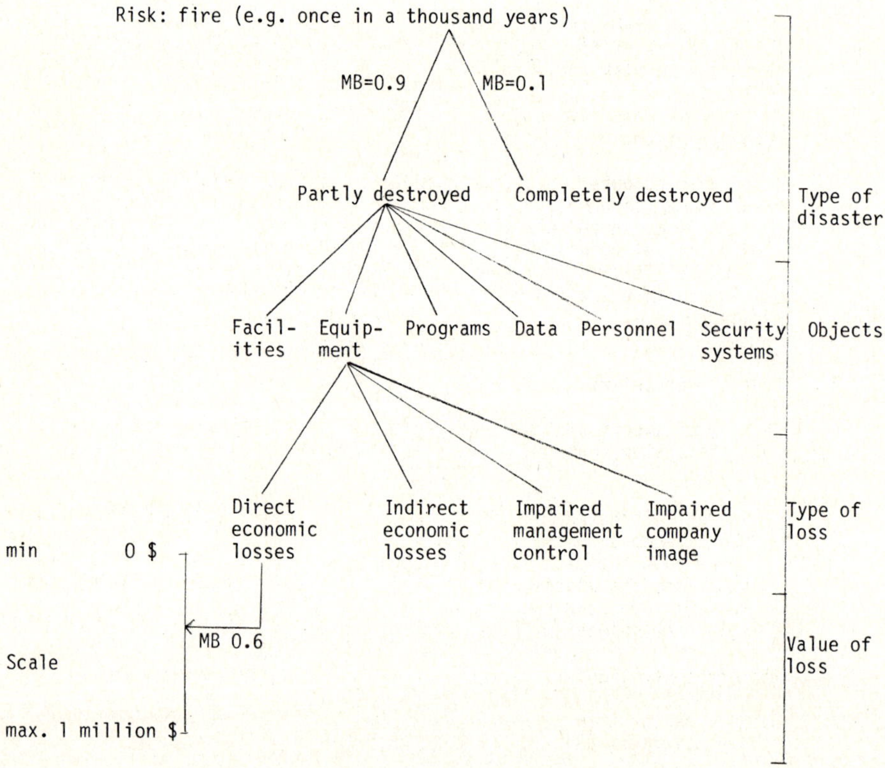

Figure 8: Calculation of consequences of risk factors

For each room/zone the risks are calculated as follows:

1. The value of the facilities is determined, either in figures or linguistically (high/low scale), and the equivalence between the scales is determined.

Example:

	very high	high	medium	low	very low
Value of the loss ($)	1 mill.	1 mill.- 100.000	100.000- 50.000	50.000- 10.000	10.000

2. Correspondingly, the value of the loss of equipment, programs, etc. situated in the room is determined.

3. Other possible losses are estimated, such as indirect economic losses, the influence of impaired management control and the influence on the company image.

4. The characteristics of the room, mainly structural protection, such as fire class of fire walls, determine whether the surrounding rooms should be risk analyzed (spreading of the risks).

5. The risks are divided into possible components, e.g. partial or total destruction.

Based on a computer supported evaluation of the risks, the security measures may then be studied according to the suggestions made by the system. Based on the characteristics of the room, e.g. size, number of access control points, etc., the costs of the security measures can be determined. This would require that unit prices, such as access control unit/door, fire extinguishing system/m^2 etc. are included in the knowledge base.

5.4 Control Mechanisms

The use of expert systems requires certain contol mechanisms to be built into the system (Barr 81). The control mechanisms have the following functions:

- Guide the construction of the knowledge base, e.g. zoning of computer rooms, access control, protection etc.
- Guide risk analysis, e.g. by suggesting only relevant risk factors
- Determine the accuracy level when vulnerability factors and security measures are studied
- Guide the selection of security measures

Through control questions the process can be guided as follows:

- Risk factor X (e.g. fire): Which level of the hierarchy should be investigated? (Answer: at zone level)

- Zone Y (e.g. production area): Do you want to look at risk factor X also by each room? (Answer: only printing area)

The control mechanisms consist of production rules. The user is asked questions which he answers either by yes/no or by giving a basic probability value. These control mechanisms make it possible for the user to manipulate diffuse knowledge in the system (Barr 81).

The risk analysis begins with a rough investigation at the company level. Based on this analysis the relevant risk/vulnerability factors and security measures are chosen (cf. section 5.1 above).

Below are some rules for the process:

1a Describe the activities of the company
1b Describe the EDP functions
1c Describe the surroundings (both physical and functional)
1d Describe security measures already taken
2 You will receive from the system a preliminary list of risk factors to be checked
3 Give a preliminary definition of the dependency and probability, linguistic value or basic probability
4 You will receive from the system a checked list of the risk factors

Example: The production process is controlled by a real time system. The value of production is X $/day, and the cost of a standstill caused by EDP is X $/h. The probability of a standstill is high.

Example: The company is situated in an industrial area where the probability of disturbances caused by different gases and dust is high.

Example: The databases do not contain sensitive material.

When zones/rooms are investigated, the production rules should prevent the selection of overlapping security measures, and when the measures are partly overlapping the rules should modify the basic probabilities. Here we are approaching a knowledge base of frame type (Barr 81).

Example:

- IF halon fire extinguishing system THEN the vulnerability decreases by X
- IF water sprinkler system THEN the vulnerability decreases by Y
- IF both THEN the vulnerability decreases by X + (Y-Z)

If the user adds new vulnerability factors and security measures to the system, it will check that the sum of the basic probabilities is equal to 1 and suggest which probabilities should be changed.

The selection of security measures is guided by the following criteria, which are also realized with production rules:

1) Decreased risks
2) The investment in security measures is profitable
3) The influence of decreased risks on the company image
4) The influences on the company management
5) The expected value of direct and indirect economic losses must not exceed X % of the turnover
6) The absolute value of direct and indirect economic losses must not exceed Y % of the turnover

Each security measure acts in a different way in each of the above mentioned areas. Each criterion should be given a linguistic weight (Nego 85).

6 AREAS OF APPLICATION IN AIR-CONDITIONING AND ELECTRICITY SYSTEM DESIGN

Areas where the expert systems can be applied are among others (Asia 85):

1. An expert system can be used as an aid in planning:
   - When creating the structure of the system, taking into account different conditions, rules and principles.
   - When planning alarm systems, operation sequences, protection principles, supervision screens and a dialogue for monitoring system operation.
   - Security analysis.
2. Expert systems can be of help when analyzing the state of the process and when choosing automatically between alternative operation sequences.
3. Expert systems can support disturbance analyses and recovery planning.
4. Expert systems can be used as an aid for selecting supervision display screens and will thus also support operation.
5. Expert systems can be used for supervising the process dynamics.
6. For control of service and maintenance.

An expert system used for the planning of air-conditioning and electricity would, for example, solve problems of the following kind (Must 85):

- How reliable is the system when the fault density of the components is known?
- How many additional air-conditioning units, compressors, pumps etc. are needed when we know the required cooling effect, the fault density of the air-conditioning units and the possibilities of decreasing the need for air-conditioning?

Below is an example of how the electricity system should be planned to ensure continuous supply of electricity (Must 85):

1. Give the type of electricity disturbance.
2. Check the equipment disturbance tolerances (e.g. voltage -10...+8 %).
3. Insert observed values.
4. Insert duration and frequency of situations when the tolerance limits have been exceeded.
5. The program compares the break tolerances derived from the risk survey with the number of breaks caused by disturbances in the electricity supply.
6. If there are too many breaks, the program suggests a solution.

7. By using the suggested solution, the number of breaks decreases by x %, is this satisfactory?

8. If not, go back to item 6.

9. Give the required power supply level.

10. The program calculates the price of the solution based on given unit prices.

11. Is the cost/benefit relation satisfactory?

When air-conditioning systems are planned, the security analysis is carried out by a team of experts (Suok 85). The importance of the security analyses has increased as the processes have become more and more complicated. One factor limiting the use of security analyses is that there are not enough experts available. A security analysis is usually carried out by an air-conditioning planner, an automation planner, an operations engineer and a maintenance engineer. These persons supply information on accidents and disturbances and on disturbance models for the process components, and based on this an expert system that makes the security analysis can be developed.

Below is an example of a deviation check:

IF the cooling air flow is too low

THEN the pump is broken or
a valve is stuck or
there is a leak somewhere or
the pressure difference is too small or
the regulator is defective.

7 SUPPORT SYSTEM FOR THE EDP OPERATOR

The water, heating, air-conditioning and electricity system of a computer center is a complicated one to control, and here an expert system could be of help. This would also have an effect on other functions of the computer center. For example, when disturbances occur in the air-conditioning the computers have to be switched off, and if this is not done in the right order, the electrical system may be wrongly charged which may damage the computer equipment. According to the authors' experience, this is one of the most common causes of disturbances or faults. The operators are not usually capable of controlling the air-conditioning and electricity systems and they do not know how to act when such disturbances occur.

A support system for the operator could:

- supervise operation
- interpret the state of the systems
- detect abnormal and dangerous situations
- make a diagnosis of disturbances
- predict the function of the systems
- automatically generate or plan control measures
- follow up the influence of measures taken

An expert system that acts as an aid for the operator would answer the following questions:

- what should be done when...
- what happens if...
- why did xxx occur...
- can activity yyy be carried out

Figure 9 shows the support system for the EDP operators and the connections of the system to the surroundings.

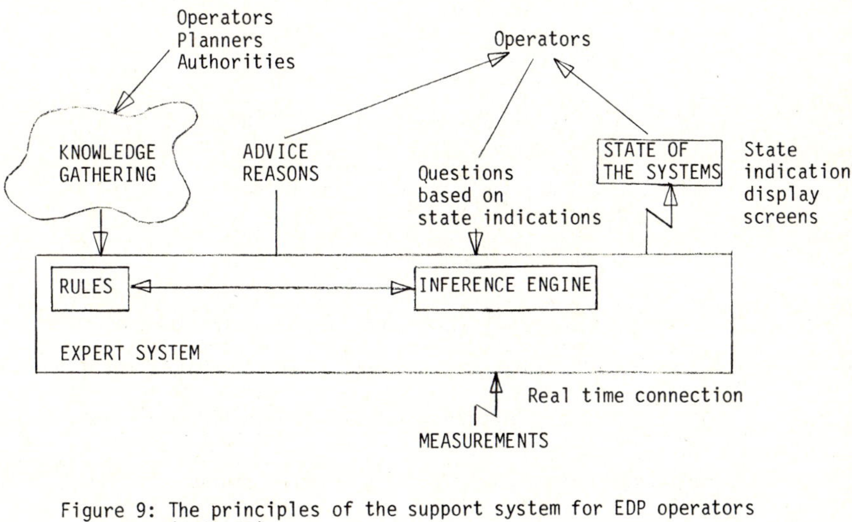

Figure 9: The principles of the support system for EDP operators (Asia 85)

The system should contain knowledge of the following kind:

1. Information about components included in the system (subprocesses, information on the regulating valves, equipment records, operation descriptions, etc.).

2. Information about events that are connected to the components (disturbance reports, alarms, fault trees, cause and effect etc.).

3. Information about how certain things should be done (regulation algorithms, model solutions, rules for planning etc.).

4. Information about what kind of knowledge is available and how it can be used (lists of documents, drawings, etc.).

Another important issue is how the knowledge is used. Some examples:

1. Collection and storing of knowledge (machinery documents etc.).

2. Search of knowledge for some special reason (scanning of directions for operational use or for disturbances, studying of system descriptions, etc.).

3. Use of knowledge for inference and problem solving (settling of disturbances, recovery plans etc.).

Below are some examples of rules connected to the air-conditioning system:

```
IF      several heat zones are affected
        heating source is enabled
        space air flow is low
        only one floor is affected
        perimeter cooling is disabled
        cooling source is OK

THEN    preheat coil is not OK (20)
        preheat coil control valve is not OK (20)
        preheat valves are leaking (20)
        fire damper fuse is not OK (20)
```

At the moment, a joint Nordic project for the development of expert systems for supervision operations of power plants is being carried out in Finland.

8 OTHER APPLICATIONS

PIDS (Perimeter Intrusion Detection System) is an already existing control system which analyzes fault alarms in the burglar alarm system (Asia 85). The system is connected to the burglar alarm system. PIDS analyzes the alarms and informs of fault alarms and their possible causes.

Diagnosis systems have been used for analyzing faults in EDP equipment and programs (Davi 83).

Digital Equipment Co. has developed an expert system for the configuration of VAX and the planning of equipment layouts (XCON and XSIRE) (Asia 85). This is a central problem in the planning of computer centers (Must 85). Unsufficient knowledge of equipment, cabling etc. may lead to serious problems and delays. However, the above mentioned systems only present a solution as far as one manufacturer is concerned.

9 CONCLUSIONS

The authors hold the opinion that further work should be carried out in order to develop risk control methods based on expert systems. One way of doing this would be to form a Working Group acting within the framework of IFIP TC 11.

REFERENCES

Aald 85 Aalders J.C.H., Herschberg I.S. & van Zanten A., Handbook for Information Security, North-Holland, Amsterdam, 1985

Asia 85 Asiantuntijajärjestelmät teollisuudessa, Insko ry, Helsinki, 1985

Barr 81 Barr A. & Feigenbaum E.A., The Handbook of Artificial Intelligence, Vol. I, Pitman Books Limited, London, 1981

Blai 71 Blair R.N. & Whitston C.W., Elements of Industrial Systems Engineering, Prentice-Hall Inc., Englewood Cliffs, NJ, 1971

Buch 84 Buchanan B.C. & Shortliffe E.H., Rule-Based Expert Systems, The MYCIN Experiments of the Stanford Heuristic Programming Project, Addison-Wesley Publishing Company, Reading, MA, 1984

Davi 83 Davis R. & Shrobe H., Representing Structure and Behaviour of Digital Hardware, Computer, October 1983, IEEE, 1983

Edma 84 Edman T., Expert system for heating, ventilation and air conditioning. In Workshop on artificial intelligence application to nuclear power technology, Organized by Electric Power Research Institute, Palo Alto, Ca, 1984

Haye 83 Hayes-Roth F., Waterman D.A. & Lenat D.B., Building Expert Systems, Addison-Wesley Publishing Company, Inc., Reading, MA, 1983

Hyvö 84 Hyvönen E., Seppänen J. & Syrjänen M. (ed.), STeP-84 Tutorial and Industrial Papers, Finnish Artificial Intelligence Symposium, Finnish Society of Information Processing Science, Espoo, 1984

Krau 80 Kraus L.I., SAFE, Security Audit and Field Evaluation for Computer Facilities and Information, Amacom, New York, 1980

Must 85 Mustonen A., ATK-tilojen suunnittelu, Rakennuskirja Oy, Helsinki, 1985

Mylo 83 Mylopoulos J., Shibahara T. & Tsotsos J.K., Building Knowledge-Based Systems: The PSN Experience, Computer, October 1983, IEEE, 1983

Nego 85 Negoita C.V., Expert Systems and Fuzzy Systems, The Benjamin/Cummings Publishing Company, Inc.,Menlo Park, CA, 1985

Park 81 Parker D.B., Computer Security Management, Reston Publishing Company, Reston, Virginia, 1981

Perr 81 Perry W.E. & Knong J.F., EDP Risk Analysis and Controls Justification, Management Advisory Publications, Wellesley Hills, MA, 1981

Raif 70 Raiffa H., Decision Analysis, Introductory Lectures on Choices under Uncertainty, Addison-Wesley, Reading, MA, 1970

SBA 83 SBA Metoden, Riksdataförbundet, Stockholm, 1983

Schu 83 Schubert L.K., Papalaskaris M.A. & Taugher J., Determining Type, Part, Color and Time Relationships, Computer, October 1983, IEEE, 1983

Smit 84 Smith S.T. & Lim J.J., An Automated Method for Assessing the Effectiveness of Computer Security Safeguards, Toronto, IFIP/Sec'84, 1984

Suok 85 Suokas J. & Karvonen I., A comparison of automatic fault free construction with hazard and operability study. Technical Research Centre of Finland, Research Reports 330, Espoo, 1985

COMPUTER SECURITY
J.B. Grimson and H.-J. Kugler (Editors)
Elsevier Science Publishers B.V. (North-Holland)
IFIP, 1985

SECURITY VULNERABILITIES IN THE AUTOMATED OFFICE

Informal Observations
for the
Third International Congress and Exhibition
on
Computer Security

Dublin, Ireland
August 12-15, 1985

Marvin Schaefer
Chief Scientist
Department of Defense Computer Security Center
Fort Meade, Maryland USA

ABSTRACT

In this paper, we describe typical office automation applications environments. Working from this description, we discuss technical security vulnerabilities of such applications with respect to preserving the privacy of documentation prepared or distributed over a system. The paper includes a description of typical shortcomings in the hardware base on which office automation systems are typically implemented. The paper concludes with suggestions for procedural controls that should be employed in current office automation systems and recommends computer security features and assurances that should be built into future office automation systems.

While the term has recently been receiving wide use, it is useful to begin with a working definition of 'office automation system'. While there are many differences in capabilities, an office automation system could be characterised as being aimed at the automated composition and preparation of documentation. Office automation systems may have several features other than just word-processing. These functions include the possibility of preparing a document or a portion thereof on one workstation, while allowing it to be electronically distributed to some other workstation(s) for printing or editorial review. It should be noted that the capability to transfer a document from one workstation to another is sufficient to implement electronic mail between individual system users. Such office automation environments often have the same security problems as does a local area network.

Since the data that can be transmitted from workstation to workstation can range from short messages to full chapters of manuals, these systems can also be used to coordinate calendars and schedule attendance at meetings. Office automation systems can also be used to reduce the paperwork in office environments. Electronic representations of briefing charts can be transferred not just for preparation by graphics departments -- they can also be distributed in advance to meeting attendees along with memoranda, notices, and other working papers. The limitations are more constrained by the imagination than by the technology.

There was a time when workstation users had to employ a special-purpose processor for document preparation. However, the wide-spread inexpensive availability of personal computers and personal computer software has permitted the easy construction of rather heterogeneous office automation work environments. The ability to simulate almost anything on a personal computer via the introduction of special purpose software has truly opened up all kinds of new avenues for creativity.

Because local area networking is often fundamental to office automation, the availability of protocol processing permits (and even encourages) even the least sophisticated of users to learn to work in networking environments. The next logical steps tend to call for expanding the local area network to permit connection to other networks external to the office environment. This form of progress invites business travelers to "dial in" to the system from other corporate offices or even from hotel rooms in order for the traveller to get his daily mail "fix" either through a commercial service network like Telenet or Tymnet, a government network like the Arpanet, or by phoning a dial-up server or modem at a convenient time of day or night, irrespective of time-zone constraints.

It also serves the purpose of allowing employers and employees to extend their workday by bringing the office into the home study or den. Employees who have personal computers in the office and at home are not even obliged to tie up their telephones at night in order to continue working, since they can carry their day's work home in their pocket on a floppy disk.

Surely, the computer security issues of such a wonderful working environment are evident. The way a local area network moves data from one workstation to another is quite simple: data moves along a cable from workstation to workstation, and a small processor inspects the traffic that passes it to determine whether it is intended for the workstation to which it is attached or not. In the event that it is, the processor grabs the data; if it is not, then the processor looks for the next "chunk" of data that passes by to see if that one is intended for its attached workstation, and so on.

This processing environment is open to fairly straightforward browsing attacks by would be interlopers. Anyone who can connect to the cable, either with a standard processor or with one of his own choosing, has the potential ability to read all the data that passes by -- unless that data is uniquely encrypted in some way that only permits it to be read by its intended destinee. For reasons to be addressed later, this problem may or may not be easily solved.

A stolen cleartext disk is easily concealed and can be more easily removed from a guarded office environment than can a quantity of paper documentation. That employees can carry data for which they have authorization home with them, also permits employees to carry home data they should not be carrying with them. A sensitive disk lying around the house is probably more valuable to some thieves than would be the equivalent stack of technical papers and reports. Many firms are tempted to encrypt all removable data storage media in order to control data privacy and data theft. If the office encrypts diskettes, then the employee would have to have the right kind of equipment at home in order to decrypt the diskettes and work with them. This would suggest that a thief would have to steal both the data-bearing floppy disks and what -- the home personal computer or the encryption software or firmware. Is this difficult to manage? If the computer uses a login and password to protect data is this sufficient to protect encrypted contents of disks, even if the personal computer is also stolen?

Lamentably, the answer is generally "no". The sad state of the computer security architecture designed into most personal computers leaves the machines wide open to profitable attack by even the least sophisticated of interlopers.[1] In many cases, it suffices simply for him either to boot a different operating system onto the word processing workstation or, in the event that security controls have been installed in the standard disk, to surreptitiously replace portions of the workstation's operating system on the distribution disk, at which point whatever security was supposed to be supported has been eliminated through simple subversion.

In either of the above subversion examples, the interloper will have removed or patched out the calls on the login routine or the password check in order to obtain access to the workstation. Following this, the interloper would attempt to find the encryption key variables in memory or, more likely, by disassembling the operating system disk to discover the logic used to make data flow through the encryption device. In doing this he may well discover the collection of encryption key variables. If this were not directly possible, e.g. because the system disk is itself encrypted, the interloper would have to analyze the memory image of the operating system -- a tedious task, but one that is feasible by exploitation of the lack of memory protection inherent to most personal computer architectures. Even the use of the BASIC interpretor or a compiled program that has the equivalent of the PEEK and POKE commands

---

[1]Unlike the majority of modern mainframe computers, most personal computer architectures fail to provide hardware features with which to implement separate address spaces for the operating system and applications programs (memory protection), nor do they provide the distinct execution privilege states that are necessary to prevent applications programs from directly performing security-relevant operations. In modern mainframe systems, at least two distinct states are provided. The combination of these two features is generally sufficient to protect the operating system and the interrupt handlers from attack by applications code. The single state architecture is not capable of defending against either an erroneous program or a malicious attack on the system.

would suffice for this kind of exploration and memory modification. The point is that unless the hardware has been modified in a very special way, the workstation must be able to boot-load its operating system, and this requires that the primitive system boot be decrypted. The literature abounds with many examples of patient 14-year olds who are capable of performing this form of analysis on Apple and Atari computers.

In short, encryption key management problems are difficult. They are even more difficult when there is no rigourously embedded security mechanism in the system that suffices to control access to the encryption keys.

As personal computers begin to replace more dedicated workstations, it becomes essential that we know the answer to the question: How secure is a traditional personal computer? The current answer is "not very."

How secure is a traditional intelligent dial-up modem? Currently the most one can say is that they are most secure when they are turned off. For once the modem has established someone's remote connection to the personal computer, the interloper has the potential ability to attack the personal computer. He may have the ability to transmit data that affects the interrupt logic of the personal computer in such a way as to permit him to obtain full access to the personal computer and its remote peripherals, even if he is incapable of passing the login challenge.

How secure is a personal computer on a network? Again, not very. Although it is clearly important, let us consider the privacy of the communications medium to be beyond the scope of this paper. It appears that most users of networks employ some commercially available general-purpose communications package rather than programming their own. (Indeed, most personal computer users buy or otherwise obtain their applications packages rather than designing and programming them themselves. This, of course, is much of the appeal of the general purpose personal computer over special-purpose workstations.) Many of the commercial communications packages come with features that permit automatic telephone dialing, automatic login on distant networks and computer hosts, automatic logging of user functions on either disks or RAM "disks", and reliable file transfer services for up- and down-line file moves.

Mass use of commercial applications and communications packages has nearly led to a semi-standardisation of what can be found on personal computers. For the moment, hypothesize a typical personal computer user. His personal computer is equipped with a systems disk containing, say, an operating system, a word processor, and a few other utilities including a commercial communications package. Examination of the standard communications packages could potentially allow an interloper to place a "smart" trojan horse in any of the standard utilities to discover which of the communications packages was in use and then to search for the user's dial-up phone numbers, access codes, passwords, etc. storing them into easily accessible files for subsequent covert release onto a distant network host. It appears to be common practice that even those users whose personal computers are not equipped with hard disks do not generally write-protect their systems disks, and hence it may be relatively straight-forward to perform the subversion. The result, of course, would be that a receptive communications server on the distant host could collect all of the user's *other* access numbers and passwords while the user remained ignorant of the transaction. Certainly such subversion is improbable. Or is it? Few users are *really* aware of the source or the integrity of the applications software they use on personal computers.

It is becoming common practice for an increasing number of organisations to make use of pirated personal computer software. Certainly, someone has purchased the original copy of an application. Often, the organisation is willing to issue software packages to all of its personal computer users. But many users tend to be fickle in their choice of applications packages, and switch from package to package. Further, many users need an application *now* and are unwilling to wait for one to be ordered. The result is that software is often copied with "lockpick" programs and used indiscriminately on personal computers other than the one on which it is generated. The fact that the software being used in such cases has been obtained illegally is certainly significant. These are cases of outright copyright or licensing violations. In addition to the lawbreaking, however, such users may be opening themselves up to the entire class of "borrowed software" attacks.[2] They are literally asking to be subverted, penetrated, or otherwise abused.

Of course it is interesting to ask from what source one gathered such observations on the personal computer subversion problem. The above examples came from a commercial EDP auditors' workshop, where a number of the participants chose to discuss "war stories" they had picked up working with clients in the private sector.

While the majority of personal computer users are not sophisticated in computing science, it is worth pointing out that the tools that are increasingly at their disposal were

[2]Cf. Lampson's paper, "A note on the confinement problem."

created by extremely sophisticated individuals. Originally, software pirates had only to use the personal computer's disk copy utility in order to make duplicates of products. The evolution of sophisticated copy protection mechanisms has been duplicated by a similar degree of sophistication amongst those who write utilities that defeat these same copy protection techniques. Through the use of disassemblers, tracing debuggers, and other analysis tools, the would-be pirates have the luxury of analyzing protected software as if it were data on a disk or as a program in execution, or as a combination of both. It is significant that these users are capable of making the once sophisticated distinction between a "subject" and an "object" in the computer security context.

Several suppliers of licensed personal computer applications have introduced "time bombs" and "Trojan horses" into their products. Some of these are set to destroy data or the source disk unless certain configuration-specific conditions are satisfied. Other attempts at protection have included the use of encryption, add-on intelligent devices, etc. There are known cases in which the licensee receives an update diskette as a function of mailing in a warrantee card, and unless code from the update disk is used to replace portions of the original code, eventual denial of service to the user may result. According to the hackers and readers of "pirates' bulletin board" systems, these sophisticated techniques have succumbed to prolonged analysis by dedicated teenagers.

The result is that many 14-year olds now have obtained fluent experience with many of the techniques developed by the "tiger teams" that penetrated operating systems in the mid-1970's. As these youngsters mature, there is an increasing likelihood that such attacks as described in this paper will be used against professional workstations.

The majority of personal computer and dedicated workstation hardware architectures are currently too weak to support the implementation of even a Class C1 trusted system[3] because of the lack of strong memory protection, separate domains of execution, and configuration control of the software base. As long as the user has the full capability of loading an arbitrary operating system into the workstation, he has the capability of supplanting whatever protections may have been built into some other operating system provided with the workstation. These fundamental security deficiencies will continue to present challenges to those who need to protect data on office automation systems. Careful security planning must be initiated soon, in order to protect the many small businesses that have entrusted *all* of their corporate data processing to these machines.

Even if the next generation of personal computers were designed with a good computer security hardware architecture, there remain a number of office automation security problems that need to be solved. If sensitive data will be processed or stored on the office automation system, then the operating system that runs on each workstation needs to incorporate a fundamental set of computer security safeguards:[4] the workstation should have hardware controls that prevent any but an authorised copy of the operating system from being booted; the operating system should be protected by the hardware from any form of modification; the workstation should authenticate

---

[3]As defined in the *Department of Defense Trusted Computer Systems Evaluation Criteria*.

[4]The full set of suggested minimal requirements are those for Class C2 in the *Trusted Computer Security Evaluation Criteria*.

the identity of each individual user (e.g., based on a unique machine-generated password known only to the user) prior to permitting any access to system resources; the system should have mechanisms that can be used to define the access rights of each individual user to each sensitive data object controlled by the system, and the user's identity should be used by the system as *the* basis for granting each separate mode of access by the user to the data; each attempt by a user to create new data or to obtain access to data controlled by the system should be placed in a protected audit file that is protected from modification by users.

Because of the possibility that subverted software might be introduced into an office automation system, it is important that strict configuration controls be employed to discourage the use of unevaluated or frequently modified applications packages. Similarly, attention should be paid to permitting external dial-up connections to the office automation system.

In addition, the local area network interfaces and the processors that interface between the workstations and the local area network should both be designed and built such that it is not possible for a workstation to obtain access to information for which the user of the workstation is not explicitly authorised.

Today's office automation systems are particularly vulnerable to attack by authorised and unauthorised users. The *Trusted Computer System Evaluation Criteria* provide a standard for measuring the strength of the controls in computer systems and should be employed by corporate management in selecting their office automation systems. In order to reduce risk, installation managers should employ careful procedural controls until and after automated security controls are available and installed in their facility.

REFERENCES

1. Butler W. Lampson, "A note on the confinement problem," *Communications of the ACM*, **16**, 10, October 1973, pp 613-615.

2. *Department of Defense Trusted Computer System Evaluation Criteria*, Department of Defense Computer Security Evaluation Center, 15 August 1983, NTIS Acquisition Number AD-A141-304, US Government Printing Office St. N° 008000004188.

AUTHOR INDEX

Beatson J.G., 251
Becker L.G., 241
Byrne W.J., 155
Carroll J.M., 1
Chainer T.J., 129
Courtney R.H.Jnr., 55
Cronhjort B.T., 397
Davies D.W., 371
Doswell R.T., 277
Ekebrink I., 233
Eloff J.H.P., 337
Essén J., 47
Fåk V., 35
Fraga J., 203
Fugini M., 17,
Goulbourn M., 297
Gundersen S.C., 129
Herschberg I.S., 27, 179
Jürgensen H., 1
Kingston P.P.C.H., 297
Kugler H.-J., 191
Lane V., 361
Lindberg B., 47
Mäkilä R., 225
McLean K.D., 39
Moeller R.R., 305
Murine G.E., 329
Mustonen A., 397
Nolan M., 163
Orlandi E., 283
Osvald T., 219
Paans R., 27, 179
Parker D.B., 175
Pohl H., 261
Powell D., 203
Power J.M., 117
Rasmussen O.S., 107
Rice R., 65
Schaefer M., 427
Stanley P.M., 313
Step J., 361
Tener W.T., 269
Todd M.A., 55
Tompkins F.G., 65
van Tongeren H., 323
Ware W.H., 379
Wilbur S.R., 117
Worthington T., 129
Williford J.D., 129
Wood C.Cresson, 347